Y0-BDF-708

Industrial Growth and Stagnation

Industrial Growth and Stagnation

The Debate in India

Edited by
DEEPAK NAYYAR

Published for
SAMEEKSHA TRUST

OXFORD UNIVERSITY PRESS
BOMBAY DELHI CALCUTTA MADRAS
1994

Oxford University Press, Walton Street, Oxford OX2 6DP

Oxford New York Toronto
Delhi Bombay Calcutta Madras Karachi
Kuala Lumpur Singapore Hong Kong Tokyo
Nairobi Dar es Salaam Cape Town
Melbourne Auckland Madrid

and associates in
Berlin Ibadan

First Published 1994

ISBN 0 19 563442 X

Typeset by Economic and Political Weekly, Bombay and printed at
All India Press, Pondicherry and published by
Neil O'Brien, Oxford University Press, Oxford House,
Apollo Bunder, Bombay-400 039

Preface

The *Economic and Political Weekly*, quite in the manner of its predecessor, *The Economic Weekly*, continues to thrive on debates and controversies. The discussions carried by it, often intense, have embraced aspects of both theory and policy, and contributed in a major way toward expanding the frontiers of knowledge and analysis. One debate the *EPW* played host to during the seventies and the eighties was on the theme of industrialisation and growth. The linkage between industry and the other sectors of the economy, the relative importance of domestic and external markets for fostering industrial growth, the role of the State in either accelerating or hampering industrial expansion were among the issues covered during the debate. Professor Deepak Nayyar graciously accepted the Sameeksha Trust's invitation to put together a selection of these articles; he has also contributed an absorbing Introduction to the volume. The selection, in our view, is extremely rich fare and should command the attention of policy-framers as well as the general readership.

ASHOK MITRA
Editor of Publications
Sameeksha Trust

December 28, 1993

Contents

Contents

Introduction

Deepak Nayyar

INDUSTRIALISATION and development is a complex theme which has aroused considerable interest and stimulated much debate among economists. There exists an extensive literature on the subject which attempts to describe, analyse and evaluate the industrialisation experience of economies in Asia, Africa and Latin America during the post-colonial era. It establishes that the pace and the range of industrialisation have, on the whole, been impressive, particularly when compared with the underdevelopment and the stagnation of the colonial past. But it also reveals that the process of industrialisation has been uneven over time and across space, both within and between countries. This pattern of development has accentuated regional disparities in industrialisation within countries. It has also increased the economic distance between nations with the 'newly industrialising countries' at one end and the 'least developed countries' at the other. Industrialisation in developing countries has thus been characterised by success stories in a few, muddling through in some and near-failure in others. The post-mortem of failures has led to a diagnosis, while the analysis of successes has led to prescriptions. These lessons from the experience of particular countries have sought to be generalised and transplanted elsewhere. Such an approach tends to ignore not only the complexities of the growth process but also the characteristics of economies which are specific in time and space. In my view, the object of research should be to contribute to our knowledge and to deepen our understanding of the industrialisation process in developing countries, rather than to provide magic recipes in the sphere of policy formulation. Towards this objective, it is necessary to examine industrial development in the wider context of structural transformation of economies and analyse the macro-economics of industrial growth. Such an approach would enable us to consider problems of industrialisation in perspective and recognise the specificities of national economies, where the focus is not simply on the industrial sector or the policy regime but on the economy as a whole.

In keeping with such a wider perspective, this introductory essay is structured as follows. First, I shall outline the contours of the debate on the industrialisation experience in India since independence, which spans a wide range of analytical, as also ideological, perspectives. Second, I shall set out the object, the scope and the theme of this book. Third, I shall highlight some strategic isssues in industrialisation: the relationship between agriculture and industry, the relative importance of the domestic market, the nature of state intervention and the development of technology. Fourth, I shall situate problems of industrialisation in a macro-economic perspective by considering the importance of supply factors on the one hand and demand factors on the other but, more important perhaps, by considering the implications of the interaction between supply and demand for industrialisation in a dynamic context.

INDUSTRIALISATION IN INDIA: THE DEBATE

The debate on industrialisation in India spans a wide range of issues and the literature on the subject is vast. The discussion is at two discernible levels. These can be categorised as alternative approaches to the problem, each of which endeavours to provide an assessment and a critique of the industrialisation experience in India since independence, but from somewhat different perspectives. The first approach, which seeks to focus on relative prices and resource allocation, is micro-theoretic in its analytical foundations. This literature, largely orthodox, is primarily concerned with an evaluation of import substitution strategies and the economic efficiency of industrialisation. The second approach, which attempts to analyse the factors underlying industrial growth, is largely macro-theoretic in its concerns; there are some micro-theoretic dimensions of this approach, particularly in the area of technology, which have remained relatively unexplored. This literature, a mix of the orthodox and the unorthodox, is concerned with the macro-economic determinants of, and constraints on, industrial growth in the wider context of structural transformation of the economy.

Orthodox economic theory, in the neo-classical tradition, provides the analytical basis for the former approach. In this context, however, the analytical construct is narrow. Significant new developments in the neo-classical tradition, whether in industrial economics or in trade theory, are almost ignored when such analysis is applied to problems of industrialisation and development. Hence this approach, which is static rather than dynamic in conception, tends to ignore intertemporal considerations, and does not quite incorporate increasing returns, market structures or externalities which are inherent in any process of industrialisation. The excessive concern with resource allocation, in terms of static allocative efficiency criteria, is perhaps misplaced. Success at industrialisation is not only about resource allocation. It is as much, if not more, about resource utilisation and resource creation. The mode of utilisation of resources is a crucial determinant of economic efficiency. The process of creation of resources is a crucial determinant of economic growth. The disproportionate emphasis on resource allocation or relative prices, in conjunction with a focus on policy regimes or on the cost and the quality of industrial output, serves a limited purpose. What is more, it fails to recognise that policy regimes are permissive rather than causal factors in the industrialisation process, which are at best necessary conditions but under no circumstances sufficient conditions. For these reasons, the elaborate literature in this school, while thematic and cohesive, remains inadequate.

The latter approach is distinctly wider in its canvas and seeks to explore the problems of industrialisation in terms of economic dynamics. The analytical basis of this approach is also much more diverse. The macro-economic analysis in many of the studies is in the tradition of Keynes and Kalecki; some of the authors are of broadly Marxist persuasion but there are others who are very much in the realm of orthodox economics. The problems posed or the issues considered, however, are similar though not the same. The macro-economics of industrialisation in India is the common concern. For one, there is an attempt to explore the complex interaction between the forces of supply and demand, over time, at a macro-level. For another, there is an attempt to examine the role of the State, beyond the policy regime, in this process of development. The problems of industrial growth, whether about its pace, its composition or its quality, are situated in the larger macro-economic context, so that growth and structural change in the industrial sector are not considered in isolation from the economy as a whole. Given the complexity of the issues, this is easier said than done and the literature, while rich in analysis and ideas, remains incomplete.

THE BOOK: RATIONALE, SCOPE AND THEME

The problems of industrialisation in India, situated in this macroeconomic perspective, were the subject of a lively debate which began in the early 1970s and continued until the early 1980s. Most of the contributions to this debate were published in the pages of *Economic and Political Weekly*, but some appeared elsewhere. This volume brings together a selection of essays, published in the *Economic and Political Weekly,* that made a significant contribution to the debate in India. The rationale is worth noting. First, such a book of readings would serve a valuable purpose for the interested student and the reader unfamiliar with the extensive literature. Second, the issues raised in this debate remain important even at the present conjuncture, although it may now be perceived as unfashionable economics. Third, the debate is relevant for studies on the experience of late industrialisers elsewhere, particularly the large semi-industrialised countries in Asia and in Latin America.

The object of the book is to present the main strands of the discussion, and the broad contours of the debate, on industrialisation in India, mainly for the benefit of the new reader. The task of the editor, I must admit, has been somewhat difficult, for there is a very large number of interesting and valuable contributions on or around this theme in *Economic and Political Weekly.* Yet, if the length of the volume had to be kept within manageable proportions, choice was inevitable. In the use of this editorial prerogative, I have attempted to be as objective as possible.

It needs to be stressed, however, that the catchment area did not extend beyond the pages of *Economic and Political Weekly.* And there are several important contributions to the debate on industrialisation in India which were published elsewhere by the authors in the form of books, monographs or articles. It was obviously not possible to include them in the present volume. All the same, this literature deserves mention particularly for the new or the unfamiliar reader. It is striking that some of the earliest contributions are in this category. Amiya Bagchi (1970), Sukhamoy Chakravarty (1974), and Ashok Mitra (1977), were among the first to explore the macro-economics of industrial growth in India and may indeed have initiated the discussion which occupies the pages of this volume. Some years later, Amiya Bagchi (1981) provided an analytical review of this literature. Similarly, Jagdish Bhagwati and Padma Desai (1970), followed by Jagdish Bhagwati and T N Srinivasan (1975), were among the first to provide an elaborate critique of industrialisation in India, from a neo-classical perspective, suggesting that the policy framework led to economic inefficiency and resource misallocation while the cumulative effect of these policies became an obstacle to growth. The same approach was reiterated and developed further by Isher Ahluwalia (1985). More recently, a survey by K L Krishna (1987) and a monograph by J C Sandesara (1992) provided a critical review of the debate and considered the available evidence. In a wider context,

Sukhamoy Chakravarty (1987), Lance Taylor (1988) and Abhijit Sen (1991) set out a macro-economic analysis of constraints on growth in India.

In retrospect, it is possible to discern three phases of industrialisation in independent India: the phase of rapid industrial growth from the early 1950s to the mid-1960s; the phase of stagnation from the mid-1960s to the mid-1970s; and the phase of revival in the late 1970s followed by growth in the 1980s. The essays in this volume endeavour to analyse the factors underlying the deceleration in industrial growth and the persistent quasi-stagnation during the second phase, with some discussion of the necessary or the sufficient conditions for a return to the path of sustained growth. The alternative hypotheses about the macro-economic determinants of, and constraints on, industrial growth in India, developed in these essays, are mostly structuralist explanations which focus on the performance of the agricultural sector, the level of investment in the economy, public investment and public expenditure on the part of the government, or income distribution and the demand factor. The issues of concern, which have been the core of the debate about the uneven pace of industrial growth in India, include inter-sectoral terms of trade between agriculture and industry, disproportionalities within and between sectors, the nexus between public investment and private investment, the significance of supply constraints and the nature of the demand constraint. It is only to be expected that different authors emphasise different factors and advance different explanations. This is, at least in part, attributable to the conjuncture and the issues of concern at the time. The overlap in the discussion, juxtaposed with conflicting perceptions, makes it difficult to group the contributions. For this reason, as also to retain the flavour of the original debate, the essays in this book are presented in the chronological order of publication.

It is customary for an editorial introduction to attempt a summary if not a synthesis of the contributions, but I have decided to depart from this practice. For one, it would be somewhat difficult to provide a summary of the essays in this volume. For another, it would serve little purpose as most of these papers are standard references. Yet, there is a need to reflect on the theme of these essays in the present context, for the issues analysed remain both relevant and significant despite the passage of time. In the remaining part of this introduction, therefore, I shall explore some strategic issues in industrialisation and situate problems of industrialisation in a macro-economic perspective. In doing so, I shall not even endeavour to provide answers to complex questions. The object is simply to highlight the issues or pose the questions. This should enable the reader to consider the debate in India in the context of the literature on industrialisation and development.

STRATEGIC ISSUES IN INDUSTRIALISATION

There are some issues which are recognised as fundamental, if not strategic, in any process of industrialisation: the relationship between agriculture and industry, the relative importance of the domestic market, the nature or the degree of State intervention, and the acquisition or the development of technology. The recognition, however, does not mean that these critical issues have received sufficient attention in the studies and research on industrialisation, in India or elsewhere. Some have, but others have not. In my judgment, the relatively unexplored questions around these issues must form an essential part of any agenda for future research.

The relationship between agriculture and industry in the process of development is an issue that has engaged the attention of scholars and occupied centre-stage in the literature on the subject. It is widely accepted that in the early stages of industrialisation, when an overwhelming proportion of output and income in the economy originates from the primary sector, the agricultural sector is crucial not only because it provides a labour surplus, but also because it provides a marketable surplus of wage goods and an investible surplus of resources. In the Lewis characterisation of surplus labour economies, therefore, the subsistence sector engaged in primary production provides the foundations for both capital accumulation and industrial growth. At the same time, the agricultural sector provides the main source of demand for industrial goods, whether inputs for production or outputs for consumption. The inter-sectoral linkages, on the supply side and on the demand side, operate through a variety of mechanisms. The nature of these linkages, combined with the inter-sectoral terms of trade between the agricultural and non-agricultural sectors, can have a profound impact on the pace of industrialisation, whether we consider market economies or the erstwhile planned economies. In most developing countries which have a rural hinterland, issues arising out of the agrarian question are strategic for industrialisation prospects, not only to begin with but also at later stages; of course, the degree and the nature of the interdependence changes over time. The importance of this proposition is borne out by the literature on the industrialisation experience in India. For one, several essays in this volume suggest that the performance of the agricultural sector, in conjunction with movements in the inter-sectoral terms of trade, has been a crucial determinant of growth in the industrial sector. For another, several contributions published elsewhere, in particular Byres (1974), Mitra (1977), Mundle (1985) and Mathur (1990), stress the impact of agricultural growth on industrial development in India.

The second question is about the relative importance of the internal market and of external markets in the process of industrialisation. The answer must obviously depend, among other things, on the size of the country. In large countries such as India, where the domestic market is overwhelmingly important, sustained industrialisation can only be based on the growth of the home market. On the other hand, in small countries the possibilities of industrialisation may be limited by the size of the domestic market. It must be stressed, however, that these possibilities are not mutually exclusive. It is simply a matter of natural emphasis and temporal sequence. In the ultimate analysis, large economies must seek to externalise internal markets whereas small economies must endeavour to internalise external markets. Therefore, industrialisation may stress manufacturing for the domestic market through import substitution or manufacturing for export to external markets. The emphasis would depend on the size of an economy and the stage of its development. Unfortunately, this basic issue has been reduced to a debate about trade policies for industrialisation or a choice between import substitution and export promotion. It is essential to get out of this false dilemma and examine the home market question in its wider context. In terms of an appropriate strategy for industrialisation, striking a balance between import substitution and export promotion is the equivalent of walking on two legs. The timing and the pace of the transition in shifting emphasis from one to the other clearly matters. However, success or failure depends not so much on the choice between inward-looking and outward-looking policies as it does on the setting in which these are introduced. An environment that produces a spectacular export performance is also conducive to efficient import substitution and rapid economic growth. It is, therefore, necessary to analyse the factors underlying success or failure at industrialisation not in terms of policy regimes at a micro-level but with reference to the macro-economic context and the conjuncture of internal and external economic factors which are responsible for the outcome. The debate on industrialisation in India has addressed some of these issues but with unequal attention and in uneven depth. Many of the essays in this volume, for example, focus on the size of the home market as a source of industrial growth or on domestic demand as a constraint on industrial growth. However, the neo-classical critique of the Indian industrialisation experience, which emphasises relative prices and resource allocation, often poses the problem as a choice between import substitution combined with inward-looking policies and export promotion combined with outward-looking policies. Such an approach is open to question. The association of export expansion with policy regimes is neither unique nor inseparable. What is more, the discussion on trade policies for industrialisation is not situated in its wider macro-economic context.

The third issue is the nature and degree of State intervention in the process of industrialisation. Our experience in the second half of the twentieth century suggests that the guiding and the supportive role of the State has been at the foundations of successful development among late industrialisers not only in the planned economies of Europe but also in the market economies of Asia. It is ironical that, at this juncture, the erstwhile centrally-planned economies of Europe which have witnessed a collapse of the system provide an unconvincing example, while the market economies of Asia which have sought to emulate the Japanese experience provide a convincing example. Even among the East Asian countries, which are often cited as success stories that depict the magic of the market place, the visible hand of the State is much more in evidence than the invisible hand of the market. In the earlier stages of industrialisation, State intervention creates the conditions for the development of industrial capitalism by establishing a physical infrastructure through government investment, by developing human resources through education, or by facilitating institutional change through agrarian reform. State intervention continues to perform an important role, beyond the initial stages, in mobilising or utilising resources that may remain outside the productive sphere and in creating a commodity composition of output more conducive to growth. In the later stages of industrialisation, State intervention is functional or strategic rather than conducive, but remains crucial. At one level, functional State intervention may seek to correct for market failures, whether general or specific. At another level, strategic State intervention, interlinked across activities or sectors, may seek to attain broader, long-term objectives of development. It is possible to cite several examples. Exchange rate policy is not simply a tactical matter of getting-prices-right but may turn out to be a strategic matter if deliberately undervalued exchange rates, maintained over a period of time, provide an entry into a world market for differentiated manufactured goods. The structure of interest rates is not just about allowing market forces to determine the price of capital, but may be a strategic method of guiding the allocation of scarce investible resources. Restriction on the use of foreign brand names is not so much an inward-looking attitude, if it is perceived as a strategic means of buying time to develop national brand names that become acceptable in world markets after a lag. In this manner, State intervention may constitute an integral part of any strategy of industrialisation that endeavours to strengthen capabilities and develop institutions rather than rely on incentives or markets alone. There is, of course, government failure just as much as market failure, for neither governments nor markets are, or can be, perfect. In theory, it may be possible to remedy market failure by State intervention. In practice, governments may lack the ability or the willingness to intervene efficiently. It is the nature and the form of State intervention that matters. The experience of India illustrates that it is possible for State intervention to create an oligopolistic situation in a competitive environment, just as the experience of the Republic of Korea illustrates that it is possible for State intervention to create a competitive situation in an oligopolistic environment, and this has had far-reaching implications for industrialisation in both countries. The experience of excessive State intervention associated with government failures, however, should not lead to the conclusion that minimal State intervention is the best or that market failures do not matter. We appear to have moved from a widespread belief, prevalent in the 1950s, that the State could do nothing wrong to a gathering conviction, fashionable in the 1990s, that the State can do nothing right. These are caricature perceptions. The reality is more complex than simplified paradigms that may be in or out of fashion. In a world of uneven development, characterised by rapid technical progress, ever-changing comparative advantage and imperfect market structures, the role of governments in the industrialisation process remains vital and could account for the difference between success and failure. For industrialisation is not only about getting-prices-right; industrialisation is also about getting-State-intervention-right. The essays in this volume do not address these issues, but it is imperative that further research on industrialisation should analyse the actual and the potential role of State intervention which may be difficult to generalise across countries.

The fourth strategic issue in the process of industrialisation relates to technology. The direction and the speed of technological development influences the pace of growth, the nature of structural change and the efficiency of production in the industrial sector. An economy that industrialises should be able to move from importation to absorption and adaptation of technology through to the stage of innovation, at least in some sectors, on the path to sustained industrialisation. In the pursuit of this objective, imports of technology and indigenous technological development need to be combined in a judicious mix. The industrialisation experience of India suggests that there are a number of sectors where the level of technological development is not adequate. There are several examples of situations where technologies were imported for particular sectors at a point of time and the absorption of such technologies has been followed by stagnation rather than adaptation, diffusion and innovation. At the same time, in many cases, indigenous development of technology has not led to widespread diffusion, let alone technological upgradation. The underlying reasons are complex. These are, to some extent, discussed in the available literature, but mostly at a micro-level. The concerns of the essays in this volume remain somewhat distant from such analysis or research. It is clear, however, that market structures and government policies have not combined to provide an environment which would accelerate the absorption of imported technology and foster the development of indigenous technology, or create a milieu which would be conducive to diffusion and innovation. It needs to be stressed that, at a macro-level, the role of the government is crucial for planning technological development across sectors and over time. This means planning for the acquisition of technology where it is to be imported, setting aside resources for technology where it is to be produced at home, or even deciding to opt out of a technology where it is not needed. For this purpose, it is necessary to formulate a policy regime for the import of technology, allocate resources for R and D and evolve government procurement policies. Such a guiding and supportive role of the State has been a necessary condition for technological development among the late-comers to industrialisation, particularly in Asia but also elsewhere.

A MACRO-ECONOMIC PERSPECTIVE

Industrialisation is associated with economic growth and structural change. The process of economic growth is characterised by a dynamic interaction between demand factors and supply factors, so that a mismatch between aggregate demand and aggregate supply, as also disproportionalities between and within sectors, which surface over time, affect either the price level or the balance of payments or both. The process of structural change reflects differences in the rates of expansion or contraction of output, employment or investment in different sectors, where the underlying factors are changes in the structure of final demand and changes in the technology of productive activities in the national context juxtaposed with changes in comparative advantage in the international context. Studies on the industrialisation experience of developing countries focus on the supply side, or on the demand side, and do not pay adequate attention to the interaction between the forces of demand and supply in a macroeconomic perspective.

On the demand side, the size of the market is an important determinant of industrialisation prospects. The relative importance of the internal market and the external market then assumes significance. On the supply side, the level of resource mobilisation, the pattern of resource allocation, the mode of resource utilisation and the potential for resource creation, taken together, shape the possibilities of industrialisation. The contribution of internal resources as compared with external resources obviously influences the nature of industrialisation. It follows that, whether we consider markets on the demand side or resources on the supply side, the mix between the internal and the external is crucial in any process of industrialisation. The relative importance depends on the size of a country or the stage of its development. In general, countries can exercise greater control or influence over internal markets and domestic resources as compared to external markets and foreign resources. Nevertheless, a recognition and utilisation of markets and resources beyond national boundaries can foster industrialisation in terms of both pace and quality.

In the realm of orthodox economics, much of the literature on industrialisation emphasises the supply side. Resources generated through greater efficiency are assumed to be automatically invested. The ideal world is one where resource allocation follows revealed comparative advantage, to choose industries and technologies in accordance with relative international prices, so that industrialisation everywhere is part of an optimal division of labour between countries in the world economy. Any divergence, the neo-classical perspective suggests, would worsen the quality and reduce the pace of industrial growth. Surely, this is an argument carried too far. Understanding industrialisation requires a recognition of supply factors but does not call for a neglect of demand factors. What is more, the interaction between supply and demand has important implications and consequences for industrialisation which cannot be ignored. It does not serve much purpose to consider a high marginal capital-output ratio or a slow total factor productivity increase as performance criteria if capital or capacities are underutilised. Unfavourable values for these variables follow as a statistical result. The emergence or existence of widespread excess capacity in many sectors of the economy cannot always be explained in terms of resource-misallocation or cost-inefficiencies. In such a context, it would be a mistake to neglect demand factors, particularly for large industrialising economies such as India, on the presumption that inadequacy of demand is not a real problem given the existence of a virtually unlimited demand for exports. Thus, it may be worth considering the significance and the composition of demand factors, in the context of industrialisation, before turning to the implications of supply-demand balances or imbalances.

Let us start from the national income accounting identity. On the expenditure side, gross domestic product can be disaggregated into its principal components: (i) private consumption; (ii) private investment; (iii) government consumption and investment taken together; and (iv) trade surplus (excess of exports over imports). From this accounting definition, it follows that aggregate demand, or the size of the market, can be expanded in four ways that are analytically distinct from each other, even if they are difficult to separate in real world situations.

First, it is possible to conceive of private-consumption-led expansion which would require a redistribution of incomes, if not assets, in favour of the poor who, it is reasonable to presume, have a higher propensity to consume. There is a diluted version, or another variant of this theme, which may be described as a consumer-durable-led expansion, where incomes are redistributed in favour of a small elite or a larger middle class which has a high propensity to consume. The former postulates an egalitarian strategy of development which may be constrained by political factors. The latter may give rise to an economic constraint manifest in the balance of payments or a social constraint in the form of income inequalities, but its capacity to alleviate the demand constraint on industrialisation would depend upon the size of the elite or the middle class as a proportion of the total population. In India, this proportion is much smaller than elsewhere in Asia or Latin America. Indeed, it is plausible to suggest that an unequal income distribution, operating through the demand factor, might constrain rather than stimulate industrial growth in an economy such as India. In the long run, the pace of industrialisation can only be sustained if there is a growth in the domestic market because, after allowing for all possibilities of export expansion, the capacities created in the producer goods sector must be matched by final demand in the consumer goods sector. But, in a market economy where the distribution of income is unequal, and made more so, the demand base may be too narrow in terms of population spread. Only a broad-based demand for mass-consumption goods can lead to a sustainable expansion of aggregate demand, and enable the manufacturing sector to realise economies of scale, which in turn requires incomes for the poor.

The second possibility is private-investment-led expansion. This can happen only if there is an improvement in the expected profitability of investment. Such profitability, however, is necessary but not sufficient, unless it is associated with animal spirits and managerial capabilities of entrepreneurs. The evidence in India, at least so far, cannot be a source of optimism on this score. Many entrepreneurs have revealed their preference for rents instead of profits or for trading instead of manufacturing activities. Few entrepreneurs have sought to promote R and D. Surprisingly enough, there is now a variation around this theme which regards profitability as both necessary and sufficient, on the assumption that inflows of direct foreign investment would, at least in the first instance, provide the entrepreneurship for industrialisation.

In my view, the structural reforms and policy changes introduced recently in India focus on these two methods of increasing aggregate demand: to create a demand for consumer goods on the part of the middle class and to create an environment where private investment, both domestic and foreign, would be profitable.

The third analytically distinct way is government-expenditure-led expansion. Such an expansion can be based either on public investment or on public expenditure. In my judgment, the first phase of rapid industrial growth in India, from the early 1950s to the mid-1960s, was characterised by government stimulus in the form of public investment, whereas the third phase of revival in the late 1970s and growth in the 1980s was characterised by government stimulus in the form of public expenditure. The strategy of public-consumption-expenditure-led expansion which supported growth in the 1980s was simply not sustainable, based as it was on external borrowing. It was only a matter of time before the government slipped into a deep fiscal crisis and the economy ran into an acute balance of payments crisis, as inflation gathered momentum and the current account deficit became unmanageable. The inevitable response in terms of macro-economic stabilisation is, of course, bound to squeeze public expenditure, but the choice of soft options in fiscal adjustment is most likely to squeeze public investment. Taken together, such macro-management by the government would lead to a contraction, rather than an expansion, of aggregate demand. But that is not all. The experience in India suggests that public investment crowds-in rather than crowds-out private investment. Insofar as this is so, a slow down in public investment may also curb private-investment-led expansion.

The fourth possibility is export-surplus-led expansion. Unlike the other three components, in this case it is the external market, instead of the internal market, which is critical in increasing the size of the market to sustain the industrialisation process. In principle, however, import substitution should have an identical effect on aggregate demand insofar as one dollar of imports saved generates the same trade surplus as one dollar of exports. While there is an obvious accounting similarity, there is an important analytical difference. A dollar saved through import substitution may decrease the propensity to import and hence increase the size of the foreign trade multiplier. A dollar earned through exports would increase the level of exports and hence enlarge the base on which the foreign trade multiplier operates. In a large continental economy such as India, however, it is domestic demand and not an export surplus that is likely to be the main source of expansion in aggregate demand. What is more, in the Indian context the macro-economic impact on national income, through the foreign trade multiplier, may be limited by two factors. First, insofar as exports and imports are a relatively small proportion of national income, the impact of the foreign trade multiplier cannot be large in terms of either its base or its size. Second, insofar as there are supply constraints, the foreign trade multiplier may work with respect to money income rather than real income.

The process of industrialisation and growth in an economy may be associated with supply-demand balances or supply-demand imbalances that emerge over time at a macro-level. In either case, interaction between the forces of supply and demand, in a dynamic setting, has important implications for the process of economic growth. *Ceteris paribus*, balances may serve as catalysts to growth while imbalances may operate as constraints on growth.

Consider first, a situation where industrialisation is associated with a balanced growth in demand and supply over time. An increase in market size facilitates the realisation of scale-economies, thus bringing about a cost-reduction, just as a reduction in costs, hence prices, induces a demand expansion. In an industrialising economy, a rapid increase in the share of manufacturing in total output may then be associated with a steady decline in average costs over time. The underlying factors would be dynamic scale-economies, which are a function of cumulative past output or cumulative production experience, and increase in labour productivity. The cost-reduction, passed on to consumers in the form of lower prices, would stimulate demand expansion in domestic, as also foreign, markets. This cumulative causation, which is complex but virtuous, is often termed the 'Kaldor-Verdoon Law'.

Consider next, a situation where industrialisation is associated with the emergence of imbalances between supply and demand over time. More often than not, this is a short-term problem but it can persist in the medium-term. If there emerges a gap between demand and supply, it can be bridged either through imports or by allowing prices to rise. Industrialisation and growth may then be disrupted by a balance of payments crisis or mounting inflation. The problem of imbalances may be exacerbated by an asymmetry, or a mismatch, between the speeds of adjustment on the demand side and on the supply side. The responsiveness of aggregate demand, through some of its principal components, is relatively fast and macro-economic policies can be deployed to adjust domestic demand expansion. Supply adjustment, on the other hand, takes longer even if all the price incentives of a market economy can be brought to perfect function. In other words, the reallocation of resources from one industry to another, one sector to another or one activity to another is a relatively slow process, for resources are neither so mobile nor so substitutable as neo-classical economics suggests. In some economies, supply may adjust particularly slowly due to problems such as the nature of agrarian relations or very inadequate infrastructural facilities, so that State intervention may be essential to coax a response on the supply side. The fast dynamics of demand and the slow dynamics of supply have two important macro-economic implications. For one, growth in aggregate demand and aggregate supply often diverge. For another, insofar as the composition of demand, guided by income elasticities, and the composition of supply, guided by relative profitabilities, do not match, sectoral problems of excess demand or excess supply often emerge. These imbalances affect both the price level and relative prices. Insofar as economies have tolerance limits in terms of an acceptable rate of inflation or a manageable current account deficit in the balance of payments, beyond a point, the persistence of supply-demand imbalances can only operate as a constraint on growth and disrupt industrialisation. Thus, orthodox programmes of stabilisation and adjustment which do not succeed can transform such imbalances into a long-term problem.

CONCLUSION

In this introduction to the book, I began by emphasising the need to examine industrial development, not in isolation, but with reference to structural transformation of economies so as to analyse the macro-economics of industrial growth and thus to consider problems of industrialisation in the wider context of development. In discussing the strategic issues and outlining the macro-economic perspective, I attempted to draw attention to some unexplored issues and some complex questions. There is a clear need for further research which would carry the debate forward and improve our understanding of the industrialisation process. It is hoped that the discussion in the preceding pages would enable the reader to situate the essays that follow in a wider perspective. This should at least contribute to an understanding of the problems, even if it cannot provide definitive answers to complex questions.

[For comments on an earlier draft, I would like to thank C P Chandrasekhar, Ashok Mitra, Prabhat Patnaik and Abhijit Sen. I would also like to thank Mrituinjoy Mohanty for his assistance with the editorial work for this volume.]

REFERENCES

Ahluwalia, Isher J (1985): *Industrial Growth in India: Stagnation since the Mid-Sixties*, Oxford University Press, Delhi.

Bagchi, Amiya K (1970): 'Long-Term Constraints on India's Industrial Growth, 1951-1968' in E A G Robinson and M Kidron (eds), *Economic Development in South Asia*, Macmillan, London.

– (1981): 'Reinforcing and Offsetting Constraints in Indian Industry' in A K Bagchi and N Banerjee (eds), *Change and Choice in Indian Industry*, K P Bagchi and Company, Calcutta.

Bhagwati, Jagdish and Padma Desai (1970): *India: Planning for Industrialisation*, Oxford University Press, London.

Bhagwati, Jagdish and T N Srinivasan (1975): *Foreign Trade Regimes and Economic Development: India*, Columbia University Press, New York.

Byres, T J (1974): 'Land Reform, Industrialisation and the Marketed Surplus in India' in David Lehmann (ed), *Agrarian Reform and Agrarian Reformism*, Faber and Faber, London.

Chakravarty, Sukhamoy (1974): *Reflections on the Growth Process in the Indian Economy*, Administrative Staff College of India, Hyderabad.

– (1987): *Development Planning: The Indian Experience*, Clarendon Press, Oxford.

Krishna, K L (1987): 'Industrial Growth and Productivity in India' in P R Brahmananda and V R Panchmukhi (eds), *The Development Process of the Indian Economy*, Himalaya Publishing House, Delhi.

Mathur, Ashok (1990): 'The Interface of Agricultural and Industrial Growth in the Development Process: Some Facets of the Indian Experience', *Development and Change*, Vol 22, pp 247-80.

Mitra, Ashok (1977): *Terms of Trade and Class Relations*, Frank Cass, London.

Mundle, Sudipto (1985): 'The Agrarian Barrier to Industrial Growth', *Journal of Development Studies*, October, pp 49-80.

Sandesara, J C (1992): *Industrial Policy and Planning: 1947-1991: Tendencies,*

Interpretations and Issues, Sage Publications, Delhi.
Sen, Abhijit (1991): 'Shocks and Instabilities in an Agriculture-Constrained Economy: India: 1964-1985' in J Breman and S Mundle (eds), *Rural Transformation in Asia*, Oxford University Press, Delhi.
Taylor, Lance (1988): 'Macro-Constraints on India's Economic Growth', *Indian Economic Review*, Vol XXIII, No 2, pp 145-65.

1

Disproportionality Crisis and Cyclical Growth

A Theoretical Note

Prabhat Patnaik

IN any underdeveloped economy, the mobilisation of the economic surplus for productive investment constitutes the chief problem of development. In addition, however, where the prospects of transformation through trade are limited, subsidiary problems may arise whereby the effective limit on investment is not the smallness of the mobilised surplus as a whole, but the smallness of some elements of it. This second is the so-called problem of disproportionality. Corresponding to the three different components of capital–fixed capital, wage goods and materials–clearly three different types of disproportionality can arise, each involving a relative shortage of one of the components. Indeed these three have been discussed in different contexts by Feldman (1964)-Mahalanobis (1955), Nurkse (1953)-Dobb (1967)-Sen (1968)-Kalecki (1965a), and Sen and Raj (1961), respectively.

Disproportionalities are clearly of secondary significance in any discussion of long-term constraints on development. Over time, substitution between different goods and different types of resources to the required degree can always be brought about through trade or through adjustments of the domestic production structure. Moreover these adjustments become more rapid and smooth, the greater the dominance of capitalist production in the different sectors of the economy. Thus disproportionality crises are simply the reflection of the uneven fashion in which capitalist development usually takes place–certain sectors spurt ahead, the sluggishness of others checks this spurt, capital is then concentrated in this second group to overcome the sluggishness, this group spurts ahead and creates the conditions for renewed spurt of the first group and so on. The basic long-term constraint continues to be the extent of mobilisation of the economic surplus as a whole. For this reason, Marxist economists with the exception of Kalecki (1965a) have placed little emphasis on disproportionality [Baran, 1957], on the whole I think justifiably. A second reason for this lack of emphasis is that the same socio-political factors lie behind both disproportionality and the overall smallness of the surplus mobilised. After all smallness of some *element* of surplus simply implies inadequate mobilisation from *certain* of the sections to whom surplus accrues.

Nevertheless certain kinds of disproportionality have played an important limiting role–notably that between agriculture, especially food production, and the industrial sector. Though the growth rate of the former is increasing and in the long-run may even increase sufficiently, this particular disproportionality has certainly been one of the elements in the inflationary recession and retains a certain relevance. Some of its implications are explored in the present paper. The discussion though formal, schematic, based on drastic simplifications, and hence unsatisfactory from several points of view, nevertheless perhaps throws some interesting light on the question. The paper's debt to Kalecki's writings will be obvious to the readers.

We shall discuss a simple model in Section I, an extended one in Section II, and the implications and conclusions in Section III.

I

Consider a closed economy with two branches of production. One, 'agriculture' produces food while the other 'industry' produces goods for luxury consumption and investment, there being no stock-holding anywhere. There are two classes in the agricultural sector–landlords and crop-sharers, who divide the crop between them in a fixed proportion. The output of the crop itself is largely determined by exogenous factors, ie,

$$A(t) = \bar{A}(t) \tag{1}$$

Industry has two classes, workers and capitalists and alongside the latter we can place the State, which acts as a gigantic capitalist. Capitalists and landlords consume only luxury goods, workers and crop-sharers only food, crop-sharers remaining outside market relations.

$$w_t = \frac{\alpha \, . \, A(t)}{N_t} \tag{2}$$

where α is landlords' relative share and w_t and N_t denote wage rate and employment respectively. Wage rate equals the total share of landlords, all of which is marketed and constitutes a sort of wage fund, divided by employment. Labour productivity in industry is given, i e, each particular good has given labour requirements and changes in industrial composition do not affect the overall ratio.

$$N_t = nO_t \qquad (3)$$

where O_t is industrial output and n is labour coefficient.

$$O_t = L_t + I_t \qquad (4)$$

i e, industrial output consisting of luxuries L_t and investment goods I_t is demand determined since unutilised capacity exists. The justification of this follows from the working of the model itself. Moreover, we abstract completely from government current expenditure.

$$I_t = \frac{dk(t)}{dt} \qquad (5)$$

where k(t) denotes the stock of fixed capital in industry at time t, i e, there is no depreciation and all investment is destined for industry, which is in line with (1) above.

We have so far ignored three important factors–population growth, use of agricultural raw materials in industry and the production of 'necessary' industrial consumption goods–and shall for the present continue to do so. Several attempts have been made to partition the total industrial sector in India into groups based on raw material requirements though interesting final use patterns often correspond. A notable example is the one by Ashok Rudra (1967) and his associates. In terms of his classification, we are roughly speaking confining our attention here to the second group, i e, 'mining and mining-based industries', while ignoring both the 'agriculture-based industries' and the 'universal intermediaries' – this last in any case is much smaller.

We now come to the two most important relationships. We postulate

$$L_t = e.O_t \qquad (6)$$

where e is a constant. The following attempt to justify this is made not so much because (6) as such is particularly necessary or realistic but in the hope that it clarifies in the process the economic structure underlying the model. We have seen that at time t, landlords sell $\alpha A(t)$ amount of food in exchange for luxuries, and this given employment determines real wages. The mechanism for this is the change in food prices in response to demand, relative to money wages. Suppose money wages are given. With unutilised capacity in the industrial sector, pricing is of the 'degree-of-monopoly' type, i e, prime cost plus a profit margin. Since wage costs are here the sole element of prime costs, money prices must be rigid as well. Thus, denoting money wages by w_m, prices of the two sectors as p_a and p_i, we have

$$\frac{w_m}{w} = p_a \text{ and } \frac{p_i}{w_m} = q$$

which denote the margin. Therefore

$$\frac{p_a}{p_i} = \frac{w_m}{w} \times \frac{1}{w_m.q} = \frac{1}{w.q} \qquad (6')$$

and

$$\alpha\, A(t) \times p_a \,/\, p_i = \alpha\, A(t)/w.q = \frac{N_t}{q} = \frac{n.O_t}{q}. \qquad (6'')$$

Since both n and q are parameters, this implies that the landlords' command over industrial goods is a fixed proportion of the latters' output. This result is clearly a special one and follows from our simple assumptions. (It is as if the workers get a fixed share of the industrial output and hand this over to the landlords in exchange for whatever the agricultural surplus happens to be.) Now, suppose the relative shares of private capitalists and the State also remain unchanged, then the distribution of O_t between the three entities is given. Then *e* in (6) is simply a weighted average of their propensities to consume luxuries, the weights being their relative shares in O_t–these propensities themselves could have any value less than 1. In case of the State, the marginal propensity may be zero, the upper bureaucrats' and managers' luxury consumption being a constant. But for convenience, we ignore the constant term. Now, the State's share of O_t is likely to be constant even if State enterprises produce only investment goods, provided that investment orders–both State and private–are distributed in a fixed ratio between these enterprises and private ones. The condition is not very restrictive though a demonstration, both tedious and perhaps unnecessary, may be safely relegated to a footnote.[1]

Investment consists of two parts–private and State–of which the former is determined by the prospects of profits. We denote investment decisions and actual investments by D and I respectively–using small letters for the corresponding variables in the private industrial sector–and government investment by g. Now suppose we have a purely private enterprise economy and no State sector, we can put

$$d_t = a\,i_t + b(O_t \,/\, k_t - u_o)\,.\,k_t \qquad (7)$$

i e, investment decisions depend upon current investment which by generating profits and finance, tends to stimulate future investment and the degree of utilisation which is some index of the state of the market – u_o being the 'normal' level of utilisation.[2] If markets themselves depended only on this sector's own investment, sustained growth will be difficult to explain. The value of *a* will be less than 1 and though there may be spurts of growth, if they collapse nothing would move the economy out of stagnation.[3] The fact, however, that growth has taken place in such economies is essentially because of the operation of a stream of factors strictly speaking outside the sector itself–e g, inventions, new external markets, etc. The magnitude of growth can be explained by looking at the intensity of these factors. This line of argument was put forward–though not in this way–by Rosa Luxemburg (1951) and developed by Kalecki (1965: ch 14 and 15). Indeed in India, as Bagchi's historical study shows, private investment had been essentially restricted by this market problem and the colonial government's unwillingness to do anything about it. Since Independence government investment has provided such an exogenous stimulus for growth. Indeed so sustained and guaranteed has this stimulus been that entrepreneurs may well have taken it for granted. We assume that the value of *a* has been above 1, i e, temporary set-backs to investment have not affected the basic optimism. With such large government investments, private profits depend rather more generally on I and not merely i. Moreover, if capacity in the state and private sectors grows over time at roughly the same rate (obviously unrealistic in the Indian context) combined with our earlier assumption about distribution of orders we can say that changes in the overall degree of utilisation and such changes for the private sector alone, proceed together. We can thus put

$$d_t = a' I_t + b(O_t - u_o . k_t) \qquad (7')$$

We further assume that the distance between the time-curve of investment decisions and actual investment is one period and that orders once given are never revoked. Then we have

$$d_t = i_{t+1} \qquad (8)$$

Incidentally the value of a′ in (7′) is obviously much less than 1. Of course in a mixed economy, the private sector will take several other factors into account–apart from utilisation–to arrive at its plans, but we ignore these. Finally we take government investment as exogenously determined. In the long run the dimensions of desired investment are derived from some plan objectives which may or may not be fulfilled. In the short run, however, i e, for any particular t, obviously other factors enter into consideration and one such is the level of real wages. We assume–and we shall give a more precise formulation below–that when real wages fall below a certain level $\bar{w}$, government investment slows down to prevent further erosion of real wages for political fears of increasingly militant working class action. Thus

$$g(t) = \bar{g}(t) \tag{9}$$

subject to restrictions we shall mention below. Putting (7′), (8) and (9) together,

$$I_{t+1} = a' \, I_t + b(O_t - u_o \, . \, K_t) + \bar{g}_{t+1} \tag{10}$$

From (4) and (6), $O_t = I_{t/1-e}$ and substituting in (10) and putting

$$c = \frac{1}{1-e} \text{ we get } I_{t+1} = a' \, I_t + b(cI_t - u_o \, . \, K_t) + \bar{g}_{t+1} \tag{11}$$

This is the basic equation and we shall retain it in this particular form in our subsequent discussion. If we look at it in isolation, there is no particular reason why growth could not take place with a uniform trend in this system. If g increased at a steady rate all other variables could get appropriately tethered to g and also increase at the same rate. This steady growth, however, breaks down if agriculture is sluggish. We have two exogenously determined functions of time and disproportionality will arise unless a certain relation holds between the two rates. Suppose both these–$\bar{g}(t)$ and $\bar{A}(t)$–have the specific form of exponential functions. Under the very rigid assumptions of our model, the two exogenous rates must be equal for balanced growth. If however the rate of growth of g exceeds that of A, wages sooner or later must fall to $\bar{w}$ and the growth of g slows down. Thus disproportionality will arise even if agriculture itself experienced no fluctuations, let alone absolute falls in output.

Moreover when the 'ceiling' has been hit, say, at time t the system does not stay there and eventually crawl along it but in fact experiences a downturn. Prior to t, industrial growth was steady and its rate exceeded the agricultural growth rate. At t private decisions are unaffected, so even if growth rate of g is lowered to equal that of A, at t+1 the industrial sector still grows at a faster rate. Therefore w falls below $\bar{w}$. But utilisation must also fall since I_{t+1} has fallen below the level warranted for normal utilisation under steady growth. The middle term in (11) becomes negative and eventually private investment also contracts relatively. When the slowing down of industrial growth has raised w to the level of $\bar{w}$, government investment accelerates and soon the recovery begins. Thus disproportionality turns into a regular cyclical phenomenon because private decisions are made independently and with reference to their own immediate experience, i e, utilisation. This is essentially a result of the anarchy of capitalism and State interference by no means eliminates it.

We have so far discussed why cyclical movements take place at all. Since they do, the system is obviously caught in their grip from the very beginning, i e, we do not really ever start with steady growth. Let us therefore look more closely at the mechanism of the cycle. We shall reformulate (9) in a new way:

$$g(t) = \bar{g}(t)$$

subject to the following constraints:

$$\text{(i)} \quad \frac{dg(t)}{dt} / g(t) > 0 \text{ for all t.}$$

$$\text{(ii)} \quad \frac{dg(t)}{dt} / g(t) \lesseqgtr r \text{ as } w_t \lesseqgtr \bar{w} \qquad (9')$$

In this r is the trend growth rate, i e, sustainable rate of steady growth with balance and obviously $\frac{dA(t)}{dt}/A(t) = r$. Condition (9′) will follow whether we give the government a conscious role or not. It may *know* that in the long run it cannot raise the trend $\bar{g}/g$ above r without inviting political trouble, so it aims at this whenever $w = \bar{w}$. Alternatively it *may not know* and may just be trying to have as much growth as possible provided w did not fall below $\bar{w}$, so that when $w = \bar{w}$, it invests an amount which it thinks is the most it can without pushing w back below $\bar{w}$. Here the trend rate r is established as a resultant of these *ad hoc* manipulations.

We have not specified more precisely the nature of these functions, etc, which would establish the amplitude and the length of the cycle. All these are irrelevant for the present purpose which is to show the existence and the causes of cyclical movements. Essentially when $w = \bar{w}$, $w \neq 0$, which as we saw above is because private investment reacts with a lag and follows its own laws which the government cannot control. It cannot even in its efforts to maintain real wages afford to predict and take account of this private investment. Of course *if somehow* the industrial sector was put on the steady growth path with rate r and appropriate proportions, etc, there would be no cycles but since there are, these continue. Starting from a boom, when $w = \bar{w}$, $\bar{g}/g = r$ but $\dot{I}/I > r$. Therefore $\bar{w} < 0$. The reverse holds when we start from a slump. Insofar as the agricultural sector itself experiences changes in growth which are totally exogenous, these act as random shocks and under certain conditions prevent the damping of cycles [Kalecki, 1965: ch 13].

The important thing here is that the cyclical growth caused by disproportionality is not because of any mistakes of the government but occurs even if the government, within its frame of reference, follows a 'sensible' policy. Before considering the implications of the model, we shall look at certain other things.

II

Disproportionality of the sort we are considering may lead to yet another kind of cyclical movement. We now introduce essential industrial goods (from now on called 'essentials') which only the workers consume. These goods–the prime example being cloth–clearly belong to Rudra's sector 1, ie, agro-based industries. Nevertheless let us make the following grossly unreal assumption on the grounds that it keeps things simple without affecting the basis of the model. We picture to ourselves a situation where these industries control their own raw material supplies which can be expanded when desired without raising the raw material prices. The implications of dropping this will be examined below. Now we have

$$O_t = E_t + L_t + I_t \qquad (4^*)$$

where E_t denotes the new element–the output of these goods–being also expandable with demand.

Since money wages are spent on two different types of goods–food and essentials–a precise expression for real wages becomes more difficult to obtain and handle. We get around this by using a 'food commanded' measure, so that w denotes w_m / p_a even though not all food commanded is actually consumed by the same worker. Instead a part of 'real wages' is spent on essentials. We assume the following expression which though restrictive is replaceable for the total essential consumption:

$$E_t = N_t.e(w_t - w') \qquad (12)$$

with $E_t > 0$, e less than but close to unity. Since w for a given money wage depends upon p_a which in turn depends on A and N, we can, by taking e and w as constants, broadly put

$$E_t = F(A_t, N_t) \qquad (12')$$

with the following property. For a given N, E increases with A, but for a given A, E may behave rather peculiarly as N is varied: over a certain range as N increases it may increase but if N continues to

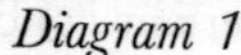

Diagram 1

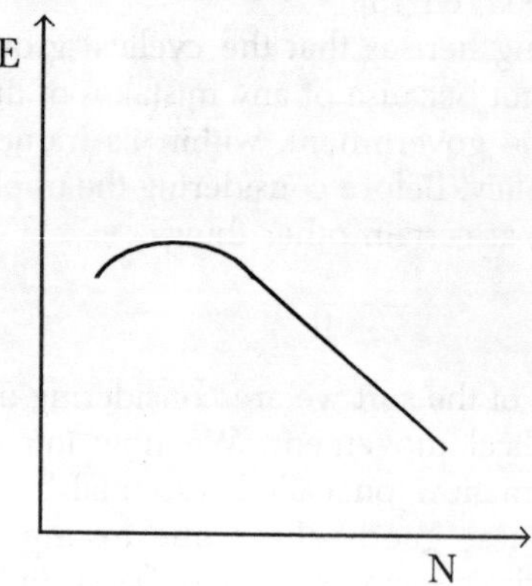

increase it must after a while fall for in the extreme case when w tends to w′, it approaches zero. So *for a given* A, the behaviour of E in response to N may look like in Diagram 1. The reason for this is obvious–essential industrial products are a kind of superior good for workers while food is an inferior good. If the latter becomes very expensive, they will restrict the consumption of the former.[4] In what follows we shall be concerned only with the downward sloping segment of the curve for this is the relevant segment for considering the effects of our kind of disproportionality.

Finally we assume that labour requirements per unit of essentials are the same as in the rest of industry and also that total consumption of luxuries bears a fixed relationship denoted by d to total investment. The latter assumption we shall drop shortly since while simplifying things in the present context it conceals certain relevant aspects. O_t now becomes $c' I_t + F(A_t, N_t)$ where $c' = 1 + d$ and since N_t again equals nO_t, we can put $O_t = G(I_t, A_t)$. Substituting this in the investment function (10) which remains the same and using (1) we now have

$$I_{t+1} = a' I_t + b \mid G(I_t, \bar{A}_t) - u_o . k_t \mid + \bar{g}_{t+1} \qquad (11^*)$$

This is our basic equation. From (11*) it is clear that even if we ignore any limits to the growth of government investment–like the one we discussed before–the sustainable rate of steady growth, consistent with the continued existence of demand for essentials cannot again exceed r, the growth rate of agriculture. A higher rate will eventually lower wages to a level where capacity utilisation in the essentials sector falls and hence investment is restricted. If, however, thanks to the exogenously determined g(t) investment in other sectors continues to increase very rapidly–making the growth rate of the total exceed r–then w will eventually fall to w′ eliminating all demand for essentials.

Even if the industrial sector grew at the trend rate r, it will nevertheless be in the grip of a cycle once it has got started. To understand its mechanism, let us assume that $\bar{g}$ grows steadily at the rate r, i e,

$$\bar{g}(t)/g(t) = r = \frac{\mathring{A}(t)}{A(t)} \qquad (9^*)$$

Clearly a particular solution to (11*) is where all variables grow at the rate r. If somehow the sector is by God's grace placed on this steady growth path, it will continue along it. But if not, or if there is a disturbance, it will move cyclically around this path. If the ratio A/N which we shall denote by μ takes the trend value μ^*, then we have a cycle when for $\mu = \mu^*$, $\dot{I}/I \neq r$. Suppose $\mu = \mu^*$ and $\dot{I}/I > r$, then I, O and hence N are growing faster than A. As a result the wages are falling, the demand for essentials is rising less and less rapidly and the growing unutilised capacity in this sector eventually lowers $\dot{I}/I$ to r. But it cannot stay there, for the unutilised capacity in luxuries and investment goods sectors caused by this very slowing down, pushes it below r. Similarly, on the other side any tendency for this to cumulatively perpetuate itself is checked by the fact that this very slowing down by raising real wages, increases the demand for essentials hence capacity utilisation in that sector. Thus we constantly have two contradictory phenomena affecting capacity utilisation in the two sectors. *Ceteris paribus*, rapid growth of investment improves capacity utilisation in luxuries and investment goods, but ultimately reduces it in the essential goods sector. The interplay of these two provides automatic ceilings and floors and keeps the cycle going. From Diagram 1, it will be clear that the position of μ^* on the curve together with the exact shape of the curve would determine the length and amplitude of the cycle given the other parameters.

This model in some sense is the mirror image of Goodwin's (1951). He used a non-linear accelerator to obtain ceilings and floors, whereas we basically have a non-linear multiplier, something like in Diagram 2. As a result we either have

$$\dot{I}/I > \dot{O}/O > r; \text{ or}$$

$$\dot{I}/I < \dot{O}/O < r.$$

This basic characteristic which gives us the cycle need not be altered when we drop the unrealistic assumption that luxury consumption bears a fixed ratio to investment. We can take capitalists'

Diagram 2

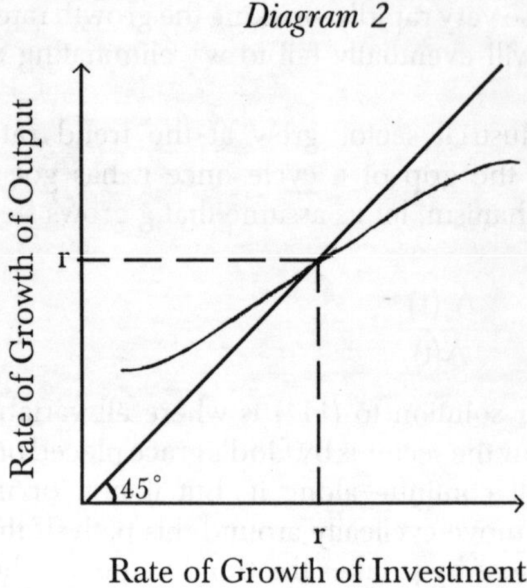

consumption for example to be growing steadily over time since it may depend on some measure of 'permanent income'. Landlords' consumption may grow less steadily—it may be affected by their real income situation with a lag. Or we may assume some other behaviour, but as long as variations in luxury consumption were not such as to systematically counterbalance the movements in capacity utilisation in other sectors, the basic logic of the model is not affected.

We have so far ignored agricultural raw materials. During the boom along with food prices, their prices will also increase. With a degree of monopoly pricing this would raise the prices of goods which use these materials, mainly essentials, relative to other industrial goods. In consequence the tendency towards reduced capacity utilisation in essentials is if anything further strengthened. However, introduction of these complicated inter-industrial price variations makes a macro analysis more difficult which is why we ignored these earlier. In an extreme case raw material shortage may directly bring a boom in such essential industries to an end even before demand has appreciably slackened—a case which we shall return to later.

We now have two distinct mechanisms through each of which disproportionality between agriculture and industry may assert itself as a process of cyclical growth. The question immediately arises: what is the relationship between the two? The two phenomena were discussed above on the basis of two different assumptions about the government's reaction (9′) and (9*). They both however have certain similar characteristics—the raising of real wages above some trend value stimulates investment which owing to disproportionality finally brings wages down; this in turn curtails investment until wages are raised sufficiently to allow a new spurt of growth. So the two mechanisms complement one another and generate an overall cycle around a trend, the wages on which can be taken to be the $\bar{w}$ of our first model and μ^* is the value of μ which corresponds to w. Without specifying more precisely the nature of government's reaction (9′), we clearly can say little about this cyclical process but now let us look at the trend.

Obviously the steady growth trend with all sectors growing at similar rates is a result of our rigid assumptions. The maintenance of intersectoral balance does not require the two sectors to grow at the same rate once we allow for changes in methods of production, sectoral composition, pattern of consumption, etc. Instead it is possible to achieve a rate of industrial growth in excess of r. Of course, cyclical movement in industry caused by disproportionality crises will continue to take place around the higher trend for exactly the same reasons as we discussed above. Moreover, even this growth may be far below what the government considers adequate. Wages on this trend will then be constant at some level $\bar{w}$ as the government would presumably wish to achieve the maximum industrial growth possible without a steady decline in wages. Obviously employment grows at the rate r, i e, less rapidly than industrial output. The output of essentials in such a case will also grow on average at this lower rate. Thus the maintenance of a high rate of industrial growth in the presence of disproportionality necessarily involves a change in the sectoral composition of the industry–a relative stagnation of industrial essentials, compared to the accelerated growth to investment goods and luxuries. This change is naturally accompanied by an increasing rate of exploitation since productivity rises faster than real wages which of course as we saw remain stagnant over time. To induce this lower growth rate and lower investment, the average capacity in the essentials sector which remains unutilised must be proportionately higher than elsewhere. This point is taken up again in the next section's discussion of the implications of the model.

III

To summarise: a slowly growing agriculture imposes strict limits on the growth of industry; these limits in a capitalist economy make their presence felt through a process of discontinuous growth, i e, booms and slumps or cyclical movements; a boom comes to an end when real wages have been pressed hard enough through a rise in food prices to reduce capacity utilisation; this comes about in the industrial necessaries sector by a fall in workers' consumption and in the other industrial sectors by a fall in investment especially of the government which is sensitive to the political implications of continuing inflation in food prices; the sensitivity of private investment to capacity utilisation creates a downward spiral leading to a slump; finally the growing unemployment and the slowing down of inflation create conditions for a new spurt of industrial growth as government investment picks up once again and so eventually does private investment.

Of course, the Indian economy in the plan period has been subject to so many different influences and factors that it would be nonsensical to expect it to exhibit a neat pattern of cycles in line with the predictions of any simple model. It cannot however be denied that cyclical movements arising from disproportionality (and now bearing in mind that agriculture itself grows discontinuously) have embedded themselves in the overall dynamics of the economy. Several writers, notably Ashok Desai (1966) and Charles Bettelheim (1968), have observed this phenomenon. The present model has addressed itself to this problem. Some of its implications specifically on inflationary recession and more generally on growth with disproportionality may be brought together briefly.

(1) The following explanation for inflationary recession in the late 1960s was advanced by A M Khusro:[5] low agricultural output depresses demand but at the same time by making raw materials scarce results in a lower output which can in fact still sell at high prices. Thus raw material scarcity was considered to be the cause for restricted output. However, though such scarcity may have limited output at certain times it is inadequate as a general explanation. The recession in cotton textiles had appeared already before the 1965-66 *fall* in agricultural output which could have affected raw material availability. Even in the 1958 recession, we find that output restriction while maintaining textile prices intact resulted in a fall in raw cotton prices.[6] Thus the explanation following from our model reverses in a sense the Khusro sequence: output shrinks because demand shrinks owing to high food prices; a simultaneous relative (and not absolute) shortage of raw materials may raise their prices but these generally get passed on in the form of high final goods prices through the prime cost-plus type of pricing.

P B Medhora[7] argued that income shifts had taken place away from the urban sector–capitalists and the government–towards the rural rich whose demand for industrial goods was limited; hence the recession. The argument while correctly emphasising the demand side is nevertheless erroneous as it stands. If income shift was the factor that reduced demand there was nothing to prevent the government from deficit financing to an appropriate extent to make up for this reduction. The fact that it could not was precisely because it did not wish to aggravate the inflationary situation, i e, further raise food prices *relative to money wages.* Thus the real limit to government action is imposed not by income shifts but by the fact that $w < \bar{w}$ and to underline this we have deliberately assumed that landlords consume the same sort of goods as capitalists.

(2) This relates to a more general point. Several writers in discussing the Indian economy emphasise the so-called conflicts of interest between the urban and rural sectors [Lipton, 1968]. The present model doubts the meaningfulness of this particular dichotomy, and emphasises instead the vertical division between capitalists and landlords on the one hand and workers on the other. That capitalists and landlords being property-owning classes have a common interest in maintaining a certain socio-economic structure is not open to doubt. But what we are saying now goes much further: if either capitalists or landlords suddenly increase their claims on social output by investing or consuming more, they do not hurt one another. These higher claims are met by utilising more capacity and employing more workers with the given wage bill–in other words by a greater exploitation of the workers. To reformulate Kalecki's aphorism, 'the workers consume what they earn while capitalists and landlords taken together earn what they consume'. We have so far kept crop-sharers outside market relations. If their share of crops is sold immediately and with the money they buy both crops and essentials later then their position is analogous to that of the workers–increased claims of capitalists and landlords hit them too.

It is true that there are limits to the extent to which capitalists and landlords at any time can increase their claims but within these, the *immediate* conflict of interests is not between them.

(3) According to the model there is always a reserve of unutilised capacity in the industrial sector. A part of it is clearly owing to the cycle but a residual element remains even at the top of the boom. The chief obstacle to its utilisation at any time in our model lies precisely in the fact that this would sharply raise the money wage bill and hence food prices. Its existence in other words is a result of disproportionality. What needs to be explained is its perpetuation over time. Why do entrepreneurs go on investing when there is this residual excess capacity even at the top of the boom? The explanation for this lies not in some psychological quirk but by the objective fact of

competition among capitalists. (This competition exists even under oligopoly hence must not be confused with the 'perfect competition' of textbooks.) Two elements can be distinguished within this residual excess capacity and each has a different explanation.

(i) The incidence of demand between the different firms is uneven. At the top of the boom, some firms have better utilisation than others. Now if each firm on the basis of past experience reckons that it may be the 'high demand' firm in the boom, it will maintain on average some spare capacity to meet this demand. Even when in certain booms it is not a 'high demand' firm, provided this fact does not destroy its reckoning, it will continue to maintain this spare capacity. Thus each firm's maintenance of some spare capacity may be justified periodically when it is actually utilised, but for industry as a whole there is always on average a certain excess capacity.

(ii) There may be an additional element even above this spare capacity–which is after all sometimes used. This additional element in fact is perhaps never used, but is maintained on game-theoretic grounds. Any single capitalist faced with the choice between adding to capacity and utilising existing capacity better is guided by what he thinks others will do. If he did not add to capacity while others did, they would be potentially better placed to meet an expanding market, so quite rationally he has to invest despite the unutilised capacity. Since all capitalists think along the same lines a certain level of unutilised capacity is maintained by all and this provides the justification for each one maintaining it. (This kind of thinking lies behind the maintenance of excess capacity in anticipation of import licences, etc, though these fall outside the assumptions of our model.) This of course does not mean that *any* level of excess capacity can be so maintained and justified, but clearly *some* level (within a certain range, depending on government policies, conditions of availability of finance, etc) can be.

Finally, if the response of utilisation in different industrial sectors is similar then the more slowly growing sectors, eg, essentials will have on average a larger element of excess capacity.

(4) We saw earlier that where industrial growth is limited by the slow growth of agriculture, real wages remain constant in the neighbourhood of subsistence level, employment grows slowly, the rate of exploitation increases and this is reflected in an altered industrial structure–essential industrial goods growing slowly compared to investment and luxury goods. Thus industrialisation takes on a 'top-heavy' character and its effects on the living conditions of the bulk of the people are negligible. By contrast when the growth

of agriculture is rapid a similar rate of industrial growth is accompanied by a rise in real wages, a strengthening of the mass industrial market, and since such industries tend to be more labour-intensive a faster growth of employment as well. It follows that if the higher agricultural growth could be 'purchased' by sacrificing a little of the industrial growth, it will still be preferable. Perhaps this is the meaning of the Chinese idea of 'walking on two legs', though such a 'purchase' may become possible only after certain institutional changes, e g, land reforms, have been implemented as in China.

(5) An important feature of 'top-heavy' industrialisation is its excessively heavy dependence on the State to maintain the perpetual stimulus of growing investment demand. We argued earlier that external stimuli, eg, opening of 'outside' markets including those arising from the State sector were necessary to maintain the tempo of capitalist development. In case of 'top-heavy' industrialisation based on a weak mass market, the necessity is all the greater. Any sudden slowing down of government investment or drying up of other stimuli which may have operated together with it throws the industrial sector into a prolonged crisis. The Indian industrial sector is experiencing such a crisis. Several stimuli, eg, the easier avenues of import substitution which operated earlier have exhausted themselves so that even if government investment followed its earlier trend a crisis would still remain. It may appear as if such a crisis would solve itself–that industry would eventually 'pick-up', even if its growth be slower it would have a better 'balance' with agriculture with a consequent shift back of emphasis to essentials and some shedding of its 'top-heavy'-ness. Economies however do not change course, move from one strategy to another so easily.

A more convincing case can be made for the view that the new-found dynamism in agriculture by initially stimulating landlords' consumption of industrial goods, would start a new spurt of growth. This may be so, but not necessarily, eg, suppose landlords exported their entire additional output and imported luxuries from abroad. Though the case does not arise in our simple model of a closed economy, it is not altogether without relevance. Anyway all these lie outside the scope of the present paper, whose purpose is to make some comments on a few issues primarily to stimulate economists better informed and more capable of dealing with such things to react to these comments.

NOTES

1 Under our conditions, State sector's profits are proportional to investment and equal say $s.I_t$. Since landlords' share is a constant proportion of O_t, say $v.O_t$, capitalists' share is $O_t - v.O_t - s.I_t$. Denote capitalists' consumption propensity by e_1 and landlords' by e_2, then $e_1 (O_t - v.O_t - s.I_t) + e_2(v.O_t) + I_t = O_t$ and on simplifying $O_t = h.I_t$ where $h = \dfrac{1-s.e_1}{I-e_1(1-v)-ve_2}$ = constant.

Hence State's share $s.I_t$ is also a constant proportion of O_t.

2 For a discussion of the effects of utilisation on investment, see J Steindl, *Maturity and Stagnation in American Capitalism*, Oxford, 1952.

3 A fuller discussion of this is contained in my paper, 'External Markets and Capitalist Development', *Economic Journal*, 1972.

4 Government of India, *Cotton Textiles Enquiry Committee Report 1958*, makes this point. See also M Kalecki, 'Financing Economic Development', *Indian Economic Review*, Delhi, 1955.

5 A M Khusro, 'Recession, Inflation and Economic Policy', *Economic and Political Weekly*, October 14, 1967. Khusro's paper is valuable and has a broader scope. We are criticising only one aspect of it.

6 See *Commerce*, Annual Number 1965, review of textiles and the *Textile Enquiry Committee Report, 1958*, respectively, for these two assertions.

7 P B Medhora, 'Income Shifts and Recession', *Economic and Political Weekly*, July 27, 1968. My criticisms are not intended to diminish the importance of his article.

REFERENCES

Bagchi, A K: *Private Investment in India 1900-1939*, Cambridge.

Baran, Paul A (1957): *The Political Economy of Growth*, London.

Bettelheim, C (1968): *India Independent*, London, Chapter IX.

Desai, A V (1966): 'Growth and Fluctuations in the Indian Economy 1951-1964', *Economic and Political Weekly*, November 19.

Dobb, M H (1967): 'Some Problems of Industrialisation in Agricultural Countries' reprinted in *Papers on Capitalism, Development and Planning*, London.

Feldman, G A (1964): 'On the Theory of Growtth Rates of National Income', Parts I and II, reprinted in N Spulber (ed), *Foundations of Soviet Strategy for Economic Growth*, Bloomington.

Goodwin, R M (1951): 'The Non-Linear Accelerator and the Persistence of Business Cycles', *Econometrica*, Vol 19, No 1.

Kalecki, M (1965): *Theory of Economic Dynamics*, London (Revised edition).

— (1965a): 'Problems of Financing Economic Development in a Mixed Economy' in *Essays on Planning and Economic Development* (Research Papers, Vol 2), Centre for Research in Underdeveloped Economies, Warsaw.

Lipton, M (1968): 'Strategy for Agriculture: Urban Bias in Rural Planning' in P P Streeten and M Lipton (ed), *The Crisis of Indian Planning*, London.

Luxemburg, Rosa (1951): *The Accumulation of Capital*, London.

Mahalanobis, P C (1955): 'The Approach of Operational Research to Planning in India', *Sankhya*, December.

Nurkse, R (1953): *Problems of Capital Formation in Underdeveloped Countries*, Oxford.

Raj, K N and A K Sen (1961): 'Alternative Patterns of Growth under Conditions of Stagnant Export Earnings', *Oxford Economic Papers*, February.

Rudra, A (1967): *Relative Rates of Growth–Agriculture and Industry*, Bombay.

Sen, A K (1968): *Choice of Techniques*, Oxford (3rd edition).

Annual Number, February 1972

2

Some Aspects of Inter-Sectoral Resource Flow

Ranjit Sau

THE early phase of industrialisation in Japan as well as in the Soviet Union is believed to have been sustained by a net resource flow out of the agricultural sector into industry. By sharp contrast, the position today in China and India is claimed to be just the reverse: resources are flowing into agriculture from industry.[1]

The modality varies. Japan extracted capital from agriculture mainly through fiscal means, while England worked through the terms of trade. During the period 1700 to 1850, redistribution of income in England came about intermittently through unfavourable terms of trade for agriculture.

It is but a short step to shift from the axes of 'agriculture-industry' to the co-ordinates of 'rural and urban', and then to correlate the inter-sectoral flow of resources with the exigencies of the prevailing political system.[2] Before doing such an exercise in political correlation analysis one should however look into the flows between agriculture and industry, or rural and urban sectors, on both current and capital accounts. This paper reports some preliminary findings in this respect. It gives an estimate of the consumption of 'industrial' and 'agricultural' goods in rural and urban areas of India over the years from 1952-53 to 1964-65. With these figures it would be possible to construct a major part of the trade between agriculture and industry, or between rural and urban sectors.

Apart from shedding light on the issue of inter-sectoral flows, this paper shows that the market for industrial consumption goods in India is, in a sense, shrinking: the percentage of per capita consumer expenditure spent on industrial goods is declining over the years rather sharply in rural India, but mildly in urban. Among various fractile groups of population, the ones at the bottom are increasingly withdrawing from the market of industrial consumer goods. In a word, Indian industry is fast approaching the walls of a restricted market. Although our data cover the period up to 1964-65, there is no reason to believe that the trend has been arrested since then.

I

METHODOLOGY

National Sample Survey (NSS) is the main source of our data. It gives item-wise consumer expenditure for the following: (a) food-grains, (b) milk and milk products, (c) meat, egg and fish, (d) edible oil, (e) sugar, (f) salt, (g) other food, (h) clothing, (i) fuel and light, (j) miscellaneous, (k) rent, and (l) taxes. By *industrial goods* we mean items (d) to (j), except that only three-fourths of item (g), namely, other food, is included under this category, the remaining one-fourth of it being considered as non-industrial, that is, agricultural product.[3] Agricultural goods is defined to consist of the first three items together with one-fourth of item (g).

Industrial goods as defined above are not necessarily produced in a factory, nor can they be always identified as urban products. Sugar which is here classified as an industrial good, for instance, consists of gur, sugar candy and sugar. But gur is typically produced in rural areas. Similarly, clothing includes cotton (mill-made, handloom and khadi), wool and silk clothing and bedding and upholstery. Handloom and khadi in particular are supplied by the small-scale cottage industry of rural India. If neither the production in a factory nor the location of their origin in urban areas is the common characteristic of the items classified here as industrial goods, what, then, is their specificity? The single thread which binds them together is that they are not a direct product of agricultural activity as such.[4] Perhaps a more appropriate term would have been 'non-agricultural goods'. But convenience of expression has dictated our choice. These industrial goods, even if they are not all produced in factory today, could be conceivably organised under factory production. If the onslaught of capitalism continues further, in due course they would be brought under the factory system. Although the classification adopted here is therefore crude from the operational point of view, it is quite clear conceptually.

NSS data are available for twelve expenditure groups.[5] For each expenditure group the percentage of per capita consumer expenditure spent on industrial goods is computed. Next, the per capita consumer expenditure of various fractile groups of population is calculated.[6] Now, for matching the NSS expenditure groups with fractile groups of population the per capita consumer expenditure is used as the indicator. In 1964-65, for instance, the rural population fractile group 70-80 had a per capita monthly consumer expenditure of Rs 30.91; while the expenditure group Rs 28-34 in NSS 19th Round (July 1964 / June 1965) had Rs 30.51. So we shall say that the consumption pattern of the former is similar to that of the latter. The expenditure group of Rs 28-34 spent 39.28 per cent of its per capita consumption on industrial goods. Accordingly, it is assumed that the fractile group 70-80 also did the same.[7]

Where such close correspondence between the two figures of per capita consumption was not found, interpolation was resorted to, by simple average of the percentages in the two adjoining, relevant expenditure groups.

In a few later years the per capita consumer expenditure of the richest 5 per cent of urban population was well above that of the top expenditure group, namely, Rs 55 and above or Rs 75 and above as the case may be. In these cases the percentage of consumer expenditure spent on industrial goods by the former has been derived by adding certain percentage points to that of the latter.

Per capita consumer expenditure, and the proportion of expenditure on industrial goods thus having been known, the calculation of the absolute amount of industrial goods consumed, at current prices, is a straightforward matter of arithmetic.[8]

II

SHRINKING HOME MARKET FOR INDUSTRY

Rural India is gradually reducing the fraction of total expenditure it spends on industrial goods. The decline is far more noticeable for the poorer fractile groups. The lower six deciles spent around two-fifths of their expenditure on industrial goods in 1952-53; twelve years later the ratio was hovering near three-tenths (Table 1). The trend in urban India is very much the same (Table 2).

In the annual aggregate consumption of industrial goods of rural areas, the lower six deciles had lost ground, proportionately (Table 3). The relative position of various fractile groups in urban areas appears to be quite volatile (Table 4). However, the richest 10 per cent of population accounts for 30 to 40 per cent of such consumption in both rural and urban areas.

The base of the market for industrial consumer goods in India is narrowing, despite the rapid growth of industrial production in the country over the last two decades. The concentration of industrial consumer goods is rising at the thin, top layer of the population.

Table 1: Percentage of Per Capita Consumer Expenditure Spent on Industrial Goods in Rural India

(Per cent)

Population Fractile	1952-53	1953-54	1954-55	1955-56	1956-57	1957-58	1959-60	1960-61	1961-62	1963-64	1964-65
Poorest											
0-5	39.44	31.24	36.14	36.29	33.35	32.62	31.15	32.46	29.41	30.72	28.28
5-10	39.44	31.24	36.14	36.29	33.35	32.62	33.41	32.57	30.15	31.02	25.10
10-20	38.91	37.24	36.14	36.29	33.26	32.50	35.67	32.69	30.89	31.96	28.90
20-30	40.25	37.24	36.78	37.76	33.18	32.41	35.68	33.10	33.00	33.53	28.83
30-40	42.21	34.81	37.42	39.24	32.36	36.91	36.30	36.59	33.83	36.08	30.60
40-50	39.46	37.94	38.84	37.66	34.30	38.59	36.83	37.92	37.88	38.32	31.17
50-60	40.99	40.86	40.79	40.55	36.23	39.69	37.37	40.58	37.85	39.40	32.62
60-70	42.74	42.37	43.32	43.19	39.35	41.52	41.64	42.54	41.71	41.49	36.36
70-80	44.98	44.65	49.13	44.65	40.96	44.22	43.47	46.40	47.44	44.32	39.28
80-90	47.20	53.15	48.67	47.29	46.46	48.67	44.93	49.11	50.45	48.09	42.74
90-95	53.01	55.96	54.69	51.91	47.91	51.79	49.72	55.41	54.92	53.63	49.02
Richest											
95-100	61.86	62.51	65.76	61.44	60.84	61.54	63.05	68.95	65.51	59.23	62.00
All	46.66	46.38	47.27	46.99	43.08	45.52	45.08	46.87	45.67	44.04	40.17

Table 2: Percentage of Per Capita Consumer Expenditure Spent on Industrial Goods in Urban India

(Per cent)

Population Fractile	1952-53	1953-54	1954-55	1955-56	1956-57	1957-58	1959-60	1960-61	1963-64	1964-65
Poorest										
0-5	41.30	31.68	39.96	36.61	36.92	38.51	39.79	33.75	34.24	36.52
5-10	43.69	36.90	39.96	38.30	36.96	39.04	38.29	39.12	38.67	37.21
10-20	45.65	42.12	40.59	39.98	38.73	39.83	40.61	43.23	39.05	37.89
20-30	47.34	41.11	46.38	43.88	41.38	43.31	43.43	44.53	43.10	39.46
30-40	50.39	43.59	46.22	45.49	42.58	44.35	45.44	46.35	43.83	40.35
40-50	50.29	44.61	47.44	48.28	45.13	46.31	47.52	47.14	46.79	43.34
50-60	53.15	46.15	48.33	49.93	48.15	49.54	49.48	50.24	50.99	44.53
60-70	55.84	49.61	54.35	52.40	50.13	50.51	50.43	51.56	51.74	45.72
70-80	55.87	49.56	55.95	54.36	52.92	53.18	53.17	54.88	54.39	46.49
80-90	62.22	56.36	57.72	56.06	54.96	56.04	56.04	59.31	60.31	55.24
90-95	66.37	60.51	66.12	57.02	66.68	62.50	60.95	62.53	61.93	56.48
Richest										
95-100	75.00	65.00	70.00	66.10	75.00	67.29	70.00	70.00	69.53	70.33
All	58.02	52.04	56.91	54.74	55.16	54.09	54.40	55.14	55.51	52.66

Table 3: Percentage of Consumption of Industrial Goods by Fractile Groups in Rural India

(Per cent)

Population Fractile	1952-53	1953-54	1954-55	1955-56	1956-57	1957-58	1959-60	1960-61	1961-62	1963-64	1964-65
Poorest											
0-5	1.04	0.82	0.97	1.00	1.09	0.99	1.08	0.99	0.87	1.05	1.04
5-10	1.44	1.25	1.28	1.35	1.49	1.14	1.62	1.33	1.23	1.46	1.26
10-20	3.67	3.71	3.18	3.41	3.65	3.34	4.20	3.55	3.26	3.67	3.61
20-30	4.81	4.48	4.02	4.49	4.42	4.02	4.95	4.05	4.11	4.67	4.38
30-40	6.06	4.75	4.83	5.55	4.99	5.38	5.76	5.20	5.03	5.85	5.40
40-50	6.56	6.04	5.78	6.16	6.09	6.51	6.60	6.11	6.56	7.10	6.33
50-60	7.70	7.45	7.04	7.76	7.34	7.66	7.49	7.49	7.57	8.34	7.60
60-70	9.26	9.10	8.87	9.77	9.19	9.25	9.53	8.95	9.64	10.09	9.71
70-80	11.66	11.36	12.19	12.23	11.31	11.67	11.90	11.46	12.97	12.50	12.24
80-90	15.14	17.07	15.43	15.89	15.80	15.91	14.81	15.30	17.00	16.45	16.24
90-95	10.97	11.48	11.34	11.01	10.37	10.82	10.19	11.13	11.62	11.28	11.49
Richest											
95-100	21.69	22.49	25.07	21.38	24.24	23.11	21.87	24.44	20.14	17.54	20.70
All	100.00	100.00	100.00	100.00	100.00	100.00	100.00	100.00	100.00	100.00	100.00

Table 4: Percentage of Consumption of Industrial Goods by Fractile Groups in Urban India

(Per cent)

Population Fractile	1952-53	1953-54	1954-55	1955-56	1956-57	1957-58	1959-60	1960-61	1963-64	1964-65
Poorest										
0-5	0.81	0.71	0.82	0.88	0.82	0.92	1.08	0.82	0.87	1.02
5-10	1.16	1.16	1.09	1.21	1.10	1.26	1.33	1.28	1.29	1.29
10-20	3.05	3.21	2.80	3.09	2.88	3.16	3.40	3.41	3.19	3.22
20-30	3.92	3.90	4.00	4.08	3.77	4.22	4.35	4.29	4.08	3.89
30-40	4.95	5.05	4.67	5.07	4.57	5.10	5.26	5.23	4.85	4.69
40-50	5.83	5.95	5.68	6.26	5.61	6.30	6.30	6.10	5.94	5.79
50-60	7.28	7.20	6.90	7.81	6.93	7.80	7.53	7.49	7.42	6.89
60-70	9.26	9.11	9.17	9.81	8.48	9.40	9.07	8.91	8.77	8.24
70-80	11.02	11.15	11.70	12.62	10.87	11.77	11.59	11.65	11.24	9.97
80-90	15.92	17.46	15.99	16.50	15.04	16.26	15.86	16.55	17.36	15.72
90-95	12.09	12.60	12.51	10.99	12.32	12.23	11.36	11.88	12.68	10.88
Richest										
95-100	24.69	22.50	24.66	21.67	27.61	21.57	22.90	22.39	22.30	28.39
All	100.00	100.00	100.00	100.00	100.00	100.00	100.00	100.00	100.00	100.00

III

RURAL–URBAN TRADE

Tables 5-8 give the estimates, at current prices, of consumption of agricultural and industrial goods in rural and urban areas. For all practical purposes, agricultural goods can be characterised as having their origin in the rural sector alone; but no such identification between industrial goods and the urban sector is permissible, for some of such goods are generated in the rural areas as well.

The rural market for industrial goods is of the order of Rs 3,000 crore to Rs 4,000 crore whereas the corresponding urban market is in the range of Rs 1,000 crore to Rs 1,900 crore (Tables 5 and 7). The preponderance of the rural market is of course largely due to the overwhelming weight of the population it bears and despite the low rate of intake per capita.

The urban market for agricultural goods had more than doubled, from Rs 760 crore in 1952-53 to Rs 1,700 crore in 1964-65, whereas the rural market for industrial goods increased much less from Rs 3,500 crore to Rs 4,500 crore during the same period (Tables 5 and 8). Now if it is assumed that rural India produces industrial goods to meet, say, one-third of its own consumption of industrial goods (and does not export much of industrial goods to urban India), it follows that the rural sector is incurring huge deficit in its trade with the urban sector insofar as consumer goods are concerned. That is to say, the net flow of consumer goods is from the urban to the rural sector in India.

To complete the picture of rural-urban trade, one, of course, has to consider other flows also such as jute, oilseeds, cotton, cement, fertiliser, machinery and so on. But these magnitudes are not likely to change the qualitative nature of the balance of trade. In any case, work is in progress to quantify these flows.

IV

IN LIEU OF CONCLUSION

Our definition of industrial goods in terms of the NSS items of consumer expenditure is broad enough to include all non-agricultural products, from home-spun khadi to the motor car that is produced in the most sophisticated factory. Yet, the rural and urban consumers are found to be reducing the proportion of their expenditure on such industrial goods. Could it be that, foodgrains being the first charge on a consumer's budget, the relative rise in foodgrains prices is eating into the market for industrial goods? Indeed the close association

Table 5: Consumption of Industrial Goods in Rural India by Fractile Groups

(Rs 100 crore)

Population Fractile	1952-53	1953-54	1954-55	1955-56	1956-57	1957-58	1959-60	1960-61	1961-62	1963-64	1964-65
Poorest											
0-5	0.370	0.249	0.269	0.272	0.316	0.331	0.372	0.431	0.373	0.469	0.471
5-10	0.512	0.380	0.356	0.365	0.431	0.454	0.557	0.578	0.530	0.649	0.571
10-20	1.305	1.124	0.888	0.924	1.054	1.124	1.445	1.536	1.405	1.638	1.633
20-30	1.710	1.359	1.121	1.217	1.275	1.350	1.704	1.753	1.770	2.082	1.982
30-40	2.154	1.440	1.348	1.504	1.441	1.809	1.985	2.250	2.164	2.607	2.444
40-50	2.331	1.831	1.613	1.669	1.758	2.189	2.272	2.647	2.825	3.165	2.863
50-60	2.737	2.258	1.965	2.103	2.119	2.575	2.580	3.247	3.257	3.716	3.440
60-70	3.291	2.755	2.475	2.646	2.654	3.109	3.282	3.878	4.150	4.496	4.393
70-80	4.141	3.443	3.400	3.313	3.266	3.924	4.099	4.962	3.584	5.569	5.538
80-90	5.378	5.172	4.305	4.307	4.562	5.351	5.100	6.626	7.314	7.330	7.348
90-95	3.897	3.478	3.164	2.984	2.993	3.640	3.510	4.822	5.000	5.025	5.196
Richest											
95-100	7.704	6.808	6.996	5.796	6.999	7.770	7.534	10.585	8.665	7.818	9.359
All	35.531	30.296	27.901	27.101	28.870	33.626	34.440	43.315	43.037	44.563	45.238

Table 6: Consumption of Agricultural Goods in Rural India by Fractile Groups

(Rs 100 crore)

Population Fractile	1952-53	1953-54	1954-55	1955-56	1956-57	1957-58	1959-60	1960-61	1961-62	1963-64	1964-65
Poorest											
0-5	0.559	0.547	0.475	0.477	0.632	0.683	0.824	0.897	0.895	1.056	1.194
5-10	0.774	0.834	0.628	0.642	0.861	0.936	1.109	1.197	1.226	1.439	1.705
10-20	2.015	1.880	1.565	1.622	2.114	2.191	2.606	3.161	3.140	3.479	4.017
20-30	2.484	2.273	1.920	2.001	2.564	2.812	3.072	3.541	3.593	4.119	4.890
30-40	2.886	2.769	2.246	2.316	3.011	3.083	3.480	3.893	4.226	4.606	5.540
40-50	3.484	2.975	2.519	2.756	3.364	3.472	3.891	4.323	4.636	5.703	6.319
50-60	3.862	3.258	2.837	3.073	3.724	3.881	4.315	4.740	5.322	5.689	7.100
60-70	4.256	3.730	3.211	3.455	4.069	4.352	4.592	5.231	5.793	6.309	7.674
70-80	4.786	4.245	3.474	4.066	4.682	4.909	5.309	5.700	6.150	6.958	8.549
80-90	5.722	4.547	4.472	4.781	5.229	5.993	6.224	6.821	7.118	7.851	9.802
90-95	3.303	2.583	2.589	2.751	3.245	3.335	3.536	3.825	4.406	4.270	5.353
Richest											
95-100	4.237	4.020	3.367	3.538	4.377	4.739	4.341	4.721	4.436	5.011	5.615
All	38.669	33.661	29.304	31.477	37.873	39.985	43.299	48.049	48.592	55.861	67.758

Table 7: Consumption of Industrial Goods in Urban India by Fractile Groups

(Rs 100 crore)

Population Fractile	1952-53	1953-54	1954-55	1955-56	1956-57	1957-58	1959-60	1960-61	1963-64	1964-65
Poorest										
0-5	0.105	0.070	0.092	0.092	0.099	0.109	0.139	0.125	0.162	0.196
5-10	0.151	0.114	0.122	0.127	0.133	0.148	0.177	0.196	0.239	0.248
10-20	0.398	0.316	0.314	0.324	0.347	0.371	0.452	0.521	0.593	0.615
20-30	0.512	0.384	0.448	0.427	0.454	0.495	0.578	0.657	0.758	0.743
30-40	0.646	0.498	0.524	0.531	0.552	0.600	0.699	0.799	0.902	0.896
40-50	0.761	0.587	0.637	0.656	0.677	0.740	0.836	0.932	1.103	1.106
50-60	0.950	0.710	0.774	0.818	0.837	0.916	1.001	1.146	1.380	1.317
60-70	1.208	0.898	1.029	1.028	1.024	1.104	1.205	1.362	1.629	1.575
70-80	1.437	1.099	1.312	1.322	1.311	1.383	1.540	1.782	2.090	1.907
80-90	2.076	1.721	1.793	1.729	1.814	1.910	2.106	2.531	3.226	3.006
90-95	1.577	1.242	1.403	1.151	1.487	1.436	1.508	1.816	2.355	2.080
Richest										
95-100	3.220	2.177	2.766	2.270	3.331	2.534	3.041	3.425	4.145	5.428
All	13.040	9.857	11.215	10.475	12.066	11.747	13.282	15.292	18.583	19.117

Table 8: Consumption of Agricultural Goods in Urban India by Fractile Groups

(Rs 100 crore)

Population Fractile	1952-53	1953-54	1954-55	1955-56	1956-57	1957-58	1959-60	1960-61	1963-64	1964-65
Poorest 0-5	0.144	0.149	0.134	0.154	0.167	0.171	0.207	0.245	0.307	0.339
5-10	0.188	0.194	0.179	0.197	0.223	0.227	0.275	0.301	0.372	0.416
10-20	0.457	0.430	0.446	0.469	0.532	0.543	0.634	0.658	0.892	1.004
20-30	0.547	0.521	0.496	0.511	0.624	0.622	0.725	0.786	0.954	1.132
30-40	0.601	0.636	0.578	0.613	0.714	0.718	0.803	0.878	1.099	1.312
40-50	0.707	0.715	0.656	0.670	0.780	0.793	0.870	0.982	1.177	1.421
50-60	0.778	0.768	0.772	0.778	0.849	0.875	0.956	1.059	1.234	1.609
60-70	0.845	0.842	0.778	0.855	0.949	1.004	0.083	1.193	1.388	1.830
70-80	0.999	1.003	0.931	1.021	1.075	1.116	1.230	1.352	1.580	2.129
80-90	1.053	1.182	1.177	1.153	1.306	1.336	1.504	1.520	1.961	2.258
90-95	0.607	0.660	0.611	0.764	0.631	0.719	0.836	0.922	1.241	1.456
Richest 95-100	0.644	0.921	0.790	0.937	0.888	1.007	0.956	1.076	1.369	2.163
All	7.569	8.021	7.549	8.122	8.738	9.131	10.079	10.972	13.575	17.067

between the upward movement of foodgrains prices and the slump in the demand for cotton textile has been observed many a time. Secondly, there is the inequality of income distribution, which stands in the way of expansion of the market for industrial goods at the lower stratum of the population.

Factory production has been replacing cottage and small-scale operations for many a consumer item. Some of the items included in the definition of industrial goods here yet continue to be allied with the agricultural activities of a family. But in principle they can be separated from agriculture and brought under the system of factory production; in course of time it may actually so happen. The category of industrial goods adopted here is broad enough to encompass all non-agricultural products. Should the classification be narrowed down to only factory-made goods, the decline in the proportion of expenditure on industrial goods may even be all the more glaring. For, in case foodgrains become more expensive and thus erode a consumer's budget for industrial goods, the axe falls first on factory-made goods before it cuts into the demand for the produce of a farm- or family-related activity. If he has now less to spend, the consumer would switch from sugar to gur, for example.

It is widely held that NSS data underestimate the consumption of the richer sections of the population. If so, the increasing degree of concentration that is observed in the consumption of industrial goods may even be actually higher than what is reported here.

There are discrepancies between the NSS and the Central Statistical Organisation of the Government of India insofar as the estimate of the private consumer expenditure is concerned. We are now doing alternative calculations with the CSO data as well. But the general conclusions reached so far are not going to be affected.

NOTES

[Research assistance of Ratan Ghosh and Manaswita Sanyal is acknowledged, without ascribing any responsibility for the findings here.]

1 Shigeru Ishikawa, *Economic Development in Asian Perspective*, 1967, Ch 4. See also John W Mellor, 'Accelerated Growth in Agricultural Production and the Intersectoral Transfer of Resources', *Economic Development and Cultural Change*, October 1973; Uma J Lele, 'Agricultural Resource Transfers and Agricultural Development: A Brief Review of Experience in Japan, England and France', Occasional Paper No 13, Cornell University, June 1970; and T H Lee, *Intersectoral Capital Flows in the Economic Development of Taiwan, 1895-1960.*

For the theoretical debate, see Alexander Erlich, 'Preobrazhenski and the Economics of Soviet Industrialisation', *Quarterly Journal of Economics*, February 1950; B F Johnston and J W Mellor, 'The Role of Agriculture in Economic Development', *American Economic Review*, September 1961.

For recent growth models, see W Arthur Lewis, 'Economic Development with Unlimited Supplies of Labour', *The Manchester School*, 1954; J C H Fei and G Ranis, *Development of the Labour Surplus Economy: Theory and Policy*, 1964; and D W Jorgenson, 'The Development of a Dual Economy', *Economic Journal*, 1961.

The importance of this issue in India has been also highlighted by S Chakravarty, 'Reflections on the Growth Process in the Indian Economy', *Indian Left Review*, June 1974.

2 See Ashok Mitra, 'Class Relations and Growth of Output', in B Singh and V B Singh (ed), *Social and Economic Change*, 1967; and M Lipton, 'Strategy for Agriculture: Urban Bias and Rural Planning' in P Streeten and M Lipton (eds), *The Crisis of Indian Planning*, 1968.

3 'Other food' includes pulses and products, vegetables, fruits and nuts, spices, beverages and refreshments. 'Miscellaneous' includes pan and supari, tobacco and products, drugs and intoxicants, amusements and sports, education, medicine, toilets, sundry goods, consumer services, conveyance, ceremonials, furniture, musical instruments, ornaments, domestic utensils, footwear and other durable and semi-durable goods and their repairing expenses including the maintenance of residential houses.

4 This is subject to the qualification that the presence of pan and supari in 'miscellaneous items' of consumer expenditure would lead to slight over-estimation of industrial goods.

5 The groups are as follows: Rs 0-8, 8-11, 11-13, 13-15, 15-18, 18-21, 21-24, 24-28, 28-34, 34-43, 43-55, and 55 and above. For some later years, further breakdown in the form of Rs 55-75, and Rs 75 and above are given.

6 Source: Planning Commission, Government of India, *Report of the Committee on Distribution of Income and Levels of Living*: Part II, 1969; NSS Reports on Consumer Expenditure; and B S Minhas, 'Rural Poverty, Land Redistribution and Development Strategy: Facts and Policy' (Table 1), *Indian Economic Review*, 1970. For the methodology, see also Ranjit Sau, *Indian Economic Growth,* 1973, pp 30-31.

7 In all calculations the following correspondence between NSS rounds and the financial years is assumed: 1964-65 (19th round: July 1964/June 1965), 1963-64 (18th round: February 1963/January 1964), 1961-62 (17th round: September 1961/July 1962), 1960-61 (16th round: July 1960/August 1961), 1959-60 (15th round: July 1959/June 1960), 1957-58 (13th round: September 1957/May 1958), 1956-57 (11th round: August 1956/February 1957), 1955-56 (10th round: December 1955/May 1956), 1954-55 (8th round: July 1954/March 1955), 1953-54 (7th round: October 1953/March 1954), 1952-53 (4th and 5th rounds combined: August-September 1952, and December 1952/March 1953 respectively).

Exception: The consumption patterns of expenditure groups of 10th and 11th rounds are applied on the estimates of monthly per capita consumption of fractile groups as of 9th round (May-November 1955) and 12th round (March-August 1957) respectively for computations relating to the years 1955-56 and 1956-57, for both rural and urban.

For the comparability of data of various rounds see Uma Datta Roy Chowdhury, 'Study of Trends in Consumer Expenditure, 1953-54 to 1960-61', *Indian Economic Review*, 1967.

8 We have taken census figures of rural and urban population for 1951, 1961 and 1971; the figures for the years in between have been estimated according to the observed growth rate over the decade. Then three-quarters of one year's figure has been added to one quarter of the following year's to convert the data from calendar year to fiscal year.

Special Number, August 1974

3

Growth and Stagnation in Indian Industrial Development

K N Raj

THAT Indian industry has made impressive strides since independence is so self-evident a proposition that it is hardly necessary to reiterate it. What we know about small-scale industrial enterprises is of course inadequate for drawing firm inferences about the nature and extent of progress in this highly decentralised segment of manufacturing activity in the country. But we have more ample and reliable data about factory enterprises, and it is clear that their net output through manufacturing has risen more than four-fold over the period 1947-74 (Table 1). As any random sample of their output would reveal, the progress made has been even greater if judged in terms of the range and sophistication of the products manufactured.

At the same time one can discern two features of the growth process in this sector which are no less striking. One is the emergence of a significant quantum of unutilised manufacturing capacity; the other is a sharp decline in the rate of growth of industrial output since the mid-sixties. The two could be interrelated but not necessarily; considerable unutilised capacity was reported even in the period 1960-64 when the rate of growth of industrial output was rising at around 8 to 10 per cent per annum. In any case, the emergence of unutilised capacity and the decline in the rate of growth of output taken together are clearly a matter for serious concern.

The decline in the rate of growth of industrial output since the mid-sixties has naturally widened the gap between the targets set in the five-year plans and the actual record of achievement in this sector. In the First, Second and Third Five-Year Plans the rate of growth of output aimed at in the sector of large-scale manufacturing were approximately 7, 10.5 and 10.75 per cent per annum respectively, while the realised annual rates touched around 6, 7.75 and 8 per cent in the corresponding plan periods. So, while there were shortfalls, they were

Table 1: Index Numbers of Industrial Production in Factory Enterprises

Category of Industry	Weights Attached in Index Numbers with Base Year of		Index Numbers of Industrial Production						
			1947	1951	1951	1956	1961	1965	1970
			1946=100.00		1960=100.00				
	1946	1960							
Agro-based industries	66.55	47.05	95.6	96.9	72.5	88.2	105.9	125.9	136.8
Mineral-based industries	13.65	15.02	102.1	124.6	54.2	76.5	105.8	138.8	173.8
Metal-based industries	9.30	9.09	96.8	115.5	42.5	61.0	117.9	186.5	208.9
Chemicals and chemical-based industries	4.92	7.26	102.7	260.2	42.4	63.7	113.4	159.3	236.5
Machinery manufacturing industries	5.58	15.43	249.2	272.3	19.9	79.1	115.2	224.9	228.7
Electricity, gas and steam	—	5.47	—	—	35.7	58.5	116.3	190.5	334.0
All Industries	100.00	100.00	97.2	117.2	54.8	78.4	109.1	153.8	180.7

Notes: 1 The index numbers of production for all industries (1960=100.00) were 186.1 for 1971, 199.4 for 1972, 200.6 for 1973, and 201.8 for the first seven months of 1974. A category-wise breakdown of the kind presented in the above table is not readily available for the period 1971-74.

2 Making allowance for the percentage increase in the output of *all* industries between 1947 and 1951, but none for the difference in the weightage attached to the various categories of industry covered by the series for the period before 1951 and for the period after, the index number of industrial production for *all* industries, with 1947 taken as base year (100.00), will be approximately 433.0 for 1974.

Source: V V N Somayajulu, 'Structural Changes and Growth in Indian Industries, 1946-1970', Table 11, *Asian Economic Review*, 1973.

not very large. The position has changed significantly since then, in fact alarmingly.

In the first version of the Fourth Five-Year Plan published in 1966 (soon after the devaluation of the rupee), the rate of growth of industrial output aimed at was about the same as in the Third Plan, i e, about 10.75 per cent per annum. The final 1969 version of the Fourth Plan, prepared after three years of Annual Plans (sometimes referred to as a period of 'plan holiday'), aimed at a still higher rate of about 12 per cent per annum, presumably to make up for the ground lost in the period 1965-68. The Draft Outline of the Fifth Plan, published towards the end of 1973, lowered the sights somewhat and fixed a rate of growth of only about 8 per cent per annum. But the realised rates of growth of industrial output since the mid-sixties have been very much lower than all this: it was only about 3.33 per cent per annum in the period 1965-70 and around 2.75 per cent per annum in the period 1970-74 (Table 2). With the population of the country growing at the rate of around 2.5 per cent per annum, the increase in per capita industrial output over the entire decade, 1965-74 could have been only marginal.

Table 2: Annual Rates of Growth of Industrial Production in Factory Enterprises

(Percentages)

Category of Industry	Annual Compound Rates of Growth					
	1947-51	1951-56	1956-61	1961-65	1965-70	1970-74
Agro-based industries	0.3	4.0	3.8	4.4	1.7	—
Mineral-based industries	5.1	7.2	7.7	7.0	4.6	—
Metal-based industries	4.5	7.5	14.1	12.2	2.3	—
Chemicals and chemical-based industries	26.2	8.5	12.2	7.9	9.0	—
Machinery manufacturing industries	2.2	32.1	7.8	18.2	0.3	—
Electricity, gas and steam	—	10.4	14.7	13.2	11.9	—
All Industry	4.8	7.4	6.8	8.9	3.3	2.8

Notes: 1 These estimates of rates of growth are based on the data presented in Table 1.

2 When 1951 is taken as the base year (and different weights attached to the industries covered according to their relative importance in that year), the annual rate of growth of output of all industries in the period 1951-56 works out to 5.8 per cent per annum. Similarly, when 1956 is taken as the base year, the rate of growth of output of all industries in the period 1956-61 works out to about 7.2 per cent per annum (Somayajulu, op cit, Tables 9 and 10).

Estimates of unutilised manufacturing capacity in India are relatively few and vary a great deal. Their conceptual and statistical bases are also often not precise enough for one to be sure how much reliance can be placed on them. For instance, according to an estimate made in 1965 within the United States Agency for International Development (to be referred to hereafter as the USAID estimate),[1] the net output of large-scale enterprises could be increased with already installed capacity (as of 1964) by over 75 per cent in the case of engineering industries; and by about 15 per cent in the case of chemical industries, if an additional shift was introduced in their operation and the necessary imports of materials (described usually as 'maintenance imports') provided for.[2] However, if one were to go by an estimate made by the National Council of Applied Economic Research (NCAER) for the period 1961-64,[3] the increase in net output that could be realised under what was described as 'desirable working conditions' was only a little over 30 per cent in the engineering industries but over 50 per cent in the chemical industries; the NCAER's estimate of the possible increase in the net output of large-scale manufacturing industries as a whole under 'desirable working conditions' was about 30 per cent.[4]

In still sharper contrast, we have estimates of 'potential-utilisation ratios', computed on a more precisely defined and dependable statistical basis by the Reserve Bank of India which indicate that the underutilisation of capacity was only around 12 per cent in all manufacturing industries taken together in the first half of the sixties (Table 3). However, in a sense, these Reserve Bank estimates beg the question, since 'potential production' for any industry is defined as nothing more than the maximum level attained by it either at the point of measurement or prior to it.

Estimation of true capacity in manufacturing industry and of the unutilised part of it is beset with many complex problems, and it is therefore not surprising that there should be such wide differences in the estimates offered. What one has to be careful about, however, are the uses to which the estimates are put.

For instance, the USAID estimate referred to above was used primarily for making quantitative assessments of the likely beneficial effects on production if the rupee was devalued and this was done along with simultaneous import liberalisation sustained by additional foreign aid. For this purpose it was implicitly assumed that the existence of unutilised capacity was an adequate basis for expecting substantial increases in industrial output. The increases in output were estimated at no less than the equivalent of $ 1 billion in the industries which would directly benefit from import liberalisation, another $ 1.4 billion

Table 3: Potential-Utilisation Ratios for Manufacturing Industries

Year	Machinery and Equipment Manufac-turing Industries (10.51)	Basic In-termediate Goods Industries (10.02)	Other In-termediate Goods Industries (25.42)	Consumer Goods Industries (36.05)	All Manufac-turning Industries (100.0)
1960	76.8	84.6	89.9	90.3	87.7
1961	80.4	89.7	88.7	91.4	88.9
1962	83.7	85.9	89.8	89.7	88.5
1963	80.5	90.5	89.3	85.7	86.7
1964	84.8	88.0	88.8	87.4	87.6
1965	84.9	86.8	89.4	88.1	87.9
1966	69.4	85.2	83.3	86.6	83.2
1967	63.5	80.8	83.2	81.9	79.8
1968	62.9	83.2	84.3	81.6	80.2
1969	61.3	87.8	79.1	85.0	80.5
1970	59.2	80.5	79.5	86.2	80.0
1971	56.9	81.0	77.0	82.6	77.4
1972	57.0	86.2	81.4	83.0	79.6
1973	61.6	82.0	80.3	79.8	

Notes: 1 The weights attached to the four major categories of manufacturing industry are given in brackets. Mining and quarrying, electricity, shipbuilding and repair, etc, are not covered, and hence all the industries covered in the index numbers of industrial production do not figure under 'all manufacturing industries' in this table.

2 The potential production for any given industry during a year is defined as the peak (maximum) level of monthly production attained by that industry at the point of measurement or prior to it. As the official index numbers of industries, the potential production of an industry for a year has been taken as the peak level reached by the monthly production index for the industry during the year under consideration. For highly seasonal industries like tea, salt and sugar, an exception has been made by considering the peak annual average production index as the potential for a particular year because otherwise the utilisation becomes much lower than that for other industries which do not show such pronounced seasonal pattern. In the case of these industries also the potential is assumed to be non-decreasing.

Source: *Reserve Bank of India Bulletin*, April 1970, March 1972, October 1973 and September 1975.

of additional output in other non-agricultural sectors of the economy, and substantial (though unestimated) gains in agricultural income induced by increased production in agro-based industries. These estimates were described as reasonable though 'crude' guesses. But the data on which the estimates were based, and the methods adopted for estimation, were not good enough, in fact quite dubious, for even 'crude' guesses.

The reasons why they were not adequate can be easily seen from the conclusions of another and professionally very much more scrupulous study of industrial capacity utilisation completed towards the end of 1965.[5] The following extracts will convey the essential points:

> The shortage of foreign exchange for the import of components, raw materials and spare parts is undoubtedly the most important single factor limiting output in the industries studied. There can be no doubt that, with greater availability of imported supplies, production can be raised almost immediately in at least the same proportion. *The demand for final products at the present time is, however, substantially less than full capacity output in the technical sense.* It would appear that nearly all firms in these industries have responded to years of shortages and high profits by steadily expanding capacity, well beyond the limits indicated in the Industries Act licences... *The accurate measurement of capacity in these is... no guide to the amount of additional foreign exchange that is required from the economic point of view. A smaller amount of foreign exchange would suffice to meet present demand in full.* Requirements will no doubt grow as demand increases from year to year; on the other hand, there may, to an extent, be import substitution in the raw materials... *In the industries that we have studied, it is demand and not capacity that would set the limit to output* if an adequate supply of components and raw materials were available. These conditions may also prevail in a number of other industries. *We consider, therefore, that the first step in any further study should be to estimate the current demand for each product* (italics mine).[6]

The lines of further investigation and analysis pointedly suggested by this study (of which the chief author was a distinguished economist, the late V K Ramaswami) do not however seem to have been pursued. This is perhaps one reason why those who took seriously the USAID estimate, and supported on that basis the policy of undertaking import liberalisation along with the devaluation of the rupee in 1966, had to regret it later.[7]

While the existence of considerable under-utilisation of industrial capacity is a matter for legitimate concern, one has to be careful therefore about the estimates offered and even more about the uses to which they are put. It seems timely to strike a note of caution, as estimates indicating massive under-utilisation in manufacturing industry are now again being put forward. A recent one places it at no less than 40 per cent of the installed capacity; and on this estimate are built various programmatic policy recommendations similar to those made a decade ago on the basis of the USAID estimate.[8] The assumptions underlying such estimates, not to mention the policy recommendations, need careful scrutiny and economic analysis.

If a measurement of unutilised capacity in manufacturing industry is at all attempted for policy-making purposes it should in fairness cover not merely the factory enterprises but the small-scale enterprises engaged in manufacturing which may be affected by the contemplated policy measures. The economic role and interests of these two categories of industry are not necessarily identical or even similar. Small-scale enterprises were left out in the USAID estimate of 1965 mainly on the ground that they did not consume much foreign exchange, but this meant that the possibility of their being competed out, by the additional imports to be made available to the factory sector through foreign aid, did not receive the attention it deserved.

The factors governing multiple-shift operation for more intensive utilisation of capacity in manufacturing industry are also of a much more complex nature than is sometimes thought.[9] So one must resist the temptation of making facile assumptions about the possibilities of such operation, however desirable it may itself be, without examining all the relevant aspects for each of the concerned industries under the given conditions and making sure that the conditions are in fact favourable for its adoption.

Actually, as in the mid-sixties, what is really important to undertake is not a more comprehensive or accurate measurement of *capacity* but an analysis of the factors governing the *demand* for manufactured products. Before attempting a disaggregated industrywise analysis, it would be useful however to confine attention to the factors governing the demand for broad categories of industry. This is what I propose to do now very briefly in order to bring out the main reasons for the trends in industrial output that have been in evidence from the mid-sixties to the mid-seventies and to indicate some of the inferences one can draw about the future course of industrial development in the country.

Essentially there are three major sources of demand: households and private enterprises within the country, government (including public enterprises), and the world outside. The demand generated within the country is in turn of three kinds: demand for consumption goods, demand for investment goods, and demand for intermediate products going into the production of consumption or investment goods. These are therefore the categories with reference to which the analysis needs to be done. For the sake of brevity, however, we shall not go into each of them in detail but confine ourselves to the broad essentials. I shall not even touch upon issues concerning world demand for Indian products as, in the present context, it will require much more detailed analysis than can be attempted in the course of this paper.

Private consumer demand in a country such as India depends to a large extent, as one should expect, on how things go in the agricultural sector. If output and income in this sector are rising rapidly, consumer demand for both agricultural and non-agricultural products can also be expected to increase rapidly, the latter even more than the former since higher proportions are generally spent on non-agricultural products as levels of income rise. Output and incomes in the agricultural sector need not of course always rise together since the effect of sharp increases in output (particularly when they are sporadic as due to exceptionally good monsoons) could well be to lower the prices of agricultural products more than proportionately; this is in fact an important factor governing agricultural incomes in some regions of the country characterised by serious year-to-year variations in climatic conditions and water supply (a theme to which we shall shortly revert).

A large segment of Indian manufacturing industry—in fact most of the traditional industries like cotton and jute textiles, tea, sugar, vegetable oils, and tobacco built up before independence—is also considerably 'agro-based' in the sense that they depend mainly on agricultural inputs. Their output is therefore directly affected when agricultural performance is not good enough. Since the demand for items such as cotton textiles, vegetable oils, tea and even sugar has a fairly broad base in the rural population dependent on agriculture, as well as among the urban population who might also be indirectly affected by what happens in agriculture, it is not surprising that the rate of growth of output in these agro-based industries should reflect the trends in agricultural output.[10]

As is now well known, the so-called green revolution has failed to raise the overall rate of growth of agricultural output in the country above the level achieved in the 15 years prior to 1965. It certainly helped to increase very significantly the output of a few crops such as wheat, bajra and maize within a short period (in the same way that similar introduction of new varieties of sugarcane, developed at an agricultural research institute in Coimbatore, brought about a doubling of its output within about 6 years in the 1930s). Expansion in the output of crops like wheat has been however partly at the expense of other crops such as cotton and groundnut (and indirectly even pulses) from which land was competed away. In any case, the output of even the few crops which had recorded sharp spurts towards the late sixties is not growing so rapidly any more. Whether there has been in consequence a deceleration in the overall rate of growth of agricultural output is not certain yet, but that it remains low is beyond doubt.

There is of course still very considerable scope for continuous scientific innovation in agriculture, and its impact may well begin to show more perceptibly in the coming years in the case of other crops such as rice and pulses. It is important however to recognise that there are serious constraints on the rate of growth of agricultural output in India on account of limited availability of readily cultivable land and either shortage or sharp variability in the supplies of water.[11] These can be overcome in a variety of ways, but not overnight. Moreover, obvious measures such as extension of irrigation have been found to be to a large extent infructuous on account of various institutional impediments arising from the pattern of land holdings and the consequent inability to adopt all the necessary and otherwise feasible steps required for efficient water management.[12] It would be therefore a serious error to repeat the mistake made earlier of believing that a rapid acceleration in agricultural growth is feasible in the immediate future if only much larger inputs such as chemical fertilisers are applied. In fact, the demand for such inputs is itself likely to grow less rapidly than otherwise on account of constraints of the kind just referred to.

A part of private consumer demand is however for products which are not agro-based in the sense of being dependent on agricultural inputs; they may, for instance, be 'chemical-based' such as synthetic textiles, plastic goods, and pharmaceuticals, or 'metal-based' such as bicycles, electrical appliances, motor cycles and cars, radios and television sets. The rate of growth of agriculture need not therefore act as a constraint on the rate of growth of output of such products, provided the demand for them is rising rapidly enough and the necessary intermediate goods (chemicals, metals, etc) are available in adequate quantity.

However, in India given the level of incomes, the consumer demand for most of these products comes mainly from the top strata of society. The rate of growth of demand for them depends therefore to a large extent on the rate at which incomes grow in the relevant range. The industrial and commercial policies followed hitherto have provided ample scope for fairly rapid growth of incomes in this range. If agricultural output does not grow rapidly enough, or even if it does grow a little faster but the increases in output are realised mainly in the larger farms, this is likely to take place only alongside further accentuation in the inequalities of income and wealth. There has been evidence of such accentuation for some time. If this continues, a pattern of industrial development based on high rates of growth of demand for 'luxury' and 'semi-luxury' products may well come to be regarded as the only way of maintaining a high rate of growth of output in this sector. It would of course be wholly contrary to the strategy advocated in the Draft of the Fifth Five-Year Plan (published towards the end of 1973); but there are many sophisticated and not-so-sophisticated ways in which a case can be made for it on 'pragmatic', 'rational' and even 'scientific' grounds.[13]

It is important however to recognise fully all the implications–social, political as well as economic–of choosing such a path. Let me quote a few extracts from a paper by the well known Brazilian economist, Celso Furtado,[14] on the experience of Brazil in this regard, as it happens to be a country in which this policy has been adopted and pursued with great vigour since the late sixties:

Brazil's high rate of growth in industrial production attained in the last five years (1968-72), after a period of seven years of relative stagnation (1961-67), has been obtained through a very successful government policy which aims at attracting the MNC (multi-national corporation) and fostering the expansion of such corporations already installed in the country...

The state has also been playing important complementary roles by investing in physical infrastructure, human capital (in an attempt to enlarge the supply of professional cadres and personnel), and in those industries with a low capital turnover. Industries producing homogeneous products such as steel, non-ferrous metals and other standard inputs of the industrial system do not rely on innovation of products to compete or generate market power... Furthermore, a policy of low prices, followed by such industries through concealed subsidies, may be defended as essential to foster the process of industrialisation. Thus, keeping this block of industries in the hands of the state, totally or partially, may be the best way for MNCs to obtain a rapid payoff, and may maximise profits and expansion.

The most complex part of this policy concerns the process of fostering and steering income concentration. To obtain the desired result, the Brazilian government has been using various instruments, particularly credit, income and fiscal policies. The first spurt of demand for durable consumers' goods originated from a rapid expansion of consumers' credit, benefiting the upper middle class... It is through fiscal policy, however, that the government has been pursuing the more ambitious objective of giving permanence to the new structures. Scores of 'fiscal incentives' have been implemented, aiming at creating a sizeable group of rentiers within the middle class. As a matter of fact, every person having to pay income tax (approximately 5 per cent of the families) has been induced to compose an investment portfolio as an alternative to the payment of part of the tax due... The apparent objective of the government in adopting this policy is to link the purchasing power of the upper middle class to the most dynamic flow of income, the flow of profits. *In this particular and important aspect, Brazil is engendering a new type of capitalism, heavily dependent upon the appropriation and utilisation of profits to generate a certain type of consumption expenditure... Nowhere has a capitalist economy been so dependent upon the state to gear demand to supply* (italics mine).

What such a pattern of development implies in social terms should be fairly obvious to a Bombay audience. Politically, Brazil has of course been under a military dictatorship, which has had to make the regime even stricter a year ago. This political tightening-up was compelled by economic factors, in particular the inability of the luxury goods industries (and of industries such as steel catering to them) to continue producing and growing as hitherto.

One should perhaps add that Brazil has been able to sustain this pattern of development so far not only on account of capital inflow through multinational corporations–they have also been remitting back their profits on a fairly large-scale–but through a sub-regional trade arrangement (Latin American Free Trade Area) under which Brazil has been able to export manufactured industrial products to its neighbours, as well as through large exports of agricultural products, such as coffee and livestock products, with its plentiful resources of land.[15] India does not have these advantages now.

The temptation to follow the Brazilian model is likely to be considerable in India for several reasons: (1) the sharp fall in the rate of growth of industrial production since the mid-sixties has been mainly because the process of import-substitution of capital goods (i e, machinery and equipment as well as related intermediate goods such as steel), accelerated by the Second Five-Year Plan, had made enough progress to sustain the rate of investment attained in the economy, except of course for some imports of these goods which would always be required on account of the particular specifications they need to satisfy (Tables 2 and 4); (2) the rate of investment in the economy has not only failed to rise since the mid-sixties but has fallen as a proportion of the national product (Table 5); (3) industries manufacturing products catering to the demand of the upper-income groups (durable consumer goods, for instance) have also been adversely affected by lack of adequate demand (Table 4); and (4) since the domestic rate of saving has not been rising rapidly enough to sustain even the current rates of investment, any stepping-up of the rate of investment, it could be argued, requires generating higher rates of saving from among those who have already incomes high enough for saving more, and also supplementing domestic saving with foreign saving (which might be available, beyond a point, only in the form of private capital inflow through multinational corporations or other similar channels).[16]

This is not to suggest by any means that the logic of economic compulsions makes it necessary or inevitable that India should now

Table 4: Index Numbers of Industrial Production According to an Alternative Classification and the Annual Rates of Growth of Output of the Different Categories, 1961 to 1974

Category of Industry	Weights Attached in Index Numbers	Index Numbers of Industrial Production (1960=100.0)				Annual Compound Rates of Growth (in percentages)			
		1961	1965	1971	1974 (January to July)	1961-65	1965-71	1971-74	1965-74
Machinery and equipment manufacturing industries	11.76	118.0	244.0	224.3	266.3	19.9	-1.4	5.9	0.9
Basic intermediate goods industries									
(a) Metals and minerals	17.69	111.0	154.1	180.5	189.9	8.5	2.7	1.7	2.3
(b) Chemicals	1.15	128.4	229.2	549.3	637.9	15.9	15.7	5.1	12.0
(c) Electricity	5.37	116.3	190.9	358.5	405.8	13.2	11.1	4.2	8.7
Other intermediate goods industries	25.88	105.8	140.2	160.4	177.7	7.3	2.3	3.5	2.7
Consumer goods industries									
(a) Non-durable	31.57	105.8	120.5	140.2	144.1	3.3	2.5	0.9	2.0
(b) Durable	5.68	110.8	166.5	268.0	273.6	10.7	8.2	0.7	5.7
All industries	100.00	109.2	153.8	186.1	201.8	8.9	3.2	2.8	3.0

shift to a pattern of development of the kind symbolised in recent years by Brazil, or that such a shift will take place as the result of an explicit statement of new policies in which the rationale of the changes being made will be clearly set out. There is, to my mind, no such inevitability

Table 5: Gross Investment and Saving in the Economy, 1950-51 to 1972-73

Year	Gross Investment		Gross Saving	
	Amount (Rs Crore)	Per Cent of Gross National Domestic Product	Amount (Rs Crore)	Per Cent of Gross National Domestic Product
1950-51	785	8.3 (5.1)	–	–
1951-52	1130	–	–	–
1952-53	938	–	–	–
1953-54	1246	–	–	–
1954-55	1290	–	–	–
1955-56	1479	14.6 (9.9)	–	–
1956-57	2037	17.4 (13.0)	–	–
1957-58	1789	14.9 (9.9)	–	–
1958-59	2034	15.5 (10.8)	–	–
1959-60	2095	15.0 (10.9)	–	–
1960-61	2541	16.9 (12.6)	2060	15.0 (10.7)
1961-62	2435	15.2 (10.7)	2090	13.9 (9.5)
1962-63	2915	17.0 (12.3)	2475	14.5 (9.8)
1963-64	3270	16.6 (12.2)	2828	14.4 (10.0)
1964-65	3737	16.2 (12.0)	3136	13.6 (9.2)
1965-66	4393	18.2 (13.8)	3793	15.7 (11.3)
1966-67	5449	19.7 (15.5)	4222	16.4 (12.2)
1967-68	5272	16.3 (12.1)	4424	13.7 (9.5)
1968-69	5421	16.2 (11.7)	5004	14.9 (10.4)
1969-70	6205	16.7 (12.2)	5963	16.0 (11.5)
1970-71	7278	18.0 (13.5)	6887	17.0 (12.5)
1971-72	7029	16.3 (11.5)	6546	15.1 (11.6)
1972-73	7985	17.0 (12.2)	7684	16.3 (12.5)

Notees: For the estimates covering the period 1950-51 to 1959-60, see K N Raj, 'Some Issues Concerning Investment and Saving in the Indian Economy', *Economic Development in South Asia*, edited by E A G Robinson and Michael Kidron, Macmillan, 1970. The percentages given for this period are as of gross national product at market prices. For the estimates covering the period 1960-61 to 1972-73, see Table 12 in *National Accounts Statistics*, 1960-61 to 1972-73, Central Statistical Organisation, Goverment of India, April 1975. The percentages given for this period are as of gross domestic product at market prices. The figures given in brackets are estimates of net investment and saving as percentages of national/domestic product.

except for sociological reasons arising from the power exercised by certain social groups over the political and administrative processes of decision-making. Precisely for that reason, a shift of this kind is not likely to be brought about by explicit statements to that effect, even if the social groups concerned have a clear and coherent picture of the direction in which they wish to move and of its underlying logic; it might be in fact politically inexpedient to be so explicit.

What is more likely to happen is that the country and the economy will move in that direction in the good old English style of 'muddling through', as the result of a series of *ad hoc* measures and policies devised apparently in a practical spirit to deal with concrete problems as and when they arise. Between the plan and the performance the gap might therefore continue,[17] perhaps even widen (unless of course the objectives set out initially and the actual programmes and policies incorporated in the plans are treated in separate compartments to an even greater degree than hitherto).

The alternative would be to recognise clearly the reasons for the tendencies towards stagnation that have been evident in the industrial sector over the last decade and trace them to their source. There should also be determination to tackle the problems at the root, even if it implies facing squarely the power groups that are in the way and there is a period of apparent dislocation in the economy while the gears are being changed and new directions set. This would require, above all, tackling the problems of agriculture in a comprehensive and thorough fashion, recognising the differences from region to region and even within each region. It would require explicitly linking the future pace and pattern of industrial development with the growth of incomes from agriculture, the needs of agricultural development, and the resources available for the purpose locally or within each region. This would imply paying much more attention to small-scale industries catering to rural needs—not merely stating that it is the objective but working out in detail what can be done in each area, how the raw materials required can be secured, and what kind of technological improvements need to be made. It might also imply in certain cases restricting or altogether preventing the growth of certain kinds of industries, and certain kinds of technological changes in the large-scale sector.

All this is of course more easily said than done. For it requires in a sense a different kind of planning from the sort we have had so far—much more aware of the inter-regional differences within the country, hence more decentralised (not merely in profession as it has been hitherto but in practice), and more genuinely experimental and innovative with fewer models, directives and guidelines imposed from above. This in turn would require naturally a more decentralised system of decision-making and therefore of political arrangements.

Let me indicate very briefly why I say this and what I have in mind. Consider, for instance, the pattern of agricultural growth that has taken place in India over a period, regionwise. The accompanying graphs, which show the movements between 1956-57 and 1970-71 (and in some cases 1971-72) in the index numbers of agricultural production constructed separately for each state,[18] bring out one feature quite sharply. It will be seen that, viewed in terms of the movements of these index numbers, the states fall broadly into six groups:

(1) those which have recorded high rates of growth of the order of 5 to 6 per cent per annum with only moderate year-to-year fluctuations—namely, Punjab, Haryana and Karnataka;
(2) those which have apparently achieved high rates of growth, ranging between approximately 5 and 7 per cent per annum, but have been susceptible to such violent fluctuations in output that the estimated growth rates will themselves vary significantly depending on the terminal years one adopts for the purpose—namely, Rajasthan and Gujarat;
(3) those which have recorded moderate rates of growth, of approximately 2.5 to 3 per cent per annum, with only minor year-to-year fluctuations in output—namely, Tamil Nadu and Kerala;
(4) those which have apparently achieved higher, or at least as high, rates of growth as Tamil Nadu and Kerala but whose output has been subject to such violent fluctuations that once again the estimated rates will themselves vary significantly depending on the terminal years chosen—namely, Orissa, Uttar Pradesh and, to a lesser degree, West Bengal;
(5) those which have recorded rates of growth of less than 2 per cent per annum (i e, rates lower than the rate of growth of their population) and at the same time have also been subject to fluctuations—namely, Andhra Pradesh and Assam; and
(6) those which have apparently had to suffer both very low rates of growth and severe fluctuations—namely, Bihar, Madhya Pradesh and, to a lesser degree, Maharashtra.

These differences even in the broad characteristics of agricultural growth have very important implications which need close investigation. For the present purpose one needs to take note of only two of them.

In the first place, since violent fluctuations in agricultural output are accompanied generally by similar fluctuations in the prices of the products affected, and such price fluctuations are not conducive to farmers taking the measures necessary for increasing their output, the phenomenon of agricultural fluctuations cannot be separated from that of agricultural growth and need to be tackled alongside the measures taken for promoting the latter. Since the fluctuations in

Index Numbers of Agricultural Production (1956-57 = 100.0)

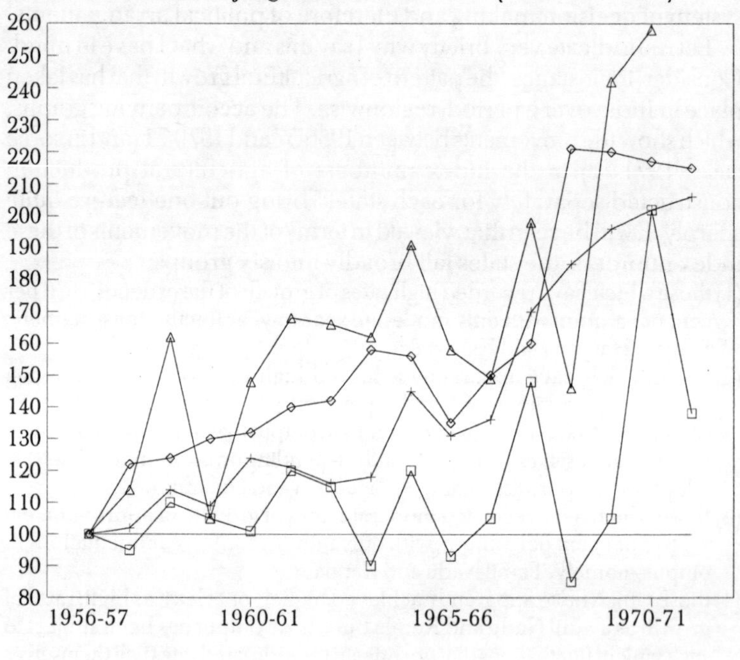

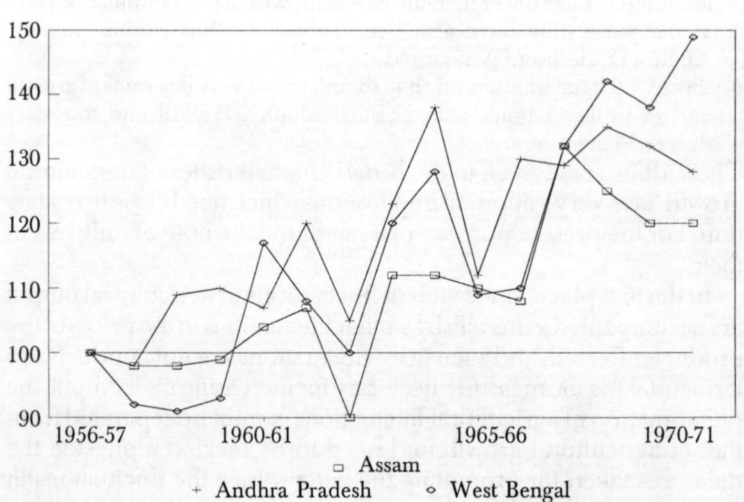

Index Numbers of Agricultural Production (1956-57 = 100.0)

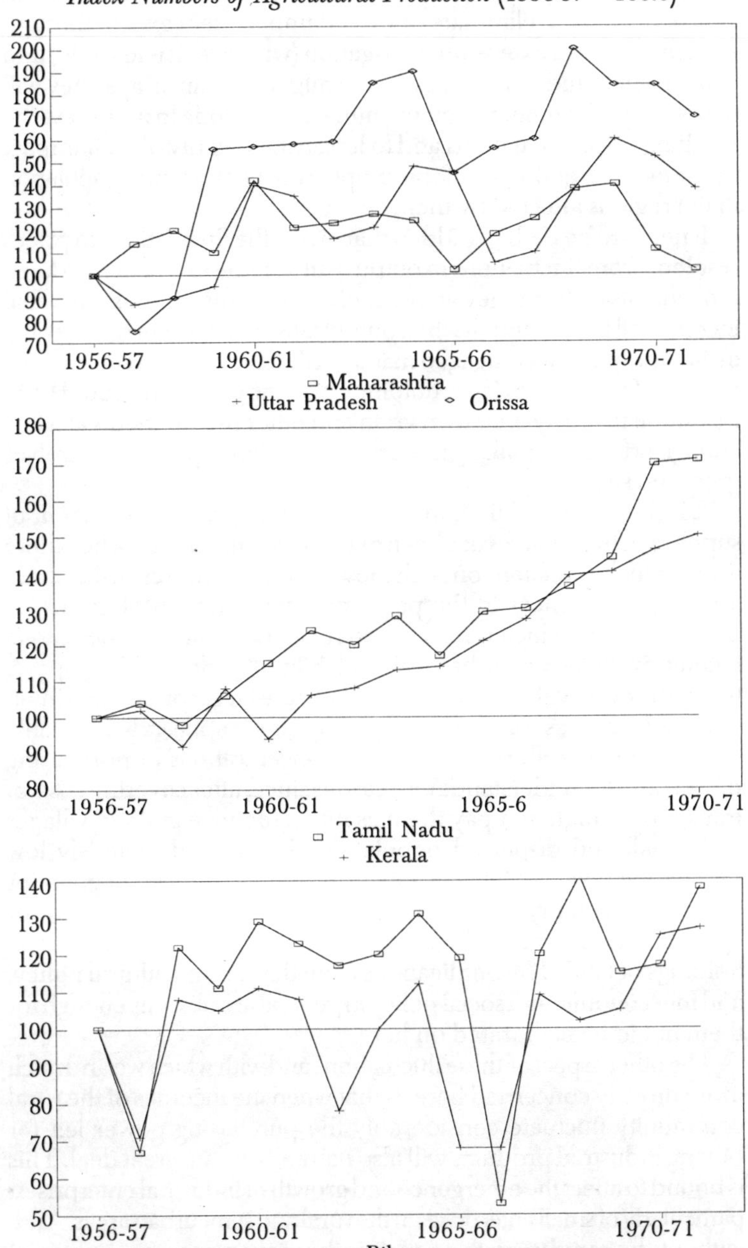

output are largely the result of climatic variations much cannot of course be done to eliminate or even dampen them except through such measures as extension of irrigation (wherever it is feasible) and evolving new and more effectively drought-resistant crops; they will necessarily take time. But many things can be done to moderate the resulting price fluctuations and to lessen the severity of their impact on the incomes and levels of consumption of the large rural population in the regions affected by them.

It needs to be perhaps added that, while the fluctuations in prices resulting from fluctuations in output will to some extent help to keep movements in the money incomes of farmers within limits, their real income will inevitably fall when output falls. This will not be true only in the case of farmers engaged mainly in the cultivation of commercial crops, or farmers with large holdings growing grain, who could be in a position to satisfy their own grain and other requirements at a low enough price while making more money on the crops they themselves grow and sell.

It has been found that, in the case of foodgrains, movement of supplies between states has been extremely limited even when there are no zonal restrictions on such movement, with the result that there are large differences in the per capita consumption of grains, as between states, which reflect not so much differences in per capita income as differences in the local availability of grains.[19] This appears to be true even within states, particularly the larger ones. Such inter-state movement as is there through private trade appears to be mainly to urban areas with relatively large concentrations of purchasing power; and for understandable reasons since, after covering costs of transport, it might not pay them as much to move grain to villages with small and dispersed population clusters and relatively low purchasing power. The consequences of poor harvests of grain for those in the countryside can therefore be imagined, particularly for agricultural labourers and even farmers with small and medium-sized holdings of land. The implications of all this for agricultural policy, and for economic and social policy in general are obvious enough for them not to be elaborated on here.

The other aspect of these fluctuations and with which we are much more directly concerned here, is that when the incomes of the rural community fluctuate considerably the purchasing power left for buying industrial products will also naturally vary a great deal. This is bound to affect the emergence and growth of industrial enterprises, particularly of small enterprises in the rural and semi-urban areas. And, without the rapid growth of such industrial enterprises, industrial growth in the larger enterprises can have but a limited impact on a relatively small section of the country's population.

Viewed from this angle, it would appear that conditions are favourable for the more extensive and rapid growth of small-scale industries in only some regions of India, i e, those which have recorded moderate to high rates of growth of agricultural output without being subject to serious fluctuations. It is probable that a large part of the favourable linkage effects have been taken advantage of more by large than small enterprises through their superior market powers. Nevertheless, the linkages which already have been or could be established in states like Punjab, Haryana, Karnataka, Tamil Nadu and Kerala need to be closely examined in the light of this analysis. Unfortunately the data available on small-scale enterprises are very meagre and unsatisfactory. But, to the extent they are available, they do support the hypothesis that the rate of growth of small-scale enterprises (particularly in the rural sector and small towns) is generally higher in states which are characterised by high or even moderately high rates of growth of agricultural output and which are at the same time not subject to sharp year-to-year fluctuations. If this is the case, more can certainly be done to establish and foster in a more systematic way the growth of linkages between agriculture and industry through small-scale enterprises in all regions. This requires however adequate recognition of all the implications of such a policy. One should above all avoid being guided by only the statistics of the growth rates in factory enterprises; they enjoy not only greater market power but also greater access to influential news media and professional analysts of all kinds (including economists), not to mention the centres of political and administrative power at still higher levels.

So far I have made no reference to questions of economic efficiency in manufacturing industry (which are often raised particularly in the context of import substitution and export promotion). It is partly for lack of time, but it is also because I have serious reservations about the way this concept is defined, interpreted and used by economists. It is so closely associated with the use of the market mechanism as it operates (and therefore with prevailing market prices), and permits so little scope for interfering with its working except through fiscal devises (which have many limitations), that it often misses the essence of the problems of developing economies. Unfortunately, a large number of persons belonging to my profession in this country, trained and fostered in neo-classical economic theory, cannot forget what they learnt from standard text-books, and from their mentors in the more advanced industrial countries which can afford this largely irrelevant luxury for dealing with this class of problems. The one thing I would like to say, and with all the emphasis I can command, is that I do not agree with much of the analysis and a large part of the policy prescriptions of such economists when they deal with the problems of countries such as India.

This does not mean that I do not attach any importance at all to the market mechanism or the desirability of using it whenever it helps. Nor am I unaware of the limitations of administrative controls and their abuse.[20] What I do not subscribe to are simple magical solutions such as devaluation and import liberalisation sustained by more foreign aid, as recommended and accepted in 1966 for the problems faced by Indian industry.[21] The pressures exerted in the mid-sixties were largely from outside agencies, there are now apparently strong pressures from within as well, and with support from influential quarters. I have similar reservations, for similar reasons, about some of the industrial policies now being followed with vigour.

The problems facing the country are complex, so are the solutions; and one should at least be humble enough to say that one does not quite know how they are all to be tackled. It is enough however if one knows the directions in which one needs to move in order to make progress and avoid following false signals and accepting false promises.

NOTES

[This is a slightly edited version of my G L Mehta Memorial Lecture delivered at the Indian Institute of Technology, Bombay, on February 6, 1976.

I wish to acknowledge with gratitude the help I have received in the preparation of this paper from my colleagues in the Centre for Development Studies. In particular, I am thankful to A V Jose for computing the state-wise index numbers of agricultural production, Chandan Mukherjee for preparing the graphs based on these index numbers and C G Devarajan for getting copies of the paper typed and mimeographed with such care. Some of my other colleagues–I S Gulati, N Krishnaji, T N Krishnan and P G K Panikar–have also helped me immensely with their comments at various stages in the preparation of the draft. I should not also forget to acknowledge the valuable assistance I have received from my son, N Gopal Raj (now enjoying a vacation in the transition from school to college), in the computation of all the compound rates of growth incorporated in the statistical tables, an intricate exercise beyond my mathematical comprehension.]

1 Daniel G Pfoutz and Miller B Spangler, 'Effects of Import Liberalisation on Increased Utilisation of Industrial Capacity: Economic Problems and Benefits (Preliminary Study)', United States Agency for International Development, October 1965. This paper was not published but circulated in mimeographed form.

2 These estimates of unutilised capacity in the paper referred to above formed

incidentally the basis of two estimates of the additional foreign exchange required annually for import liberalisation; the higher of these two estimates approximately $ 900 million, figured prominently in the discussions leading up to and following the devaluation of the rupee in 1966 as well as in the related negotiations for foreign aid. The estimates made in the paper led also to the following 'reasonable but crude guesses' as to the contribution that import liberalisation and consequent fuller utilisation of plant capacity would make to the implementation of the Fourth Five-Year Plan: '(a) A $ 1 billion gain in annual national income from firms directly affected by liberalisation of imports. (b) An indirect gain of $ 1.4 billion in income in other non-agriculture sectors stimulated by the former. (c) Substantial, but unestimated, gains in agricultural income induced by the increased productions of agro-based industries through a fuller utilisation of their capacities. (d) A reduction of unemployment by the creation of about 2 million new jobs by industrial firms directly and indirectly affected by import-liberalisation as well as stimulation effects on other non-agricultural sectors of the economy. (e) A very substantial increase in the potential for capital formation both in the private and public sectors through increased entrepreneurial profits and increased public revenues. (f) Energising the attainment of productive efficiencies resulting in cost-reducing measures and improved quality of products which will add to the real income of the economy. (g) Promotion of substantial export earnings which, in turn, would have stimulative effects on the economy of the types enumerated above since the resulting increased availability of foreign exchange would permit a further liberalisation of imports to include even more industries.'

3 National Council of Applied Economic Research, *Underutilisation of Industrial Capacity*, New Delhi, 1966. See Table 2 in particular.

4 This is not an estimate made by the NCAER itself but one which can be derived from its estimates of average underutilisation of capacity in the various categories of manufacturing industry; the weights attached to the different categories, for this particular exercise, are the same as for the official indices of industrial production with 1960 as the base year.

5 V K Ramaswami and D G Pfoutz, *Utilisation of Industrial Capacity*, a joint pilot study sponsored by the Government of India and United States Agency for International Development, December 1965. V K Ramaswami was Economic Advisor in the Department of Economic Affairs, Ministry of Finance and D G Pfoutz the Supply Advisor in the USAID.

6 D G Pfoutz, it will be observed, was also a joint author of the earlier estimate prepared within the USAID in October 1965. The reasons for Pfoutz taking a different position in the earlier paper will be evident from the following extracts from it:

> ...various Mission personnel including the Director pressed the subject of fuller utilisation with responsible Indian officials and late in May the GOI agreed to a formal, combined study. In the early part of June the first serious steps were taken to inaugurate the study. Results of the initial meeting were somewhat disappointing in that, instead of a relatively quick study of broad areas, the GOI suggested a pilot study of five industries over a period of six to eight weeks... While the pilot study has since been progressing at a reasonable rate, few results are yet available as a basis for quantifying the foreign exchange requirements at various levels of utilisation

of existing capacity. The major specific benefit thus far derived from the pilot study is an even clearer realisation of the almost complete inadequacy of the industrial data available to the GOI for decision making...

One further note seems appropriate as a prelude to the estimates to follow. It is the writers' belief that the actual ability of Indian industry to absorb additional maintenance imports is so great or, conversely, that installed capacity is so grossly understated that any estimate of foreign exchange needs is likely to be too low rather than too high (Daniel G Pfoutz and Miller B Spangler, op cit).

It will be evident from a comparison of these extracts with those from the paper jointly authored with V K Ramaswami that the underlying assumptions and perhaps the objectives were somewhat different.

7 There is little doubt that the USAID estimates of unutilised capacity in manufacturing industry, and of the additional foreign exchange needed for putting it to work through imports of intermediate goods, had considerable influence on the policies urged upon the government of India by international agencies like the World Bank and which were ultimately adopted by it in June 1966. Of the $ 1.6 billion of foreign aid which the World Bank undertook to organise for India in 1966-67, $ 900 million was to be set apart for the import of urgently-needed raw materials, components and parts (see *The Times of India*, June 11, 1966); this corresponded precisely to the 'crude estimate of $ 900 million' for additional maintenance imports arrived at by the USAID in the paper referred to above.

In this context it is interesting to note the observations made in an earlier draft of the same paper prepared in June 1966, about the role of the USAID in promoting import liberalisation in Pakistan:

Since the objectives of the GOP in this move parallel those we in India are trying to promote, it will be useful to describe some of the Pakistani circumstances which are similar (or dissimilar) to circumstances here in India which would have a bearing on joint AID-GOI efforts toward liberalising imports for a fuller utilisation of capacity. Both the Harvard Advisory Group and AID Mission to Pakistan played leading roles in persuading the GOP to liberalise. A major increase in USAID non-project loans plus additional commitments from the World Bank and other Consortium members paved the way for the creation in 1964 of a free list of 51 import items some of which (e g, iron and steel, fertilisers, pesticides, diesel locomotive spares) were purchasable from the US only... The major persuasive forces in the GOP were principally the MOF supported by the Planning Commission. President Ayub's role is not known but is believed to have been a rather passive but open-minded one.

...the climate in India is perceptibly becoming more receptive than ever before to making an important change. The incentive of additional non-project aid on an appropriate scale might well tip the balance in favour of a measure of decontrol or simplification of import control procedures that the US would deem as desirable on behalf of promoting economic development and laudatory in promoting a freer economic system in which the private sector will benefit even more than the public sector.

8 According to a report in *The Hindu* of January 22, 1976, this estimate has been made by the Federation of Indian Chambers of Commerce and Industry and mentioned by its president. Harish Mahindra, in a key-note address at a seminar on 'Strategy for Accelerated Economic Growth' held in Madras on January 21, 1976. 'Sample surveys had shown that the average degree of utilisation of capacity in industry in 1975 was only around 60 per cent. Industries which had suffered most from under-utilisation included

mini-steel plants, railway wagons, steel pipes, etc. A FICCI survey showed that power shortage was still the single major constraint on capacity utilisation in about 28 per cent of the industries; credit squeeze and inadequate final demand were together responsible for nearly 50 per cent of the under-utilised capacity in the industrial sector.' He mentioned these figures only to indicate the magnitude of the problems and the causes relative to the situation. In his address, Mahindra put forward also a four-point programme for promoting economic development and exports: (1) increasing foodgrain production to 140 million tonnes, (2) doubling industrial production, (3) raising the rates of investment and saving in the economy to 20 per cent and 16 per cent respectively of the national income, and (4) opening 'the doors wider' to private foreign investment so as to increase the annual inflow from less than Rs 50 crore now to Rs 500-600 crore for covering the gap between investment and saving within the country. The suggested target for exports was Rs 5,000 crore by the end of the decade, to be achieved by the adoption of a 'consortium approach' between industry and government. The estimated rate of growth of national income, as a result of the adoption of these measures was reported to be 7 per cent per annum.

9 See, for instance, R Marris, *The Economics of Capital Utilisation: A Report on Multiple-Shift Work*, Cambridge University Press, 1964.

10 It has to be borne in mind, however, that in several industries for so-called 'unorganised sector' of small-scale enterprises may be important enough for the production trends in the factory enterprises to be more than neutralised by the trends in the small-scale sector. A good example is the cotton textile industry in which it has been the official policy for some time to revive, expand and modernise the handloom units. This policy has in turn involved placing certain restrictions on the output of woven cotton cloth in the mill sector. Estimates of the rate of growth of output in each of these sectors and for cotton cloth as a whole, between 1960-61 and 1973-74 are given in Table A.

There could be some other industries in which too the output in small-scale establishments has registered a high rate of growth while the output in the factory establishments has been growing slower or declining. On the other hand, there may be industries in which the reverse has been the case, i e, where expansion of output in large-scale factory enterprises is more than neutralised by reduction of output in small-scale enterprises. It could have taken place on a significant scale in the case of industries in which the pace

Table A

	Output of Cotton Cloth (Million Metres)		Compound Rate of Increase (+) or Decrease (–) Per Annum (Per Cent)
	1960-61	1973-74	
Mill sector	4649	4083	–1.0
Decentralised sector	2089	3863	+4.8
Total cotton weaving	6738	7946	+1.3

Source: *Economic Survey 1974-75*, Government of India, February 1976, Appendix, Table 1.16.

of technological change, or market control through advertisement of competing products has made it difficult for the small enterprises to withstand competition and survive. This may have benefited some agro-based industries (such as sugar manufacturing) in the factory sector. Displacement of small-scale enterprises seems likely to have happened to some extent even in the steel industry in which re-rollers and electric arc furnaces (the so-called 'mini-steel plants') have recently had to face severe competition from the main steel plants.

11 See in particular Dharm Narain, 'Growth and Imbalances in Indian Agriculture', Technical Address, Indian Society of Agricultural Statistics, March 1972, reprinted in *Economic and Political Weekly*, Review of Agriculture, Vol VII, No 13, March 25, 1972.

12 See B S Minhas, 'Rural Poverty, Land Redistribution and Development Strategy: Facts and Policy' *Sarkhya* (C), Volume 36, Nos 2 and 4, December 1974. Also, K N Raj, 'Agricultural Development and Distribution of Land Holdings', *Indian Journal of Agricultural Economics*, Vol XXX, No 1, January-March 1975.

13 The following statement made by Siddhartha Shankar Ray, Chief Minister of West Bengal, on January 22, 1976 appears to be a straw in the wind:

> Refrigerators, air-conditioners, television sets and even bicycles, motor scooters and household goods are not being purchased in the number in which they should have been. Inventories are increasing in these as well as other industries. I have received reports that even in paper and cement industries goods are not being lifted. I think time has come when the government of India should take a second look at the structure of income-tax payable by assessees all over India. We should drive all black money out of circulation and to achieve this every step, however strong, must be taken. But at the same time some relief should perhaps be given to the tax payer in the sphere of income-tax so that he has some additional money to purchase particularly consumer goods (*Indian Express*, January 28, 1976).

The plea has been made of course in the context of inventories accumulating from production out of existing capacity; but it would need only one more step (perhaps not even that, since the logic of such tax policy can be expected to take its own course) to rationalise a pattern of industrial development relying heavily on demand for such products.

14 See Celso Furtado, 'The Brazilian Model', *Social and Economic Studies*, Kingston, Jamaica, Volume 22, No 1, March 1973, pp 122-31; also K N Raj, 'Linkages in Industrialisation and Development Strategy: Some Basic Issues', in *Journal of Development Planning*, No 8, United Nations, 1975.

15 Actually Brazil had depended fairly heavily on foreign private capital even in the fifties and recorded a rate of growth of output of around 5 to 6 per cent per annum till 1961. Subsequently the rate of growth fell sharply to about 3.5 per cent per annum till 1966. See Robert D Daland, *Brazilian Planning*, The University of North Carolina Press, 1967, ch 2, p 25.

16 The lines along which the case is likely to be made is already evident from a report on the proceedings of the three-day session of the Indo-US joint business council which began in New Delhi on February 2, 1976. Orville Freeman, the chairman of the US delegation (who was the Secretary for Agriculture in the US Government in the mid-sixties), prefaced his remarks by pointing out that, though his delegation was attending the meeting not as representatives of their government, he was hopeful that they could

influence their government in policy formulations. "Mr Freeman devoted a substantial part of his speech to the 'key role' multinational corporations could play in economic development. These corporations had collectively the 'brains and muscle to save the world from self-destruction'. They were the 'masters of new technology; have the skills and innovative strength to engineer change; and the organisation and management skills, together with the cash flow and borrowing power, to launch desperately needed, new, large, problem-solving international enterprises'." Harish Mahindra, the leader of the Indian delegation, is reported to have said: "Our two countries are large and our economies are complementary. You have sophisticated technology and vast capital resources. We have abundant labour, both skilled and unskilled. This diversity of factor endowment can be a sound foundation for an expanding two-way trade" (*The Economic Times*, February 3, 1976).

At the end of the session, Freeman told newsmen that "the clarifications given to the US delegation by Indian officials had gone a long way towards removing the misunderstanding among American businessmen that India did not want foreign investment" and that a policy statement now from the Prime Minister would have 'a dramatic effect on the business community in the US'. It has been further reported that "the need for a flexible approach in administering the Foreign Exchange Regulation Act (FERA) was emphasised both by Mr Freeman and Mr Harish Mahindra" (*The Times of India*, February 5, 1976).

These two reports became available only after the preparation of this paper but have been added since then in view of their obvious significance.

17 Unfortunately, 'muddling through' in this way will involve continuing much wasteful investments in highly capital-intensive industries such as steel. I had recently an opportunity of learning something about the colossal scale on which such waste can take place, during my brief tenure as a member of the Board of Directors of the Steel Authority of India. The most unfortunate part of it is that the arrogance of power, which exists as much (or perhaps even more) in the public sector, comes in the way of considering reasonable solutions which are less wasteful. When managerial personnel trained in the private sector (sometimes selling soap and toilet articles) are inducted into the public sector, they also bring with them the capacity to conceal more effectively what is being done, through public relations and various other cosmetic methods. This makes it worse, not better, as far as the genuine interests of the public (for which the public sector is supposed to exist) are concerned.

18 These are index numbers constructed in the Centre for Development Studies with the available data: they need to be improved upon with the further data that might be available in the Ministry of Food and Agriculture.

19 See Chapter II of *Poverty, Unemployment and Development Policy: A Case Study of Selected Issues with Reference to Kerala*, prepared by the Centre for Development Studies, Trivandrum in April 1975. This is being published by the Centre for Development Planning, Projections and Policies of the United Nations, and will be available in print by April, 1976.

20 My views are from the Report of the Committee on Steel Control (published in October 1973 by the Ministry of Steel and Heavy Industries, Government

of India). Raj Krishna, K S Krishnaswamy and I were members of the committee of which I was also the chairman.

21 Jagdish Bhagawati, K Sundaram and T N Srinivasan wrote a lengthy paper nearly 3½ years ago on 'Political Response to the 1966 Devaluation' in *Economic and Political Weekly*, Volume VII, Nos 36-38, September 2, 9 and 16, 1972. In the course of their analysis they have made the following observations:

"The Prime Minister again took the opportunity to put the devaluation across as a decisive and bold piece of action. 'We were not pressurised'; and, without denying that the IMF and World Bank had advised in favour of the devaluation, she pointedly noted that: 'We were also advised by our own economists as well as economists outside the government not only now but for a very long time. In fact, one renowned economist who is supposed to not supprt devaluation now had supported it in an article just six months before we took the action'."

"This and subsequent quotes from the prime minister's speech are from 'Lok Sabha Debates' Volume 57, Columns 2699-2705. The reference to the 'renowned economist' is presumably to K N Raj of Delhi University."

"...the Finance Ministry had before it an extensive report on the current export subsidies and the merits of a devaluation which it had commissioned from J Bhagwati, then at Delhi University during mid-1965. Besides other economists, such as K N Raj, had also written in support of a new parity."

"And one of us (Bhagwati) who was consulted by the prime minister (Indira Gandhi) prior to the devaluation decision, distinctly remembers her probing questions (to which he could respond only fumblingly) on how certain prominent, senior economists and well known newspapers would react."

"Most of the prominent economists' papers and writings have been reprinted in *Devaluation of the Rupee and Its Implications*, Institute of Constitutional and Parliamentary Studies, New Delhi, 1968. In addition, see K N Raj, 'Food, Fertiliser and Foreign Aid', *Mainstream*, April 30, 1966."

It would appear from these extracts that K N Raj had acted like a weathercock and therefore been rightly exposed in the Parliament by the prime minister. The facts of the matter are that K N Raj was in favour of rupee devaluation from 1964; had written an article in *The Times* of London some time around September 1965 stating that export subsidies were creating various problems and abuses of administration, and needed to be done away with as far as possible through an adjustment of the exchange rate of the rupee; later learnt, early in February 1966 (in circumstances which he does not wish to divulge as it would acutely embarrass some of his professional friends, both Indian and foreign), that devaluation of the rupee was being considered actually along with import liberalisation on the promise of massive foreign aid from the United States; therefore, when requested by the prime minister later in February 1966 to prepare a confidential paper stating his views on the problems that might come up in the course of her forthcoming discussions with the president of the United States, gave one entitled 'Economic Aid from the United States' in which it was argued that, while devaluation might help India in export promotion (if rightly timed), its being tied to import liberalisation and massive aid would *not* be to the long-run interests of the country; it was the essence of this paper which was later published as an article 'Food, Fertiliser and Foreign Aid' in the *Mainstream* of April 30, 1966. Here is an extract:

...the World Bank insists not only on the devaluation of the rupee but on relaxation of import controls all along the line. Though devaluation of the rupee may not help to raise export earnings very significantly in the immediate future (and would require imposition of additional export duties on some commodities to maintain the existing level of earnings) there is certainly a case for considering it as a substitute for measures of export promotion that have now the effect of diverting the foreign exchange earned to low-priority uses and of generally distorting the pattern of use of scarce resources. On the other hand, while export promotion schemes are certainly responsible in part for such diversion of resources, basically it is the pattern of income distribution in the economy and the kind of consumer goods industries it fosters that has led to the absorption of scarce foreign exchange directly and indirectly in low priority uses. Since only direct imports of consumer goods have been restricted and little has been done either to reduce the rate of growth of demand for the less essential consumer goods or to make it unattractive for private industry to go into the production, our industry structure is still heavily oriented towards consumption and a large part of even the output of industries like steel (to which we attach high priority for other reasons) has been finding its way into it. Devaluation by itself will not therefore correct the diversion of resources to low priority uses, unless followed immediately by other measures such as much heavier taxation of the less essential consumer goods and withdrawal of the development rebate and such tax concessions from consumer goods industries.

What is being advocated by the World Bank on the other hand is a simultaneous relaxation of the import controls all along the line together with devaluation. This would help the low-priority industries to consolidate themselves, encourage them to expand further, and result in a much larger amount of foreign exchange getting absorbed in uses of no consequence from the point of view of the development of the economy at this stage...

The purpose of liberalisation is said to be the fuller utilisation of installed capacity in industry–and the case for it is certainly strong in certain engineering industries–but if a general relaxation of import controls is allowed on this ground it is almost sure to be used at the next stage as an argument for shifting priorities in favour of a pattern of industrial development for which both foreign private capital and aid will be more easily forthcoming in the future.

This is practically an exact reproduction of some of the paragraphs in the paper given to the prime minister earlier. It is therefore a pity that the authors of this review of the 'politics' of the 1966 devaluation did not examine more closely the contents of the article to which they themselves referred in a footnote. If it is the case that when the prime minister referred to the change in the position of a 'renowned economist' she had in mind K N Raj, this has certainly not been conveyed to *him.*

All this is old history, and of no great importance. But the record needs to be set right. If it was not done earlier, it was only because such personalised analysis of economic issues and decisons was not considered necessary or relevant; and partly because on account of the pledge given to the prime minister in February 1966 that the confidentiality of the paper given to her would be kept. A decent interval of at least a decade had to be allowed to pass before divulging some of these facts.

Annual Number, February 1976

4

Export-Led Growth and Import-Substituting Industrialisation

Amiya Kumar Bagchi

THE disappointing performance in the field of growth of industrial output, and more emphatically, in the field of private industrial investment, has led many people in India to advocate a strategy of growth through increase in exports. The main argument of this note is that the dichotomy between the strategy of export-led growth and the strategy of import-substituting industrialisation *in its latest phase* is largely irrelevant in India today; shifting the emphasis on either policy is similar to changing the pressure from the left foot to the right foot, and back again, and not at all comparable to changing the mode of transport altogether. The contradictions which foul up a strategy of import-substituting industrialisation in its later phases will also upset the policy of *long-term growth* through exports, and the contradictions between class and class, and between the propertied rich and the propertyless poor are themselves likely to be aggravated. The *quality* of growth achieved mainly through increased exports in the present circumstances can be questioned; but such questions need be raised only if the *feasibility* of long-term export-led growth can be demonstrated in the first place.

The experience of import-substituting industrialisation can be roughly divided, for our purposes, into three phases. The first phase, lasting roughly up to the middle of the First Five-Year Plan, witnessed the substitution in imports of such ordinary consumer goods as cotton textiles and sugar, and other crude basic and intermediate goods, such as steel, cement and paper.[1] While there was some development of basic goods and even of capital goods in this period, the perspective of continued and sustained growth was lacking. So the growth remained rather meagre.[2] From around 1953-54, began a determined thrust towards substitution in basic and capital goods industries with a view to *raising* the rates of growth of demand for and supply of capital goods industries. However, this second phase of import-substitution was already dogged by the spurt in consumer expenditures by upper income classes. And, from the middle of the Third Five-Year Plan period, the third phase of import substitution, primarily based on the domestic fabrication of goods demanded by the richer income groups, took over. Our note is addressed towards analysing the links between this phase of import substitution and the advocacy of export-led growth.[3]

The most important link here is that, in the class-divided society that India is, with a capitalist and managerial class primarily dependent on models from advanced capitalist countries for their techniques, products, and organisational framework, an increase in exports generally leads to an increase in imports. Furthermore, given that the contribution of technical change to growth in Indian industrial output is rather small in a world in which most of the advanced countries derive a major part of output growth from such technical change, any major thrust in industrial exports has to be borne by the wage-earners producing the output and the poorer consumers releasing part of their consumption for exports. In the field of agricultural or mineral exports also, the same kind of reasoning would apply. The 'green revolution', whatever its reality in other areas, has left untouched such products as jute or lac or oilseeds, and a sustained increase in exports is generally associated with a rise in the share of the *exporters* of the crude or fabricated products.[4] This is brought about primarily because of the oligopolistic control exercised by the wholesalers and manufacturers in these markets.

Turning to the other side, it has been observed that the import-intensity of luxury consumption in India is higher than that of the consumption of necessities.[5] On the basis of plausible assumptions about patterns of consumption of the propertied and managerial class, this would imply that a relative rise in their income will lead to a rise in the share of imports of consumer goods in total consumption; and conversely, a relative rise in the incomes of wage-earners, poor peasants and the poor tradesmen and artisans will lead to a fall in the share of imports of consumer goods in total consumption.[6] The import-intensities of industrial investment and defence expenditure are also almost certainly higher than the import-intensity of consumption of necessities. To the extent that a rise in industrial investment and a rise in defence expenditure is associated with a rise in the share of the incomes of the propertied and managerial classes, we can lump together consumption expenditures of the upper class, investment in the organised sector, and defence expenditure, and postulate a direct positive relationship between these entities and imports.

Against this perspective, many of the policies of the government which are aimed at raising the share of exports can also be seen as implying a rise in the share of incomes of the propertied and managerial classes; and conversely, many of the policies that are aimed at restraining a rise in real wages of workers or in the incomes of the poorer peasantry would lead, other things remaining constant, to an increase in exports of crude manufactures, and agricultural products that are primarily mass consumption goods.

Take, for instance, a policy of general devaluation of the rupee. This would lead to a rise in the value of exportable products in rupee terms. In the case of agricultural products, crude or processed, most of the gains would be captured either by the manufacturers exporting the processed products or by the big traders engaged in exports. The real wages of industrial workers or of agricultural workers would not rise much in the general situation of weak trade unions and an ever-rising reserve army of labour, although money wages might respond—with a lag—to any rise in prices occurring in the wake of decreased absorption in the economy. Similarly, the incomes of the poorer peasants are unlikely to benefit much from the devaluation-induced rise in prices since they generally have to sell most of their crop within a short period of the harvest and are also often indebted to moneylenders, traders, and landlords. The artisanate are also deprived of most of their potential gains through inadequate access to markets and through chronic indebtedness to the wholesale merchants. What we have said about devaluation would also apply to schemes of export subsidies.

In the paragraphs below, I shall assume, for the sake of concreteness, that the government effects a redistribution in favour of property-owners by means of devaluation. While I talk only about 'property income', it must be understood that this includes the incomes of (a) people who derive the major part of their income from ownership of property on the one hand (and thus excludes the petty property-owners whose main income is derived from work) and of (b) those who derive their income from managerial or supervisory roles in private and public enterprises, and governmental and semi-governmental bureaucracies. Correspondingly, wage income would include not only the incomes of agricultural and industrial wage-earners but also the incomes of poorer peasants and 'self-employed' petty artisans and tradesmen. The border between the two categories is likely to be marked by a band rather than thin line in real life, but the distinction is quite clear nonetheless.

With these preliminaries over, we now set out a simple formal model which helps to bring out some of the problems associated with export-led growth and the intimate connection between the present form of import-substituting industrialisation and the emerging pattern of export-led strategies.

Let X, M, Y, W and P denote exports, imports, national income, 'wage income' and 'property income' respectively. The smaller case letters denote parameters. Then we have:

(1) $X = a + bP$
(2) $M = cW + dP$
(3) $P = e + fY$
(4) $M = X + g$
(5) $Y = P + W$
(6) $a > 0, b > 0, c > 0, d > 0, e > 0, f > 0.$
(7) $d > b + c$

With the restrictions on the parameters given in (6) and (7), the other five equations will generate positive solutions for the ranges of values of the five variables that we have in mind. We have not placed an a priori restriction on the value of g in equation (4), which is best regarded as the target balance of payments equation. If the government is planning to generate a current balance of trade surplus, in order either to build up foreign exchange reserves or to generate funds for investment abroad, or to service debt payments, then the value of g can be negative. In that case, if the absolute value of g is abnormally high, then the positivity of the solutions can be endangered. We simply rule out such values of g. In a case in which the government is planning to have a current balance of trade deficit, the value of g will be positive, as in the case of the values of other parameters.

Before I discuss the properties of the solutions something more should be said about the equations themselves. The equations have been kept simple and linear, in order that we understand the properties of small changes in the policy parameters better. Introducing non-linearities or complicating the equations in other ways will generally make the analysis more complicated without giving us much insight into the problem.

Equation (1) simply says that exports respond positively to property income, but there is a positive intercept of exports, so that, in the limit, even were property income as near zero as it would be realistic to assume, there still is a substantial volume of exports. In fact, we assume that a is rather large and b rather small. This is to take account of the fact that most of our exports still originate in traditional sectors whose outputs are more sensitive to the weather and other exogenous factors than to the plans of the capitalists and managers, and that while a fall in wage income will release some part of the home-consumed exportables, the rate of release will not be fast, because such exportables partake of more of the nature of necessities than of luxuries. We could make the equation (1) more general by writing (la)

$X = a' + b' W + c' P; a' > 0, b' > 0, c' > 0, \text{ and } c' > b,$

but a little experimentation will show that this would not alter the nature of the conclusions.

There is not much to say about equation (2). Here we assume that imports increase with an increase in both wage-income and property-income, but imports rise more strongly with a rise in property-income than with a rise in wage-income. (The restriction $d > b + c$, when all the parameters are positive, would imply $d > c$). Equation (3) is the government policy equation. When the government raises f, it raises the share of P in Y, when e is given. A policy of devaluation, or a policy of wage freeze, or a policy giving tax concessions to income tax payers, or a policy imposing more indirect taxes on ordinary consumer goods could all lead to a rise in f. If a government pursued a policy of making lump-sum transfers (unrelated to the level of current national income in any way), that could be interpreted as raising the value of e. At any moment of time, property-owners have a claim to a certain amount of income, independently of government fiscal and monetary policies (but not, of course, independently of the government's policy towards property or privilege as such). This is reflected in the positive value of e.

We have already explained the function of equation (4). Equation (5) gives the usual national income identity. Now we set out the solutions of the equations in terms of the parameters.

We put $c + f(d - b - c) = \Delta$

Then we have

$$(8)\ P = \frac{ce + f(a + g)}{\Delta}$$

$$(9)\ W = \frac{a + g - e(d - b) - f(a + g)}{\Delta}$$

$$(10)\ Y = \frac{a + g - e(d - b - c)}{\Delta}$$

$$(11)\ X = \frac{ac + af(d - c) + b(ce + fg)}{\Delta}$$

$$(12)\ M = \frac{c(a + g) + f(a + g)\ (d - c) + bce}{\Delta}$$

Before commenting on the character of these solutions, I shall illustrate the logic of the working of the system by means of a diagram.

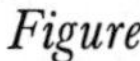

Figure

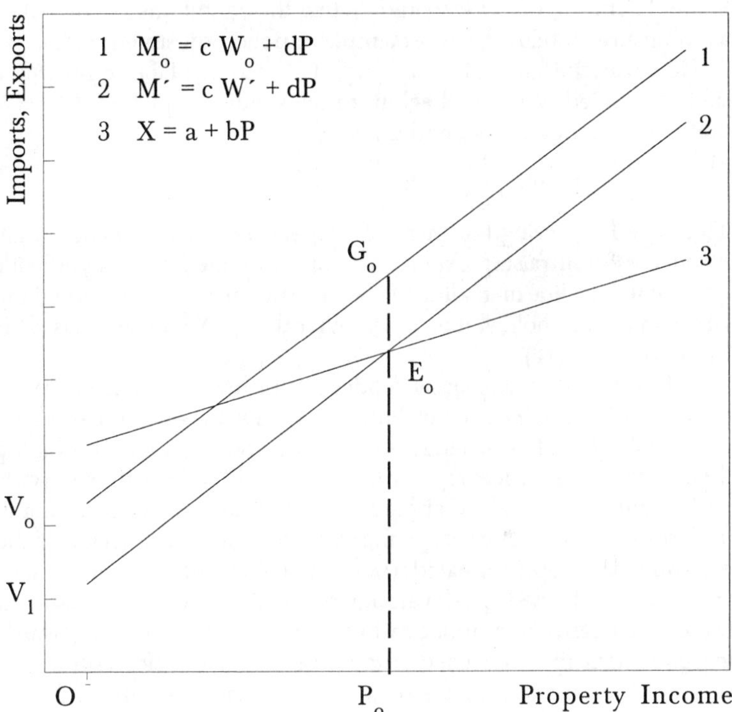

In the figure, in the initial situation, OP_0 is property income and W_0 (not shown in the figure) is the wage income, so that the Y-intercept of the import function, $OV_0 = cW_0$. At that point, there is a gap between imports and exports which is represented by $G_0 E_0$. (We have given the import functions with a much steeper slope than the export function, in line with the assumption that c > b). If the gap is to be eliminated without touching property income, the government may devalue the rupee or provide export subsidies so as to raise f in equation (3). In order to effect this the Y-intercept of the import function has to be lowered. This means lowering the imports arising from wage incomes to OV'. At that point, exports $E_0 P_0$ again equal the imports. But in the process wage income has to be lowered by a multiple equal to $1/c$ and national income has to be lowered.

The main objection against this type of analysis would be that it is comparatively static in nature and does not say much about the adjustment path. Constructing a truly dynamic model which is realistic would be useful but the usual dynamic models have to take the putative point of equilibrium too rigidly for granted. One conventional defence in our case would be that the conditions are rigged so as to ensure stability for most simple-minded adjustment paths.

However, the figure gives only a partial account of the comparative statics involved. We can check from the solution equations (8)–(12) that with our boundary conditions,

$$\frac{df}{dX} > 0. \ \frac{dp}{df} > 0 \text{ and } \frac{dw}{df} < 0, \ \frac{dy}{df} < 0.$$

Thus a policy raising the share of property in national income may be successful in raising exports and property income and yet leads to an actual decline in income. If the government succeeds in lowering g by some other policy, then given other things, Y will fall, as is clear from equation (10).

Before we reject the basic model out of hand, because of these strong results, let me point out that this is mainly the outcome of taking the assumptions of export-led growth models seriously and combining them with the empirical regularities in the field of growth of exports and imports.[7] It could be argued that what has happened in many underdeveloped economies is that a larger and larger sector of the economy has simply retreated from a situation in which their fortunes are strongly affected by developments in the field of international trade. This can come about in two ways: one is a retreat towards various forms of subsistence farming or production for home consumption and the other is the building up of linkages within different sectors of the economy on both the sides of demand and supply, which almost entirely exclude any influence emanating from the field of international trade. I am not sure that, in typical underdeveloped economies, the second type of disengagement from international trade has dominated over the first type. In fact, there is a third type of development we must think of: that is the phenomenon of gradual pauperisation of large segments of the population who have neither the resources for production for self-consumption nor the steadiness of employment for continual involvement in the market. Both the strategies of export-led growth and import-substituting industrialisation come to grief on these rocks of what may be called last-resource subsistence farming and increasing pauperisation.

So the strong results of the model, instead of damning it utterly, may be a point in its favour. The model as we have formulated it, is essentially short-run. For interpretation in the long run, most of these results have to be taken in relative terms. That is, for example, a rise in the *share* of exports in national income will lead to a *fall in the rate of growth* of national income, rather than to a decline in absolute income. Appropriate modifications may be made to the model to take such considerations into account without altering its basic structure.

Another feature of the model which some people may find disquieting is the implication that a growth in national income would *require* a fall in the share of property income to the total. This is in strong contrast, for example, with the Kaldorian theory of distribution, in which profits, through investment, have a strongly positive relation with the growth of income. Such a contrast in itself would not say much about the reasonableness or otherwise of our analytical structure. But the contrast is helpful in pointing out the essentially passive role that property income plays in relation to investment and growth of income in our perspective. This is because investment, particularly private investment, is very much dependent on various exogenous factors such as the growth of public expenditure, the availability of foreign technology on favourable terms, and innovations in types or qualities of products and methods of production going on abroad. A rise in property income may simply stimulate luxury consumption because the property-owners find the prospective rate of profit on productive investment too low in comparison with the rate which they consider 'normal'. A thorough discussion of the determinants of private investment in India is not attempted in the present paper,[8] and the following remarks are in the nature of a drastic condensation of a number of connected issues.

The rich in India, as in other third world countries, derive their consumption standards from abroad, and the types of goods they demand continually change. But the size of the class which can afford to buy modern consumer durables is quite small, and income and wealth are extremely unequally distributed within that class as well. So, while the top income earners can vie with their peers abroad with regard to their consumption of new types of luxuries (while retaining much of the feudal style of living with numbers of retainers in their employ), the demand for consumer durables at the lower range of the property-owning and managerial class is quickly saturated. This at the same time keeps the propensity to import of the rich quite high, and creates problems for the consumer durable industries that get established. After only a few years, the latter find their demand tapering off to the level of replacement demand plus the demand on the part of the new entrants to the ranks of the rich. On top of this, once import substitution starts in a particular line, everybody with the requisite capital and connections rushes in, and excess capacity soon builds up. Because of the oligopolistic nature of industry, competition rarely results in price-cutting. With the prevailing income distribution, the price elasticity of demand is not likely to remain very high for long either. But the prevailing business ethos does not favour price competition any way. So the prospects appear quite dim to a new investor surveying an established field. What has been said about consumer durables applies with even greater force to mass consumption goods. Un-coordinated investment in any field adds to the deadweight of excess capacity without generating much demand for other industries. The longer such a depression persists the more intractable the problem appears to be.

While the market for a particular type of consumer durable appears depressed, new types of consumer durables are always appearing—*abroad*. Some stimulation in the market for consumer goods can be expected from this source, but here the total inability of our capitalists to effect any major innovations on their own and their dependence on foreigners for technology in any new field whatsoever come in the way. This incapacity has deep historical and structural roots. Suffice it to say that the long divorce in third world countries of science and learning from production, the gradual squeezing out of ordinary people from any skilled participation in the production process in the name of modern production technologies, the resulting (relative) shrinkage over time of the production base on which research and development can build, the continuous temptation to any private entrepreneur (or manager of a public enterprise for that matter) to abrogate any agreement to use indigenous technology only and bring in a more immediately profitable foreign technology—all these play havoc with any simple-minded attempt to remove contradictions arising out of the social structure by some elitist science policy.[9] However, because of this technological and managerial dependence, the demand bottleneck is further constrained by a supply bottleneck. Such a supply bottleneck can only be eased in the short run through import of foreign technology, and what is perhaps equally important, of assurance given by a foreign name. The ordinary people, through whose efforts exports and foreign exchange earnings are generated pay heavily for this result, to the benefit again of the richer income groups.[10] Thus there are spurts of demand for luxury goods or comforts by property-owners which temporarily stimulate investment and production in the respective lines, but these spurts are ended either through the saturation of the market or through the aggravation of the balance of payments deficit.

I will not try to relate this model to Indian experience in any detail. The upshot of our analysis would appear to be that both import substitution and export-led strategies come up against the contradictions of a class-riven retarded society. A very large fraction of the poor remain outside the purview of stimulation sought to be provided by these strategies, both on the demand and on the production sides. The process of economic change works by excluding people from an active production process, and converting them into 'waste products'. These waste products can then hardly be expected to help either in raising productivity in industry and agriculture and enabling indigenous capitalists to compete with advanced capitalist countries at home and abroad, or in expanding the market in the long-term and thereby raising the long-term profitability of investment. There may be other strategies for raising industrial growth and achieving self-reliance, but their discussion would require the blueprint for an alternative society as the appropriate background.

NOTES

[I am indebted to Ajit Biswas and Asim Das Gupta for searching comments on an earlier draft of the paper, and to Sudip Chaudhuri for help in checking the algebra. None of them is responsible for any remaining errors.]

1 According to a UN study, the structure of employment in the organised industrial sector in India changed as in the table (figures are percentages of the yearly totals).

	1911	1921	1936	1948
Finished consumer goods	82	76	67	58
Other finished goods	8	13	15	16
Intermediate materials	10	11	18	26

See UN: *Processes and Problems of Industrialisation in Underdeveloped Countries*, United Nations, New York, 1955, p 138.

2 For a survey of industries other than consumer goods industries at the time of independence, see P J Thomas, *India's Basic Industries*, Orient Longman, Calcutta, 1948.

3 For critiques of the strategy of import substitution in the Indian context, see V V Desai, (a) 'Import Substitution and Growth of Consumer Industries', *Economic and Political Weekly*, March 15, 1969; and (b) 'Pursuit of Industrial Self-Sufficiency: Critique of the First Three Plans', *Economic and*

Political Weekly, May 1, 1971. For more general critiques, see J H Power, 'Import Substitution as an Industrialisation Strategy', *The Philippine Economic Journal*, 5 (2), 1966; A O Hirschman, 'The Political Economy of Import-Substituting Industrialisation', *Quarterly Journal of Economics*, 82 (1), February 1968; and David Felix, 'The Dilemma of Import Substitution–Argentina' in G F Papanek (ed), *Development Policy–Theory and Practice*, Harvard University Press, Cambridge, Mass, 1968.

4 Cf Reserve Bank of India, *Report on Currency and Finance for the Year 1975-76*, Bombay, 1976, pp x-xi.

5 cf B R Hazari, 'Import Intensity of Consumption in India', *Indian Economic Review*, New Series, October 1967.

6 Similar regularities have been observed in Argentina. See W B Reddaway, 'A Visiting Economist's Questions', *The Review of the River Plate*, September 21, 1963; C F Diaz Alejandro, *Essays on the Economic History of the Argentina Republic*, Yale University Press, London, 1970, Chapter 7; and Clarence Zuvekas, Jr, 'Economic Growth and Income Distribution in Post-War Argentina', *Inter-American Economic Affairs*, 20(3), Winter 1966.

7 Cf Pramit Chaudhuri, 'A Note on the Irrelevance of Trade', *Economic and Political Weekly*, Annual Number, February 1976.

8 For a preliminary discussion, see my paper, 'Some Characteristics of Industrial Growth in India', *Economic and Political Weekly*, Annual Number, February 1975.

9 I have dealt with some of these problems in an unpublished paper 'Choice of Techniques: A Critique of Non-Neoclassical Orthodoxy'.

10 It is noticeable that most of our exports still originate in agriculture or in crude manufactures, and not in the technology-intensive, foreign-collaboration-ridden, 'modern' industries. This is in line with the experience of other Asian countries. See Angus Hone, 'Multinational Corporations and Multinational Buying Groups: Their Impact on the Growth of Asia's Exports of Manufactures–Myths and Realities', *World Development*, 2(2), February 1974; and B I Cohen, *Multinational Firms and Asian Exports*, Yale University Press, New Haven, Conn, 1975.

Annual Number, February 1977

5

Economic Performance since the Third Plan and Its Implications for Policy

T N Srinivasan
N S S Narayana

THE final version of the Fifth Five-Year Plan, an unusually slim volume, has been recently released, nearly three years after the publication of the draft volume. Presumably work on the approach to and the dimensional hypotheses of the Sixth Plan is about to begin in Yojana Bhavan.

We would like to take this opportunity to review the performance of the Indian economy since the beginning of planning for national development and draw some policy conclusions. In doing so, we shall concentrate mainly on some macro-economic indicators such as real capital formation, public saving, foreign capital inflow, and growth of output of selected industries. Our aim is not to build any elaborate econometric model of Indian planning or analyse in detail (and depth) policies pursued but the limited one of drawing broad conclusions suggested by the available data.

The year 1966 marks a watershed in recent Indian economic and political history–it marked the end of the Third Five-Year Plan, the devaluation of the Indian rupee and a second serious drought in succession. It also marked the postponement of the start of the Fourth Five-Year Plan eventually by three years, and the beginning of the first three so-called 'annual' plans. It is, therefore, natural to examine whether the trends in crucial economic magnitudes established during the first three five-year plans continued in the subsequent period, 1966-75. While it is not our argument that the trend of the first three plans should necessarily have been continued beyond, it is obvious that any *downward* departures from past trends, particularly in respect of real investment and such other macro-variables, is a cause of concern since it is nobody's claim that there are no potential investment opportunities in the Indian economy that could be exploited without running into diminishing returns.

We begin with Figures 1-3 in which the data on real gross fixed capital formation (at 1960-61 prices converted into an index with the base 1960-61) in the economy as a whole as well as the public and private sectors have been plotted. An exponential trend line fitted to the annual data up to 1965-66 is also marked in each of these graphs. The graphs on public sector and total investment show similar striking results, namely, that the period after 1965-66 represents a departure in the downward direction from the trends established during the first three plans. This is particularly so in respect of the public sector–after growing at the trend rate of around 11.5 per cent per annum during the first three plan periods, gross real fixed capital formation in the public sector *declined* during the years 1967-68 to 1971-72 and the recovery after this year did not bring it back anywhere near the previous trend.

It appears that private sector investment did not slacken after 1965-66, and in fact, until 1970-71 the observations are above the trend line. However, there is a puzzling aspect to the data on private savings and investment: household savings in the form of physical assets (mainly housing, minor irrigation and inventories) show a quantum jump in the period from 1966-67; at current prices this item approximately ranged between Rs 300 crore and Rs 800 crore in the period 1960-61 to 1965-66 while it exceeded Rs 1,600 crore in every year after 1965-66 and by a substantial amount in some years. The data on domestic capital formation by type of assets reflects the same phenomenon– investment in private sector construction jumps to substantially higher levels than before from 1966-67. While it is conceivable that households invested more in real estate in later years as a hedge against inflation, it would be surprising that a shift of the order indicated above could be due only to this factor.

It is well known that the methodology of estimating savings and capital formation rely on diverse sources of information that include yearly data on commodity flows and ratios obtained from bench-mark surveys conducted at longer intervals than a year. Only for some components of saving and investment, direct and fairly reliable data are available. Other components have to be estimated indirectly making heavy use of bench-mark ratios. Household savings in the form of physical assets are particularly vulnerable to changes in the methodology as well as to revisions in data since this item is obtained as a residual–by subtracting from the total physical asset formation the shares of other sectors. There is no alternative estimate against which this residual can be compared. Though we have no evidence that some errors or biases crept in only after 1965-66, a deeper probe

Figure 1: Index of Real Gross Fixed Capital Formation: Public and Private Sectors (1960-61 = 100)
(Y-axis represents the logarithmic value of this index to the base 'ten')

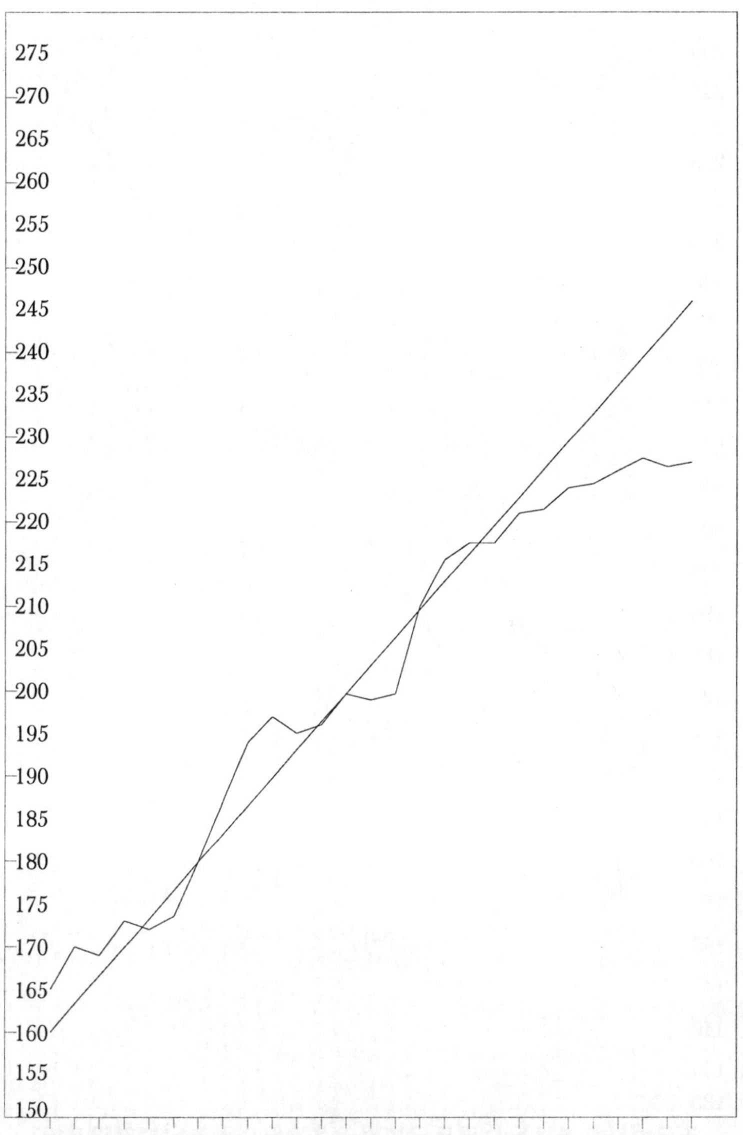

Figure 2: Index of Real Gross Fixed Capital Formation: Public Sector (1960-61 = 100)

(Y-axis represents the logarithmic value of this index to the base 'ten')

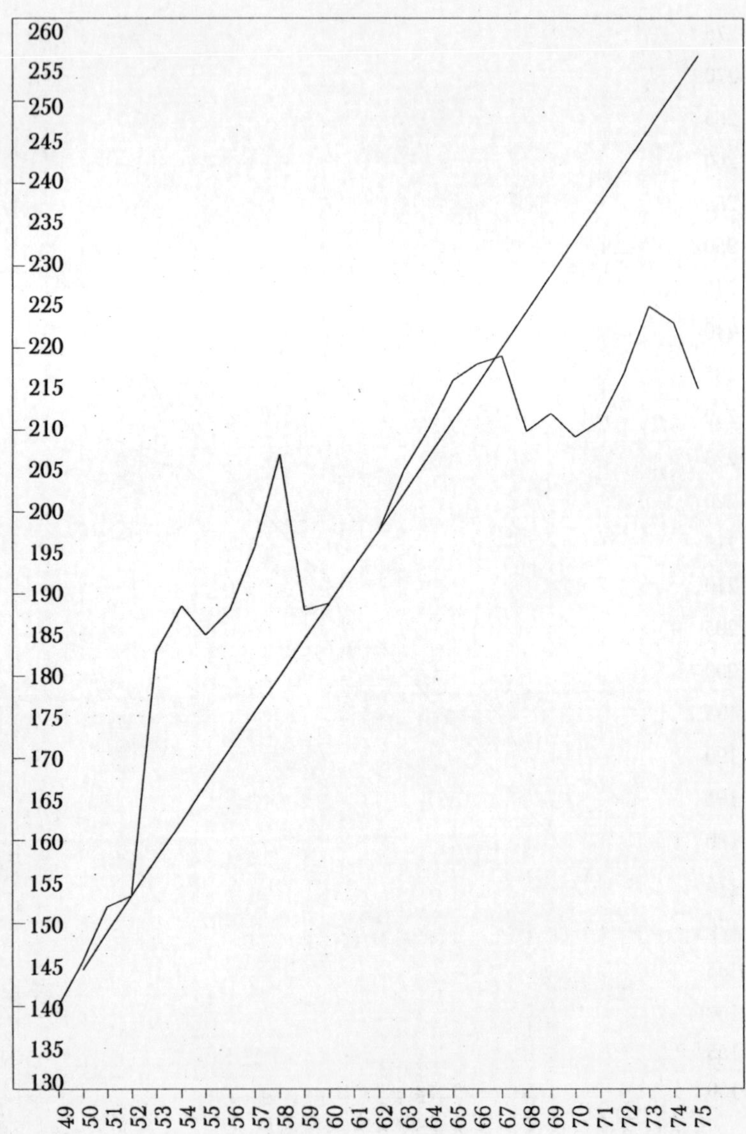

Figure 3: Index of Real Gross Fixed Capital Formation: Private Sector (1960-61 = 100)

(Y-axis represents the logarithmic value of this index to the base 'ten')

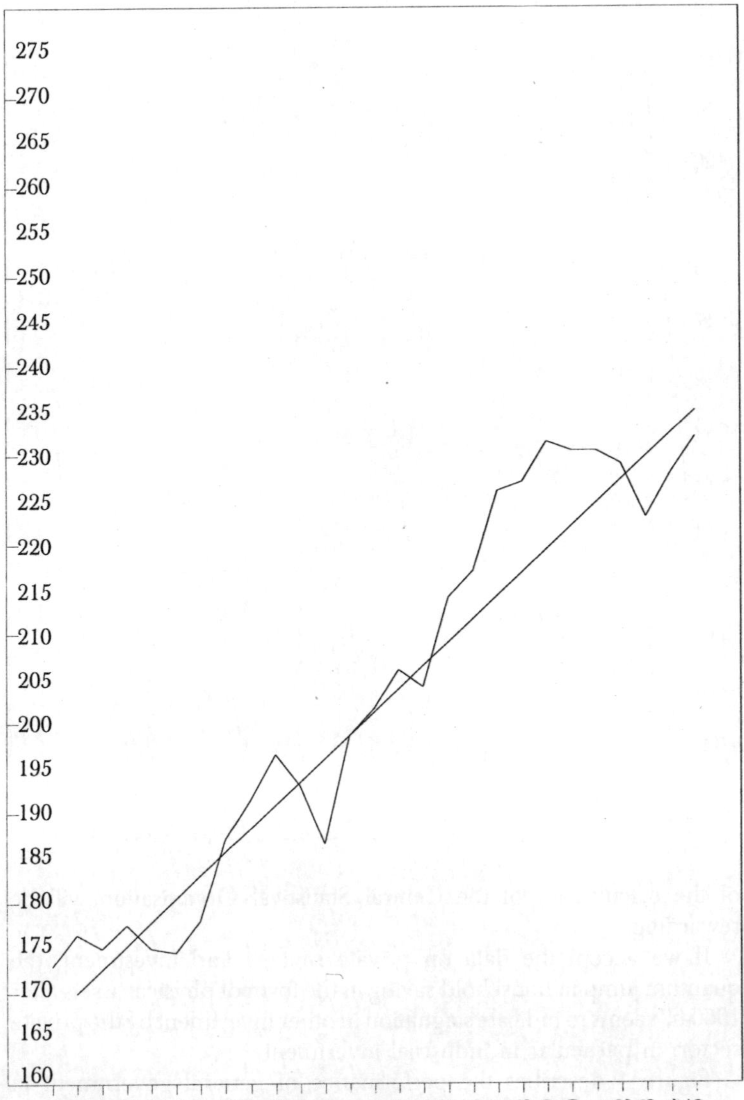

Figure 4: Savings of General Government as a Proportion of Receipts

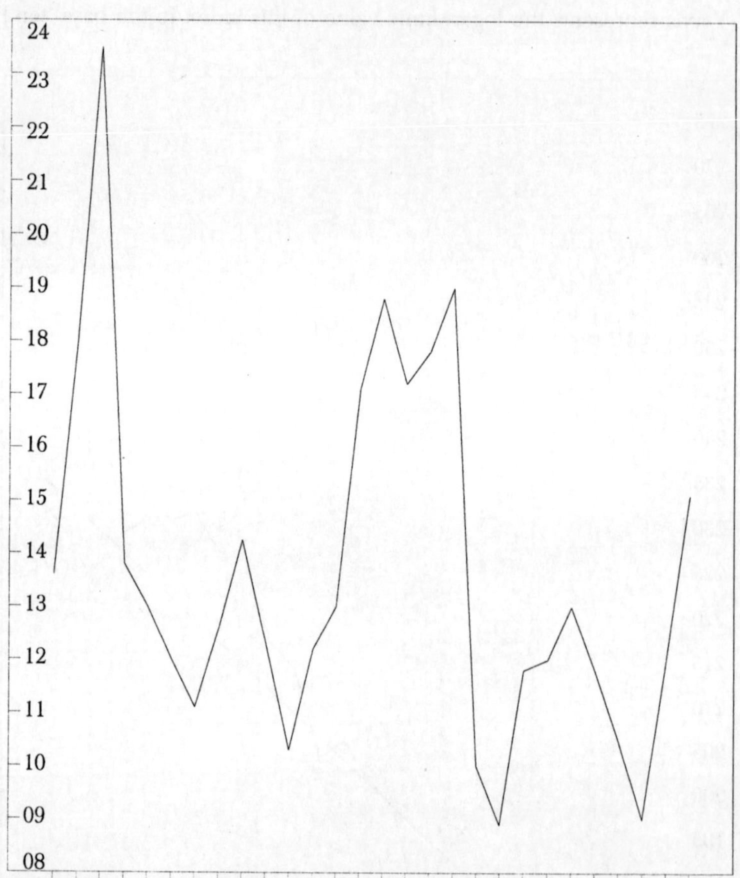

of the calculations of the Central Statistical Organisation will be rewarding.

If we accept the data on private savings and investment, the quantum jump in household saving in the form of physical assets after 1966-67 seems to indicate stagnation in other investment by the private sector, in particular in industrial investment.

Figure 4 describes the performance of general government in respect of the proportion it saved from its receipts. Clearly there is no visible trend in this ratio and the fluctuations from year to year

Figure 5: Net External Aid

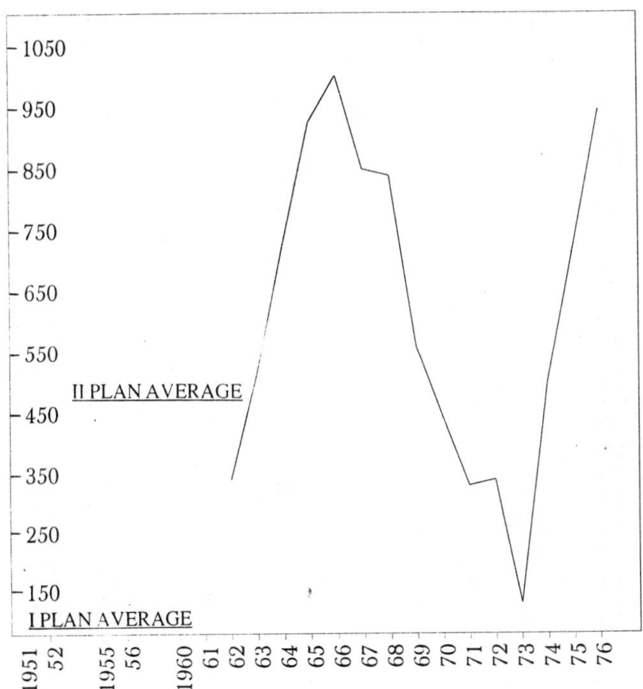

have been extreme. Thus the hopes that were entertained at the beginning of the planning era that the public sector will generate increasing volume of resources for its investment have not apparently materialised. Further, even though there is no trend, it appears that the savings ratio fluctuates around a lower mean since 1965-66 as compared to the period before, thus explaining in part the slackening in public investment in the later period.

In Figure 5 we have plotted the data on net external aid. In the period ending in 1965-66 there was a rapid rise in net aid, followed by a sharp decline until 1972-73 and a subsequent rise. It is perhaps not entirely a coincidence that public sector investment rose rapidly when aid rose and fell when aid inflow fell. Of course it is too facile to suggest that availability of aid determined the volume of public investment; but given the fact that in the period prior to 1965-66, aid such as under PL-480 programme did constitute a source of budgetary support to the government, the hypothesis that in adjusting to a

Figure 6: Index of Real Fixed Capital Formation in Mining, Quarrying, Manufacturing and Construction, (1960-61 = 100)
(Y-axis represents the logarithmic value of this index to the base 'ten')

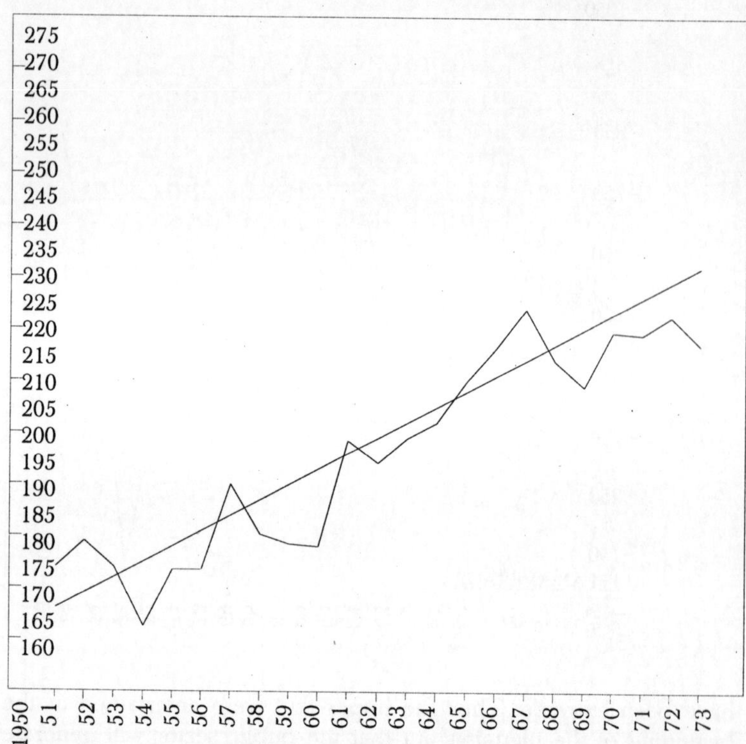

reduction in aid the axe fell mainly on public investment is plausible. Indeed, public consumption expenditure on defence, health, education, etc, has a momentum of its own and, reducing its growth over time so as to maintain the growth of investment requires political will.

We now look at the broad sectoral composition of real investment. The sectors considered are (i) agriculture, (ii) mining, quarrying, manufacturing and construction, (iii) transport, storage and communication, and (iv) electricity, gas and water supply. The aggregation into these particular sectors was dictated by the fact that we wished to utilise the data put together by R N Lal for the period up to 1960-61 with the data published by the Central Statistical Organisation. The results are shown in Figures 6-8. It is clear that the sectors that normally account for a substantial proportion of public sector investment, namely, transport and communication, electric power, etc, departed

Figure 7: Index of Real Fixed Capital Formation in Transportation, Communication and Storage (1960-61 = 100)

(Y-axis represents the logarithmic value of this index to the base 'ten')

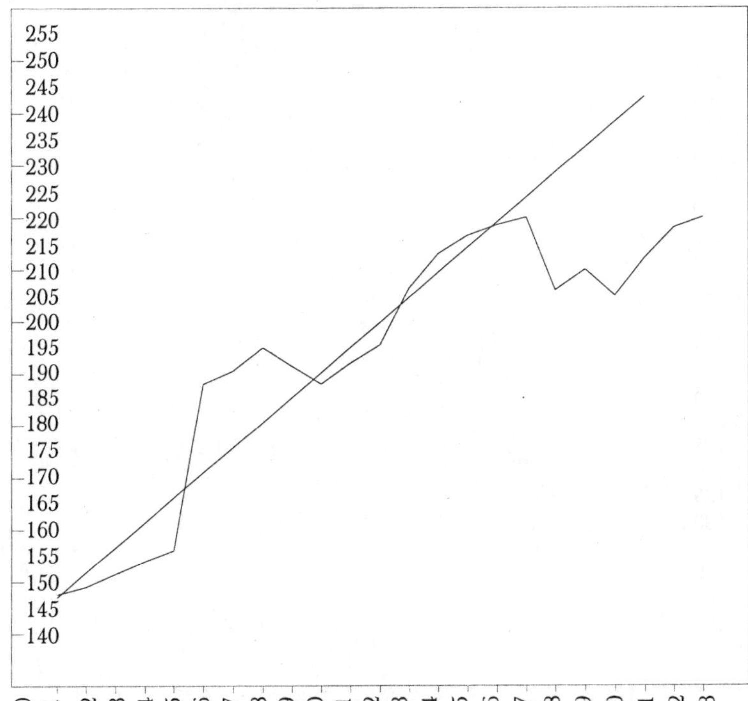

significantly in the downward direction from their trend growth in investment established during the first three plan periods.

Let us now turn to the consequences of the investment stagnation in the economy. It is to be expected that growth in capacity creation will be slowed down sooner or later if investment growth is reduced, sooner (later) in the case of industries with short (long) gestation lag between investment expenditure and capacity creation. Unfortunately we do not have a reliable time series on installed capacity. We have therefore got to use production as a proxy variable for capacity. Of course, to the extent rates of capacity utilisation vary over time, using production as a proxy can be misleading in the sense that shortfalls in growth in demand will get confounded with shortfalls in growth in potential supply as represented by growth in capacity. This has to be kept in mind in interpreting what follows.

Figure 8: Index of Real Fixed Capital Formation in Electricity, Gas and Water Supply (1960-61 = 100)

(Y-axis represents the logarithmic value of this index to the base 'ten')

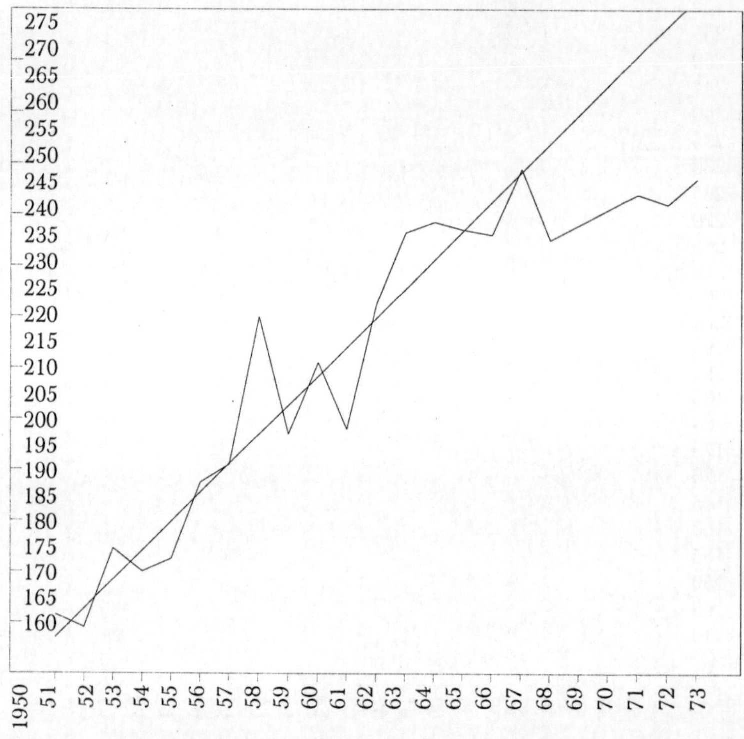

Figures 9-13 show the trends in general index of industrial production, index of production of electricity, cement, machinery (other than electrical) and transport equipment. The general index and that of electricity output are broad indicators of industrial activity as a whole. Both show clearly a slow-down in growth from their trend rates (around 7 per cent and 12 per cent per annum respectively in the cases of the general index and electricity output) during the first three plans. The indices of output of investment goods such as cement and transport equipment show substantial downward deviations from trend, this being particularly marked in the case of transport equipment. This is to be expected since growth in domestic demand for investment goods in general is related to the growth in investment in the economy. Only part of the reduction in the growth of this demand could be accommodated by reduction in equipment imports and an

Figure 9: Index of Industrial Production: General (1956 = 100)
(Y-axis represents the logarithmic value of this index to the base 'ten')

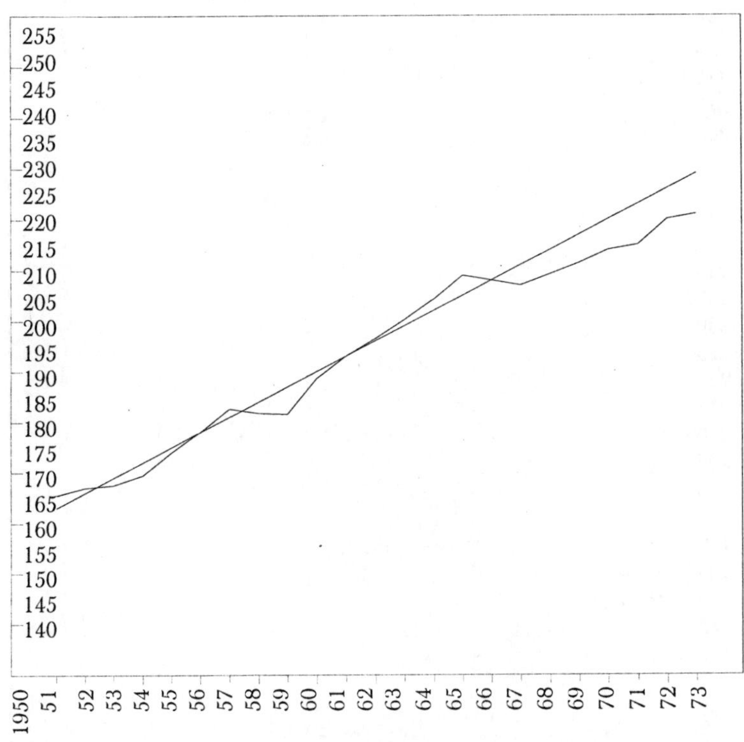

increase in exports (particularly steel and engineering goods), the rest being accommodated by slowing down the growth of domestic output.

To sum up the findings so far: In the decade since 1966 the Indian economy seems to have departed significantly from the growth trends established during the first three plans. Growth of real investment by the public sector, a sector which was envisaged by the planners to take on an increasingly dominant role in the economy, declined substantially. Public sector savings as a proportion of its receipts showed no perceptible trends either during the first three plans or later except that the average of this ratio in the later period seems to have been lower. The vigorous growth in public sector investment during the first three plans and its later stagnation appears to have been associated with the rapid growth and later generally rapid decline in net foreign aid. The stagnation in investment seems to have affected

Figure 10: Index of Industrial Production: Electricity (1956 = 100)
(Y-axis represents the logarithmic value of this index to the base 'ten')

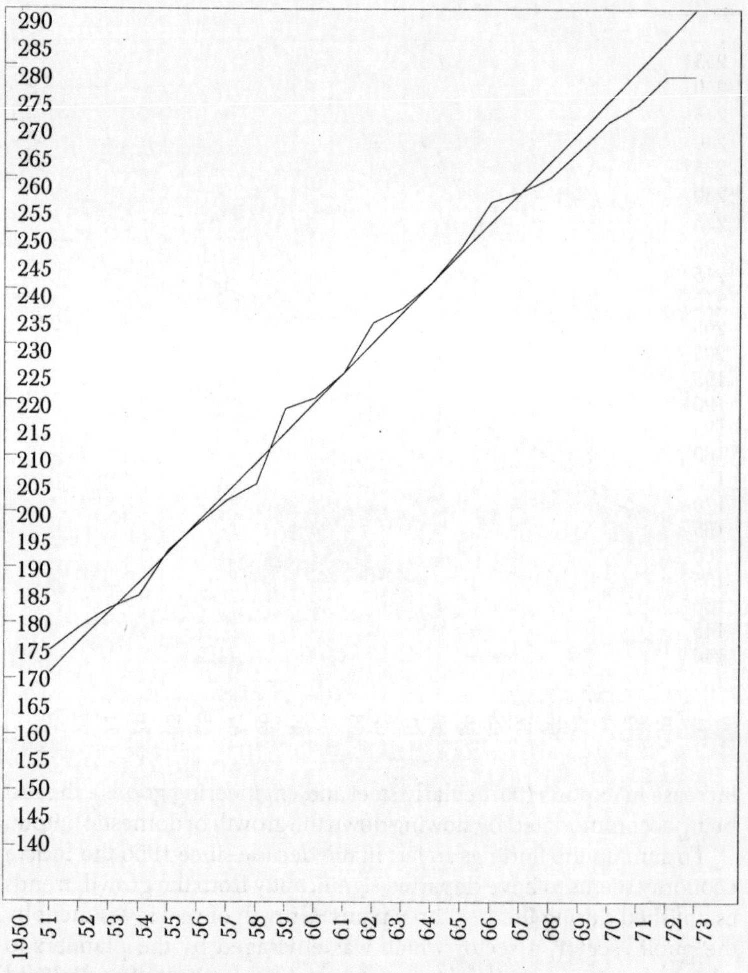

the performance of capital goods producing sectors of the economy significantly.

Let us reiterate, however, that it is not our contention that the trends in investment and production established prior to 1966 could have been continued without a major restructuring of policies. For instance, the opportunities for rapid industrialisation through import substitution had been nearly exhausted by 1966. Also, the problems of

Figure 11: Index of Industrial Production: Cement (1956 = 100)
(Y-axis represents the logarithmic value of this index to the base 'ten')

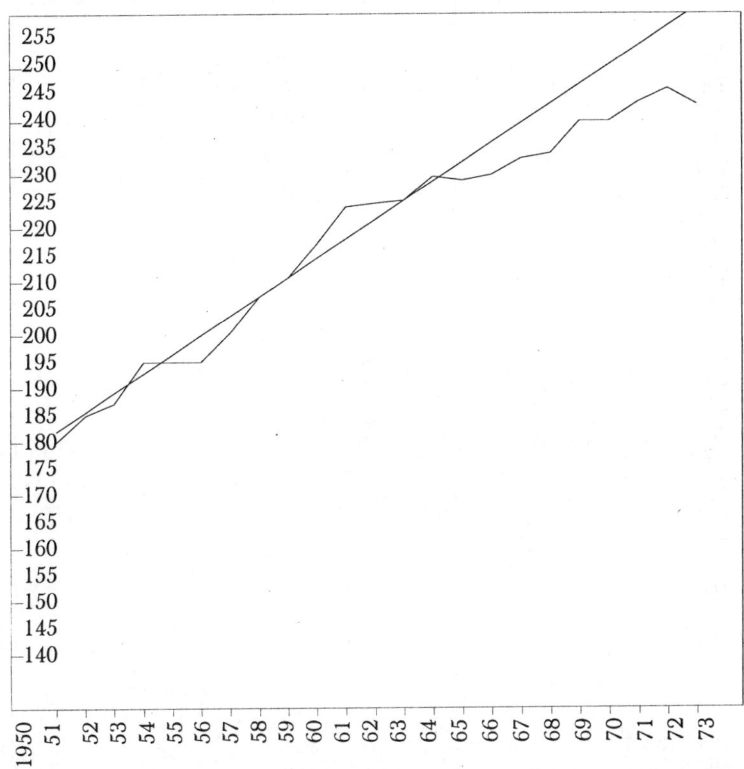

management and operation of public sector enterprises were becoming acute. Further, even if the severe droughts of 1965 and 1966 had not occurred, the problem of relatively slow agricultural growth, particularly the rate of growth of output of foodgrains, would have had to be faced. Finally, the problem of sustaining public investment in the absence of growth of public savings and a decline in aid could not be wished away. *All* these problems had become apparent even before 1966 and what is more, some hesitant steps were being taken to face them, such as, for instance, the devaluation of 1966 and associated liberalisation measures. However, and this is our main contention, these steps did not either go far enough, such as, for instance, the extent of devaluation, or were reversed altogether.

Before we turn to policy conclusions to be drawn from our discussion, it may be worthwhile to document the progressive scaling

Figure 12: Index of Industrial Production: Machinery Except Electrical Machinery (1956 = 100)
(Y-axis represents the logarithmic value of this index to the base 'ten')

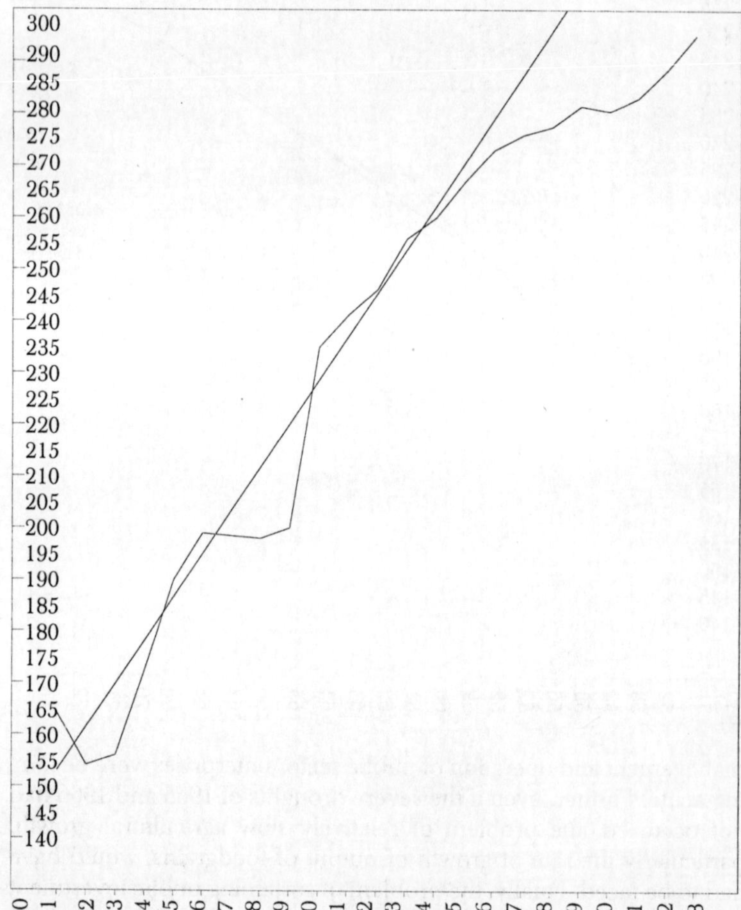

down during 1966-75 of plan targets in respect of crucial economic magnitudes. The data we use (see the table) have all been taken from publications of the Planning Commission: three documents from the Perspective Planning Division (*Perspective of Development: 1961-76, Implications of Planning for a Minimum Level of Living*, circulated in 1962; *Notes on Perspectives of Development: India 1960-61–1975-76*, published in 1964; *Material and Financial Balances Relating to the*

Figure 13: Index of Industrial Production: Transport Equipment (1956 = 100)

(Y-axis represents the logarithmic value of this index to the base 'ten')

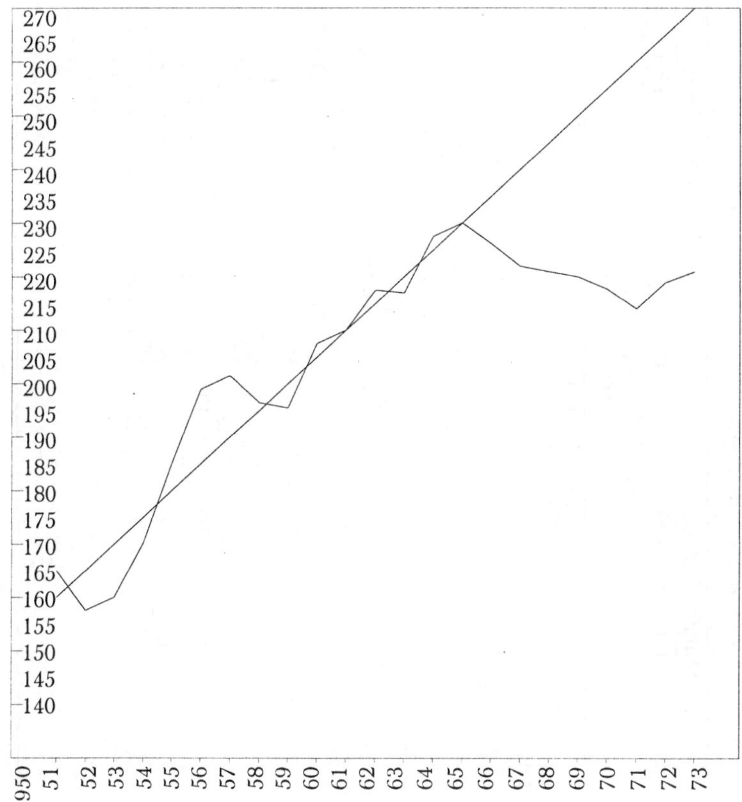

Fourth Plan, published in 1966), the two drafts of the Fourth Plan published in 1966 and 1969 and the three versions of the Fifth Plan. The target for output of foodgrains has been scaled down from 152-154 million tons for the year 1975-76 as contained in the 1966 PPD document to 125 million tons for the year 1978-79 in the final Fifth Plan. Steel target goes down from 27.4 million tons for 1975-76 in the 1962 PPD document to 8.8 million tons for 1978-79 in the final Fifth Plan. Of course it could be and has been argued that earlier targets were wildly unrealistic. However, it is equally clear that achievements in relation to targets has apparently not improved markedly as the targets got progressively lower! Be that as it may, the important point

Table: Major Targets

	Target Year	Perspective Planning Division			Five-Year Plans				
		1962	1964	1966	IV Plan		V Plan		
					Draft (1966)	Draft (1969)	Approach	Draft	Final
Foodgrains (million tonnes)	1970-71		122	166	120				
	–74					129		144	
	–76	148	151	152-154					
	–79					156	140	140	125
	–81					167			
	–84							162	
	–86							170	
	–89								161-170
Steel (finished) (million tonnes)	1970-71		115	8.8	8.8				
	–74					8.1		5.4	4.7
	–76	27.4	21.5	15.5					
	–79					12.5	9.4	9.4	8.8
	–81					15.0			
	–84							17.1	
	–86							20.5	
	–89								
Coal (million tonnes)	1970-71		140	106	106				
	–74					94			
	–76	255	210	158				79	
	–79					130	141		
	–81					145		135	124
	–84								
	–86							203	
	–89							238	

(Contd)

Table: Major Targets (Contd)

	Target Year	Perspective Planning Division			Five-Year Plans				
		1962	1964	1966	IV Plan		V Plan		
					Draft (1966)	Draft (1969)	Approach	Draft	Final
Electric power consumption (billion kwh)	1970-71		79	78	80				
	–74					82		72	72
	–76	144	126	126					
	–79					145	129	120	116-117
	–81					175			
	–84							200	
	–86							245	
	–89								
Cement (million tonnes)	1970-71		23	20	20				
	–74					18		16	15
	–76	51	36	30					
	–79					27	27	25	21
	–81					32			
	–84							38	
	–86							45	
	–89								
Railway freight (million tonnes/km)	1970-71		224	170	308*				
	–74					265*	–	215*	
	–76	441	297	250					
	–79							300*	250-260*
	–81								
	–84								
	–86								
	–89								

* Originating traffic (million tonnes).

to note is that in early 1964, prior to the death of the then chairman of the Planning Commission, Jawaharlal Nehru, when the PPD notes were taking their final shape, there was a consistent perspective on the future growth of the economy based on a target of 7 per cent per annum growth in real national income. The growth envisaged then in respect of crucial sectors such as domestic capacity to produce capital goods, technical education, transportation, etc, became no longer relevant as the planned growth of income did not materialise. Excess capacities began to grow particularly in investment-related industries and employment opportunities even for technically trained people did not grow rapidly enough to absorb the supplies that had been planned for a more rapid growth in the economy.

The discussion so far leads us to conclude that if the Indian economy is to break away from its recent stagnation, a return to a vigorous growth in public sector investment as a part of a return to planned development is essential. It is possible that this step-up can be achieved only with increasing net aid inflow. In this context, it is interesting to note, firstly, that the final Fifth Plan document does not mention the zero net aid target of the draft volume nor does it comment on, other than stating, the fact that net aid inflow during the first three years of the plan has been far above what had been assumed in the draft. Indeed, one could argue that whatever improvement in plan investment took place in the first two years of the Fifth Plan is probably a consequence of the larger than expected aid inflow. The second point to be noted in this context is that there is a certain inconsistency between our eloquent arguments in international forums for a large transfer of resources from developed to the developing countries and our own policy objective of zero net aid by the end of Sixth Plan! While we do not wish to suggest that aid on any terms should be accepted, we do hold the view that emphasis should be on defining the terms acceptable to us rather than on the quantum of aid. If increasing volume of aid on acceptable terms becomes available, no shibboleth such as a zero net aid target should be allowed to come in the way of our accepting such aid.

It is also worth emphasising that our argument is really for *planning for the absorption* of a larger volume of aid on acceptable terms. Otherwise it may easily degenerate into using aid for rescue operations, i e, to cushion the economy from failures of economic policy. Indeed such failures as well as lack of clarity in defining the terms on which we would accept or seek aid have been responsible in the past for aid or threatened denial of it to be used for political ends. Of course, these arguments may turn out to be irrelevant if the prospects for larger volume of resource transfer from the rich to the poor countries do not become far brighter than they appear now.

Our emphasis on public sector investment arises, apart from the accepted policy of enlarging the share of public sector over time, also from the hypothesis that in the Indian economy the profitability of private sector investment is influenced more by the growth in demand generated by a vigorous growth in public sector investment than by fiscal incentives.

It is also likely that an enlarged public sector investment appropriately allocated will have considerable impact on achieving the objectives of increasing the volume of employment creation and reducing the extent of poverty. Almost surely, investment in minor irrigation and development of ground water resources, land consolidation and development, rural roads, water supply, sanitation, etc, will have to be stepped up. If lack of adequate number of projects in these areas is a constraint in the short run, at least for the Sixth Plan such a constraint should be eased considerably by devoting sufficient resources for project identification and preparation.

Our emphasis on increasing investment should not be taken to mean that we think that efficient operation of the economy, both in public and private sectors, is not important. We do not go into this issue here firstly because it has been receiving wide attention (see for instance Bhagwati and Desai (1970), and Bhagwati and Srinivasan (1974), and secondly, because the impetus to growth arising out of improvements in efficiency would be a once and for all contribution, though not necessarily negligible. In any case, there are encouraging signs of improving efficiency, particularly in the public sector, since mid-seventies. This trend ought to be reinforced by a conscious dismantling of regulations and controls that have outlived their utility and serve only as shackles on efficient resource allocation and utilisation.

We now turn to the question whether a substantial step-up in public investment is feasible in the short run and in the long run. It is obvious that in the long run, a solidly-based vigorous growth in public sector investment is limited (apart from external aid) only by the growth in public savings. One cannot emphasise enough the need for generating an increasing volume of public savings. In the short run, there could be an 'absorptive capacity limit' to investment though it is absurd to suggest the existence of such a limit in the long run for a supposedly planned economy. Indeed, some may even argue that the accumulation of stocks of foodgrains and foreign exchange reflects this in the sense that unplanned inventory (food and foreign exchange) investment is a consequence of lack of investment opportunities elsewhere in the economy. While there may be some truth in this argument, it is equally important to observe that this inventory accumulation is also a result of unanticipated increase in supplies due to favourable weather in the case of foodgrains and vigorous export growth as well as increased inflow of aid, in the case of foreign exchange. There is also the question whether the existing levels of food and foreign exchange reserves are 'excessive'. We do not propose to explore this issue in detail here and proceed further on the assumption that some release from these stocks is possible without reducing their levels to 'risky' limits.

It will not be out of place here to note in passing that the performance on the export front is explained, apart from the slackening of domestic demand discussed earlier, by the decision to link the rupee to the sinking pound in 1971 (and more recently to a basket of currencies). The across-the-board incentives provided by the implicit devaluation of the rupee in relation to most currencies other than the pound were perhaps more important in boosting exports than the plethora of specific subsidies, explicit and implicit, that have been characteristic of the Indian export promotion schemes.

Coming back to 'absorptive capacity', it is possible that there are not enough worthwhile projects (lying on the shelves of the Planning Commission) and this may provide in the short run an 'absorptive capacity limit'. There is also another aspect. Given the inflationary record until 1974-75 and the resurgence in price rise during the whole of 1976, it is possible that fears of rekindling inflationary fires may be inhibiting the planners from proposing a substantial step-up in investment. But with the existence of inventories of food and foreign exchange, this argument is essentially a confession of a lack of faith in the government's ability to influence the course of prices through suitable releases from the inventories of food and foreign exchange. Given the performance of the public sector in respect of release of food stocks in 1973 and, more recently, its intervention in the vegetable oil markets, this lack of faith may indeed be warranted. It will be a tragedy, however, if this is allowed to come in the way of a substantial step-up in investment.

It will be an even greater tragedy if certain naive proposals for the use of accumulated foreign exchange are implemented. One such proposal starts from the assumption that the problem in boosting public sector investment is one of 'rupee finance'. It is argued that one way of solving this rupee finance problem is to use foreign exchange to import such items as scooters and sell them and thereby raise 'rupees'. The economic rationale, if any, behind such proposals is hard to discern. At one level, the problem of the use of excess inventories of food and foreign exchange is one of converting them into presumably more productive assets and at this level, it is by no means certain that scooters are the relevant assets! At another level, the very same stocks could be used to meet the demands of wage goods and other inputs arising out of an expansion of investment activity. At this level again, it is by no means obvious that the best way of achieving it is through the release of resources that would have been spent by scooter buyers on other commodities, if they are not supplied with scooters! The very fact that such ideas are gaining currency suggests an abdication of responsibility by planners. The obvious solution to the alleged problem of 'rupee finance' is deficit financing. The risk of rekindling inflationary fires through recourse to deficit financing is minimal, given the available stocks of food and foreign exchange. On the use of foreign exchange reserves, the liberalisation of import controls, particularly in respect of equipment imports should be extended further.

We should like to conclude by pleading for a return to serious planning for national development. With the return to normalcy in other spheres, a really bold effort in planning is called for now.

APPENDIX

Sources of Data

(A) Publications of Central Statistical Organisation:
 (i) *National Accounts Statistics* (defined hereafter as the *White Paper* or WP), various issues.
 (ii) *Estimates of Gross Capital Formation in India: 1948-49 to 1960-61.*
 (iii) *Monthly Statistics of Production of Selected Industries*, issues of January-June 1967, January-February 1968, March 1972 and March 1974.

(B) R N Lal, *Capital Formation in India.*

(C) Several publications of the Planning Commission as indicated in the text.

Processing of Data

White Paper (WP) gives data on total gross fixed domestic capital formation (FCF) at current prices from 1960-61 to 1974-75 sector-wise (i e, public and private) by types of assets, i e, construction and machinery and equipment. At constant prices (1960-61 prices), this information is given only by types of assets. Asset-wise proportions of public and private sector investments were calculated from the data in current prices for each year and these proportions were used in splitting constant price data of FCF to arrive at asset-wise distribution of investment at constant prices in the two sectors.

The data on fixed CF for the years prior to 1960-61, i e, from 1948-49 to 1960-61, at constant (1958-59 prices) prices are available sector-wise, i e, public and private sectors, in document A (ii) above.

Taking 1960-61 as base year, indices of fixed capital formation (for public, private and total) were constructed.

Investment at constant prices relating to the following industries for the years 1950-51 to 1970-71 were taken from R N Lal's book:
(1) Agriculture including forestry, logging and fishing.
(2) Mining, quarrying, manufacturing and construction.
(3) Electricity, gas and water supply.
(4) Transport, storage and communications.

WP contains data on sector-wise gross capital formation only for the years 1960-61 to 1974-75. To arrive at the fixed capital formation figures, the gross capital formation figures were multiplied by the ratio of the total gross fixed capital formation to total gross capital formation, year-wise. Again taking 1960-61 as base, indices were constructed.

Data on Index of Industrial Production for the years 1951-1966 with base 1956 were taken from documents A (iii) above. The data for years after 1966 are available only with 1960 as base. To convert them to 1956 base, the year-to-year growth rates of the indices *with 1960 as base* were applied to the relevant index for 1966 *with base 1956.*

[The views expressed in this note are those of the authors and are not necessarily shared by their organisations. T N Srinivasan presented some of these results at a Symposium on the Fifth Plan organised recently by the Institute of Economic Growth, Delhi. Thanks are due to M S Ahluwalia, M R Shroff, S D Tendulkar and Jean Baneth for their comments and useful suggestions.]

REFERENCES

Bhagwati, J N and P Desai (1970): *India: Planning for Industrialisation*, Oxford University Press, London.

Bhagwati, J N and T N Srinivasan (1974): *Foreign Trade Regimes and Economic Development: India*, Columbia University Press, New York.

Lal, R N (1977): *Capital Formation in India*, forthcoming.

Annual Number, February 1977

6

Constraints on Growth and Policy Options

A Vaidyanathan

THIS paper argues that (a) the sluggish growth of output and investment since the mid-sixties was in a large measure due to the meagre growth in agricultural production; (b) the impediments to agricultural growth are not such as can be removed by larger investments alone and any significant improvement over past performance is improbable; (c) with low agricultural growth, the economy cannot maintain the overall growth rates of either output or investment visualised by the revised Fifth Plan unless there is a quantum jump in export growth and/or a dramatic improvement in the state's ability to achieve a high marginal savings rate in a non-inflationary manner; and (d) since neither of these conditions is likely to be met, it would be wiser, though not easier, to trim the goals of overall growth nearer to feasible levels and ask ourselves what can be done to promote the equity and employment objectives within this limit.

In stressing the rate of agricultural growth as the principal constraint on the growth of overall output and investment, the paper presents a somewhat different viewpoint from that advanced by Srinivasan and Satyanarayana.[1] They argue that the stagnation of real investment, especially in the public sector, is among the most important causes of sluggishness of the economy during the last decade and that, therefore, the central thrust of policy to pull the economy out of its present stupor should be a vigorous expansion of public investment, if need be by the recourse to deficit financing. They point out that, properly utilised, the available reserves of food and foreign exchange, which are unusually large, are sufficient protection against inflationary pressures. Much the same line of thinking is apparent in the formulations of the pre-budget *Economic Survey*, as well as in the pronouncements of spokesmen for the private sector. In absolute terms reserves of food and foreign exchange are indeed comfortable; but it is well to remember that the external reserves are equivalent to only 6-7 months' value of imports and that, allowing for a reasonable buffer stock, the food reserves are equivalent to barely 10 per cent of annual consumption. The level of reserves can be drawn down to support larger investment and output, but only for a while. It is therefore important to focus on the long-term constraints and this is what the present paper attempts to do.

PERFORMANCE DURING SIXTIES

There can be of course little doubt that stagnation of investment since the mid-sixties adversely affected the overall growth rate. Since the increase in the aggregate real investment fell from an average of over 8 per cent a year between 1960 and 1966 to under 2 per cent a year in the subsequent six years, the demand for products of industries producing capital goods and their inputs must have suffered a severe set-back which in turn would have dampened production as well as new investments in these sectors. But given the small fraction of total GDP derived from these activities, their slow-down is unlikely to have been a significant factor in the deceleration of overall growth.[2] The slackening of the pace of new investments is likely to have had a much bigger impact on overall growth by slowing down the rate of additions to productive capacity. However, there are strong reasons to doubt whether the deceleration of GDP growth in the sixties can be adequately explained by investment trends alone.

The sixties in fact witnessed a significant increase in fixed investment in agriculture which is reflected in the higher rate of expansion of irrigation potential, soil conservation, and other capacity-creating investments in the sixties compared to the fifties; the absorption of current inputs (notably fertilisers), which are a major source of output growth, also accelerated during this period; and this was the period of major technological development symbolised by the high-yielding varieties. And yet, the rate of agricultural growth in the sixties (2.1 per cent) was much lower compared to the fifties (3.3 per cent per annum).[3] Even in the industrial sector, the persistence of underutilised capacity suggests that output could have increased more than it in fact did, even though the rate of capacity expansion might have been slower on account of the failure of the rate of investment to rise.

It could be argued that the marked deceleration in overall growth, as well as in the growth of manufacturing industry and investment beginning in the mid-sixties was due in considerable measure to the fall in the rate of agricultural growth. The direct effect of the latter on overall growth–agriculture and related activities after all account for close to half the total GDP–must have been quite substantial.[4] The deceleration in output growth during the sixties was more marked for such industrial crops as fibres and oilseeds, than for foodgrains. The possibilities of importing agricultural raw materials being constrained by foreign exchange shortages, a shortfall in agricultural production meant a shortfall in supply of raw materials to an important segment of industry: food, drink, tobacco and textiles, whose principal raw materials are derived from agriculture, accounted for over half the value added by manufacturing in the early sixties. Slower-than-targeted growth of agriculture also meant slower-than-targeted growth of domestic demand for manufactures. Since exports absorb such a small proportion of output, the extraordinarily rapid growth of manufactured exports in recent years could not compensate for the slack in domestic demand. Consequently, the inducements to undertake new industrial investments must have been considerably dampened.

Slow agricultural growth also compounded the problems of mobilising savings partly because of its depressing effect on the growth of real income and hence on voluntary private savings; and, more importantly, because the resulting shortages of essential commodities and rising prices severely restricted the scope for increasing public sector savings. Since the sixties agricultural production has barely kept pace with the population and, despite larger imports, the per capita availability of essential items of food and clothing has not shown any improvement; in fact, in several years the availability was less than in the early sixties.

The prices of essential commodities were under severe pressure through much of this period. The public distribution system could not protect the poorer segments of the population against shortages and inflation. In this context, measures to augment public revenues (whether by additional taxation or through higher prices for products of public enterprises) had to contend with greater political resistance. Such additional revenues as could be raised were neutralised by the growth of non-development expenditure–partly reflecting increased commitments for defence and police, but in large part due to increased salaries, and food subsidies, to mitigate the effects of inflation on public sector employees and urban consumers. Faced with a demand recession, efforts to improve public enterprise surpluses, by better use of capacity or by price adjustments, did not make much headway either. Altogether, the savings of the public sector, which were slated to be the principal source of increased savings, recorded a decline in relation to GDP. In the circumstances, cut-backs in the public investment programme were inevitable. But the available resources were inadequate to finance even the trimmed-down programme and recourse to central bank funds remained at high level during much of the period. This only aggravated the inflationary pressures already latent in the stagnation of per capita food supplies.

FACTORS AFFECTING AGRICULTURAL GROWTH

The reasons for the slow growth of crop production in the recent past and the constraints on future growth have been discussed by me at some length elsewhere.[5] To recapitulate briefly: The failure to realise targeted growth of agricultural production in the decade 1965-1975 was due to three major factors. First, the rate of additions to cropped area during the sixties was much lower than in the fifties. Second, the additions to irrigation and fertiliser use fell much short of plan targets. And third, the productivity of inputs turned out to be significantly below expectations.

In the future, too, there is little prospect of achieving faster growth of crop area than in the recent past. While there is a large untapped potential for irrigation, the pace of exploitation visualised by the plans may be difficult to achieve on account of both organisational and financial constraints. Qualitative improvement of irrigation, which is perhaps more important than quantitative expansion, is not likely to be rapid, in part because it is not receiving sufficient attention in the plans and more importantly because crucial institutional aspects of the problem are not being tackled under existing programmes. The projected rapid expansion of fertiliser use is also in serious doubt unless the productivity of plant nutrients under conditions of mass application is substantially improved. The scope for such improvement is apparently large, but far too little is known about the reasons for the divergence between actual and potential response to formulate remedial action. The quality of irrigation is one of the factors, but, for reasons cited above, the pace of its improvement is likely to be slow. The cumulative effect of likely shortfalls in irrigation, slow improvement in irrigation quality, and shortfalls in fertiliser use makes the realisation of targeted long-term agricultural growth rate (4-4.5 per cent) extremely doubtful. Even to recover the pre-Third Plan growth rate of 3.2 per cent per annum would call for a degree of improvement over current performance which cannot be taken readily for granted. If we were to take the latter as a more realistic projection of agricultural growth in the coming decade—and this seems the prudent thing to do—the configuration of the overall plan, in terms of the overall growth rate target, the composition of output and investment, as well as the policies of improving the conditions of the poorest classes and regions will have to be drastically different from the perspective outlined in the revised Fifth Plan.

IMPLICATION OF SLOW AGRICULTURAL GROWTH

The long-term perspective outlined in the revised Fifth Plan[6] postulates (a) the rate of population growth being brought down from the present 2.4 per cent per annum level to 1.1 per cent by 1986-1991; (b) the average annual growth rate to rise from an expected 4.4 per cent in the Fifth Plan period to 5.6 per cent and 6 per cent in the Sixth and Seventh Plans respectively; (c) the rate of investment to rise from 15.2 per cent in 1973-74 to 19 per cent in 1988-89; and (d) a marginal savings rate of 24 per cent. The long-term projection of exports, imports and balance of payments are left undefined, though in the course of the Fifth Plan exports are projected to rise by 8.5 per cent a year; and the current account deficit from Rs 1.2 million to Rs 5.3 billion. The plan also indicates the pattern of sectoral output growth which is consistent with the specified macro-economic magnitudes and constraints, and which satisfies the requirement of supply/demand balance at the sectoral level, given the structure of input-output relations. On this basis, the gross output of agriculture is required to grow by 3.9 per cent a year in the Fifth Plan and 4.3 per cent a year in the Sixth and the Seventh Plans.

Suppose, however, that agricultural production increases by only 3.2 per cent a year. In principle if we are interested in somehow maintaining the overall rate of growth we could try and compensate for the shortfall in agriculture by a faster expansion of non-agricultural output than currently visualised. Assuming that the elasticity of value added to gross output in agriculture as well as the elasticity of tertiary sector output to GDP are the same as implicit in the Fifth Plan projections, the growth rate of mining, manufacturing, electricity and transport[7] will have to be stepped up from the projected 6.9 per cent a year to around 8 per cent a year. This may seem only a marginal step-up but it has to be borne in mind that even the attainment of the revised Fifth Plan target of growth in these sectors is contingent on a substantial improvement in the quality of planning, construction and management of projects (especially in the public sector) and on improving the rate of capacity utilisation all round. The problem, moreover, is not merely one of achieving a faster growth of industries and related activities; it is also a question of finding the outlets for the extra output of manufacturing.

While the targeted growth rate can, in an arithmetical sense, be achieved by a different combination of sectoral growth rates than that indicated in the plan, any departure from the latter is apt to upset the internal consistency and balance of the economy unless certain other adjustments are made. Specifically, a 3.2 per cent agricultural growth and an 8 per cent annual expansion in the secondary activity would, other things remaining the same, mean a substantial deficit in the supply of agricultural products and a corresponding excess of manufactured goods, in relation to domestic demand.

On a rough estimate, if the plan targets of population and real income are fulfilled, and agricultural production grows by only 3.2 per cent a year over the period 1973-74 to 1988-89, the latter will meet only 80 per cent of the domestic demand in 1988-89. The absolute value of the deficit in farm products will be close to Rs 90 billion at 1973-74 prices.[8] On the other hand, the output of mining and manufacturing will be correspondingly larger than internal demand. This imbalance can be corrected without resorting to inflation in either of two ways:[9] (1) by exporting the surplus manufactures and using the proceeds to meet the deficit of agricultural products through import; or (2) increasing the marginal rate of saving and hence total investment above currently postulated levels to generate larger demand for investment goods and their inputs. In either case the *structure* of manufacturing output will have to be different from that visualised by the plan, the nature of the change depending on which of the above two courses are pursued: Under alternative (a), it is the export opportunities which will determine the pattern of additional manufacturing output, while (b) would call for raising the output of investment related industries. The crucial question is whether either of the above alternatives is really feasible.

THE EXPORT ALTERNATIVE

The revised Fifth Plan does not give any projections of export earnings beyond 1978-79. The long-term perspective outlined in the Draft Plan is predicated on a 7–8 per cent annual increase in real exports. Practically all the increase is expected from non-traditional items (like marine products, minerals, handicrafts and manufactures based on non-agricultural materials) whose exports are projected to grow by 12-13 per cent per annum. As mentioned earlier, if the domestic agricultural output grows by no more than 3.2 per cent a year and the real income target is unchanged, the economy will need to import an additional (at least) Rs 90 billion per year by 1988-89. Assuming that additional foreign aid to meet this increased import requirement will not be sought, or is unlikely to be forthcoming, the objectives of price stability and viable balance of payments cannot be safeguarded unless the economy increases its exports by an equivalent amount. This means stepping up the overall growth rate of aggregate exports to 12 per cent (from the actual level of 1973-74) and that of non-traditional items by over 20 per cent a year.[10] If, as seems likely, the exports of marine products and ores cannot be increased much above levels already visualised (whether because of supply or of demand constraints), the required growth rate of manufactured exports will have to be even higher.

Few countries have been able to achieve and sustain such a high rate of growth of aggregate exports in real terms though many have reached or exceeded these levels in nominal terms. In the case of India, there are some apparently favourable factors: one of these is that it is still one of the minor trading nations of the world accounting, in 1974, for barely half a per cent of world exports and about 4 per cent of the exports of non-oil developing countries.[11] With its large and diversified industrial base and the emergence of large potential markets in the Middle East, it would seem that given determination and the 'right' policies, quite high rates of export growth based on manufactures could be achieved. Assuming that world trade, excluding OPEC countries, grows in real terms by seven per cent a year, and that developing countries as a whole manage to arrest the declining trend in their share of world trade, a $ 16 billion export from India in 1988-89 would increase its share to barely one per cent in world exports, and 6.5 per cent in the developing countries' exports. Prima facie, these dimensions may not appear implausibly large. And if it can be accomplished, there are obvious advantages by way of faster growth of non-agricultural employment opportunities. However, even if the conditions of the world market and especially the attitude of developed countries were favourable, far-reaching changes in our policies will be needed if this course is to be successful.

Sustained growth of manufactured exports at the required rate cannot be achieved by relying, as we have tended to, on temporary excess capacity in industries meant for the domestic market. It requires a clear commitment to creating capacities oriented primarily to export markets. Also, since the projected growth of manufactured exports is faster than that of domestic manufacturing output, the pattern of export demand will become progressively more important in shaping the pattern of industrial investments and production.[12] But as of now, ideas on what appropriate pattern of exports should be (taking into account the emerging pattern of world demand, the policies of major importing countries, as well as India's technological and factor endowments) remain quite ill-defined. And there is hardly any conscious planning for expansion of export capacity.

Detailed long-term planning of export capacities may not be feasible because of the many uncertainties about the future and because a significant part of potential exports fall within the ambit of the private sector. According to conventional wisdom, the focus of policy under these conditions should be on providing adequate incentives (through appropriate exchange rate and fiscal policies) to make exports profitable, and building the necessary institutional infrastructure to stimulate exports. However, the growth of exports depends on a great deal more than exchange rate and subsidies. The ability of the government to contain inflationary process within tolerable limits, the extent to which productivity can be raised and the degree to which various classes (especially those with the power to enforce their claims for an inordinately large share of the output) co-operate, or are made to co-operate, in sharing productivity gains in a manner which maintains competitiveness in export markets, are just as important.

There are also questions of a much broader political nature. In the past, a good part of the expansion in our exports has been directed to the Soviet Union and eastern European countries. It seems unlikely that this group of countries can, or will, absorb our manufactured exports on the scale implied in the above scenario. Therefore, if the export-led growth is to be successful, a significant shift of strategy aimed at aggressive expansion of trade to the developed market economies seems essential. Being a relative newcomer to the world market in manufactures, India has to establish marketing channels. Other countries seem to have done this, at any rate in the initial stages, by producing on contract for multinational corporations and other private firms from developed countries, the latter providing both know-how and ready access to established marketing outlets. The marked preference of the foreign collaborators for private enterprise, and the argument that public enterprise cannot be resilient enough to adapt production and marketing strategies to changing conditions, may be used to force a change in the relative roles of public and private sectors in favour of the latter. The performance of the public sector, no doubt, leaves much room for improvement. But to whittle down its role in the name of exports, rather than tackling the admittedly difficult problems of improving their management, would be to give up what is potentially one of the most effective means for regulating distribution of income and wealth.

Altogether, a shift in strategy which seeks to compensate for slow agricultural growth by making the economy consciously more export-oriented has far-reaching implications for the patterns of production, organisation, and economic management within the country as well as in its external postures. Such changes touch issues which cannot, at any rate are not, decided purely on economic calculations. And since economic calculation alone is not in a position to convincingly demonstrate in advance that the gains will be dramatic and reasonably assured, its ability to persuade major shifts of policy is not likely to be significant.

OPTION OF INCREASING DOMESTIC INVESTMENT

The second alternative, namely, stepping up domestic investment to absorb the larger output of manufactures, is not feasible either because the degree of additional resource mobilisation required to sustain it will be unmanageable. If this is to be sustained in the face of a 3.2 per cent agricultural growth, the marginal rate of savings will have to be around 34 per cent,[13] compared to the 24 per cent postulated by the plan.[14] Even the plan target of savings, not to speak of significantly higher rates, will be difficult to achieve.

One aspect of the problem is to restrain the growth of overall consumption to the required degree and in a manner which is equitable in the sense that the restraint operates more on the relatively well-to-do than on the poorer classes. This necessarily requires a purposeful use of fiscal instruments. Fiscal incentives for stimulating private savings (either by way of a tax on consumption expenditure or of fiscal concessions for savings) may increase aggregate savings, but it is doubtful whether savings of the order required will be generated; moreover, such incentives would result in further accentuation of the inequalities in the distribution of wealth and income, and therefore goes directly contrary to the objectives of a more egalitarian income distribution. On the other hand, experience has also demonstrated the immense difficulties of enforcing a truly progressive fiscal policy. Under the existing distribution of political power, such a policy (whether by way of increased taxation, or of higher prices for product of public enterprises, or of reduction in subsidy elements of public expenditure) is bound to affect the interests of precisely those classes (namely, the business interests, the upper strata of the peasantry and workers in the organised sectors of the economy) who wield effective political power. Under these conditions any attempt to maintain higher levels of investment by recourse to deficit financing will further aggravate inflationary pressures and the attendant distortions in income distribution and resource allocation.

Given past experience, it would be naive to hope that the effect of inflation on the poorer classes can be mitigated by a comprehensive system of public procurement and distribution of essential consumer goods. In the first place, this will require a vast increase in the coverage of the public distribution system in terms of commodities, classes and regions. At present public distribution is largely limited to foodgrains and to urban areas; except in very bad years, like 1965 and 1966, it barely accounts for 10-12 per cent of the total consumption of foodgrains and that too largely on the basis of imports.[15]

An expanded public distribution system will work only if the government is able to procure vastly larger quantities of foodgrains and other essential commodities from the domestic producers and at prices which do not burden the budget with inordinate amount of subsidies. The problem is manageable if the marginal saving rate is raised to a level which ensures reasonable balance between the aggregate supply of and aggregate demand for consumer goods. If, as seems highly probable, savings on the required scale cannot be mobilised by fiscal means, there is bound to be an excess demand for consumer goods. Since, in a situation of shortages, producers stand to benefit by selling in the free market while consumers are interested in keeping the rise in price to the minimum, the conflicts between these groups will be inevitably aggravated, the intensity of the conflict being naturally greater as the degree of shortage increases. Under these conditions, attempts at compulsory procurement at prices below market prices, which in effect mean a tax on the producers, will face strong resistance from farmers. Past experience provides ample corroboration of the power of the farmers to make their interests prevail and there is no reason to expect the future will be very different. Therefore, the odds against being able to compensate for slow agricultural growth with a higher level of investment and industrial output than currently visualised, and without risking severe inflation, are very heavy indeed.[16]

Severe inflation is not the only penalty for persisting in a programme of investment (in terms of level and pattern) based on an unduly optimistic assumption regarding agricultural growth and/or possibilities of resource mobilisation and of public distribution. Such a course also gives rise to considerable distortions in resource use. Once adopted, the five-year investment allocations under the public sector plan serve as the basis for the operating ministries and departments to programme their activities. Many of these activities have to be planned several years ahead and cannot be switched on or off at short notice without heavy cost. And in many cases facilities have to be expanded in relation to certain expected long-term demand growth. If the latter should fail to materialise, imbalances between capacity and demand emerge resulting in idle capacity in some segments and shortages in others.

Another source of distortion is the tendency to start too many projects and thereby to spread the resources thinly over a wide compass. The inclusion of a project in the 'original' five-year plan has tended to be viewed as a commitment from which it is politically difficult to withdraw. There are strong pressures to start as many of the projects included in the five-year plan as possible, even when the emerging trends in the economy warrant (for lack of demand or for lack of finance) some of them being postponed or dropped. With the real resources available being much smaller than originally expected and the costs of projects (quite apart from inflation) underestimated, this means spreading available resources on far too many projects, thereby delaying the completion of all. While no precise quantification is possible, the swelling pipeline of unfinished projects may be one factor explaining the sharp rise in the overall capital-output ratio observed during the last two decades. To the extent a more 'realistic' target reduces the scope for such distortions, it should also improve the realised productivity of investment as measured by the ICOR. The overall ICOR may also be brought down by the change in the composition of investments associated with lower growth rates.[17]

Although in principle, these distortions can be corrected by revising production targets and investment allocations in the light of actual experience, this seldom happens in reality. In the past, financial stringency and inflation have of course resulted in a pruning of the real investment programme. But this adjustment is made not on the basis of a coherent revision of the plan as a whole, but in a haphazard and *ad hoc* fashion depending in part on unplanned delays in preparing and implementing projects, and sometimes by such arbitrary devices as across-the-board cuts in allocations. The quinquennial planning exercise should, in principle, provide the occasion to attempt a full-scale revision of the overall plan perspective both in terms of overall growth rate and of the composition of output and investment. But the persistent gap between targets and realisation suggests that this process has not been as thorough as it ought to have been.

ARGUMENT FOR LOWER GROWTH TARGETS

Altogether, the apparently severe constraints on expansion of agricultural output at rates currently planned and of exports at rates much beyond present targets, would seem to argue for a lowering of overall growth targets in the interests of price stability and minimising wasteful distortions. With agriculture growing by 3.2 per cent a year, exports at 7-8 per cent a year and a marginal savings rate of 25 per cent, the maximum sustainable non-inflationary growth is around 4 per cent a year. Unless we have reasonable assurance that the performance in the above critical areas can be substantially better than the levels assumed—and they call for a far clearer appreciation of the policy changes required as well as their political feasibility than is apparent now—it would be imprudent to base the scale and pattern of development on any higher target of growth. An important consequence of accepting a lower growth rate would be a substantial scaling down of the targets for manufactures, especially in the investment goods.[18] This is so because (a) lower growth rates would mean a much slower step-up of investment and, hence, the demand for capital goods; and (b) many of the capital goods industries have capacities substantially in excess of present domestic requirements.

This would of course mean a retreat from the bold formulations or the vision which characterised earlier plans. Regrettable as this is, we have to recognise that the vision has in any case eroded progressively[19] in deference to actual experience and our demonstrated inability to implement the necessary policy changes. A degree of optimism may well have been justified until the early sixties—though even at that time there were many voices urging caution. But the actual record and our analysis of the constraints, which, let it be recognised, are fundamentally political, make a sober reassessment of our long-term perspective an imperative.

It will no doubt be argued that trimming the growth targets would mean slowing down the pace of diversification and the rate of new employment creation, thereby making the prospects of solving the problem of abject poverty recede further into the future. However, this is not a meaningful question: The relevant comparison is not between what can be done for the poor with hypothetically high and low growth rates, but between what is being accomplished and what can be done with appropriate policies, given the fact of a modest overall growth. Viewed from this angle, the problem takes on a somewhat different complexion.

Recognition of severe constraints on the realisation of even the modest growth targets of the revised Fifth Plan implies that if the attainment of minimum income objectives is to be pursued seriously, redistribution measures which enable the incomes of the poor to rise at a higher rate than average must be given greater weight in policy. Programmes to help the poor improve their income and welfare are of several different types. Ceilings on land ownership, protection of tenancy rights, and other elements of land reform aim at giving more land to the small cultivator, some land to the landless, and a higher share of the produce to the tenants. All measures which lead to the redistribution of land in favour of the marginal farmers and the landless have a strong employment aspect in that it creates opportunity for self-employment. Stimulation of small-scale enterprise (through a combination of protection and positive measures to increase their competitive capacity *vis-a-vis* large enterprises) and attempts to evolve appropriate technology are all designed to create larger employment for a given level of output, and also achieve a wider spatial dispersion of benefits. A third category consists of such programmes as 'minimum needs', rural public works, drought-prone area programmes, programmes for tribal areas and scheduled castes, all of which are explicitly focused on improving the welfare skills and productivity of specific, well-identified, segments of the poor.

Redistribution measures operating through land reform, ceilings on urban incomes and property and similar other measures are certainly desirable and there is considerable room for improvement in the implementation of law already in force. Nevertheless, it is unrealistic to expect these measures to make a significant difference to income distribution. All these reforms have a direct adverse effect on the economic status of the classes which are in control of the instruments of power; and the poor simply are not organised to press their claim in any effective manner. Less direct and drastic measures emphasising redistribution through the fiscal mechanism and through programmes which help increase productivity and employment of the poor are widely believed to be a more promising answer. While this course also involves acceptance of 'sacrifices' on the part of the well-to-do it is arguable that the only course open is to push along this road as far as possible. The focus of such programmes has to be primarily, if not exclusively, on increasing the absorption of labour in agriculture and related activities by increasing the scale and improving the effectiveness of the third category of programmes mentioned above.

SCALE OF ANTI-POVERTY PROGRAMMES

The scale of anti-poverty programmes depends on the scale on which resources, both financial and real, can be mobilised. And since the whole point of the programme is to redistribute real incomes in favour of the poor, it is imperative that the resources are mobilised mostly from the richer segments of the population. It is possible that a trimming of the overall growth targets, more in line with the possibilities of expanding agricultural production and exports, might improve the efficiency of investment and thereby release more resources for anti-poverty programmes. While the investment required to sustain a 4 per cent annual growth would need to be worked out in detail, it seems probable that this could be achieved by an appropriate restructuring at the current rate of investment (namely, 15-16 per cent of GDP). And if the targeted 25 per cent marginal savings is realised something like 10 per cent of the additional incomes could be set apart for anti-poverty programmes.

The nature of the measures needed for this purpose (namely, restructuring the tax system, reduction of subsidies, and improvement in the operation of public enterprises) are sufficiently well known.[20] And so long as fiscal policy is effective in restraining the overall consumption increase within the limit set by the available supplies of agricultural commodities, changes in the product mix to match shifts in the commodity composition of demand associated with a more equal distribution of income can be accomplished, in principle, by appropriate adjustments in relative prices. But since markets are not perfect and adjustments in relative price changes may not be adequate, the state may still have to intervene with a public distribution system to make the necessary supplies available at reasonable prices. The public distribution system will naturally have to play a much more important role if fiscal policy is not carried to the full extent necessary. And it need hardly be emphasised that, whether it be fiscal policy or public distribution, the problem, being one of forcing the well-to-do to accept a slower growth of income and consumption, is fundamentally political.

EFFECTIVENESS OF ANTI-POVERTY PROGRAMMES

There is also much room for improvement in the effectiveness of anti-poverty programmes. The variety of programmes currently in operation is justified insofar as it reflects an attempt at discriminating between the needs of different classes of the poor. The emphasis is, and rightly, on using these programmes to build productive assets as the basis for a lasting increase in employment opportunities and incomes in rural areas rather than simply as a vehicle for somehow providing jobs to the poor. Judging by the experience of other Asian countries, notably China and Japan, there seems to be vast scope for increasing the amount of labour in Indian agriculture.[21] Properly designed programmes, both in terms of type of works and of their geographical distribution could make a significant impact in raising the employment and income levels of the poor regions and the poor classes.

However, as presently conceived, these programmes have a large overlap with the normal development activities and, where such overlap exists, the arrangements for co-ordination are less than adequate. Ideally, such a co-ordination should be based on an overall programme for agricultural and rural development of the selected areas prepared after a systematic study of the potentials and constraints specific to each area. Though the need for such area plans has been recognised and repeatedly emphasised, little in fact has been achieved. Further, the choice of areas for anti-poverty programmes are determination of the intensity of poverty, unemployment and future production potentials. And, in an effort to placate as many constituents as possible, the anti-poverty programmes also tend to be spread widely among regions and projects thereby diluting their effectiveness.

As a first step towards rationalisation of the anti-poverty programmes, it would be desirable to group the numerous schemes which qualify for inclusion into the following three broad categories according to type of activities and the group of people which form their focus: (1) the 'minimum needs' programme, which as conceived by the Fifth Plan, seeks to ensure that all parts of the country and all sectors of society will have, within a specified period, a certain minimum standard of education and health facilities, drinking water supply, access to roads, and such other amenities. The activities will improve the general welfare of the population and strengthen the social infrastructure, but their effects on production are neither immediate nor direct. (2) Programmes of the area development type focusing primarily on districts or taluks with a high incidence of poverty whether due to a very low level of average per capita real incomes or due to their maldistribution. The focus of effort in these areas, which should be possible to identify on a fairly objective basis, ought to be on preparing and implementing projects for increasing the production potential, preferably on the basis of an integrated long-term development programme. Once this is done, all projects in the area could be brought under a single administrative aegis. (3) Programmes aimed at improving productivity and income of particular groups of poor, like small farmers, marginal farmers and rural artisans. Since these categories are spread all over the country including the relatively better-off areas, they will necessarily have a much more diffused geographical focus.

A second step would be to set apart a certain portion of the public sector plan funds explicitly for these three categories of anti-poverty programmes but giving a much greater priority for categories (1) and (2). (Such an idea was in fact advocated in the early stages of the discussion of the Fifth Plan in respect of the minimum needs programme but did not make much headway.) Whether and in what manner funding of such programmes can be done within the context of the federal structure and the existing conventions governing centre-state financial relations are questions which need further consideration. Quite clearly, since most of the programmes fall within the sphere of the state governments, the latter will have to be persuaded to the idea of a separate minimum needs and backward areas programme, of funding them separately, and of deciding the selection of the areas and projects on an objective basis.

The acceptance of anti-poverty programmes as a separate and high priority activity should introduce greater purposiveness and objectivity in the use of public resources towards this goal. Its success, however, requires a high degree of decentralisation of actual planning and implementation so that the selection of projects as well as the design of organisations for planning and implementation are adapted to local conditions. Effective decentralisation is thus the third important requirement. This does not mean only autonomy in spending and strengthening the administration underpinning for the programme; it is just as important to have effective representative local institutions which can participate and manage this activity with a sense of stake and involvement, rather than serve (as they have tended to so far) as mere lobbies for larger assistance from higher levels of government or as agents for disbursing such assistance as is received. The acid test of this would be in the willingness and ability of the local institutions to raise at least a part of the cost of development projects from within its community.

The ability to build effective local institutions is of central importance for the success of not only anti-poverty programmes but of rural development generally. In part, this is a matter of getting people to accept the twin principles that the beneficiaries of development works share at least a part of the costs of such works and that the better-off beneficiaries should pay more. But the role of institutions goes far beyond this. The effective exploitation of the potentials for increasing yield may require planning of land-use patterns, lay-out of irrigation systems, and of cropping patterns by villages and groups of villages. And once developed there is also the problem of ensuring that scarce inputs like water are so allocated and used as to maximise overall output. This is an extremely difficult and complex problem, but one which demands imaginative solutions if agricultural development generally, and anti-poverty programmes in particular, are to achieve desired results.

The restructuring of institutions in a manner which facilitates the interests of the poor sections of the populations and the backward areas to find a fuller expression in the process of planning necessarily means a radical shift in the locus of power. The nature of the institutional changes and the manner in which they are to be brought about will naturally vary according to social and political configurations in different parts of the country. The important thing is to permit and, indeed actively encourage, forces which can bring about these shifts. Without this, professions of a 'new order' will remain empty slogans.

To sum up, it is the contention of this paper that: (a) The possibilities of accelerating overall growth, even to the degree visualised in the long-term projections given in the revised Fifth Plan, are doubtful essentially because of the severe constraint on the possibility of stepping up the growth of agriculture and export. (b) The constraints on agriculture are in part technological and in large part institutional while in the case of exports the ramification of a significantly more outward-oriented growth may involve changes in many fundamental, tenets, including political, of current development policy. (c) To continue committing investment programmes (both the level and the composition) without regard to the above constraints exposes the economy to risks of inflation and wasteful use of limited investible resources. (d) With a modest growth, it is inevitable that redistributive measures should play a much bigger role in efforts to improve the conditions of the poor, the more so because with slow growth the possibility of the poor getting jobs and maintaining the real wage level is greatly reduced. (e) A larger anti-poverty programme, consisting essentially of employment generating growth, infrastructural and productive agricultural projects concentrated in the poor areas, is possible provided that the fiscal instrument is effectively used to contain the consumption of the rich. There is also much scope for increasing the impact of such programmes by greater care in selecting areas and in planning and implementation of the projects. (f) Both with anti-poverty and agricultural programmes, the development of viable and responsible local institutions is critical to success.

This is by no means an exhaustive treatment of the various facets of India's development problems. It is easy to list many other aspects which are important but which have not been touched upon: e g, organisation of the public sector, the urban problem; the apparatus for regulating the private sector, the chaotic state of the pricing and distribution system, regional balance, etc. However, the intention was not to be exhaustive but to focus on what seemed to be fundamental constraints on the speed with which the problem of abject mass poverty can be tackled. There could be different opinions on whether what have been identified as fundamental constraints are in fact so, on the judgments regarding the factors underlying the constraints, and on the means by which, and the speed with which, they can be overcome. The time is ripe for a fresh look at the whole range of these issues.

NOTES

[I am grateful to I S Gulati and K N Raj for valuable comments on an earlier draft.]

1 T N Srinivasan and N S S Narayana, 'Economic Performance since the Third Plan and Its Implications for Policy', *Economic and Political Weekly*, Annual Number, February 1977.

2 The growth rate of total GDP fell from around 3.9 per cent a year in the fifties to 3.5 per cent a year in the sixties. These rates are computed on the basis of three-year averages of real GDP for 1950-51 to 1952-53, 1960-61 to 1962-63, and 1970-71 to 1972-73 as estimated by CSO. The deceleration is much more striking if we exclude public administration and defence which recorded a much higher growth rate in the sixties compared to the earlier period. The average annual growth rate of GDP (excluding public administration and defence) works out to 3.2 per cent for the sixties as against 3.8 per cent for the fifties.

3 The index of agricultural production rose by 38 per cent between 1950-51/1954-55 and 1960-61/1964-65; and by 23 per cent between 1960-61/1964-65 and 1970-71/1974-75.

4 The reduction of one percentage point in the agricultural sector growth would mean a half percentage point reduction in the overall growth rate.

5 A Vaidyanathan, 'Performance and Prospects of Crop Production in India', *Economic and Political Weekly*, Special Number, August 1977.

6 Government of India, Planning Commission, *Fifth Five-Year Plan*, 1974-79 1976, Chapter 2.

7 These are average annual rates over the period 1973-74 to 1988-89 taken as a whole. Since substantial shortfalls are likely even in relation to revised targets for 1978-79, the required rates of growth in the Sixth and Seventh Plans will be higher.

8 This estimate is based on the following data and assumptions:
   (a) Population, aggregate real income, savings and investment grow as projected in the revised Fifth Plan through 1988-89.
   (b) Elasticity of demand for agricultural products in relation to per capita private consumption is 0.83. (This is the value implicit in the Draft Fifth Plan projection.)
   (c) Gross value of crop production in 1973-74 was Rs 270 billion (CSO, *National Accounts Statistics*, 1960-61 to 1973-74, Disaggregated Tables).

9 The effects of a shortfall in agriculture relative to targets of the version of long-term plan prepared in 1962 have been examined by Ashok Rudra in a more *rigorous* and quantitative fashion. He drew attention to the

inflationary and balance of payments consequences of the shortfall. However, he did not consider the export option or the possibility of increasing domestic investment. See, Ashok Rudra, 'Relative Rates of Growth: Agriculture and Industry', *Economic Weekly*, November 7, 1964.

10 According to the Draft Fifth Plan projections, total exports are to rise from an estimated Rs 20 billion in 1973-74 to Rs 48 billion in 1985-86; over the same period, the earnings from non-traditional exports, defined as above, are projected to rise from Rs 6 billion to Rs 25 billion. Extrapolating these figures, non-traditional exports in 1988-89 would be Rs 35 billion, and total exports Rs 59 billion (all estimates at prices and exchange rates of 1973-74). This is roughly equal to the projected import needs of Revised Fifth Plan.

According to the Draft version of the plan, real GDP was to be approximately doubled between 1973-74 and 1985-86. Over the same period, non-food imports were also projected to be doubled (see GOI, *Planning Commission, Draft Fifth Five-Year Plan, 1974-79*, Ch 1). Applying in the implicit unit elasticity of imports relative to GDP to the projected growth in the revised plan (which would more than double the GDP between 1973-74 and 1988-89) and taking actual non-food imports in 1973-74 at Rs 25 billion, total non-food imports in 1988-89 works out to Rs 55 billion. If the projected deficit of agricultural products arising from a shortfall in domestic production of the order assumed were to be met by imports, total imports (and hence exports) would have to be of the order Rs 140-150 billion; and non-traditional exports around Rs 120-130 billion.

11 In 1974, according to *UN Trade Year Book*, total world export amounted to $ 850 million and exports of non-oil developing countries to $ 97 billion. Indian exports in this year were $ 3.9 billion.

12 Total exports of ores and manufactures (including the traditional items) was of the order of Rs 1,600 crore in 1973-74, and represents 15 per cent of the gross value added in mining, manufacturing, electricity and transport in that year. If the exports of these items is to reach the level estimated, total exports of these items in 1988-89 would have to be over Rs 10,000 crore which would be about 35 per cent of the value added in this group of sectors. As a proportion of gross output the proportion will of course be smaller but the central point regarding the share increase in export dependence remains valid.

13 Assuming that the incremental capital-output ratio is not affected by the change in product mix compared to that projected in the plan. Insofar as investment goods industries are more capital intensive, this assumption is open to question.

14 These calculations are based on the revised Fifth Plan estimates of the gross domestic saving rate for 1973-74 (14.4 per cent and the targeted saving rate assumed to be equal to the targeted investment rate), of 18.9 per cent in 1988-89.

15 GOI, *Economic Survey, 1976-77.*

16 There is an extensive literature on the problems of public procurement and distribution. See, for instance, I S Gulati and T N Krishnan, 'Public Distribution and Procurement of Foodgrains', *Economic and Political Weekly,* May 24, 1975, and the discussion which followed in the same journal. See

also, B S Minhas' Presidential Address to the Indian Society of Agricultural Economics, 1976. All of these show that the magnitude of public distribution required to effectively protect the poor needs to be much bigger and more comprehensive than at present, and that correspondingly the public procurement will have to be larger. Several schemes for procurement have been advanced; all of them assume that, given the 'political will', procurement on the necessary scale is possible, even if it involves implicit taxation of the rural areas.

17 The demand for largely capital-intensive goods (i e, high capital-output ratio) and services (like metals, construction materials, energy and transport) are, to an important degree, determined by the rate of growth of investment.

18 It should be noted that the rapid growth rates envisaged for these and related industries in the past plans *followed logically* from the expectation that the overall rate of growth could be stepped up progressively and stabilised at a relatively high (6-7 per cent per annum) level. The latter, of course, rested, among other things, on the assumption that agricultural growth could be accelerated. The strategy went wrong in good part because what then seemed to be realistic expectation of agricultural growth was not fulfilled.

19 Thus the Third Plan targeted real national income (valued at 1960-61 prices) to reach Rs 330-340 billion in 1975-76; the Fourth Plan (1969-74) implicitly postponed the target date for reaching this level by 3-4 years (to 1978-79); and the latest version of the Fifth Plan expects it to be reached only after 1985-86. Similarly, one version of the long-term plan for 1961-76, prepared in 1962, was built around a minimum per capita consumption target of Rs 20 per month (in 1960-61 prices) to be achieved by 1975-76. Though subsequent plans continue to speak of the minimum income objective, the persistent shortfalls in growth and the preoccupations with short-term problems resulted in this commitment getting blurred to a point that the revised version of the Fifth Plan does not even mention it.

20 It would seem however that the question of rationalising implicit and explicit subsidies through the budgets and the operation of public enterprises as well as the distribution of the benefits from these subsidies as between different classes, deserve greater emphasis than has been given so far. If, as widely suspected, a disproprotionate share of these subsidies benefit the relatively well-to-do, a reconsideration of the principles and policies governing them will be very much in order. The objective should be to ensure that the extent of benefits to the better-off segments is reduced as much as possible.

21 Ester Boserup, *The Conditions of Agricultural Growth*, 1965 and S Ishikawa, *Economic Development in the Asian Perspective*, 1976 have drawn attention to the fact that China, and generally the east Asian countries, use several times more labour per hectare of cropped area than India. The reasons for this striking difference have not been adequately explained.

September 17, 1977

7

Structural Retrogression in the Indian Economy since the Mid-Sixties

S L Shetty

I
INTRODUCTION

BOTH in comparison with the overall economic performance during the first fifteen years of planning as well as by certain absolute standards, the performance of the Indian economy from the mid-sixties to the mid-seventies was very unsatisfactory. There have been studies on the subject but they have generally dealt with only individual segments of this economic performance.[1] No systematic study appears to have been attempted of the performance of the economy during this period in its totality and of the causes of its poor performance.

One study in early 1977 has tried to establish that the decade since the mid-sixties has been characterised by 'a marked neglect and even mismanagement of the economy' [Panandikar and Varde, 1977]. But it is based on a few macro-level indicators. Though this hypothesis of economic drift and deterioration is incontrovertible, the macro indicators employed by that study appear to be insufficient to establish it beyond doubt. The behaviour of these macro indicators during the period is capable of a variety of interpretations. For instance, it could be argued, based on irreproachable data, that the overall growth rate of real national income from 1966-67 to 1976-77 has not been far below the trend rate observed earlier; this is so even when we exclude the exceptionally bad years of 1965-66 and 1966-67. Similarly, the peak levels of investment to national income ratio achieved in the initial years of the sixties were made possible at least partly because of the sizeable net inflow of foreign resources. The appropriation of large investible funds by defence expenditure since the mid-sixties had its origin in the military conflicts with China and Pakistan of 1962 and 1965 and it could not probably be reversed entirely. Likewise, while the persistent deterioration in India's share of world trade, which had begun in the early fifties, has not been reversed since the mid-sixties, it cannot be denied, judging by conventional yardsticks, that the following decade saw a significant diversification in India's export trade, both region-wise and commodity-wise; now the export trade consists relatively more of high value-added commodities and covers a larger number of countries; also the country's exports as a proportion of its national income have risen, albeit fractionally.

It should be conceded at once that many of these quantitative indicators of good economic performance have been more apparent than real; many of them have been adventitious; some of them like higher exports in fact, reflect the poor performance of the economy domestically; and, more importantly, all of them hide the continued and systematic retrogression in the structural characteristics of the economy which has virtually completely undermined whatever achievements that had been made in the earlier decade and a half. The Pai Panandikar-Varde study has noticed some of the adventitious factors like the growth in agricultural production following the so-called Green Revolution since the mid-sixties, but the thesis of sustained neglect of the economy and the consequential weakening of the developmental process deserves a much more thorough-going analysis.

It must be recognised that the recent weakening of the developmental process may not have entirely got reflected in the quantitative data which we employ in different sections of this paper. This is partly because of the continued structural rigidity of the economic system following the failure to effect any significant institutional and organisational reforms since independence and partly because economic performance, even prior to the mid-sixties, was not as striking as that of, say, Japan or China. If desirable institutional changes like land reforms were effectively brought about and if the system were not so structurally rigid or if the earlier performance had been more outstanding, the drift and neglect of the planning and developmental process of the recent period would have attracted sharper reaction and manifested itself in many economic indicators much more noticeably.

Nevertheless, the impact of the absence of sustained developmental efforts is seen, for instance, in the generation of apparent surpluses of foodgrains and foreign exchange reserves on a sizeable scale in the midst of rising malnutrition, poverty and unemployment on the one hand, and persistent sluggishness in domestic investment on the other. The phenomenon of sizeable stockpiling was also observed in 1975-76 and 1976-77 in steel, coal, cement and even cotton cloth. The spectacle witnessed in 1976-77 of aggregate domestic investment (estimated at 14.0 per cent of net national product at current market prices) failing to absorb even the meagre level of domestic saving (16.0 per cent of NNP) is a sad commentary on the developmental process.[2] Many other quantitative indicators are cited in subsequent paragraphs in support of the neglect and drift in economic management and planning. Nevertheless, even all of them put together would not probably be sufficient to bring out the enormity of the qualitative damage done in terms of weakening the instruments and institutions of economic planning in the country.

II

COMPARISON OF GROWTH PERFORMANCE

As depicted in Table 1, the compound growth rate during the eleven-year period from 1966-67 to 1976-77 was 3.67 per cent per annum as compared with 3.50 per cent per annum during the preceding fifteen-year period (1951-52 to 1965-66). But, as is widely known, the two transitional years of the mid-sixties, namely, 1965-66 and 1966-67, had experienced exceptionally bad drought conditions and hence may be excluded while constructing the compound growth rates; with this, the first fourteen years of planning (up to 1964-65) show a compound real income growth of 4.11 per cent, while the last ten years (up to 1976-77) have registered an expansion of 3.94 per cent per annum. The difference between the two is thus not very significant. Be that as it may, a closer look at the statistical indicators does bring out the poorer performance in unmistakable terms.

Firstly, there was greater steadiness in the annual growth rates during the first fourteen years than in the latter period; this being seen in a significantly lower coefficient of variation in the growth rates of the first period than for the latter period, the same being 0.6375 and 0.8296, respectively. This has serious welfare implications [Dave, 1973]. A moderately higher but unstable growth can cause more harm than a relatively lower but steadier growth in terms of price fluctuations, income shifts between classes and sectors, and instability in and setback to saving and investment.

Secondly, whenever the individual years of the latter period have experienced significant growth rates in real national income, the increases have almost invariably been attributable to bumper agricultural crops, the contribution of registered manufacturing sector to the growth rate in this period being considerably lower than in the first period (Table 2). This raises a number of issues such as that the benefits of improved agricultural output of the recent period have not percolated in the form of sustenance of a high industrial growth rate nor in the form of improved saving and investment nor, as seen in the period from 1966-67 to 1976-77, in relative price stability, a subject to which we shall revert. Suffice it to say for the present that a good

Table 1: Growth Rates in Real National Income and Per Capita Income During Plan Periods

Period	National Income (at Constant Prices)	Per Capita Income (at Constant Prices)
First Plan (1951-52 to 1955-56)	+3.66	+1.79
Second Plan (1956-57 to 1960-61)	+4.14	+2.10
Third Plan: first four years		
(1961-62 to 1964-65)	+4.63	+2.36
(i) 1965-66	(–)5.06	(–)7.19
Annual Plans		
i) 1966-67	+0.90	(–)1.16
ii) 1967-68	+8.19	+5.86
iii) 1968-69	+2.89	+0.49
Fourth Plan		
i) 1969-70	+6.36	+4.16
ii) 1970-71	+5.99	+3.64
iii) 1971-72	+1.33	(–)1.10
iv) 1972-73	(–)1.57	(–)3.66
v) 1973-74	+5.42	+3.30
Fifth Plan		
i) 1974-75	+0.75	(–)1.28
ii) 1975-76	+8.70	+6.63
iii) 1976-77	+1.36	(–)0.61
First fourteen years (1951-52 to 1964-65)	+4.11	+2.07
First fifteen years (1951-52 to 1965-66)	+3.50	+1.45
The latest eleven years (1966-67 to 1976-77)	+3.67	+1.48
The latest ten years (1967-68 to 1976-77)	+3.94	+1.74

Notes: 1 National and per capita income figures used here are those at 1960-61 prices up to 1970-71 and for the years thereafter, those at 1970-71 prices.

2 Growth rates for Plan periods or for groups of years represent averages of respective annual percentage variations (which is very similar to the geometric or compound rate based on exponential trend fitting through the equation $Y=ab^t$).

Sources: 1 CSO: *National Accounts Statistics : 1960-61–1974-75*, New Delhi, October, 1976.

2 Uma Datta Roy Choudhury and Pratap Narain : 'Current National Income Statistics: What They Tell', *Economic and Political Weekly*, September 27, 1975, pp 1540-52.

3 Government of India: *Economic Survey: 1977-78*, New Delhi, 1977, p 57.

Table 2: Growth Rates in Net Domestic Product Originating in Primary, Secondary and Services Sectors (At 1960-61 Prices)

Year/Period	Primary Sector		Secondary Sector		Total of	Services Sector			
	Total	Agriculture	Total	Registered Manufac-Turing	Primary and Secondary Sectors	Total	Transport Storage and Communi-cation	Banking and Insurance	Public Adminis-tration and Defence
(1)	(2)	(3)	(4)	(5)	(6)	(7)	(8)	(9)	(10)
			(Rs in Crores)						
					(2+4)				
1950-51	5196	4936	1498	575	6694	2428	332	77	332
1955-56	5997	5699	1906	771	7903	2967	423	117	386
1960-61	6965	6580	2549	1071	9514	3749	576	160	538
1964-65	7682	7224	3467	1546	11149	4879	744	215	799
1965-66	6667	6148	3553	1585	10220	5014	788	223	823
1966-67	6594	6050	3588	1520	10182	5183	811	224	874
1975-76	9423	8712	5023	2279	14446	7599	1213	394	1672
			Cumulative Percentage Increase over Specified Periods						
1955-56 over 1950-51 (5 years)	15.4	15.5	27.2	34.1	18.1	22.2	27.4	52.0	16.3
1960-61 over 1955-56 (5 years)	16.1	15.5	33.7	38.9	20.4	28.8	36.2	36.8	39.4
1964-65 over 1960-61 (4 years)	10.3	9.8	36.0	44.4	17.2	27.7	29.2	34.4	48.5
1975-76 over 1965-66 (10 years)	41.3	41.7	41.4	43.8	41.4	51.6	53.9	76.7	103.2
1975-76 over 1966-67 (11 years)	42.9	45.0	40.0	49.9	41.9	46.6	49.6	75.9	91.3
			Annual Compound Growth Rates in Percentage during Specified Periods						
1955-56 over 1950-51 (5 years)	2.9	2.9	4.9	6.0	3.4	4.1	5.0	8.7	3.0
1960-61 over 1955-56 (5 years)	3.0	2.9	5.9	7.0	3.8	5.2	6.4	6.4	6.9
1964-65 over 1960-61 (4 years)	2.5	2.4	8.0	9.6	4.0	6.3	6.6	7.6	10.4
1975-76 over 1965-66 (10 years)	3.5	3.5	3.5	3.7	3.5	4.2	4.4	5.9	7.4
1975-76 over 1966-67 (11 years)	4.0	4.2	3.8	4.7	4.0	4.3	3.7	5.3	7.5

Source: CSO: *National Accounts Statistics : 1960-61 to 1974-75,* New Delhi, October 1976, and other issues.

part of the relatively higher increases in national income during individual years such as 1967-68 to 1970-71, 1973-74 and 1975-76 was attributable to a combination of factors like favourable weather and rainfall conditions and the Green Revolution mainly in wheat, that is, primarily adventitious factors. This is the reason why the fluctuations in the growth rates in national income during the second period have also been rather sharp. However, despite the existence of propitious conditions such as higher agricultural output in some years and the existence of a fairly sound industrial base, the growth rate in industry by and large, remained niggardly.

One of the most disappointing aspects of the performance of the Indian economy from the mid-sixties to the mid-seventies relates to the deceleration in the growth of output in organised industry, accompanied by sluggish investment, vast underutilisation of capacity and very meagre increase in employment in organised industry. As presented in Table 3, there occurred a noticeable acceleration in the compound (annual) growth rate over the first three plan periods up to 1965 from 5.7 per cent in the First Plan to 7.2 per cent in the Second Plan and further to 9.0 per cent in the Third Plan. During the next eleven-year period (1966 to 1976), the annual growth rate dwindled to about 4.1 per cent including the 10.6 per cent increase in 1976; excluding it the ten-year average works out to 3.7 per cent. The growth rate during the latter period has been particularly depressing in capital goods industries or, under an input-based classification, in agro-based and metal-based industries (Table 3).

In a comprehensive study 'Growth and Stagnation in Industrial Development', K N Raj (1976) has pointed out that two striking features of the industrial growth experience between the mid-sixties and the mid-seventies are a sharp decline in the rate of growth of industrial output since the mid-sixties and the existence of large unutilised manufacturing capacity. He made a very significant observation in this respect:

> The decline in the rate of growth of industrial output since the mid-sixties has naturally widened the gap between the targets set in the Five-Year Plans and the actual record of achievement in this sector. In the First, Second and Third Five-Year Plans, the rate of growth of output aimed at in the sector of large-scale manufacturing were approximately 7, 10.5 and 10.75 per cent per annum respectively, while the realised annual rates touched around 6, 7.75 and 8 per cent in the corresponding Plan periods. So, while there were short-falls, they were not very large. The position has changed significantly since then, in fact alarmingly.
>
> In the first version of the Fourth Five-Year Plan published in 1966 (soon after the devaluation of the rupee), the rate of growth of industrial output

Table 3: Annual Compound Growth Rates in Index Numbers of Industrial Production : Overall and Group-Wise

Groups (1)	1947 to 1951[d] (4 Years) (2)	1951 to 1955[c] (4 Years) (3)	1955 to 1960[b] (5 Years) (4)	1960 to 1965[a] (5 Years) (5)	1965 to 1970[a] (5 Years) (6)	1970 to 1976[a] (6 Years) (7)	1975 to 1976[a] (11 Years) (8)
I Use-based or Functional classification							
(1) Basic industries	–	4.7	12.1	10.4	6.2	6.8	6.5
(2) Capital goods industries	–	9.8	13.1	19.6	(–)1.4	6.0	2.6
(3) Intermediate goods industries	–	7.8	6.3	6.9	2.6	3.3	3.0
(4) Consumer goods industries	–	4.8	4.4	4.9	4.1	2.9	3.4
(a) Consumer durable goods	–	–	–	11.0	8.5	4.3	6.2
(b) Consumer non-durable goods	–	–	–	–	2.8	2.9	2.8
II Input-based classification							
(1) Agro-based industries	0.3	4.0	3.8	4.0	1.7	1.8	1.7
(2) Metal-based industries	4.5	7.5	14.1	18.2	0.7	5.1	3.1
(3) Chemicals-based industries	26.2	8.5	12.2	9.0	9.8	7.3	8.4
III Classification based on Sectoral Indicators[d]							
(1) Transport equipment and allied industries	–	–	–	14.4	(–)2.2	4.8	1.6
(2) Electricity and allied industries	–	10.4	14.7	14.4	11.8	6.8	9.1
General Index	4.8	5.7	7.2	9.0	3.3	4.7	4.1

Sources and Notes: a For columns (5) to (8), see various issues of the Reserve Bank of India's Monthly Bulletins. In these, annual Compound Growth Rates represent simple averages of individual (point) annual growth rates analogous to compound rate derived on the basis of exponential trend fitting. For the periods 1960 to 1965 and 1965 to 1970, the CSO's Index Number series used is the one with base 1960=100 and for the period 1970 to 1976 the series with base 1970=100.

b For column (4), see RBI : *Report on Currency and Finance: 1966-67*, Statement 8 (pp s 16-17). For the period 1955 to 1960, the CSO's index number series with 1956=100 has been used. The compound growth rate is based on the conventional formula using initial and terminal figures.

c For column (3), the group indices have been specially worked out by us, using the RBI classification and the CSO's index number series with base 1956=100. See CSO: *Monthly Statistics of the Production of Selected Industries of India for July and August 1966*. The compound growth rate is as in (b) above.

d For column (2) and under II and III classification columns (3) and (4) see K N Raj: 'Growth and Stagnation in Industrial Development', *Economic and Political Weekly*, Annual Number, February 1976, p 225-i.

aimed at was about the same as in the Third Plan, i e, about 10.75 per cent per annum. The final 1969 version of the Fourth Plan, prepared after three years of Annual Plans (sometimes referred to as a period of 'plan holiday'), aimed at a still higher rate of about 12 per cent per annum, presumably to make up for the ground lost in the period 1965-68. The Draft Outline of the Fifth Plan, published towards the end of 1973, lowered the sights somewhat and fixed a rate of growth of only about 8 per cent per annum. But the realised rates of growth of industrial output since the mid-sixties have been very much lower than all this: it was only about 3.25 per cent per annum in the period 1965-70 and around 2.75 per cent per annum in the period 1970-74... With the population of the country growing at the rate of around 2.5 per cent per annum, the increase in per capita industrial output over the entire decade, 1965-74, could have been only marginal.

In agriculture, the decade since the mid-sixties has no doubt seen an appreciable increase in the index of overall output. Nevertheless, there is now a growing realisation—even by the government[3]—that (a) despite the Green Revolution, the overall growth rate of agricultural production as well as per hectare productivity in the country has failed to get accelerated over the level achieved in the fifteen-year period prior to 1965-66; (b) this was because the impact of the new agricultural strategy was restricted (i) to a few crops such as wheat, bajra, and maize and (ii) to a few regions in Punjab, Haryana, parts of UP, and parts of the southern states; and (c) even in respect of these crops and regions, the impact of the Green Revolution seems to have got exhausted because of, among other things, the reduced scope for increases in acreage under crops, flattening of the productivity curve, and above all, the lack of institutional reforms and the persistence of acute inequality in the distribution of land and assets in the farm sector.

This imbalance in the production structure has been brought about both by technological changes in and price support operations for superior cereals like wheat, resulting in a substantial shifting of acreage away from coarse cereals and pulses as well as from key cash crops. According to Dharm Narain (1972), 'many crops like jowar, ragi, barley, small millets, gram, tur, and other pulses, and among cash crops, cotton, have lost their share in the total area under all crops during the triennium ending 1972-73 as compared with that ending 1961-62'. Dharm Narain (1976) has also brought out 'how the principal factor pulling down the growth rate of agricultural output was of course the slowing down in the rate of expansion of cropped area. But the fact that even in the absence of technological change, the growth rate of per hectare productivity in the 1950s got sufficiently stepped up to maintain the growth rate of output, whereas in the subsequent decade, despite technological change, the improvement in the growth rate of productivity turned out to be too small to even neutralise the effect of the slow-down in area expansion call for a closer look into the sources of productivity growth.'

The above deceleration in growth rate of agriculture output appears more glaring when it is related to the growth of population. A study by Vaidyanathan (1977) comes to a very revealing conclusion in this respect:

> The concern has been further heightened by the apparent slowing down of agricultural growth during the last decade which, in the context of an acceleration in population growth, has resulted in a near stagnation of agricultural output per capita and in turn severely constrained the growth of the rest of the economy. Thus, as against the target of 4-4.5 per cent a year, the trend rate of growth in crop production has been only 2.6 per cent a year since 1950-51. The average annual growth rate between 1950-51/ 1954-55 and 1960-61/1964-65 was over 3 per cent in the aggregate, and 1 per cent per capita. In the subsequent decade, ending 1970-71/1974-75, the overall growth, of crop output was around 2.1 per cent. With population growing at 2.4 per cent a year, this meant a slight reduction in per capita crop ouput in the latter period.

Thirdly, the differential growth rates in commodity and non-commodity segments of the national product have corresponding welfare implications. Since the inception of planning, the growth rate in the non-commodity segment of the national product has been as expected, slightly higher than that in the ouput of commodity producing sectors. But what is conspicuous about this latest period is that while infrastructural sectors like transport and communication have shown a significant deceleration in growth rate *pari passu* with the sluggishness in overall economic activity, there has nevertheless been a phenomenal step-up in the growth rate in the incomes (at 1960-61 prices) originating in (a) 'public administration and defence' and (b) 'banking and insurance', particularly the former. During the decade from 1965-66 to 1975-76, the compound (annual) growth rate of the incomes from 'public administration and defence' worked out 7.4 per cent against 3.5 per cent growth in the incomes of the commodity producing sectors (primary and secondary sectors together) during the same period. Alternatively, during the same ten-year period, while income originating in public administration and defence increased by 103 per cent, that originating in commodity producing sectors rose by 41 per cent.

Fourthly, while making an aggregative analysis of the growth rate, it is more appropriate to do so in per capita terms. Per capita real income has certainly grown at a lower rate during the decade ending in the mid-seventies than in the first fourteen years, the compound (annual) rates being 1.74 per cent and 2.07 per cent respectively. Also, there was a steady and significant increase in per capita income at 1960-61 prices in the initial period, from 1.79 per cent in the First Plan to 2.10 per cent in the Second Plan and further to 2.36 per cent in the first four years of the Third Plan. But no such steady trend is discernible in the subsequent years and, if anything, the growth rate in per capita income has deteriorated over the period 1966-67 to 1976-77.

III

STRUCTURAL MALADIES

It is true that for an economy with acute inequalities in income and wealth distributions and where abject poverty and malnutrition of the vast masses of people coexist with relative affluence of a small section, the average per capita income is a meaningless number. Besides, what is relevant is not so much the extent as the type of growth witnessed during the period under examination. In other words, one could have still found some merit in the achievement of somewhat subdued real income growth in per capita terms during the past decade, if during the same period there had occurred a structural transformation of the economy in furtherance of wider socio-economic objectives of diminution of malnutrition, removal of poverty and unemployment and better distribution of income and assets. Such an expectation was obviously justified on the ground that during the first three Plan periods, a fairly sound base for further development was already laid. But despite this, not only has there been lower growth in per capita terms, but also a perceptible structural deterioration.

This structural deterioration has taken many forms. The share of the 'secondary' sector in net domestic product (at 1960-61 prices), which was continuously rising earlier, remained stagnant or declined somewhat. In other words, despite the creation of sizeable capacities in a wide range of organised industries during the Second and the Third Plan periods, the structure of output has moved against the 'secondary' sector and a substantial part of the capacity created therein has remained unutilised. This has been in turn due to the diversion to non-productive purposes of a significant proportion of resources mobilised in the name of development and elimination of poverty. Because of the misallocation of resources, the share of national product earmarked for domestic saving and investment declined for quite some years and has made only marginal improvement in the mid-seventies; even in 1976-77, the investment rate remained below the peak level reached in the mid-sixties. Following the disquieting performance of the public sector in this respect, the private sector failed to get the necessary impetus to invest and hence performed miserably. Even so, the investible funds made available from the public term-financing institutions at relatively cheap cost has induced the private corporate sector in particular to substitute on a rising scale loan capital for equity (and for the promoter's personal stake), resulting in absence of cost consciousness. An atmosphere of permissiveness in the deployment of industrial control mechanisms instituted earlier in direct investment according to Plan priorities has tended to distort investment and production structures in the country. Following significantly higher capital intensity even in the meagre investment activity during the period 1966-67 to 1976-77, the employment growth has been still more meagre. Concurrently, the high rate of inflation has helped to shift at a faster rate real incomes in favour of rich farmers, petty businessmen, traders, and merchants, industrial manufacturers, and non-fixed-income professionals like doctors, lawyers and chartered accountants. As it is, inflation was ingrained in the system of the concentration of economic power and vast inequalities. In the agricultural sector, the benefits of increased output have not been allowed to percolate to the economy as a whole in terms of reduced prices because of increases in procurement prices, which have further strengthened the holding power of the rich farmers. One of the fall-out effects of the new farm strategy has been increased inequality at the sectoral and household levels in rural areas. All of these put together have helped to sustain a blatantly elite-oriented production structure. In sum, the decade from 1966-67 to 1976-77 is characterised by serious distortions in investment and production structures, a sharp increase in income and asset inequalities, and unemployment reaching critical proportions, and poor generally becoming poorer.

The most damaging aspects of the developments of this latter period are a steady decline in the per capita domestic availabilities of key wage goods and the increase in the number of people below the poverty line.

Some of these structural problems were in evidence even in the first fifteen years of planning but in many the trends were more satisfactory then and in respect of those structural maladies such as the widening inequality which did exist earlier, first, they became more acute over the decade under review and, secondly, there were in the initial period, at least partly compensating factors in the form of higher growth of per capita income and investment and employment in organised industries, better fiscal discipline, and generally the laying of a foundation for future development; there was also probably no significant increase in the proportion of people below the poverty line.

The phenomenon of structural retrogression is evident at the aggregative level in the CSO's data on sector-wise distribution of national income. The share of the 'secondary' sector in net domestic product (at 1960-61 prices), which had continuously risen and reached the peak of 23.3 per cent in 1965-66 and 23.4 per cent in 1966-67 and which, as a corollary to the development process, should have continued to rise, has instead thereafter remained almost always below those peak levels; in 1975-76, it stood at 22.8 per cent. This share has in fact moved against the commodity producing sectors and in favour of the 'tertiary sector' (Table 4). And within the 'tertiary sector' it is the share, as indicated earlier, of 'public administration and defence' which has risen the fastest in the decade 1966-67 to 1976-77. At constant prices, this share was 3.6 per cent in 1950-51, 3.5 per cent in 1955-56, 4.0 per cent in 1960-61 and 5.4 per cent in 1965-66 (consequent upon increase in the defence expenditure following the military conflicts with China and Pakistan); but it had risen to 7.8 per cent in 1974-75 and 7.6 per cent in 1975-76. The share of the sub-group 'banking and insurance' also edged upwards; in contrast, that of 'transport and communications' remained static at 16.2 per cent in 1965-66 and 16.4 per cent in 1975-76. By and large the same trend is observed in industry-wise NDP at current prices.

Within the industrial sector, the structural retardation has taken place at two stages: first, the growth of basic and capital goods industries has been slower than in the past and also slower than even the meagre average growth in industrial ouput; and secondly, where growth has been moderately high, a majority of the industries belonged either directly or indirectly to elite-oriented consumption goods sectors. Output of industries catering to the requirements of mass consumption like cotton textiles has gone up only marginally. Even within cotton textiles, the share of coarser varieties of cloth has declined drastically.

Table 5 presents the weights obtaining for different functional categories of industries constructed by the Reserve Bank of India, based on the CSO's different series of the index of industrial production (weights generally being in proportion to their share in value added in organised manufacturing sector), the weight of capital goods industries expanded from 4.71 percentage points in 1956 to 11.76

Table 4: Net Domestic Product at Factor Cost by Broad Industrial Groups of Origin (At 1960-61 Prices)
(Percentage Distribution)

Year	Primary Sector		Secondary Sector		Total of Primary and Secondary Sectors	Services Sector			
	Total	Agriculture	Total	Registered Manufacturing		Total	Transport, Storage and Communication	Banking and Insurance	Public Administration and Defence
(1)	(2)	(3)	(4)	(5)	(6)	(7)	(8)	(9)	(10)
1950-51	57.0	54.1	16.4	6.3	73.4	26.6	3.6	0.9	3.6
1951-52	56.8	53.9	16.0	6.4	72.8	27.2	3.8	0.9	3.6
1952-53	57.7	55.0	15.5	6.2	73.2	26.8	3.6	1.0	3.6
1953-54	58.4	55.9	15.5	6.1	73.9	26.1	3.6	0.9	3.5
1954-55	57.0	54.4	16.4	6.5	73.4	26.6	3.6	1.0	3.6
1655-56	55.2	52.4	17.5	7.1	72.7	27.3	3.9	1.1	3.5
1956-57	57.9	52.1	18.0	7.4	72.9	27.1	3.9	1.0	3.6
1957-58	53.2	50.2	18.2	7.7	71.4	28.6	4.0	1.2	4.0
1958-59	54.5	51.7	17.8	7.3	72.3	27.7	3.9	1.2	3.9
1959-60	52.6	49.7	18.7	7.8	71.3	28.7	4.2	1.3	4.1
1960-61	52.2	49.3	19.1	8.0	71.3	28.7	4.3	1.2	4.0
1961-62	50.9	47.9	19.8	8.5	70.7	29.3	4.5	1.3	4.1
1962-63	48.7	45.7	20.8	9.2	69.5	30.5	4.7	1.4	4.6
1963-64	47.4	44.4	21.7	9.6	69.1	30.9	4.8	1.4	4.9
1964-65	47.9	45.1	21.6	9.7	69.5	30.5	4.7	1.4	5.0
1965-66	43.8	40.4	23.3	10.4	67.1	32.9	5.1	1.5	5.4
1966-67	42.9	39.4	23.4	9.9	66.3	33.7	5.3	1.4	5.7
1967-68	45.5	42.2	22.2	9.0	67.7	32.3	5.1	1.4	5.5
1968-69	44.5	41.3	22.6	9.2	67.1	32.9	5.4	1.5	5.7
1969-70	44.4	41.4	23.1	10.1	67.5	32.5	5.3	1.5	5.8
1970-71	45.4	42.3	22.4	9.8	67.8	32.2	5.1	1.6	5.9
1971-72	44.0	40.9	22.4	10.0	66.4	33.6	5.3	1.8	6.6
1972-73	41.5	38.3	23.5	10.4	65.0	35.0	5.4	1.9	7.1
1973-74	42.7	39.7	22.9	10.8	65.6	34.4	5.2	1.8	7.3
1974-75	41.2	38.0	23.4	10.9	64.6	35.4	5.5	1.7	7.8
1975-76	42.7	44.0	22.8	10.4	65.5	34.5	5.5	1.8	7.8

Source: CSO: *National Accounts Statistics, 1960-61 to 1974-75* New Delhi, October 1976 and other issues.

Table 5: Changes in the Weights of Major Industrial Groups in the Index of Industrial Production

Groups (1)	1956= 100 (2)	1960= 100 (3)	1965 (4)	1970= 100 (5)	1976 (6)
Use-based or functional classification					
1 Basic industries	22.13	25.11	26.84	32.28	36.14
2 Capital goods industries	4.71	11.76	18.67	15.74	16.76
3 Intermediate goods industries	24.59	25.88	23.60	20.95	19.27
4 Consumer goods industries	48.37	37.25	30.89	31.03	27.83
a) Consumer durable goods	–	5.68	6.15	2.92	2.78
b) Consumer non-durable goods	–	31.57	24.75	28.11	25.19
General index	100.00	100.00	100.00	100.00	100.00

Source and Notes: Columns 2, 3 and 5 are as per RBI's classification of individual industries into four functional categories based on the weighting diagram worked out by the CSO for its respective Index Number Series. Their sources are as in Table 4.
The crude weights for 1965 and 1976 are derived by us by applying the extent of percentage increase in the respective group index numbers during 1960 to 1965 and 1970 to 1976 respectively.

percentage points in 1960 and further to 18.66 per cent in 1965; susbsequently it declined to 15.74 per cent in 1970.

A reclassification of the CSO's industry-wise estimates of net value added into three major groups, viz, investment goods, intermediate goods, and consumer goods, for all the years since 1951-52 shows almost an identical trend. The share of investment goods industries in total net value added in the registered industrial sector at 1960-61 prices, which steadily increased from 31 per cent during 1951-53 to the peak of 46.6 per cent in 1965-67, declined to 44 per cent and remained at that level throughout thereafter until 1976-77 (Table 6).

The structural changes achieved prior to the mid-sixties and the subsequent structural retrogression can be appreciated better if we have a look at the progress made by some individual industries. In respect of a large number of specific industries which showed impressive growth rates during the first half of the sixties, the growth in the decade thereafter has been stifled to such an extent that for many years after 1965-66 their ouptput levels remained lower than those in 1965-66. The average annual increase between 1965-66 and 1976-77 is almost insignificant compared with the average from the previous five-year period. The outstanding industries in this group are the entire ferrous metals groups, viz, pig iron, steel ingots, finished

Table 6: Category-Wise (Functional) Distribution of Net Value Added in Mining and Quarrying and Registered Manufacturing Sectors

Functional Category	Net Value Added At 1960-61 Prices (Averages)						Net Value Added At Current Prices (Averages)			
	1951-52 and 1952-53	1955-56 and 1956-57	1960-61 and 1961-62	1965-66 and 1966-67	1970-71 and 1971-72	1973-74 and 1974-75	1960-61 and 1961-62	1965-66 and 1966-67	1970-71 and 1971-72	1973-74 and 1974-75
(1) Investment goods (basic and capital goods)[a]	20985	32431	51259	83245	94109	109619	50390	98166	153427	249103
Percentage to total	(31.1)	(35.6)	(40.5)	(46.6)	(44.3)	(44.8)	(40.0)	(45.9)	(44.5)	(45.1)
(2) Intermediate goods[b]	7832	11414	18660	28456	41563	45923	19144	31149	64828	99471
Percentage to total	(11.6)	(12.5)	(14.7)	(15.9)	(19.5)	(18.8)	(15.2)	(14.6)	(18.8)	(18.0)
(3) Consumer goods[c]	38657	47293	56679	67221	77134	88897	56379	84087	126576	204169
Percentage to total	(57.3)	(51.9)	(44.8)	(37.6)	(36.3)	(36.4)	(44.8)	(39.5)	(36.7)	(36.9)
(4) Total	67474	91128	126598	178793	212771	244424	125913	213652	344831	552743
	(100.0)	(100.0)	(100.0)	(100.1)	(100.1)	(100.0)	(100.0)	(100.0)	(100.0)	(100.0)

Notes: a Investment (basic and capital) goods – Comprise industrial groups: 14 to 19 and mining and quarrying
b Interest goods – Comprise industrial groups: 6 and 9 to 13
c Consumer goods – Comprise industrial groups: 1 to 5, 7, 8 and 20
} as per source

Sources: 1 For years up to 1969-70 see CSO: *National Accounts Statistics (1960-61 to 1972-73): Disaggregated Tables,* New Delhi, March 1975, pp 9-11 and 42-45.

2 For 1970-71 onwards, see similar disaggregated Table in CSO: *National Accounts Statistics*: *1960-61 to 1974-75,* New Delhi, October 1976, pp 98-101.

steel, steel castings, and forgings, steel pipes and tubes, steel structurals, which are the pace setters for industrialisation, followed by the whole gamut of mechanical engineering industries including a wide variety of industrial machinery, machine tools and railway equipment, and by cement, refractories, paper, etc. During the same period, many industries which directly or indirectly cater to the requirements of the rich and upper middle class sections of the community have registered phenomenal growth rates. For want of sufficiently disagregated data in respect of individual industrial items, it is difficult to make a more systematic analysis of this phenomenon. However, disproportionately large increases in the ouput of man-made fibres, beverages, perfumes and cosmetics, commercial, office and household equipment, watches and clocks, finer varieties of cloth—all signify the emergence of an output structure that was increasingly getting elite-oriented. It was not merely a question of these low-weighted commodities showing large output increases but rather the emergence of a pattern of final output that tended to establish an organic link with the rest of the industrial sectors such as even basic, capital and intermediate goods industries—and appropriated a large amount of investible resources directly or indirectly. The establishment of a vast network of luxury hotels, breweries, and units producing perfumes and cosmetics, tooth-paste and tooth-powder, baby food, radio sets, refrigerators, room air conditioners and what have you—all at the cost of allocation of investible funds for mass consumption goods—bears testimony to this phenomenon.

Distrotion in Output Structure: Classic Experience of 1976-77

In this respect, it is not without significance that when organised industry is supposed to have responded to the Emergency during 1976-77, the distortion in the structure of output was at its height. While output of goods catering to the requirments of the general masses registered either an absolute reduction or very moderate increase, that of patently elite-oriented products experienced astronomical increases. Thus, in that year (1976-77), when output of coal increased by 2.1 per cent, of cotton yarn by 1.8 per cent, of cotton cloth in the decentralised sector 3.4 per cent, soap by 4.9 per cent and cloth production in the mill sector actually declined by 1.4 per cent, beer output rose by 66.2 per cent, tooth-paste by 55.7 per cent, infant milk food and biscuits by 23.0 per cent each and cigarettes by 10.9 per cent. In the transport equipment sector, production of railway wagons declined by 1.6 per cent and output of commercial vehicles rose by 5.9 per cent and of bicycles by 14.9 per cent; against this, production of cars shot up by 67.6 per cent, scooters by 39.0 per cent and jeeps by 17.3 per cent. Among rubber tyres and tubes, cycle tyres and tubes, and giant tyres and tubes meant for commerical vehicles suffered a setback but tyres and tubes other than giant ones registered output increases of 32 per cent each and tractor tyres of over 18 per cent. (Production of many of these goods is controlled by multinational corporations.) Similarly, in the chemicals and petrochemicals group (other than fertilisers), output of basic products like caustic soda and soda ash increased by 8.1 per cent and 2.3 per cent, respectively, while polyester fibre output rose by 36.3 per cent, optical bleaching powder by 39.9 per cent, polystyrene by 45.7 per cent, vat dyes by 21.8 per cent, solubilised vats by 80.2 per cent, azo dyes by 33.8 per cent, and glycerine by 24.9 per cent. In the non-electrical machinery sector, the highest increases in production took place in room air-conditioners (108.4 per cent), air-conditioning and refrigeration plants (39.0 per cent) and domestic refrigerators (34.9 per cent). While some machinery items have shown significant expansion in output, reduction in output of paper machinery (–16.9 per cent), of dairy machinery (–7.0 per cent), of stationary diesel engines (–18.4 per cent) and of a whole set of metal products is a pointer to the continuing distortion in the production (and investment) structure. Among non-metallic products, while cement output increased only by 9.0 per cent, glazed tiles expanded by 42.5 per cent and sheet and plate glass by 54.9 per cent.

In this respect, one glaring example of distortion in the production structure is the change in the pattern of output of different varieties of cloth in the mills sector. As brought out in Table 7, the share of coarse and medium varieties of cloth in the total output steadily declined after the mid-sixties. In 1964, the share of these varieties of cloth in total mill cloth output was 50.4 per cent but it steadily declined to 38.9 per cent in 1971; even in 1976 its share was only 43.3 per cent. The government reduced the obligation on the mills to produce controlled varieties from 40 per cent of output to 25 per cent, but even this reduced obligation was never fulfilled. The story of cotton cloth is only one example indicating how the production structure has moved against the consumption requirements of the masses.

To cite yet another example, according to the Industry Ministry's Annual Report for 1977-78, 'the cosmetics and toiletry industry is well established in the country. A wide range of products like tooth-paste, tooth-powder, face-powder, cream, shampoo, etc, are being produced by a large number of units both in the organised as well as in the small-scale sector. In the organised sector, the industry is presently domi-

Table 7: Variety-Wise Production of Cotton by Mills

(In million metres)

Calender Year	Production by Mills							Production of Handloom and Powerloom Cloth	Aggregate Cloth Production (8+9)	Share of Decentralised Sector in Aggregate Cloth Production (9 as Per Cent of 10)
	Coarse	Lower Medium	Coarse and Lower (2+3)	Higher Medium	Fine	Superfine	Total Mill Cloth (2 to 7)			
(1)	(2)	(3)	(4)	(5)	(6)	(7)	(8)	(9)	(10)	(11)
1951	332	1903	2235		1232	260	3727	1013	4740	21.4
	(8.9)	(*)	(60.0)		(33.0)	(7.0)	(100.0)			
1956	657	3472	4129		406	317	4852	1663	6515	25.5
	(13.5)	(*)			(8.4)	(6.5)	(100.0)			
1961	790	1528	2318	1986	179	218	4701	2372	7073	33.6
	(16.8)	(32.6)	(49.3)	(42.2)	(3.8)	(4.6)	(100.0)			
1964	869	1475	2344	1808	195	307	4654	3066	7720	39.7
	(18.7)	(31.7)	(50.4)	(38.8)	(4.2)	(6.6)	(100.0)			
1965	803	1404	2207	1840	219	321	4587	3056	7643	40.0
	(17.5)	(30.6)	(48.1)	(40.1)	(4.8)	(7.0)	(100.0)			
1966	720	1130	1850	1862	209	318	4239	3097	7336	42.2
	(17.0)	(26.7)	(43.6)	(43.9)	(4.9)	(7.5)	(100.0)			
1967	683	1144	1827	1768	170	332	4097	3179	7276	43.7
	(16.7)	(27.9)	(44.6)	(43.2)	(4.1)	(8.1)	(100.0)			
1968	709	1274	1983	1822	208	353	4366	3530	7896	44.7
	(16.2)	(29.2)	(45.4)	(41.7)	(4.8)	(8.1)	(100.0)			
1969	608	1214	1822	1845	177	324	4168	3538	7706	45.9
	(14.6)	(29.1)	(43.7)	(44.3)	(4.2)	(7.8)	(100.0)			

(contd)

Table 7 (contd)

(In million metre)

Calender Year	Production by Mills							Production of Handloom and Powerloom Cloth	Aggregate Cloth Production (8+9)	Share of Decentralised Sector in Aggregate Cloth Production (9 as Per Cent of 10)
	Coarse	Lower Medium	Coarse and Lower (2+3)	Higher Medium	Fine	Superfine	Total Mill Cloth (2 to 7)			
(1)	(2)	(3)	(4)	(5)	(6)	(7)	(8)	(9)	(10)	(11)
1970	579	1108	1687	1866	219	385	4157	3692	7849	47.9
	(13.9)	(26.6)	(40.6)	(44.9)	(5.3)	(9.3)	(100.0)			
1971	503	1038	1541	1753	247	416	3957	3399	7356	46.2
	(12.7)	(26.2)	(38.9)	(44.3)	(6.3)	(10.5)	(100.0)			
1972	590	1192	1782	1917	205	341	4245	3777	8022	47.1
	(13.9)	(28.1)	(42.0)	(45.2)	(4.8)	(8.0)	(100.0)			
1973	605	1279	1884	1559	368	358	4169	3602	7771	45.9
	(14.5)	(30.7)	(45.2)	(37.4)	(8.8)	(8.6)	(100.0)			
1974	554	1272	1826	1957	277	256	4316	3968	8284	47.9
	(12.8)	(29.5)	(42.3)	(45.4)	(6.4)	(5.9)	(100.0)			
1975	558	1125	1683	1829	252	268	4032	4002	8034	49.8
	(13.8)	(27.9)	(41.7)	(45.4)	(6.2)	(6.7)	(100.0)			
1976	553	1130	1683	1788	164	246	3881	4064	7945	51.1
	(14.2)	(29.1)	(43.4)	(46.1)	(4.2)	(6.4)	(100.0)			

Note: * For years 1951 and 1956, combined figures for higher medium and lower medium are shown under column for lower medium figures in brackets indicate percentages to total.

Source: *Handbook of Statistics on Cotton Textile Industry* (Tenth Edition) by the Indian Cottom Mills' Federatiion August 1977, pp 21-22.

nated by foreign concerns and MRTP houses'.[4] That is not all; there is also some import content in the domestic output of cosmetics and toiletry which is of direct and identifiable nature, the indirect import content being immeasurable. 'Production of cosmetics and toilet products is now based mostly on indigenous raw materials except for import a peppermint oils, Iris Mose extract, a few perfumery chemicals, etc, *required to maintain the quality of the products*. The import content of this industry constitutes now 2 to 4 per cent of factory value of production.'[5]

Distorted Production Structure Even in Agriculture

Interestingly, the same phenomenon is noticed in the agricultural sector also. Among cereals, for instance, the output of coarse cereals, which are largely produced in the relatively backward districts of the country and consumed mainly by the farm and non-farm labouring and other poor classes, has remained either static or even declined in absolute terms. Thus, the output of jowar was 9.80 million tonnes in 1965-66 but it almost consistently remained below that level even in the best agricultural years, such as 1975-76 when its output was estimated at around 9.52 million tonnes. (The only exception, in eleven years, was 1974-75 when jowar output was 10.4 million tonnes.) So also has been the case with bajra, but more conspicuous has been the case of pulses which are the major source of protein for the poor. Pulses output which touched 12.4 million tonnes in 1964-65 remained around 10 to 11 million tonnes during the next 10 years and only increased to 13.1 million tonnes in 1975-76; in 1976-77, pulses production was again estimated to be lower at about 10 million tonnes.[6]

In a study on agricultural growth and poverty, Hanumantha Rao (1977: p 1369) has made a pointed reference to this feature of recent agricultural development. He has concluded that 'the composition of foodgrains output has been changing in favour of superior cereals like wheat and rice at the expense of millets and pulses. This is due particularly to the technological change which has favoured wheat and rice and partly to the price policy which has, in effect, ensured support prices for these two crops.'

In addition to the distortion in production structure, the agricultural development of the past decade or so has created the following three types of imbalances which have begun to hinder the growth process: (i) accentuation of disparity in economic development between regions and, within regions between irrigated and non-irrigated areas; (ii) further widening of inequality in the distribution of income and wealth among households within the farm sector; and (iii) gradual extension of farm mechanisation resulting in reduced employment per unit of ouput, particularly in those areas which have appropriated the bulk of the gains from recent agricultural development. We consider each of these in turn.

Inter-Regional Disparity

First on inter-regional disparities. This widening of inter-regional disparities is a feature particularly of the period from 1966-67 to 1976-77. Earlier, there was a slow trend towards closing of the gap at least insofar as the average per capita incomes of the states were concerned. Such inter-state comparisons of income disparities or disparities in economic advancement over time is beset with many conceptual and measurement problems but suffice it to say that analytical studies of the type undertaken by Uma Datta Roy Choudhury and Grace Majumdar (1977) have brought out that irrespective of the type of measure used for indicating the level of economic progress or backwardness–composite index of commodity production activity or index of state domestic product or per capita consumer expenditure–broad conclusions regarding the existence of glaring inter-state inequalities as between, say, Punjab and Haryana at one end of the spectrum and Bihar, Orissa, Assam, and Rajasthan, at the other end, are the same; the data presented in their study on per capita state domestic product and per capita consumer expenditure confirms the suggestion that these inter-state inequalities have widened, particularly since the mid-sixties.

It is arguable, as Dantwala (1976: p 45) has pointed out, that 'whatever may be the strategy of agricultural development, regions poorly endowed with soil-climate conditions cannot gain in the same proportion as the better endowed regions'. But this argument cannot be extended to conclude, as Dantwala has done, that 'it would be irrational to blame a particular innovation or the policy which promoted it for such a consequence'. This argument could be charged with 'the fallacy of single factor analysis' [Dantwala, 1976: p 43]. A thorough analysis of the subject of inter-regional disparities will not just restrict itself to such disparities being noticed in the development of a few individual agricultural crops in whose growth of output some regional specialisation is understandable. It is also understandable that the regions with favourable soil-climate conditions would produce quicker results. But the essential questions are: First, has the government opted for soft options in concentrating on the richer regions or has it made an earnest effort simultaneously to raise the level of productivity in the rest of the regions? Many studies have brought out how efforts in this direction have been lukewarm and inadequate. Secondly, what efforts have been made to share the gains of the Green Revolution that are concentrated in a few regions with the rest of the community? Have attempts been made to raise more resources from the farm sector through fiscal and para-fiscal measures? It is now evident that such an integrated look into the development of different regions of the country needed more purposeful and comprehensive economic planning, which has been absent during the past decade. Lastly, and more importantly, have not many aspects of government policies helped to accentuate the shift of incomes in favour of the developed rural regions? To cite only a few of those policies: (i) relatively high procurement prices and sympathetic increases in the open market prices resulting in considerable improvement in the terms of trade–in whatever way it is judged–in favour of agricultural commodities; (ii) providing farmers with a variety of inputs like fertilisers, seeds, pesticides, machinery, electricity and water and also credit at subsidised prices the benefits of which have largely been appropriated by the richer regions; and (iii) finally, absence of any attempt to tax rich farmers so that investible funds could be mobilised for developing the poorly developed regions and, further laxity in collecting even the already prescribed land revenue, agricultural income-tax, power tariffs and irrigation charges, and even in ensuring repayment of institutional loans.

Widening Inter-Class Disparities

Apart from the accentuation of inter-state and inter-regional disparities, the second outstanding characteristic of the period 1966-67 to 1976-77 is the widening of inter-class disparities in the distribution of assets and incomes as well as the perceptible deterioration in the situation relating to poverty and unemployment. As for assets distribution in rural areas, data presented in Table 8 brings out (i) the enormity of the inequality pattern; and (ii) the rising tendency of inequality. According to Divatia's comparative study of the two survey results, the share of the lowest 30 per cent of the rural households in the total rural assets has slipped from 2.5 per cent to 2.0 per cent and that of the top 30 per cent has increased from 79 per cent to 81.9 per cent. These conclusions are corroborated by another study by Pathak, Ganapathy and Sarma (1977: p 507). The latter study, however, brings out that the increase in inequality in rural asset holdings has been sharper. According to it, the highest decile group not only held a higher percentage share (61.79 per cent) in total assets than that

Table 8: Pattern of Asset-Holdings of Rural Households, 1961-62 and 1971-72

Household Category	Percentage Share in Asset Value	
	1961-62	1971-72
Lowest 10 per cent	0.1	0.1
Lowest 30 per cent	2.5	2.0
Top 30 per cent	79.0	81.9
Top 10 per cent	51.4	51.0

Source: V V Divatia: 'Inequalities in Asset Distribution of Rural Households', *Reserve Bank Staff Occasional Papers*, Vol I, No 1, June 1976, p 15.

revealed by Divatia's compilation (51 per cent) but also improved its share from 58.71 per cent in December 1961 to 61.79 per cent in June 1971. The study concludes that the share of top asset-holders had registered varying degrees of increases in most of the states, resulting in increased overall inequality between 1961-62 and 1971-72. Despite the conclusive evidence contained in his study, Divatia (1976) is cautious in his conclusions. Nevertheless, one of his observations in this respect is very instructive: 'The fact that over the period 1961-62 to 1971-72, the CR [concentration ratio] value and the shares of the lowest 10 to 25 per cent households in the total assets both for all classes and cultivator classes at all-India as well as state level have remained more or less the same, seems to indicate that if any efforts were made to reduce inequality, say, through land reforms, etc, in some parts of the country during this decade, there has not been any visible impact by and large in terms of reduction of overall rural inequality of wealth. It may be that simultaneously with such reformatory efforts, other factors had their impact offsetting the benefits flowing from these reforms.' As against this, Pathak, Ganapathy and Sarma (1977: p 517) emphatically state that: 'If at all, the share of top asset holders had registered varying increases in most of the states resulting in marginally higher magnitudes of overall inequality'. This is as it should be, for many critical evaluations of such measures as land reforms have revealed that 'land reforms were relatively more important in the fifties in bringing about these changes in the structural distribution' [Hanumantha Rao, 1976]. Yet another study by Laxminarayan and Tyagi (1976) comes to the same conclusion that 'most of the changes in redistribution of land took place between 1954-55 and 1961-62'. It also brings out that major factors responsible for increase in area under small-holdings are sub-division of land due to inheritance, etc, and notional transfers and subdivisions within families with a view to evading ceiling legislations. This apparent, not real, change in the distribution of family holdings of land during the sixties partly explains the dilemma which C H Shah (1976: p 76) has brought out in a recent study. However, two facts are significant. First, despite the ceiling laws, the concentration of ownership of land has not changed much in the recent period. Secondly, despite a marginal decline in the concentration of land ownership, the concentration of asset holdings has tended to increase.

After the effects of the zamindari abolition in the fifties, there has been widespread scepticism regarding the effective implementation of ceiling legislation which alone could make a marked impact on the distribution of land. 'Ceiling levels of this magnitude were in themselves a deterrent to the land reform programme's success. In the final analysis, there was very little land to distribute. Between the early 1960s and the beginning of 1970s, the states of Bihar, Mysore and Orissa had no land to distribute...Summing up for the country as a whole, by the end of 1972, declared surplus was only 2.5 million acres and area distributed even half or 0.3 per cent of one per cent of the total cultivated land in India.'[7] Towards the end of 1972, national guidelines were issued to bring about some uniformity in regard to various aspects of the ceiling laws–the levels, unit of application, exemptions, compensation and distribution of surplus land. This was done because, as explicitly stated in the draft Fifth Plan (1969-74), 'the results achieved have been meagre due to the high ceiling level, large number of exemptions from the law, mala fide transfers and poor implementation'.[8] However, 'under the revised and scaled-down ceiling laws to-date (mid-1976), about 3.5 lakh hectares have been declared surplus, of which about 1.6 lakh hectares have been acquired and 43 thousand hectares distributed' [Dantwala, 1976: p 47]. These 3.5 lakh hectares compare with 1,621.24 lakh hectares of gross cropped area or 3,058 lakh hectares of the country's reporting area.

If the ceiling laws have not brought about any basic change in the ownership pattern of land in rural areas, it is hard to find any of the governmental measures effected since the sixties which would have prevented the natural deterioration in the share of the poor in total asset holdings in rural areas. If anything, measures like asset-based advances, high support prices for surplus farmers and subsidised inputs and above all, the government's failure to implement a progressive system of taxation have all perforce brought about a shift in assets in favour of the richer segments of the farm community. And the circular causation of concentration in assets ownership leading to concentration of incomes and savings and to further concentration of assets ownership is grounded in sound empirical evidence, as shown by C H Shah (1976: pp 71-92) in a comprehensive review of such empirical data. Also, almost every field survey of the distribution of the gains of the new agricultural strategy whether in Punjab or Haryana or UP has confirmed that the gains have largely accrued to the richer segments of the farm community. A third and final aspect relates to the impact of new technology on farm employment which in totality seemed to be negative.

What is relevant to emphasise here is that the adverse structural effects of agricultural growth since 1965-66 on the distribution of income, savings and assets as well as on employment and real wages of the poor was not entirely unavoidable. As Dantwala (1976: p 45) has emphasised, 'such aggravation [of inter-class disparities] could have been arrested by appropriate policy measures, especially in view of the fact that the application of high-yielding varieties is technologically neutral to scale and has lowered the technical threshold of non-viability'. That was apparently the view held by the then government in 1973 and its Planning Commission: 'one of the major merits of the biological innovations which have been introduced in modern agriculture is that they can be adopted regardless of size, provided credit and infrastructural facilities are planned appropriately'.[9] None of those facilities has been planned appropriately. Institutional finance continues to be based on asset and hence gets appropriated by the large farmers rather disproportionately.[10] Surplus farmers continue to enjoy the benefits of higher procurement prices and subsidised inputs. Terms of trade have moved decidedly in favour of agricultural sector, to the benefit of the richer farmers. There exists even considerable inter-personal variations in the prices received, the average price per quintal rising generally with the increase in the quantity offered for sale.[11] Land reform, particularly relating to imposition of ceilings, has failed miserably. No attempt has been made to siphon off at least a part of the large surpluses of rich farmers through increased direct taxes on the farm sectors or through other para fiscal measures. An aspect of the favoured treatment of the rich farmers is seen, in the reduction in the amount of tax collections through the agricultural income-tax from Rs 14.00 crore in 1969-70 to Rs 10.50 crore in 1970-71 and Rs 12.8 crore in 1971-72. Against this large losses are incurred by irrigation and power projects, amounting to subsidisation of farmers who also benefit from public investments.

Concurrently with the pursuit of policies which have tilted the gains of development in favour of the rich, an attempt has been made during the past decade or so (since 1966-67) to offer solutions to the problems of poverty among the weaker sections–small and marginal farmers, agricultural labourers and others–isolated from the overall developmental programmes.[12] These solutions have been in the form of Small Farmers' Development Agency (SFDA), Agency for Marginal Farmers and Agricultural Labourers (MFAL), Crash Scheme for Rural Employment, Drought Prone Area Programme and Integrated Tribal Development Projects. A critical review of these programmes has concluded that 'it is now recognised that even in 1975-76, after their full implementation, the coverage and imapct of these schemes has been rather meagre'.[13] What is more, as Dantwala (1976: pp 49-50) has emphasised, 'there is a widely shared view that most of the benefits under the schemes have been diverted and appropriated by better-off farmers with political influence. From this a general conclusion is drawn that in property relations and socio-political power structure, such reformist measures...will make little impact on the conditions of the rural poor and in fact tend to be unproductive and as such add to the inflationary pressure in the economy.' In a later section of this paper, it is shown that substantial budgetary allocations earmarked for such schemes, including drought relief measures during 1970-71 to 1973-74, and the consequential increase in the deficit spending in those very years were partly responsible for accentuating inflationary pressure in the economy.

Growing Incidence of Poverty

With the all-pervasive structural retrogression–distortions in production structure, increased inter-regional and inter-class inequalities in the distribution of assets and incomes, and growing unemployment–poverty and malnutrition have got considerably accentuated during this period. This is evident from the fact that while there is disagreement on whether the proportion of rural households below the poverty line had increased or not till about the mid-sixties, no such doubt exists for the period thereafter. Among the studies that provide some time series data on the extent of 'poverty' for the period up to 1967-68 or so, four are well known, viz, Dandekar and Rath (1970), Minhas (1970), Bardhan (1970,1971) and Vaidyanathan (1971). Two of them, namely, Dandekar-Rath and Bardhan have concluded that the proportion of rural population below the 'poverty line' increased between 1960-61 and 1967-68, while those by Minhas and Vaidyanathan have come to the conclusion that the proportion of people below the poverty line had declined during the period. Based on the original estimates thrown up by the NSS data on consumer expenditure for the year 1967-68 compared with those for 1960-61, Dandekar and Rath (1970: p 37) could not find that the 'poverty' had relatively increased; they made adjustments in the NSS estimate of per capita consumption for only the year 1967-68 on the ground that the expenditure estimate was more than 10 per cent below the official estimate based on national income aggregates, and they attributed this to the possible tendency that 'the upper middle and the richer households have become increasingly inaccessible to the NSS investigators'. Rebutting this contention, Mukherjee, Bhattacharya and Chatterjee, who have made a detailed study of the divergence between the NSS estimates of consumer expenditure and the estimate of private consumption expenditure derived from the official national income statistics, make two convincing observations: First, taking into account conceptual differences and making allowances for lags between production and consumption, 'one should be struck by the degree of agreement between the NSS series on the one hand and the two official (national income) series on the other. Indeed, such an agreement validates all the series to a great extent' [Mukherjee, Bhattacharjee and Chatterjee, 1974: p 34; see also Mukherjee and Chatterjee, 1973]. Secondly, if there were discrepancies, as there were since 1964-65, 'there is no reason why the official national income estimates should be preferred to the NSS based estimates whenever there is any sizeable discrepancy between them. The empirical basis of the official national income estimates is weaker than that of the NSS estimates.'

This is not to belittle the importance of Dandekar-Rath study as a pioneering work. But because of the generally better performance of the economy during the first fifteen years of planning, particularly in structural terms–saving and investment, resource mobilisation for development, expansion of non-farm employment (which is examined in a later section) and, above all, increase in per capita availability of key wage goods–it could be, as the studies by Minhas (1974) and Vaidyanathan (1974) have brought out, that the proportion of the population below the poverty line had not increased till about the mid-sixties. Even the Dandekar-Rath (1970: pp 34-44) study concluded that while the character of rural poverty has remained the same as before, it was the character of urban poverty that had 'deepened further' because of rural migration to urban areas and the consequential raising of the proporition of urban people at the lower rungs of the income scale.

In regard to the other study by Bardhan, which revealed a staggering increase in the proportion of poor in rural India from 38 per cent in 1960-61 to 45 per cent in 1964-65 and further to 54 per cent in 1968-69, Mukherjee and others (1974: p 13) argue that Bardhan's price index might have led to over-estimation of the rise in cost of living and hence to some over-estimation in the proportion of people below the poverty line in the latter years.

This leaves us with the results of Minhas (1974) and Vaidyanathan (1974), both of whom using the same NSS data and almost the same norm of Rs 20 per capita per month consumption at 1960-61 prices as the threshold of poverty, have come to the conclusion that either the proportion of rural poor showed a steady decline from 65 per cent in 1960-61 to 50.6 per cent in 1967-68 [Minhas, 1974: p 69] or has remained almost the same at 58.8 per cent in 1960-61, 56.9 per cent in 1964-65 and 57.8 per cent in 1967-68 [Vaidyanathan, 1974: pp 12-13](Table 9).

Declining Per Capita Availability of Wage Goods

What makes the results of Minhas and Vaidyanathan plausible is that they have corroborative evidence in certain macro-level trends in the economy. For instance, given certain structural characteristics of consumption at different income levels, one could hypothesise a priori that if per capita real supplies of key wage goods are on the increase in the community for a fairly long period of years, the poor may also get a share, however small of such increase. This should be so when the rate of increase in the prices of wage goods is not exceptionally high and when the growth in employment–which is the only source of succour for the people below the poverty line–shows some significant rise. Two interrelated characteristics of consumption expenditure, which are empirically indisputable and on which this hypothesis is based, are (i) expenditure-elasticity for wage goods is low or even negative; and (ii) a preponderant part of the consumption basket of those below the poverty line, however, defined, is taken up by cereals, pulses, edible oils, sugar, gur and khandsari and cotton cloth, while these key wage goods form a significantly smaller proportion of the total consumption expenditures of the rich and the middle classes.

From available evidence, it could be justifiably surmised that when per capita availabilities of wage goods have increased over a period, the consumption of the poor in real terms may not have gone down. This was the situation obtaining till the mid-sixties. Per capita availability of mass consumption goods–cereals, pulses, sugar

Table 9: Trend in the Proportion of People Below the 'Poverty Line'

	Population Below 'Poverty Line'[1]							Proportion of People Below 'Poverty Line' Consumption Data Used[2]			
Year:	1956-57	1957-58	1960-61	1961-62	1963-64	1964-65	1967-68		1960-61	1964-65	1967-68
(i) Number in million	215	212	211	206	221	202	210	(i) NSS	59.5	60.4	67.8
(ii) Per Cent of Population	65.0	63.2	59.4	56.4	57.8	51.6	50.6	(ii) Official Series	58.8	56.9	57.8
Per Capita Consumption at 1960-61 prices (Rs)	232	243	258	257	247	266	273				

Sources and Notes: (1) Minhas, B S (1970), 'Rural Poverty, Land Distribution and Development Strategy: Facts and Policy', *Indian Economic Review*, Vol I, pp 97-128. Persons consuming less than Rs 240 per annum at 1960-61 prices were considered as those below the 'poverty line'.

(2) Vaidyanathan, A (1971), 'Some Aspects of Inequalities in Living Standards in Rural India'. A paper presented at the Seminar on Income Distribution in India (Delhi). Vaidyanathan also treated those consuming less than Rs 20 per month as persons below the 'poverty line' at 1960-61 prices.

gur and khandsari, edible oils and vanaspati, and cotton cloth–had registered by and large steady increases upto the mid-sixties. The period also experienced significant increase in employment in non-farm activities and there was no phenomenal increase in the prices of wage goods.

Extending the same logic, it could be justifiably argued that the period since the mid-sixties in contrast has seen a steady decline or stagnation in the overall per capita availabilities of wage goods, large increase in their prices, and very negligible employment growth, and that it is hence very obvious that poverty has deepened. Per capita net availability of cereals and pulses together, which was 430.9 grams per day in 1956, steadily increased to 480.2 grams in 1965; thereafter it not only always remained below this level but the highest reached was only 467.3 grams in 1972. The decline has occurred both in cereals and pulses, but it has been very steep in pulses. Though there had been some decline in availability of pulses during the first half of the sixties the reduction from 61.6 grams in 1965 to around 41 grams in 1974 and 1975 and to 51.5 grams in 1976 is perhaps the steepest amongst various consumption goods. Cotton cloth is yet another commodity in which per capita availability has steadily declined since the peak reached in 1964-65. Per capita availability of milk, edible oils and vanaspati, and sugar, gur and khandsari has fluctuated since the mid-sixties and has by and large remained stagnant. Reviewing these data, the Centre for Monitoring Indian Economy (CMIE) has come to the following conclusion: 'Some improvement was achieved in respect of most of the items by about 1964-65. But during the subsequent years, the per capita consumption of most of the key items has shown either stagnation or some decline.'[14]

This implies that the situation relating to poverty has obviously deteriorated during the period from 1966-67 to 1976-77, unless, as a perceptive observer has put it, 'one believes that in these years the poor in the country have somehow managed to appropriate a relatively larger share of the mass consumption goods whose availability per capita has declined!'[15] It could not have in any case been possible for the people below the poverty line to derive a higher share because during this period, domestic investment has been perceptibly low, generation of employment, particularly in non-farm activities, has been lower still, and due to poorer employment growth accompanied by higher rates of inflation than in the past, there has been no scope for improving the purchasing power of the poor in real terms (except probably in some pockets).

Niggardly Employment Growth

Tables 10 and 11 present data relating to the growth of employment in different segments of non-farm activities. Employment in the factory sector (not presented in these tables), which grew very moderately by 1.55 lakhs during the five-year period (1950-55) broadly coinciding with the First Plan or at a compound rate of about 1.0 per cent per annum, made a significant advance thereafter, i e, by 6.50 lakhs or at an annual rate of 3.5 per cent in the Second Plan and by 9.66 lakhs or at 4.3 per cent per annum during the Third Plan. Thus, during the ten-year period of the Second and Third Plans, there was an addition of 16.16 lakhs to factory employment in the country. By contrast, during the next entire ten-year period (1965-75), the addition to factory employment totalled only about 9.88 lakhs, a compound rate of about 2.0 per cent per annum. A small part of the increase in this is also accounted for by improved coverage of the reporting system.

More comprehensive data on employment in non-farm private and public sector establishments, available since March 1961,[16] also bring out the same phenomenon of a perceptibly poor growth in non-farm employment since the mid-sixties as compared with the growth during the first fifteen years of planning, particularly in the Second and Third Plan periods. The annual compound growth rate in total employment in the organised sector works out to 6.03 per cent for the Third Plan period but only to 2.29 per cent for the subsequent eleven-year period upto March 1977. More importantly, in terms of absolute numbers, the latter eleven-year period experienced an addition of only 44.81 lakhs[17] to employment in the organised sector as compared with the addition of 41.02 lakhs in just the five years of the Third Plan (1960-61 to 1965-66).

Also, of the total increase during the recent period, the bulk has been in non-manufacturing activities like banking and insurance and government administration. Manufacturing activities and even important infrastructural facilities like transport and communications have hardly absorbed any significant quantum of additional employment. During these eleven years, the manufacturing activities in private and public sectors together absorbed only 8.51 lakhs of additional employment whereas in the preceding period of five years (1960-61 to 1965-66), the corresponding addition was 11.39 lakhs. Similarly, under the head 'transport, storage and communications' in the private and public sectors together, the increase in employment during the eleven-year period has been 3.19 lakhs against 4.13 lakhs in the preceding five-year period. On the other hand, increases under the

Table 10: Growth of Employment in the Organised Sector in India

(Number in thousands)

Year (April-March)	All Organised Sector						Manufacturing Sector					
	Public Sector		Private Sector[a]		Total of Organised Sector		Public Sector		Private Sector		Total Manufacturing	
	Number	Percentage Increase Over Previous Year	Number	Percentage Increase Over Previous Year	Number	Percentage Increase Over Previous Year	Number	Percentage Increase Over Previous Year	Number	Percentage Increase Over Previous Year	Number	Percentage Increase Over Previous Year
(1)	(2)	(3)	(4)	(5)	(6)	(7)	(8)	(9)	(10)	(11)	(12)	(13)
1955-56	5234											
1960-61	7050		5040		12090		369		3020		3389	
Compound growth rate of 1960-61 over 1955-56		4.85										
1961-62	7417	+5.21	5160	+2.38	12577	+4.03	421	+14.09	3050	+0.99	3471	+2.42
1962-63	7953	+7.23	5450	+5.62	13403	+6.58	509	+20.90	3270	+7.21	3779	+8.87
1963-64	8454	+6.30	5590	+2.57	14044	+4.78	581	+14.15	3420	+4.59	4001	+5.87
1964-65	8957	+5.95	6040	+8.05	14997	+6.79	635	+ 9.29	3600	+10.53	4245	+6.10
1965-66	9379	+4.71	6813	+12.80	16192	+7.97	670	+ 5.51	3858	+7.17	4528	+6.67
Compound growth rate between 1960-61 and 1965-66		+5.88		+6.28		+6.03		+12.79		+6.05		+5.99
1966-67	9634	+2.72	6680	(–)1.95	16314	+0.75	695	+3.73	3750	(–)1.83	4445	(–)1.83
1967-68	9802	+2.08	6530	(–)2.25	16332	+0.11	731	+5.18	3710	(–)1.07	4441	(–)0.09
1968-69	10095[b]	+2.99	6530[b]	—	16625	+1.79	757	+3.56	3770	+1.62	4527	+1.94

(contd)

Table 10 (contd)

(Number in thousands)

(1)	(2)	(3)	(4)	(5)	(6)	(7)	(8)	(9)	(10)	(11)	(12)	(13)
1969-70	10374	+2.76	6685	+2.37	17059	+2.61	782	+3.30	3898	+3.40	4680	+3.38
1970-71	10731	+3.44	6742	+0.85	17473	+2.43	806	+3.07	3955	+1.46	4761	+1.73
1971-72	11305[c]	+5.35[c]	6769[c]	+0.40	18074	+3.44	885	+9.80	3982	+0.68	4867	+2.23
1972-73	11975	+5.93	6849	+1.18	18824	+4.44	962	+8.70	4104	+3.06	5066	+4.09
1973-74	12486	+4.27	6794	(–)0.80	19280	+2.42	1027	+6.76	4179	+1.83	5206	+2.76
1974-75	12868	+3.06	6804	+0.15	19672	+2.03	1019	(–)0.78	4109	(–)1.68	5128	(–)1.50
1975-76	13363	+3.85	6844	+0.59	20207	+2.72	1113	+9.22	4158	+1.19	5271	+2.79
1976-77	13819	+3.41	6854	+0.15	20673	+2.31	1222	+9.79	4157	(–)0.12	5379	+2.05
Compound growth rate between 1965-66 and 1976-77		+3.62		+0.69		+2.16		+5.67		+0.79		+1.50

Notes: a Between March 1961 and March 1966, data relate to non-agricultural establishments in the private sector employing 25 and more workers and thereafter the coverage was extended so as to include establishments employing 10 to 22 workers also on a voluntary basis.

b With effect from June 1972, the figures of Jammu and Kashmir are being covered and from March 1970 onwards those in Goa, Daman and Diu also figures derived after the transfer of employment data in respect of 14 nationalised banks from private sector to public sector.

c The government take-over of cooking coal units has resulted in an increase of employment in 1971-72 following better statistical reporting.

Sources: (i) Government of India: *Economic Survey*, 1970-71, pp 109-110; 1975-76, pp 82-83; 1976-77, pp 79-80; 1977-78, pp 80-81.
(ii) CSO: *Monthly Abstract of Statistics*, August, 1977, pp 4-5.

Table 11: Employment Exchange Statistics–Trends in Registrations and Placements

Year	Number of Exchanges at the End of the Year**	Average Monthly Number of Employers Using the Exchanges	Number of Registrations During the Year ('000)	Number of Vacancies Notified During the Year ('000)	Number of Placements Effected During the Year ('000)	Percentage of (5) to (4)	Percentage of (6) to (4)	Percentage of (6) to (5)	Number of Applications on the Live Register at the End of Period ('000)
(1)	(2)	(3)	(4)	(5)	(6)	(7)	(8)	(9)	(10)
1951*	126	6364	1375	487	417	35.4	30.3	86.0	329
1952*	131	6023	1477	430	358	29.1	24.2	83.3	438
1953	126	4320	1409	257	185	18.2	13.1	72.0	522
1954	128	4360	1466	240	162	16.4	11.1	67.5	610
1955	136	4880	1584	281	170	17.7	10.7	60.5	692
1956	143	5346	1670	297	190	17.8	11.4	64.0	759
1957	181	5632	1775	297	193	16.7	10.9	65.0	922
1958	212	6485	2204	365	233	16.6	10.6	63.8	1183
1959	244	7476	2472	424	271	17.2	11.0	63.9	1421
1960	296	8807	2733	520	306	19.0	11.2	58.8	1606
1961	325	10397	3230	708	404	21.9	12.5	57.0	1833
1962	342	11472	3845	790	458	20.5	11.9	58.0	2380
1963	353	12475	4152	909	536	21.9	22.9	59.0	2518
1964	365	13742	3832	917	545	23.9	14.2	59.4	2493
1965	376	13938	3958	946	570	23.9	14.4	60.3	2585
1966	396	13000	3871	852	507	22.0	13.1	59.5	2622
1967	399	11000	3912	699	431	17.9	11.0	61.6	2740

(Contd)

Table 11 (Contd)

(1)	(2)	(3)	(4)	(5)	(6)	(7)	(8)	(9)	(10)
1968	405	12000	4039	714	424	17.7	10.5	59.4	3012
1969	416	12000	4201	722	432	17.2	10.3	59.8	3424
1970	429	13000	4512	744	446	18.1	9.9	59.9	4069
1971	437	13000	5124	814	506	15.9	9.9	62.2	5100
1972	453	13000	5832	858	508	14.7	8.7	59.2	6896
1973	465	13000	6144	871	519	14.2	8.4	59.6	8218
1974	481	11000	5176	673	397	13.0	7.7	59.0	8433
1975	504	11000	5444	682	404	12.5	7.4	59.2	9326
1976	517	13000	5620	846	497	15.1	8.8	58.7	9784
1976 (Jan-March)	507	12667	1283	194	120	15.1	9.4	61.9	9353
1977 (Jan-March)	520	12333	1045	193	119	18.5	11.4	61.7	10239

Notes: * The figurers include those for the 'mobile sections' of employment exchange which were discontinued subsequently.
** Excludes University Employment Information and Guidance Bureaus.

Sources: (1) Planning Commission, Government of India: *Report of the Committee of Export on Unemployment Estimates*, New Delhi, 1970, p 117.
(2) RBI: *Report on Currency and Finance,* 1973-74, Bombay, 1974, p 46.
(3) Various monthly issues of the *Indian Labour Journal,* Labour Bureau, Government of India.

heads of 'trade and commerce' at 5.80 lakhs and 'community, social and personal services' at 20.21 lakhs have been relatively large and comparable with those achieved during the first period (2.31 lakhs and 17.93 lakhs, respectively). In mining, the increase during the recent period is reportedly more due to better reporting following the nationalisation of coal mines.

Yet another revealing aspect of employment growth in the organised sector during this decade or so is the absolute stagnation in employment in the private sector (after making allowance for the transfer of banks, general insurance and coal mines from the private to the public sector). This is particularly true of the manufacturing segment of the private sector in which there was an addition of 8.38 lakhs to employment during the five-year period 1960-61 to 1965-66, but the comparable addition was only 2.51 lakhs during the subsequent eleven-year period. In evaluating the beneficial effects of public policy, this relative stagnation in private sector employment, primarily in its manufacturing segment, ought to be described as very disquieting because it has coincided with the emergence of large all-India term-financing institutions which have provided enormous amounts of loan capital as well as share capital support almost entirely to the private manufacturing sector.

Employment Exchange Statistics are yet another important source of information on the growth of job opportunities as well as the backlog of the unemployed in urban areas. It is quite revealing that these statistics, despite some of their limitations,[18] also provide a distinct indication that job opportunities in relation to the number of job seekers, were growing rather rapidly precisely up to 1965 and that the failure of the economy to recover from the setback it received around that period is reflected in a persistent and perceptible downward drift throughout thereafter up to the first quarter of 1977. Thus, the number of vacancies notified steadily increased from 17.8 per cent in 1956 to 19.0 per cent in 1960 and further to the peak of 23.9 per cent in 1965; thereafter it steadily declined to the lowest proportion of 12.5 per cent, a decade hence in 1975. Similarly, 'placements' as a percentage of registrations reached the peak of 14.4 in 1965 and drifted to the lowest level of 7.4 per cent in 1975 (Table 11).

This rather lengthy review of the growth of employment in non-farm activities has brought out that the situation relating to the creation of employment opportunities has deteriorated since the mid-sixties. In respect of the farm sector, however, such systematic information is not available. Even so, a perceptive study by Raj Krishna proves the same point. To quote an observation based on this study:

'However, a recent study using NSS data concludes that the degree of unemployment and underemployment in rural India which had fallen perceptibly during the late fifties and early sixties, has again registered a sharp rise.'[19]

Thus, if it is conceded that the growth of employment opportunities has got significantly slackened during the decade since the mid-sixties, it follows that the incidence of unemployment and underemployment which are the primary causes of poverty, should have increased sizeably, particularly in the wake of a sharp rise in the labour force. While this is self-evident, it is difficult to produce auithoritative data thereon. Up to the unimplemented Fourth Plan (1966-67 to 1970-71), Planning Commission used to present estimates of backlog of unemployment, of growth in labour force, of additional employment created, and finally, of backlog left behind during each successive plan period, but this practice was unfortunately discontinued on the advice of the Committee of Experts on Unemployment Estimates (Dantwala Committee). As observed by Raj Krishna, 'it will always remain an intellectual mystery that the Expert Committee on Unemployment (1970) took great pains not to present any estimates'.[20] As Raj Krishna has argued, the Committee has created unnecessary scepticism about the concepts used and the results thrown up by the NSS data on labour force and unemployment in India. If the phenomenon of unemployment in any economy like that of India is 'too heterogeneous to justify aggregation into single-dimensional magnitude', the Committee could have presented different estimates based on alternative criteria. Amartya Sen was also equally emphatic that 'the solution to be sought is in presenting a set of figures reflecting different aspects of unemployment, and not in scrapping whatever figure one has; the alternative to choose should be a multi-dimensional approach'.[21] This is what Raj Krishna, another Committee on Unemployment (the Bhagvati Committee, 1973), and Amartya Sen have attempted to do. Their estimates also were close to each other. Distinguishing between those (i) unemployed, (ii) severely underemployed, and (iii) moderately underemployed as has been done in the NSS framework itself, Raj Krishna estimates for the country as a whole for 1971 (i) unemployed at 9.25 million; (ii) severely underemployed and available for additional work at 12.20 million; and (iii) underemployed and available for additional work at 7.84 million. Excluding (iii), total unemployed in 1971 worked out to 21.45 million and including (iii) to 29.29 million.[22] Likewise, the Committee on Unemployment (1973) said that 'the likely number of unemployed persons in 1971 may reasonably be taken as 18.7 million, including

9.0 million who were unemployed and 9.7 million who worked for less than 14 hours a week and who may be treated on a par with the unemployed'.[23] Amartya Sen has arrived at an estimate of 21 million as the minimal number of job seekers on the recognition approach.[24]

While these estimates could be accepted as broad magnitudes of unemployment prevailing in 1971, we are obviously on a weak wicket while comparing the trend of unemployment over time. However, none of the studies or the Committee reports has opined unequivocally that the earlier estimates presented in the Five-Year Plan documents were substantial underestimates. Also, the estimates made by Raj Krishna and the Bhagvati Committee based as they were on NSS data could at best be the lower limits of unemployment in the country.[25] Therefore, an attempt has been made to present a comparison, for whatever it is worth, of the growth in the backlog of unemployment at different years, extending it even to the year 1976 by a rough estimate of the increase in labour force and of the employment generated during the past decade (Table 12). While two alternative figures of the increase in labour force during the decade (1966-76) have been estimated based on different participation rates, we have indulged in a heroic venture of estimating single dimensional magnitudes of employment generation on farm and non-farm activities during the decade.

If these figures, as presented in Table 12, are to be believed, the sluggish performance of the economy, in terms of poor investment and employment generation, has anywhere between tripled and quadrupled the number of unemployed in a period of ten years–from about 10 million in 1966 to the range of 28 million or 38 million in 1976. In relating this growth in unemployment to the deterioration in the conditions of the poor, it must be borne in mind that there is a degree of regressivity in the incidence of unemployment on the lowest income groups. For, with the average household size being inversely related to income (or expenditure)[26] there would be a larger number of persons to share the income at lower levels; also, their bargaining strength in the economic system being limited, the employed poor have to face the incidence of unemployment of their kith and kin for longer periods.

Acute Inflation

The deleterious effects of the incidence of growing unemployment on the levels of living of the poor and lower income groups get compounded in a situation of acute inflation. On all counts, the inflation rate obtaining during the eleven year period has been very much higher than that during the first fifteen years of planning (Table 13).

Along with the increase in the general inflation rate, the tendency of faster increases in the prices of commodities entering the consumption basket of the poor has also continued even as their employment opportunities have dwindled. This is brought out by a comparative study of the behaviour of the wholesale price index number on the one hand and that of the three sets of consumer price index numbers on the other.

Besides, it cannot be said that in such an environment of sharp inflation, growing unemployment, reduced per capita availability of wage goods, and sharply widening inequality of incomes, the people below the poverty line could have improved their real consumption of basic goods even in absolute terms. Even in organised industry where there is some semblance of bargaining power for labour at least in some pockets, there is a general consensus that the real earnings of workers has tended to decline during the recent period. For the period of the sixties and even upto 1963, studies have indicated that real earnings of factory workers may have remained static over a period of 13 years or so,[27] but thereafter though money incomes have risen, they have generally failed to keep pace with the increase in the official indices of consumer prices. To quote but one authoritative study in this respect, 'there was thus a considerable erosion in the emoluments of workers, particularly during 1964-67, and after showing a marginal improvement during 1969-72, the situation worsened again in 1973 due to a sharp increase in consumer price index. The situation in 1974 is likely to be much worse.'[28] In fact, subsequent official data for 1974 revealed a staggering erosion in real earnings. While per capita nominal daily earnings of relevant factory employees remained static in 1974 (Rs 10.15 against Rs 10.10 in 1973), there was an increase of 28.8 per cent in the consumer price index for industrial workers in the same year. This was followed by another increase of 5.6 per cent in 1975 and a decline of 7.8 per cent in 1976. In 1976, the all-India consumer price index number (1960=100) was 56 per cent higher than in 1971. There was yet another cause for the loss of money incomes of the labouring class in the organised sector. That is, due to a variety of reasons, the number of man-days lost on account of strikes and lock-outs during the decade since the mid-sixties has been almost five times larger than in the preceding decade. The average number of man-days lost was 5.70 millions for the period 1961 to 1965. In the nine-year period from 1967 to 1975, it ranged from 17.0 millions to 40.0 millions. In 1976, it declined to 12.75 milions

Table 12: Backlog of Unemployment over Different Plan Periods

(In millions)

	First Plan[a] (1951-52 to 1955-56)	Second Plan[a] (1956-57 to 1960-61)	First and Second Plans[b] (1951-52 to 1960-61)	Third Plan[b] (1961-62 to 1965-66)	Original Fourth Plan (1966-67 to 1970-71) Target	Original Fourth Plan (1966-67 to 1970-71) Estimated Actuals[c]	Ten-Year Period Estimated Actuals
(1) Backlog of unemployment at the beginning of the period	3.3	5.3	3.3	7.1	9.6	9.6	9.6
(2) New entrants to the labour force during the period	9.0	11.8	20.8	17.0	23.0	23.0	43.0[d] (53.0)
(3) Total of (1) and (2)	12.3	17.1	24.1	24.1	32.6	32.6	52.6[d] (62.6)
(4) Additional employment likely to have been generated	7.0	10.0	17.0	14.5	19.0	12.0	25.0
(a) Non-agricultural sector	(5.5)	(6.5)	(12.0)	(10.5)	(14.0)	(7.0)	(16.0)
(b) Agricultural sector	(1.5)	(3.5)	(5.0)	(4.0)	(5.0)	(5.0)	(9.0)
(5) Backlog of unemployment at the end of the period	5.3	7.1	7.1	9.6	13.6	20.6 (18.6)	27.6[d] (37.6)

(Contd)

Table 12 (Contd)

Sources and Notes: a National Commission on Labour (Government of India): *Report of the Study Group on Employment and Training*, New Delhi, 1969. See also Planning Commission (Government of India), *Report of the Committee of Experts on Unemployment Estimates,* New Delhi, 1970, p 7.

b Planning Commission (Government of India): *Fourth Five-Year Plan, A Draft Outline,* New Delhi 1966, pp 106-108.

c Ministry of Labour and Rehabilitation (Government of India): *Report of the Committee on Unemployment*, Volume I: Part A, New Delhi, May 1973, pp 155-159. The Committee has made a detailed examination of the labour force figures based on the participation rates as revealed by the 1961 and 1971 Censuses, and the different Rounds of NSS and those estimates by a separate Committee of the Planning Commission (under the Chairmanship of the Registrar General of India) and came to the conclusion that the likely number of unemployed persons in 1971 may reasonably be taken as 28.7 million (p 158). The Committee also felt that their estimate coincided with those made by Raj Krishna at 28.5 million consisting of 19.1 million persons who were wholly unemployed and 9.4 million persons who were 'severely' unemployed and available for additional work. Raj Krishna also made another estimate of 29.3 million persons including those underemployed but available for work. There is a slight discrepancy between the original figures cited in Raj Krishna's Presidential Address and those quoted in the Committee Report, p 155. For Raj Krishna's Study see 'Unemployment in India', *Indian Journal of Agricultural Economics*, January-March, pp 7-8. Also see the text here. Based on our estimate of employment growth, the backlog arrived at by us is 20.6 million persons for 1971.

(d) Figures in brackets indicate the labour force estimate based on the Export Committee estimates presented in the *Report of the Committee on Enemployment* (Volume I, Part A), op cit, p 151. The principal figures are derived from the lower participation rates as revealed by the 1971 Census and used in the *Draft Fifth Five-Year Plan, 1974-79* (Vol I), pp 2-3. Employment estimates are based on the partial data available for the organised sector including those from the Employment Statistics.

Table 13: Trends in Index Numbers of Wholesale Prices

Year	All Commodities		Manufactured Products		Agricultural Commodities		Derived Indices with 1950-51=100		
	Index Number	Percentage Increase	Index Number	Percentage Increase	Index Number	Percentage Increase	All Commodities	Manufactured Products	Agricultural
(1)	(2)	(3)	(4)	(5)	(6)	(7)	(8)	(9)	(10)
Base Year: 1952-53=100									
Weights	(100.0)		(29.0)		(46.1)				
1950-51	111.8		101.8		110.0		100.0	100.0	100.0
1955-56	92.5		99.6		88.0		82.7	97.8	80.0
1956-57	105.3	+13.8	105.6	+ 6.0	104.5	+18.8	94.1	103.7	95.0
1957-58	108.4	+ 2.9	108.2	+ 2.5	107.4	+ 2.8	96.8	106.3	97.7
1958-59	112.9	+ 4.2	108.1	(–)0.1	114.0	+ 6.1	100.9	106.2	103.7
1959-60	117.1	+ 3.7	111.3	+ 3.0	116.5	+ 2.2	104.6	109.4	106.0
1960-61	124.9	+ 6.7	122.8	+10.3	123.8	+ 6.3	111.6	120.7	112.7
1961-62	125.1	+ 0.2	124.6	+ 1.5	122.9	(–)7.3	111.8	122.5	105.0
Base Year: 1961-62=100									
Weights	(100.0)		(32.30)		(33.2)				
1962-63	103.8	+ 3.8	103.2	+3.2	102.3	+ 2.3	116.0	126.4	107.4
1963-64	110.2	+ 6.2	105.9	+2.6	108.4	+ 6.0	123.2	129.7	113.8
1964-65	122.3	+11.0	109.4	+3.3	130.9	+20.8	136.8	134.0	137.5
1965-66	131.6	+ 7.6	117.0	+7.0	141.7	+ 8.3	147.2	143.4	148.9
1966-67	149.9	+13.9	125.3	+7.1	166.6	+17.6	167.7	153.6	175.1
1967-68	167.3	+11.6	129.1	+3.0	188.2	+13.0	187.2	158.2	197.9
1968-69	165.4	(–)1.1	132.8	+2.9	179.4	(–)4.7	185.2	162.8	189.0
1969-70	171.6	+ 3.7	139.7	+5.2	194.8	+ 8.6	192.1	171.3	205.3

Table 13 (Contd)

(1)	(2)	(3)	(4)	(5)	(6)	(7)	(8)	(9)	(10)
Base Year: 1970-71=100									
Weights	(100.0)		(49.87)		(40.4)				
1971-72	105.6	+ 5.6	109.5	+ 9.5	100.4	+ 0.4	214.1	201.0	212.7
1972-73	116.2	+10.0	121.9	+11.3	110.3	+ 9.9	235.5	223.7	233.8
1973-74	139.7	+20.2	139.5	+14.4	139.2	+26.2	283.1	255.9	295.1
1974-75	174.9	+25.2	168.8	+21.0	169.9	+22.1	354.4	309.6	360.3
1975-76	173.0	(–)1.1	171.2	+ 1.4	157.3	(–)7.4	350.5	313.9	335.5
1976-77	176.4	+ 2.0	175.1	+ 2.3	158.4	+ 0.7	357.7	321.1	337.8

Annual Compound Rate of Increase

(1)	(3)	(5)	(7)
Frist Plan (1950-51 to 1955-56)	–3.7	-0.4	–4.4
Second Plan (1956-57 to 1960-61)	+6.3	+4.3	+7.2
Third Plan (1961-62 to 1965-66)	+5.8	+3.5	+6.0
Ten Years (1956-57 to 1965-66)	+6.0	+3.9	+6.6
Eleven Years (1966-67 to 1976-77)	+8.7	+7.8	+8.1
Ten Years (1967-68 to 1976-77)	+8.2	+7.8	+7.2

Source: Government of India's *Economic Survey for 1970-71, for 1972-73 and for 1976-77.*

but a conspicuous aspect of that year was that nearly 80 per cent of the man-days lost were due to lockouts against 20 to 23 per cent in everyone of the earlier years.

If such is the story of sharp erosion in the real earnings of the organised labouring class in the Indian economy, what should have been the position of the poverty-stricken people who were, to begin with, below the poverty line and almost all of whom belong to the unorganised sectors of the economy?

IV

CAUSES OF STRUCTURAL RETROGRESSION

This scenario of consistent structural deterioration since the mid-sixties was primarily the result of a series of policy actions and inactions including the downgrading of the planning process; this was reflected in many policy-controlled variables and manifested in significant distortions in the functioning of the economy. Saving and investment efforts particularly in the public sector were curtailed, the public sector plan outlays were slashed initially and thereafter their growth was arrested, funds for the maintenance of past plan projects were not allocated adequately, resource mobilisation efforts were both inadequate and inequitous, deficit financing was resorted to indiscriminately, and finally, a significant proportion of the total public outlays was frittered away in non-development expenditure in the form of higher subsidies of various sorts from the national exchequer, transfers to the state governments on such pretexts as drought reliefs, and in many other forms. Simultaneously, the rigours of industrial controls—price and distribution controls, industrial licensing, capital issue controls, etc,—were drastically reduced, giving rise to many distortions in the production and investment patterns in the private sector. Though the period had seen the initiation of some sporadic progressive measures such as the stepping up of the marginal tax rates on personal incomes (to 97.75 per cent) and wealth (to 8 per cent), the enactment of the Monopolies and Restrictive Trade Practices Act, 1969, introduction of government monopoly in wholesale trade in wheat, the progressive posture was purely temporary and blatantly half-hearted and insincere. The government made a quick retreat; while the tax rates were slashed to unusually low levels the MRTP Act was made operationally defunct, and the monopoly trade in wheat was given up. Hence, these should be considered as aberrations of the period which was otherwise characterised by policy distortions and comparative neglect of the developmental process. In the following sections, some causes of structural retardation are identified.

Declining Trend in Domestic Investment

Both net domestic saving and net domestic capital formation by and large steadily rose over the first three plan periods, particularly during the Second and Third Plan periods when the total investment at 1960-61 prices increased at the (simple) average rate of 12.6 per cent per annum. The investment programmes of the Third Plan had their spillover effects in 1966-67 when investment, both at currrent and constant prices, reached its unprecedented level (though partly in the form of higher inventories, as discussed in a subsequent section). Thereafter, almost for five years from 1967-68 to 1971-72, the absolute level of net investment in real terms was lower than that in 1966-67. For the nine-year period from 1966-67 to 1975-76, the average growth rate in real investment worked out to 3.1 per cent per annum against 12.6 per cent during the preceding decade (i e, Second and Third Plan periods together).

In terms of their ratios to NNP at market prices, net domestic saving and capital formation had no doubt shown some year-to-year fluctuations, but the overall trend had been one of a significant increase, reaching the peak levels in 1966-67 (12.0 per cent and 15.5 per cent, respectively). Thereafter, there occurred a precipitate decline in the investment rate by 3.1 percentage points from 15.5 per cent in 1966-67 to 12.4 per cent in 1967-68 mainly because a 2.4 percentage point shrinkage in saving ratio from 12.0 per cent to 9.6 per cent. This was partly the result of severe drought conditions of 1965-66 and 1966-67 but partly that of the initiation of a pause in planning efforts which has persisted almost continuously thereafter. Thus, despite some improvement in agricultural output from 1967-68 to 1970-71, the rate of saving remained up to 1971-72 below or equal to the level obtained in 1965-66 or 1966-67; the rate of domestic capital formation remained so even further up to 1976-77 (Table 14). Excluding 'change in stocks' the net domestic fixed assets formation as percentage of NNP at market prices remained stubbornly static at a little over 10.0 per cent in all the years from 1967-68 to 1974-75; it was at 10.4 per cent in 1974-75 while the comparable ratios were 12.6 per cent in 1965-66 and 12.8 per cent in 1966-67; it was only in 1975-76 that the ratio reached 12.3 per cent which was nevertheless lower than that achieved in the mid-sixties.

In other words, the major source of strength of the economy during the eleven-year period from 1955-56 to 1966-67 was from the average growth of over 12 per cent per annum in fixed assets formation. By the same logic, the major factor responsible for the ills of the national economy during the subsequent decade is the failure to achieve a commensurate increase in fixed assets formation. The actual increase during this decade worked out to a little over 2.0 per cent per annum as compared with over 12 per cent during the preceding decade. Even in the First Plan, the increase had averaged about 7.0 per cent per annum.

No Shift in Investment Strategy Either

Here, it could be argued that in evaluating the performance of the economy in regard to investment during the past decade, the emphasis should not be so much on the level and its growth because:

(i) the economy could probably achieve any of the desired objectives with lower investment, as substantial installed capacities were already created in a wide spectrum of basic and capital goods industries;

(ii) there may have been during this period a planned re-orientation of the investment strategy in favour of 'agriculture' as against 'manufacturing', in favour of mass consumption goods (assuming that these have lower capital-output and higher employment-output ratios); and

(iii) finally, investment requirements within the industrial sector may have been reduced because of a shift in the techniques of production, preferring projects and industries with higher employment content and lower capital intensity.

Before we look closely at these hypotheses, a general observation could be made, namely, that any of these shifts in strategy required a coherent medium-term plan (like the Five-Year Plan) designed on the basis of a systematic evaluation of physical and financial resources and with the help of a definite policy frame. Any student of India's economic affairs will recall how the government failed to put forth during the decade ending 1976-77 a coherent plan and implement it vigorously as was done during the Second and Third Plans. Instead, the planning process during this period meant just the formulation of Annual Plans for a part of the public outlays. This is evident from the fact during this period two Five-Year Plan blueprints remained unimplemented and a third one was almost entirely restructured when it was half-way through. The original Fourth Plan draft (1966-67 to 1970-71), prepared in 1966, was shelved and there were formal Annual Plans for the period from 1966-67 to 1968-69. Similarly, the Draft Fifth Plan (1974-75 to 1978-79), which was published in 1973 and which was one of the most systematic plan documents ever produced in this country, was also not implemented. Instead, after three years of the start of the Fifth Plan, a truncated final document was published in 1976 and, in the meantime, plan programmes were being carried out basically in terms of the annual budgetary allocations.

The final version of the Fifth Plan drastically reduced its real investment content. Roughly, the shortfall works out to 16.0 per cent for the plan as a whole, but the entire shortfall has been in public sector investment in which the cut is over 27 per cent.[29] Research studies published on th eve of the release of the Draft Plan had indicated that even the investment levels proposed in the original draft Fifth Plan were meagre in relation to past performance and in relation to the needs of the economy, particularly for facilitating the utilisation of capacities built in the industrial sector.

In this regard, all evidence goes against popular explanations. First, it is not true that having achieved substantial capacities in basic and capital goods industries, the economy could make do with slower expansion in investment; the Indian economy has obviously not reached such a phase of development. The utilisation of capacity in investment goods sectors perforce requires sizeably more investment elsewhere, besides the continuing need for additional investments in those areas themselves such as coal, iron ore, steel, non-ferrous metals, machine tools, machinery, cement, commercial vehicles, and many others. Instead, these industries present the sorry spectacle of considerable under utilisation of rated capacities for want of investment demand.

Secondly, there was also no perceptible re-orientation of investment programmes in favour of 'agriculture' as against 'manufacturing' or within 'manufacturing', in favour of mass consumption goods. As is evident from sector-wise distribution of gross capital formation (GCF), the average share of 'agriculture' in GCF at current prices was 15.4 per cent during the Third Plan period and about 18.0 per cent during the five-year period 1970-71 to 1974-75. This slight increase in favour of 'agriculture' was also at the cost of investment in infrastructural facilities (which generally has a higher employment potential) and not that of 'manufacturing'. The share of 'manufacturing' continued to be as high as that obtaining during the Third Plan; it averaged 27.5 per cent of the gross capital formation during the latest five-year period 1970-71 to 1974-75 against 25.8 per cent for the five-year period of the Third Plan.

It is true that the investment content of the expenditure outlays in 'agriculture' should be lower than in 'manufacturing'. However, even when we take the sector-wise distribution of total Public Sector Plan outlays, as distinguished from investment, it is confirmed that changes

Table 14: Trends in Rates of Capital Formation and Saving

Year	At Current Prices							At 1960-61 Prices		
	Net Domestic Capital Formation Adjusted for Errors and Omissions	Net Domestic Saving	Net Capital Inflow	Net National Product at Current Market Prices	Investment Ratio Percentage of (2) to (5)	Saving Ratio Percentage of (3) to (5)	Ratio of Foreign Inflow Percentage of (4) to (5)	Net Domestic Product at Market Prices	Net Domestic Capital Formation	Capital Formation as Per Cent of NDP
(1)	(2)	(3)	(4)	(5)	(6)	(7)	(8)	(9)	(10)	(11)
1950-51	585	606	–21	9169	6.38	6.61	–0.23		885	
1951-52	770	588	182	9661	7.97	6.09	1.88		856	
1952-53	312	346	–34	9500	3.28	3.64	–0.36		553	
1953-54	388	401	–13	10000	3.88	4.01	–0.13		623	
1954-55	716	693	23	9375	7.64	7.39	0.25		761	
1955-56	924	872	52	9875	9.36	8.83	0.53		1187	
1956-57	1348	989	359	11279	11.95	8.77	3.18		1484	
1957-58	1210	735	475	11524	10.50	6.38	4.12		1229	
1958-59	1038	664	374	12824	8.09	5.18	2.92		1160	
1959-60	891	660	231	13163	6.77	5.01	1.75		1281	
1960-61	1808	1327	481	14210	12.72	9.34	3.38	14282	1808	12.66
1961-62	1626	1281	345	15067	10.79	8.50	2.29	14898	1565	10.50
1962-63	1984	1544	440	16059	12.35	9.61	2.74	15341	1845	12.03
1963-64	2265	1825	440	18543	12.21	9.84	2.37	16353	2000	12.23
1964-65	2623	2023	600	21785	12.04	9.29	2.75	17617	2221	12.61
1965-66	3161	2562	599	22719	13.91	11.28	2.64	16989	2506	14.75

(Contd)

Table 14 (Contd)

(1)	(2)	(3)	(4)	(5)	(6)	(7)	(8)	(9)	(10)	(11)
1966-67	4035	3112	923	26030	15.50	11.96	3.55	16870	2827	16.76
1967-68	3776	2939	837	30478	12.39	9.64	2.75	18232	2494	13.68
1968-69	3427	3011	416	31338	10.94	9.61	1.33	18886	2233	11.82
1969-70	4370	4129	214	34665	12.61	11.91	0.70	20104	2722	13.54
1970-71	4893	4499	394	37985	12.88	11.84	1.04	21365	2838	13.28
1971-72	5025	4546	479	40404	12.44	11.25	1.19	21804	2799	12.84
1972-73	5627	5530	297	44242	13.17	12.50	0.67	21690	3044	14.03
1973-74	7156	6764	392	54555	13.12	12.40	0.72	22541	3278	14.54
1974-75	9576	8500	1076	64695	14.80	13.14	1.66	22576	3398	15.05
1975-76	11058	10013	1045	67807	16.31	14.77	1.54	24645	3618	14.68
	Revised Series at Current Prices							Revised Series at 1970-71 Prices		
1974-75	9514	8862	652	65969	14.42	13.43	0.96	40142	5650	14.08
1975-76	9887	10002	–115	68298	14.48	14.64	–0.17	43640	5451	12.49
1976-77	10090	11517	–1427	72169	13.98	15.96	–1.98	44099	5435	12.32

Sources: (i) For years from 1960-61, see CSO: *National Accounts Statistics: 1960-61 to 1974-75,* New Delhi; October 1976, pp 30-31 and CSO's Press Notes on *Estimates of National Product, Saving and Capital Formation 1976-77,* January 1978.
(ii) Ram N Lal: *Capital Formation and Its Financing in India* Allied Publishers, 1977, pp 94, 207 and 209.

in such distribution over different plan periods have been rather insignificant (Table 15). Plan outlays earmarked for 'agriculture and allied sectors' and 'irrigation and flood control' together had formed about 21 per cent each in the Second and the Third Plans; the corresponding proportions for the Fourth Plan were 23.3 per cent and 21.6 per cent.

At this stage, it is necessary to be mindful of the analytical inaccuracies in this evaluation of the shifting investment strategies. First, as Dantwala (1976: p 33) has emphasised, 'industry-agriculture linkages make it inappropriate to talk in terms of "shares" of sector in public expenditure. What is relevant is investment for agriculture, rather than investment in agriculture.' In this respect, it is difficult to arrive at a systematic picture of the size of investment (or outlays) earmarked for agricultural sector and agriculture-oriented industries in different plans. But an attempt of a first approximation type does reveal that:

(i) investment programmes of the Second and Third Plans did not neglect the overall requirements of the agricultural sector, particularly when one considered the relative importance assigned to irrigation and power projects and to fertiliser plants; and

(ii) interestingly, during the Fourth Plan when there was a slight increase in the share of public sector (direct) outlays earmarked for agricultural sector including irrigation, there was a relatively negligible allotment for fertilisers; on the other hand during the Fifth Plan, the outlay for the fertiliser industry was raised but the relative share of direct outlays on agriculture and irrigation was reduced. There was thus hardly any shift in the overall investment strategy during the past decade.

Such a sharp shift was also not possible because the absorbing capacity of agriculture under the existing institutional structure was limited; it was just that capacities laid in metallurgical and machine-building sectors during the earlier plans facilitated a somewhat accelerated investment in fertilisers, pesticides and agricultural machinery during the recent years. But this does not mean that any basic structural change has been brought about in the investment patterns which would have implied lower investment requirements in this period.

This is true with regard to the distribution of investment even within the 'manufacturing' sector. There has not been, for instance, any shift in emphasis in favour of mass consumption goods. While the public sector has not made any major entry into the consumption goods sectors (except in drugs and watches and to some meagre extent in

Table 15: Public Sector Plan Outlays by Heads of Development–Plan Periods

(Rupees crores)

Heads of Development	First Plan 1951-56 Actuals	Second Plan 1956-61 Actuals	Third Plan 1961-66 Actuals	Annual Plans 1966-69 Actuals	Fourth Plan 1969-74 Original Outlay	Fourth Plan 1969-74 Actuals	Fifth Plan 1974-79 Outlay	Final Fifth Plan 1974-79 Outlay
(1) Agriculture and Allied Sectors	290	549	1089	1107.1	2728.2	2320.4	4730.0	4643.0
	(14.8)	(11.8)	(12.7)	(16.7)	(17.2)	(14.7)	(12.7)	(11.8)
(2) Irrigation and Flood Control	434	430	665	471.0	1086.6	1354.1	2681.0	3440.2
	(22.1)	(9.2)	(7.8)	(7.1)	(6.8)	(8.6)	(7.2)	(8.8)
(3) Power	149	452	1252	1212.5	2447.6	2931.7	6190.0	7293.9
	(7.6)	(9.7)	(14.6)	(18.3)	(15.4)	(18.6)	(16.6)	(18.6)
(4) Village and Small Industries	42	187	236	126.1	293.1	242.6		NA
	(2.1)	(4.0)	(2.8)	(1.9)	(1.8)	(1.5)	8964.0	10200.6
(5) Industry and Minerals	55	938	1726	1510.4	3337.7	2864.4	(24.0)	(26.0)
	(2.8)	(20.1)	(20.1)	(22.8)	(21.0)	(18.2)		
(6) Transport and Communications	518	1261	2112	1222.4	3237.3	3080.4	7115.0	6881.4
	(26.4)	(27.0)	(24.6)	(18.5)	(20.4)	(19.5)	(19.1)	(17.5)
(7) Others	472	855	1493	975.9	2771.7	2985.2	7570.0	6827.8
	(24.1)	(18.3)	(17.4)	(14.7)	(17.4)	(18.9)	(20.3)	(17.4)
Total	1960	4672	8573	6625.4	15902.2	15778.8	37250.0	39287.5
	(100.0)	(100.0)	(100.0)	(100.0)	(100.0)	(100.0)	(100.0)	(100.0)

Notes: Figures within brackets represent percentages to total.
Sources: *Respective Plan documents.*

paper and textiles), investment in the private sector has largely gone in favour of all types of chemicals and petrochemicals, synthetic fibres and intermediates and engineering goods. On the other hand, private sector investment in basic consumer goods has been niggardly. Fixed assets formation (at current prices) by the existing cotton textile companies worked out to an average of 11.0 per cent per annum during the eleven-year period 1956-57 to 1966-67, but it dwindled to an average of 5 per cent per annum for the nine-year period from 1967-68 to 1975-76. Besides, these assets are at current prices; if they are reduced to real terms, the increase in the latter period is likely to be entirely wiped out. The year-to-year behaviour of this ratio is still more revealing; net fixed assets formation was 10.8 per cent in 1961-62, 14.8 per cent in 1962-63 and 11.0 per cent 1965-66 but it steadily declined to 1.5 per cent in 1968-69, to 0.3 per cent in 1969-70, and to 2.9 per cent in 1970-71; thereafter it registered some improvement but mainly due to increases in the value of assets. On the whole, it could be said without a grain of doubt that the most damaging aspect of the performance of the decade ending 1976-77 has been the very meagre growth in investment (and output) in mass consumption goods industries.

It is equally true that, if anything, within the manufacturing sector a large chunk of investment has been absorbed by capital-intensive industries, giving rise to smaller employment absorption. Also, in other industries, capital intensity has certainly deepened over this period, as is evident from the negligible growth in employment in private sector industries despite some increases in fixed assets formation. There is, in other words, an obvious link between reduced investment expansion, reduced employment content of whatever investment that has taken place and niggardly industrial employment growth of the past decade. In any case, it cannot be argued that the sluggishness in investment is even remotely attributable to smaller investment requirements following any shifts in investment strategy.

The root cause of the persistent sluggishness in domestic investment is to be found in the failure of domestic savings that had slumped to unusually low levels in 1967-68 partly following drought conditions, to recover quickly and to expand commensurately with the increase in output and with the requirements of the economy to exploit the production potentials built during the earlier period. As brought out earlier, the saving ratio in relation to NNP at market prices which had receded to low levels in 1967-68 and 1968-69 did not make any significant headway until 1973-74 and when it did improve in 1974-

75 and 1975-76, the increase was largely absorbed by higher inventories of goods rather than by direct investment.

Declining Role of Public Sector

This whole subject of poor saving and investment during this period is inexorably linked with the performance of the public sector which was expected to play an increasing role in the planned development but failed to do so (Table 16). Independent estimates made by the CSO and research scholars make an interesting revelation in this regard. The share of public sector in net domestic product (NDP) at current prices (factor cost) steadily increased, reaching over 15.7 per cent in 1972-73 and 14.5 per cent in 1973-74 and far surpassing the level of 13.2 per cent achieved in 1965-66. Yet the percentage of public sector saving to the sector's share in NDP declined from 16.4 per cent in 1970-71 to 14.1 per cent in 1971-72 and further to 12.4 per cent in 1972-73; it was at 16.0 per cent in 1973-74. This whole trend implied a negative marginal rate of saving (leave alone a marginal rate of saving of 73.5 per cent).[30]

This picture of rising share of income in favour of the public sector accompanied by a declining share of its saving both in relation to its own income and in relation to the total domestic saving, is at the heart of the deep malaise into which the national economy has been pushed during the past decade or so. Behind this phenomenon lies the most glaring financial profligacy and indiscipline–a theme which can be established only with a little more probing.

Financial Profligacy

The crux of the problem is that even as the public sector obtained higher and higher amounts of domestic resources through taxation, through market borrowings and through resorting to deficit spending for the apparent purposes of development and defence, it spent smaller and smaller proportions of the total outlays in favour of development and defence or in favour of productive investment. A series of tabular data (Tables 17 to 19) on different dimensions of government finances are presented to substantiate this theme. Fairly meaningful classification of budgetary expenditures into economic and functional categories is available only with respect to the central budget.

According to the latter data as presented in Table 17, development expenditure of the central government[31] had formed 59.4 per cent of the total expenditure in 1964-65; thereafter it almost steadily declined to such a low proportion as 46.6 per cent in 1971-72 and 46.2 per cent in 1973-74. Excluding subsidies included under 'social and economic

Table 16: Shares of Public Sector in Net Domestic Product (NDP) and in Net Domestic Saving

Year	Net Saving of Public Sector at Current Prices (Rs Crores)	Percentage Share of Public Sector Net Saving to Total Net Domestic Saving	Percentage Share of Saving to Net Domestic Product of Public Sector	Percentage Share of Public Sector in Net Domestic Product (Factor Cost) at Current Prices
(1)	(2)	(3)	(4)	(5)
1950-51	123	18.8	16.8	–
1951-52	206	31.9	27.2	–
1952-53	99	23.7	13.5	–
1953-54	79	14.9	10.4	–
1954-55	100	16.0	13.5	–
1955-56	104	10.6	12.4	–
1956-57	161	14.5	17.1	–
1957-58	172	20.6	17.5	–
1958-59	154	19.7	14.5	–
1959-60	161	14.6	13.5	–
1960-61	309	23.3	21.7	10.7
1961-62	363	28.3	22.7	11.4
1962-63	408	26.4	22.2	12.3
1963-64	539	29.5	25.3	12.5
1964-65	611	30.2	25.7	11.8
1965-66	592	23.1	21.6	13.2
1966-67	407	13.1	13.3	12.7
1967-68	355	12.1	10.2	12.2
1968-69	522	17.3	13.3	13.6
1969-70	645	15.6	14.4	14.0
1970-71	830	18.5	16.4	14.5
1971-72	800	17.6	14.1	15.5
1972-73	779	14.1	12.4	15.7
1973-74	1158	17.1	16.0	14.5
1974-75	1989	23.4	21.9	15.5
1975-76	2174	21.7	20.9	17.1
Revised Series				
1974-75	2190	24.7	22.9	16.1
1975-76	2506	25.1	22.2	18.6
1976-77	2302	20.0	18.8	18.9

Note: – means data is not available.

Sources: (i) See Pratap Narain, A K Sarkar and Girish Chandra: *Public Sector Investment and Its Financing 1950-51 to 1974-75*, a paper submitted at Eleventh General Conference of the Indian Association for Research in National Income and Wealth, held at Shillong on October 20-31, 1977.

(ii) CSO: *National Accounts Statistics 1960-61 to 1974-75,* New Delhi, October 1976, pp 44-45 along with CSO's *Press Notes for 1975-76 and 1976-77.*

Table 17: Functional Classification of Central Government's Total Expenditure

(Rupees crores)

	Third Plan			Annual Plan	Fourth Plan						Fifth Plan			
	1960-61	1965-66	Total	Total	1969-70	1970-71	1971-72	1972-73	1973-74	Total	1974-75	1975-76	1976-77 Revised Estimate	Total
1. Total Expenditure	1806	3940	15207[+]	13481	4925	5576[a]	6710	7849*	8131	33191	9785	12037	13499	35321
A+B	(100.0)	(100.0)	(100.0)	(100.0)	(100.0)	(100.0)	(100.0)	(100.0)	(100.0)	(100.0)	(100.0)	(100.0)	(100.0)	(100.0)
A. Developmental	–	2340	–	6893	2352	2659	3126	3949	3754	15840	4975	6473	7367	18815
Expenditure (i)+(ii)	–	(59.4)	–	(51.1)	(47.8)	(47.7)	(46.6)	(50.3)	(46.2)	(47.8)	(50.8)	(53.8)	(54.6)	(53.3)
							(45.2)[s]	(49.2)[s]	(44.8)[s]		(49.6)[s]	(51.9)[s]	(51.2)[s]	
i. Social services	–	326	–	851	304	364	452	664	601	2385	592	733	815	2140
	–	(8.3)	–	(6.3)	(6.2)	(6.5)	(6.7)	(8.5)	(7.4)	(7.2)	(6.0)	(6.1)	(6.5)	(6.1)
ii. Economic	–	2014	–	6042	2048	2295	2674	3285	3153	13455	4383	5623	5780	15786
services[b]	–	(15.1)	–	(44.8)	(41.6)	(41.2)	(39.9)	(41.8)	(38.8)	(40.6)	(44.8)	(46.5)	(45.8)	(44.7)
B. Non-Developmental	–	1600	–	6588	2573	2917	3584	3900	4377	17351	4810	5735	6009	16554
Expenditure (i+ii)	–	(40.6)	–	(48.9)	(52.2)	(52.3)	(53.4)	(49.7)	(53.8)	(52.2)	(49.2)	(47.4)	(47.7)	(46.9)
i. General services	–	1089	–	3914	1492	1777	2018	2329	2452	10068	2618	3314	3201	9133
	–	(27.6)	–	(29.0)	(30.3)	(31.9)	(30.1)	(29.7)	(30.1)	(30.3)	(26.8)	(27.4)	(25.4)	(25.2)
ii. Unallocable	–	511	–	2674	1081	1140	1566	1571	1925	7283	2192	2421	2808	7421
	–	(13.0)	–	(19.9)	(21.9)	(20.4)	(23.3)	(20.0)	(23.7)	(21.9)	(22.4)	(20.0)	(22.3)	(21.0)
2. Defence	281	885	3575	2910	1101	1199	1525	1652	1681	7158	2112	2472	2615	7199
Expenditure	(15.6)	(22.5)	(23.5)	(21.6)	(22.4)	(21.5)	(22.7)	(21.0)	(20.7)	(21.6)	(21.6)	(20.5)	(19.4)	(20.4)

Notes: + Excludes Rs 53 crore in 1965-66 and Rs 207 crore in 1966-67 as additional payment to IMF, IBRD, IDA and ADB following changes in par value of the rupee.

a Includes compensation paid to nationalised banks estimated at Rs 84 crore and additional subscription to IMF and IBRD in the form of non-negotiable; non-interest bearing rupee securities estimated at Rs 114 crore.

b Includes block grants and loans.

* Excludes transfer of Rs 421 crore on account of Centre's assistance to States for clearing their overdrafts with the RBI.

Figures in brackets represent percentage to total expenditure.

s Figures within brackets represent percentage based on figures excluding subsidies forming part of the developmental expenditure.

– Not available.

Source: 1 *Economic and Functional Classification of Central Government Budget.*

2 *RBI Reports on Currency and Finance.*

Table 18: Proportion of Gross Capital Formation and Total Expenditure for Purposes Other than Capital Formation in Total Expenditure

(Rupees crores)

Year	Total Expenditure (Rs)	Gross Capital Formation Out of the Budgetary Resources of the Central Government (Rs)	Total Expenditure for Purposes Other than Capital Formation (Rs)	Gross Capital Formation as Percentage of Total Expenditure	Total Expenditure for Purposes Other than Capital Formation as Percentage of Total Expenditure	Financial Resources Provided to Third Parties for Purposes Other than Capital Formation: Total	To States and Union Territories	To Other Parties*
(1)	(2)	(3)	(4)	(5)	(6)	(7)	(8)	(9)
1950-51	504 —	129 —	375 —	25.6	74.4	140 (27.8)	—	—
1951-52	610 (+21.0)	203 (+57.4)	407 (+ 8.5)	33.3	66.7	175 (28.7)	—	—
1952-53	585 (– 4.1)	185 (– 8.9)	400 (– 1.7)	31.6	68.4	162 (27.7)	—	—
1953-54	661 (+13.0)	246 (+33.0)	415 (+ 3.8)	37.2	62.8	168 (25.4)	—	—
1954-55	921 (+39.3)	488 (+98.4)	433 (+ 4.3)	53.0	47.0	178 (19.3)	—	—
1955-56	974 (+ 5.8)	483 (– 1.0)	491 (+13.4)	49.6	50.4	222 (22.8)	—	—
First Plan	3751	1605	2146	42.8	57.2	905 (24.1)	—	—
1956-57	1118 (+14.8)	546 (+13.0)	572 (+16.5)	48.8	51.2	256 (22.9)	—	—
1957-58	1550 (+38.6)	802 (+46.9)	748 (+30.8)	51.7	48.3	350 (22.6)	—	—
1958-59	1639 (+ 5.7)	896 (+11.7)	743 (– 0.7)	54.7	45.3	331 (20.2)	—	—
1959-60	1710 (+ 4.3)	800 (–10.7)	910 (+22.5)	46.8	53.2	507 (29.6)	—	—
1960-61	1806 (+ 5.6)	861 (+ 7.6)	945 (+ 3.8)	47.7	52.3	512 (28.3)	—	—
Second Plan	7823	3905	3918	49.9	50.1	1956 (25.0)	—	—
1961-62	2040 (+13.0)	963 (+11.8)	1076 (+13.9)	47.3	52.7	598 (29.3)	291 (14.3)	307 (15.0)
1962-63	2533 (+24.2)	1178 (+22.3)	1355 (25.9)	46.5	53.5	695 (27.4)	294 (11.6)	401 (15.8)
1963-64	3207 (+26.6)	1525 (+29.5)	1682 (+24.1)	47.6	52.4	679 (21.1)	276 (8.6)	403 (12.5)
1964-65	3488 (+ 8.8)	1681 (+10.2)	1808 (+ 7.5)	48.2	51.8	802 (22.9)	332 (9.6)	470 (13.3)
1965-66	3939 (+12.9)†	1806 (+ 7.4)	2133 (+18.0)	45.9	54.1	1024 (25.9)	472 (12.0)	552 (13.9)

(Contd)

Table 18 (Contd)

(1)	(2)		(3)		(4)		(5)	(6)	(7)		(8)		(9)	
Third Plan	15207		7153		8054		47.0	53.0	3798	(25.0)	1665	(11.9)	2133	(14.0)
1966-67	4458	(+13.2)†	1793	(– 0.7)	2665	(+24.9)	40.2	59.8	1453	(32.6)	665	(15.0)	788	(17.6)
1967-68	4497	(+ 0.9)	1675	(– 6.6)	2822	(+ 5.9)	37.2	62.8	1542	(34.2)	733	(16.2)	809	(18.0)
1968-69	4526	(+ 0.6)	1660	(– 0.9)	2866	(+ 1.6)	36.7	63.3	1480	(32.6)	730	(16.1)	750	(16.5)
Annual Plan	13481		5128		8353		38.0	62.0	4475	(33.2)	2128	(15.8)	2347	(17.4)
1969-70	4925	(+ 8.8)	1612	(– 2.9)	3313	(+15.6)	32.7	67.3	1836	(37.3)	961	(19.5)	875	(17.8)
1970-71	5576	(+13.2)**	1888	(+17.1)	3688	(+11.3)	33.9	66.1	2019	(36.2)	910	(16.3)	1109	(19.9)
1971-72	6710	(+20.3)	2161	(+14.5)	4549	(+23.3)	32.2	67.8	2494	(37.2)	1234	(18.4)	1260	(18.8)
1972-73	7849	(+17.0)††	2627	(+21.6)	5222	(+14.8)	33.5	66.5	2960	(37.7)	1440	(18.3)	1520	(19.4)
1973-74	8131	(+ 3.6)	2665	(+ 1.4)	5466	(+ 4.7)	32.8	67.2	3153	(38.7)	1350	(16.6)	1803	(22.1)
Fourth Plan	33191		10953		22238		33.0	67.0	12462	(37.5)	5895	(17.8)	6567	(19.8)
1974-75	9785	(+20.3)	3676	(+38.0)	6108		37.6	62.4	3241	(33.1)	1068	(10.9)	2173	(22.2)
1975-76	12037	(+23.0)	4664	(+26.8)	7489		38.7	61.9	3924	(32.6)	1295	(10.7)	2811	(23.2)
1976-77(RE)	13499	(+12.1)	5158	(+10.6)	7699		38.2	61.1	4719	(35.0)	1311	(10.4)	2862	(22.7)
Fifth Plan	35321		13498		21296		38.2	60.3	118854	(33.6)	3674	(10.4)	7846	(22.2)

Notes: Figures in brackets indicate percentage variations over the previous year.

* Comprise non-developmental commercial undertakings, local authorities, foreign governments, etc.

† Excludes Rs 53 crore in 1965-66 and Rs 207 crore in 1966-67 as additional payment to IMF, IBRD, IDA and ADB following changes in par value of the rupee.

** Includes compensation paid to nationalised banks estimated at Rs 84 crore and additional subscription to IMF and IBRD in the form of non-negotiable, non-interest bearing rupee securities estimated at Rs 114 crore.

†† Excludes transfer of Rs 421 crore on account of Centre's assistance to states for clearing their overdrafts with the RBI.

Sources: (1) 'Review of Trends in Budgetary Transactions of the Central Government: 1951-52 and 1968-69', *Reserve Bank of India Bulletin*, October 1968, pp 1275-1300.

(2) Various issues of *An Economic and Functional Classification of the Central Government Budget*, Government of India.

Table 19: Trends in Combined Receipts and Disbursements and Deficits of Central and State Governments

(Rupees crores)

Year	Combined Revenue and Capital Receipts				Combined Revenue and Capital Disbursements					Combined Budgetary Surplus(+) or Deficit(–)		
	Combined Receipt	Per Cent of Net National Product at Current Market Prices	Tax Receipts	Per Cent of Net National Product at Current Market Prices	Combined Disbursement	Per Cent of Net National Product at Current Market Prices	Developmental Expenditure	Per Cent of Net National Product at Current Market Prices	Developmental Expenditure as Per Cent of Combined Disbursements	Centre	States	Total
(1)	(2)	(3)	(4)	(5)	(6)	(7)	(8)	(9)	(10)	(11)	(12)	(13)
1950-51	911	9.9	627	6.8	—	—	—	—	—	—	—	—
First Plan												
1951-52	—	—	—	—	1144	11.8	453	4.7	39.6	+44	–48	–4
1952-53	—	—	—	—	1004	10.6	452	4.8	45.0	–64	–27	–91
1953-54	—	—	—	—	1160	11.6	527	5.3	45.4	–81	+19	–62
1954-55	—	—	—	—	1278	13.6	657	7.0	51.4	–142	+40	–102
1955-56	1287	—	768	—	1504	15.2	891	9.0	59.2	–160	Neg	–160
Second Plan												
1956-57	—	—	—	—	1739	15.4	1057	9.4	60.8	–185	–65	–250
1957-58	—	—	—	—	2117	18.4	1289	11.2	60.9	–459	–29	–488
1958-59	—	—	—	—	2221	17.3	1422	11.1	64.0	–222	+54	–168
1959-60	—	—	—	—	2568	19.5	1497	11.4	58.3	–170	+16	–154
1960-61	2986	21.0	1355	9.5	2917	20.5	1708	12.0	58.6	+117	–58	+59

(Contd)

Table 19 (Contd)

(1)	(2)	(3)	(4)	(5)	(6)	(7)	(8)	(9)	(10)	(11)	(12)	(13)
Third Plan												
1961-62	2968	19.7	1537	10.2	3120	20.7	1824	12.1	58.5	–114	–80	–194
1962-63	3743	23.3	1855	11.6	3871	24.1	2078	12.9	53.7	–156	+65	–91
1963-64	4468	24.1	2313	12.5	4640	25.0	2413	13.0	52.0	–167	–35	–202
1964-65	5180	23.8	2585	11.9	5313	24.3	2762	12.7	52.0	–172	+36	–136
1965-66	5602	24.7	2902	12.8	5842	25.7	3177	14.0	54.4	–173	–179	–352
Annual Plans												
1966-67	6511	25.0	3240	12.4	6812	26.2	3290	12.6	48.3	–295	+118	–117
1967-68	6730	22.1	3423	11.2	6974	22.9	3395	11.1	48.7	–206	–74	–280
1968-69	7099	22.6	3727	11.9	7373	23.5	3891	12.4	52.8	–262	–120	–382
Fourth Plan												
1969-70	8111	23.4	4182	12.1	8098	23.4	3792	10.9	46.8	–46	+59	+13
1970-71	8421	22.2	4735	12.5	8847	23.3	4392	11.6	49.6	–285	–141	–426
1971-72	9703	24.0	5565	13.8	10511	26.0	5314	13.2	50.6	–519	–289	–808
1972-73	11443	25.9	6432	14.5	12319	27.8	6770†	15.3	55.0	–869	–7	–876
1973-74	12928*	23.7	7363	13.5	13482*	24.7	7284†	13.4	54.0	–328	–226	–554
Fifth Plan												
1974-75	15503	24.0	9206	14.2	16255	25.1	7846†	12.1	48.3	–721	–31	–752
1975-76	19610	28.9	11155	16.5	19901	29.3	9413†	13.9	47.3	–366	+75	–291
1976-77 (RE)	22035	31.2	12031	17.1	22541	32.0	10970†	15.6	48.7	–425	–81	–506

Notes: * Excludes PL 480 transactions of Rs 1,764 under the Indo-US Agreement, 1974.
† Exclude food subsidy expenditure.

Sources: (1) RBI, *Reports on Currency and Finance*.
(2) GOI, *Economic Survey*.
(3) RBI's Annual articles of Central and State Government Finances.
(4) Combined Finance and Revenue Accounts of the Central and State Governments in India.

services' which were negligible earlier and which have risen to a sizeable figure recently, this proportion was only 45.2 per cent of total expenditure in 1971-72 and 44.8 per cent in 1973-74. Though there have been sporadic improvement in this ratio, the average for the Fourth Plan period (1969-70 to 1973-74) worked out to about 47.0 per cent and that for the subsequent three years to around 51.0 per cent.

This erosion in the share of development expenditure of the central government is not, as is commonly believed, attributable to rising defence expenditure. Defence expenditure in relation to total expenditure reached the peak level of 25.4 per cent in 1963-64 following the military conflict with China. The most conspicuous feature of that period had been the maintenance of development expenditure at a high level of about 60 per cent of the total expenditure despite galloping defence expenditure. Between 1960-61 and 1965-66, when total expenditure of the central government expanded by 118 per cent defence expenditure shot up by 215 per cent. By contrast, during subsequent eleven-year period (1966-67 to 1976-77) when total expenditure rose by 243 per cent, defence expenditure as well as development expenditure rose to the same extent of about 195 per cent each. Thus, both development and defence expenditures in relation to total expenditure have remained significantly lower during the second period than in the first period.[32] Conversely, it is the disproportionate growth of non-development expenditure that has been responsible for the erosion in developmental efforts.

Slump in Capital Formation

The same development is brought out more sharply when we analyse the economic classification of the Centre's total budgetary allocations. Total capital formation expenditure had formed 25.6 per cent of the aggregate expenditure in the pre-plan period (1950-51); it rose to 42.8 per cent in the First Plan period and further to 49.9 per cent in the Second Plan; it stood at a high level of 47.0 per cent in the Third Plan despite a sharp 215 per cent spurt in defence expenditure during the same five-year period (Table 18). Thereafter, the proportion of capital formation expenditure slumped to 38.0 per cent during the Annual Plans period and further to 33.0 per cent in the Fourth Plan. The average for the first three years of the Fifth Plan (1974-75 to 1976-77) at about 38.2 per cent is just comparable to the period of the Annual Plan but far below the levels of the first three plans periods.

A glaring aspect of economic management of the period relates to financial indiscipline, reflected in significant diversion of public funds in favour of non-development expenditure including subsidies and unallocable transfers[33] to state government (for purpose other than development and capital formation). This financial indiscipline also got reflected in a distorted system of resource mobilisation; this took the form of (i) refusing to touch the richer segments of the farm community who mainly benefited from the new agricultural strategy; (ii) reducing the marginal tax rates on personal incomes and wealth in the non-farm sector; (iii) continuing to rely on indirect taxes which are regressive in their incidence; and (iv) resorting to a disproportionate amount of deficit spending.

Backlog of Development

By the beginning of 1973-74, it had become clear that the massive financial liquidity generated into the economic system, following the sizeable increases in non-developmental expenditure financed by budgetary deficits, had begun to put excessive pressure on commodity markets. Growing unemployment from the mid-sixties had resulted in narrowing down the market for basic consumption goods drastically. As the public sector did not generate sufficient investment and employment, the private sector found no incentive for increased output and investment. By then, the seriousness of the government's radical postures in terms of 'Garibi Hatao' (removal of poverty), self-reliance, control over monopoly, government monopoly over wholesale trade in wheat, etc, came to be widely questioned. Selective shortages of agricultural commodities, the fuel oil crisis and the massive monetary expansion of the past few years together helped to generate exuberant price expectations and triggererd off the unprecedented inflationary situation of 1973-74 and 1974-75. By then, even the formal adherence to progressive measures was given up and a series of tax concessions and subsidies were permitted; these tended to arrest the growth of public revenues and the government faced a serious resources constraint. Nevertheless, the government had to put up a show of tremendous developmental effort. Accordingly a new device was deployed, particularly in 1975-76 and 1976-77, whereby exaggerated claims of high developmental outlays were put forth by exhibiting phenomenal increases (for instance, 30 per cent) in plan outlays. This was achieved by withholding funds required for the maintenance of past plan projects, which is obvious from the fact that in 1974-75, when public sector plan outlays were raised by 18.1 per cent, the total developmental outlays of the central and state governments together were raised by only 7.6 per cent (Table 20). This gap widened in the subsequent two years. There was an increase of 30.3

Table 20: Trends in Plan Outlays, Developmental Expenditure and Capital Formation

(Rupees crores)

Year	Net National Product at Current Market Prices (Rs)	Public Sector Plan Outlays[a] (Rs)	Public Sector Plan Outlays as Per Cent of NNP at Current Market Prices (Rs)	Combined Developmental Expenditure of Central and State Governments[b] (Rs)	Developmental Expenditure as Per Cent of NNP at Current Market Prices	Total Net Domestic Capital Formation Adjusted for Errors and Omissions at Current Prices	Total Net Domestic Capital Formation as Per Cent of NNP at Current Market Prices	Public Sector Plan Outlays as Per Cent of Developmental Expenditure of Central and State Governments	CSO's Investment Deflator (1960-61=100)
(1)	(2)	(3)	(4)	(5)	(6)	(7)	(8)	(9)	(10)
1960-61	14210	1118.0	7.9	1708	12.0	1808	12.7	65.5	100.0
1961-62	15067	1127.9 (+0.9)	7.5	1824 (+6.8)	12.1	1626 (−10.1)	10.8	61.8	103.9
1962-63	16059	1385.8 (+22.9)	8.6	2078 (13.9)	12.9	1984 (+22.0)	12.4	66.7	107.5
1963-64	18543	1709.3 (+23.3)	9.2	2413 (+16.1)	13.0	2265 (+14.2)	12.2	70.8	113.3
1964-65	21785	1981.8 (+15.9)	9.1	2762 (+14.5)	12.7	2623 (+15.8)	12.0	71.8	118.1
1965-66	22719	2291.4 (+15.6)	10.1	3177 (+15.0)	14.0	3161 (+20.5)	13.9	72.1	126.1
1966-67	26030	2164.5 (−5.5)	8.3	3290 (+3.6)	12.6	4035 (+27.6)	15.5	65.8	142.7
1967-68	30478	2084.9 (−3.7)	6.8	3395 (+3.2)	11.1	3776 (−6.4)	12.4	61.4	151.4
1968-69	31338	2376.0 (+14.0)	7.6	3891 (+14.6)	12.4	3427 (−9.3)	10.9	61.1	153.5
1969-70	34665	2209.9 (−7.0)	6.4	3792 (−2.5)	10.9	4307 (+25.7)	12.6	58.3	160.5
1970-71	37985	2523.5 (+14.2)	6.6	4392 (+15.8)	11.6	4893 (+13.6)	12.9	57.5	172.4
1971-72	40404	3130.3 (+24.0)	7.7	5314 (+21.0)	13.2	5025 (+2.7)	12.4	58.9	179.5
1972-73	44242	3727.3 (+18.9)	8.4	6770 (+27.4)	15.3	5827 (+16.0)	13.2	55.1	191.4
1973-74	54555	4187.8 (+12.4)	7.7	7284 (+7.6)	13.4	7156 (+22.8)	13.1	57.5	218.3
1974-75	64695	4944.6 (+18.1)	7.6	7846 (+7.7)	12.1	9576 (+33.8)	14.8	63.0	281.8
1975-76	67807	6442.7 (+30.3)	9.5	9413 (+20.0)	13.9	11058 (+15.5)	16.3	68.4	305.6
1976-77	70926[c]	7851.9 (+21.9)	11.2	10970 (+16.5)	15.6	–	–	71.6	–

Notes: Figures in brackets represent percentage variations over the previous year.
(a) From 1968-69 onwards, plan outlays includes buffer stock expenditure as follows: Rs 140 crore for 1968-69, Rs 25 crore for 1969-70, Rs 50 crore for 1971-72, Rs 25 crore for 1972-73 and Rs 24 crore for 1973-74.
(b) Inclusive of loans and advances to third parties as shown in the Capital Accounts of the central and state governments.
(c) This is obtained by increasing previous year's observation by 4.6 per cent.
(–) means not available.

Source: Government of India, *Economic Survey*.

per cent in plan outlays in 1975-76 when developmental outlays increased by 16.0 per cent, and in 1976-77, the corresponding increases were 21.9 per cent and 16.5 per cent, respectively. This phenomenon of the Plan outlays showing a significantly higher order of increase than the combined developmental outlays was a new development which manifested itself after the beginning of the Fifth Plan.

More importantly, the recent increases in Plan outlays have to be deflated by the increase in the cost of investment for gauging their real impact on the economy. During the Third Plan, the plan outlays increased by an annual rate of about 12.5 per cent in real terms, whereas for the eleven years from 1965-66 to 1976-77, the corresponding increase works out to 3.7 per cent per annum. Hypothetically, if the public sector plan outlays had been rising at the rate of about 12.5 per cent per annum in real terms since the mid-sixties also, the figure of plan outlays in 1976-77 should have been *ceteris paribus* of the order of about Rs 20,000 crore (at current prices) against the actual for the year of Rs 7,852 crore. In a rough way this indicates the extent to which the clock of progress has been wound backwards by a drift as well as downright financial mismanagement.

In summing up this discussion on the performance of the public sector, it could be said that the single most important factor responsible for the relative stagnation in domestic investment in the past decade or so lies in this diminishing role of the public sector in the overall development plan. It was anachronistic that at a time when the major commerical banks were nationalised ostensibly to secure commanding influence over the economic system, there was failure to improve the government's own role in Plan programmes.

Tables 21 and 22 bring out clearly how the share of public sector in total plan outlays as well as in total Plan investment declined precisely after the mid-sixties, reversing the previous rising trend. Thus, the share of public sector investment in total plan investment had consistently risen from 46.4 per cent in the First Plan to 54.6 per cent in the Second Plan then further to 62.8 per cent in the Third Plan. This was followed by a steady decline in its share. Excluding the interregnum of the annual plans period, the public sector share drifted downwards from 62.8 per cent in the Third Plan to 60.4 per cent in the Fourth Plan and further to 55.5 per cent in the final Fifth Plan. This is reflected even in the CSO's estimates of gross capital formation (GCF) according to which the public sector share in GCF had reached the peak about 50.0 per cent at constant prices and 48 per cent at current prices in the Third Plan. Subsequently, it followed a down-

Table 21: Financial Outlays of Different Plans

(Rupees crores)

Plan Period	Public Sector Outlay			Private Sector Investment	Aggregate	
	Investment*	Current Outlay	Total**		Plan Outlay (4+5)	Investment Outlay (2+5)
(1)	(2)	(3)	(4)	(5)	(6)	(7)
1 First Plan (1951-52 to 1955-56)	1560 (46.4)	400	1960 (52.1)	1800	3760	3360
2. Second Plan (1956-57 to 1960-61)	3731 (54.6)	941	4672 (60.1)	3100	7772	6831
3. Third Plan (1961-62 to 1965-66)	7129 (62.8)	1448	8577 (67.2)	4190	12767	11319
4. Annual Plans (1966-67 to 1968-69)	—	—	6625	—	—	—
5. Fourth Plan (1969-70 to 1973-74)	13655 (60.4)	2247	15902 (63.9)	8980	24882	22635
6. Draft Fifth Plan (1974-75 to 1978-79)	31400 (66.0)	5850	37250 (69.7)	16144	53394	47544
6A. Revised Fifth Plan (1974-75 to 1978-79)	33703@ (55.5)	5700	39403 (59.3)	27048	66451	60751

Notes: @ Excluding inventories of Rs 3,000 crore.
— means not available.
* Figures in brackets are of public sector investment as percentage of aggregate investment outlay.
** Figures in brackets are of public sector outlay as percentage of aggregate plan outlay.

Sources: Respective Five-Year Plan Documents.

ward course, reaching a little over 41 per cent in the Fourth Plan period and thereafter.

Wasted Potential

On the face of it, it may appear that the above is a mechanical presentation of the potential losses to the developmental process without realising the socio-political compulsions of the period or without perceiving the technical and organisational constraints in undertaking a bigger developmental effort. Far from it. In fact, if one analysed the period from these angles, it becomes obvious that the socio-political environment of the period was far more conducive for rapid structural changes than even before the mid-sixties. Besides the laying of an industrial base, the country had also advanced significantly in terms of technological know-how and technical expertise which could be harnessed for sustained economic advancement, if only there was the genuine desire and attempt on the part of the government to bring it about.

For instance, reviewing the expansion of engineering personnel in the country during the Third Plan, the Fourth Plan document brought out that 'the existing facilities for engineering education should be sufficient to meet the Fourth and the Fifth Plan requirements. No shortages are expected. The problem will be primarily of effective deployment and better utilisation of persons trained.'[34] The Third Plan had provided for a massive expansion of facilities for engineering education both at the degree and diploma levels. Again following the military conflict with China in 1962, 'it was decided to accelerate the expansion of facilities for engineering education to meet the urgent additional requirements arising from the new developments. In the event, the targets set for the period of the Third Plan were execeeded by 1963-64'.[35] This shows that the atmosphere of serious developmental effort and growing employment opportunities of the period helped to stimulate higher intake in engineering education. But, as the Fourth Plan reported, 'There was virtually no increase in sanctioned intake in the degree and diploma levels of engineering education after 1965, but admissions dropped in 1967-68 and much more steeply in 1968-69—33 per cent below the level of previous year.'[36] And the reasons were obvious: 'A decline, and later stagnation, in the tempo of industrial development, the slowing down of the rate of investment, the severe control on government expenditure—these features of the years 1966-67 and 1967-68 restricted the opportunities for employment of engineers, while new out-turn continued on the basis of admissions three to five years earlier.'[37] Thus, while improvement in

Table 22: Sector-Wise Gross Saving and Gross Capital Formation

(Rupees crores)

Period	Gross Domestic Saving at Current Prices				Gross Capital Formation at Current Prices				Gross Capital Formation at 1960-61 Prices		
	Households Sector Saving	Private Corporate Sector Saving	Public Sector Saving	Total Saving	Households Sector Capital Formation	Private Sector Corporate Capital Formation	Public Sector Capital Formation	Total Gross Capital Formation	Public Sector Capital Formation	Private Sector Capital Formation	Total Gross Capital Formation
(1)	(2)	(3)	(4)	(5)	(6)	(7)	(8)	(9)	(10)	(11)	(12)
1951-52 to 1955-56	3848 (73.8)	522 (10.0)	847 (16.2)	5217	2928 (54.1)	694 (12.8)	1789 (33.1)	5411	2300 (33.1)	4651 (66.9)	6951
1956-57 to 1960-61	5982 (72.9)	860 (10.5)	1364 (16.6)	8206	3969 (39.2)	1802 (17.8)	4350 (43.0)	10121	4769 (42.7)	6407 (57.3)	11176
1961-62 to 1965-66	9109 (63.6)	1817 (12.7)	3395 (23.7)	14321	4581 (26.0)	3727 (21.1)	8418 (47.8)	16726	7452 (50.4)	7314 (49.6)	14766
1966-67	3292 (75.3)	414 (9.5)	668 (15.3)	4374	2689 (50.8)	492 (9.3)	2114 (39.9)	5295			
1967-68	3431 (76.3)	399 (8.9)	667 (14.8)	4497	2193 (38.6)	1183 (20.8)	2311 (40.6)	5687	4396 (40.1)	6568 (59.9)	10964
1968-69	3412 (72.6)	427 (9.1)	858 (18.3)	4697	2190 (39.7)	1183 (21.4)	2146 (38.9)	5519			
1969-70 to 1973-74	26590 (71.7)	3795 (10.2)	6684 (18.0)	37069	15690 (39.1)	8017 (20.0)	16435 (40.9)	40142	8703 (40.8)	12614 (59.2)	21317
1974-75	7670 (64.4)	1509 (12.7)	2735 (23.0)	11914	4709 (34.6)	3396 (24.9)	5517 (40.5)	13622			

(Contd)

Table 22 (Contd)

(Rupees crores)

(1)	(2)	(3)	(4)	(5)	(6)	(7)	(8)	(9)	(10)	(11)	(12)
CSO's Revised Series											
1974-75	8324	1450	2874	12648	5778	2876	5941	14595*			
	(65.8)	(11.5)	(22.7)		(39.6)	(19.7)	(40.7)				
1975-76	10008	1086	3308	14402	6138	2525	7480	16143*	Not available		
	(69.5)	(7.5)	(23.0)		(38.0)	(15.6)	(46.3)				
1976-77	12141	954	3190	16285	7851	1759	7749	17359*			
	(74.6)	(5.9)	(19.6)		(45.2)	(10.1)	(44.6)				

Notes: Figures in brackets represent percentages to totals.

* The totals and their distribution are without adjusting for errors and omissions.

Sources: See Pratap Narain, A K Sarkar and Girish Chandra: *Public Sector Investment and Its Financing 1950-51 to 1974-75,* a paper submitted at Eleventh General Conference of the Indian Association for Research in National Income and Wealth held at Shillong, on October 20-31, 1977. Also CSO's *Press Note on Estimates of National Product Saving and Capital Formation, 1976-77* (January 1978).

the quality of technical expertise was a continuing process, its availability as such could no longer be considered as a serious constraint on development if rapid development was genuinely desired.

Similarly in regard to the strengthening of the organisational framework to keep pace with the increasing variety and complexity of the developmental functions, the Draft Fifth Plan stated, 'some of the basic weaknesses in the process of implementation have been identified from time to time. Thus the Administrative Reforms Commission, the National Commission on Agriculture, the Irrigation Commission and a large number of reports of special committees, tasks forces and evaluation studies have brought out in detail the structural, procedural and institutional weaknesses and suggested specific remedies'.[38] In spite of this, if there has not been any significant improvement in the levels of performance, it is primarily attributable to the fact that the planning process itself had been downgraded. The original Draft Fifth Plan, which for the first time devoted a separate comprehensive chapter to 'Plan Implementation', held out the hope that some of the steps that had been taken or those proposal to be taken at the level of government departments and the public sector undertakings concerning the whole gamut of plan formulation, implementation and follow-up would facilitate the achievement of desired objective. But the Plan was a virtual non-starter.

Trends in Private Sector Investment

By the end of the Third Plan, the public sector with about 50 per cent of total domestic investment or with over 75 per cent of investment in organised industry had carved out a predominant role for itself. 'It bears repetition that the level of investment in the public sector plays a catalytic role in sustaining and accelerating the overall level of capital formation in the economy. The declining trend of investment in the public sector in recent years had its repercussions on the level of capital formation in the private sector. As alluded to elsewhere in this Survey, excluding that part of the activity which has been financed by the term financing institutions investment activity in the private sector has been in recent years generally subdued.'[39] This largely sums up the picture relating to the private sector investment in organised industry during this decade. Nevertheless, certain deeper issues are involved in the role of the private sector during this period, essentially arising from one aspect of public policy or the other. Analysing these issues, the major conclusions arrived at are summarised below:

First, the declining trend of investment in the public sector since the mid-sixties has had its reverberating effects on private sector output, employment and investment; among these parameters, the worst to get affected has been private sector employment and not investment. Secondly, a preponderant part of the investible funds deployed by the private manufacturing sector during this period has been provided by the public financial institutions, mainly as loans but partly also as investment in shares and debentures, and the funds so provided appear to have been disproportionate to the investment requirements of the private sector; they were certainly disproportionate to the niggardly growth in private industrial employment. Lastly, with the very large amount of funds extended to the private sector, there was hardly any worthwhile impact on the investment climate in general and on employment growth in particular, partly because of preference for more capital-intensive projects and partly because the funds were siphoned off through inflated project costs and cost over-runs by the project promoters in an atmosphere of governmental laxity, financial indiscipline both in government and private sectors, and liberal availability of public funds at relatively cheap cost.

Table 23 depicts the trends in three key dimensions of industrial activity, viz, output, employment and investment in the private manufacturing sector. Following the sizeable cut-back in public sector investment in the mid-sixties, there was an immediate setback to output in many basic and capital goods industries mainly in the private sector such as steel pipes and tubes, steel castings and forgings, heavy structurals, many items of industrial machinery, machine tools, metallurigical and other heavy equipment, commercial vehicles and the entire railway equipment industry. This was also reflected in significant underutilisation of capacity in all of them, ranging from 50 per cent to 75 per cent.[40] Many of them have continued to experience serious demand constraints and hence, their output has hardly improved. Output growth in the major traditional industries has also been sluggish, as a result of which the General Index of Industrial Output made very slow progress during the decade 1966 to 1975-76.[41] The situation relating to employment growth in the private sector organised industry has been worse still, as discussed earlier.

By contrast investible funds absorbed by the private manufacturing sector have been disproportionately large. The rate of gross fixed assets formation (at current values) in respect of the RBI sample of medium and large public limited companies in the private sector had worked out to 10 per cent during the period from 1950-51 to 1968-69. Subsequently, only for a short period of four years from 1968-69 to 1971-72 that the gross fixed assets formation rate receded a bit; it ranged from 6.8 per cent to 7.4 per cent during this period. As this

Table 23: Key Indicators of Private Investment, Output and Employment in the Industrial Sector

Year	Gross Fixed Assets (Rupees Crores)	Gross Fixed Assets Formation at Currrent Prices* (Rupees Crores)	Gross Fixed Assets Formation at Current Prices (Per Cent)	Gross Fixed Assets Formation Reduced to 1960-61 Prices (Per Cent)	Percentage Rates of (at currrent prices): Net Fixed Assets Formation	Gross Capital Formation	Net Capital Formation	Percentage Growth in Industrial Output (General Index)	Percentage Growth in Private Sector Employment**	Debt-Equity Ratio
(1)	(2)	(3)	(4)	(5)	(6)	(7)	(8)	(9)	(10)	(11)
1950-51	550,69	—	—	—	—	—	—	—	—	—
1951-52	582,98	32,29	5.9	—	2.5	11.1	11.7	—	—	—
1952-53	628,87	45,89	7.9	—	7.0	3.0	0.6	3.1	—	—
1953-54	677,23	48,36	7.7	—	7.3	3.6	1.5	2.6	—	—
1954-55	740,69	63,46	9.4	—	9.9	7.5	6.8	6.8	—	—
1955-56	825,86	85,17	11.5	—	13.9	10.2	10.6	10.6	—	—
1955-56	950,95	—	—	—	—	—	—	—	—	—
1956-57	1089,70	138,75	14.6	—	18.8	16.9	20.2	8.8	—	—
1957-58	1268,38	178,68	16.4	—	8.3	14.3	9.1	4.2	—	—
1958-59	1417.42	149,04	11.8	—	25.2	8.4	14.3	3.4	—	—
1959-60	1523,32	105,90	7.5	—	6.5	6.1	5.0	8.5	—	—
1960-61	1645,94	122,62	8.1	—	3.9	10.6	9.0	11.3	—	—
1960-61	1812,71	—	—	—	—	—	—	—	—	18.4
1961-62	2000,11	187,40	10.3	9.9	8.5	10.5	9.5	9.2	1.0	17.6
1962-63	2191,48	191,37	9.6	8.9	7.7	9.3	8.1	9.7	7.2	17.2
1963-64	2424,58	233,10	10.6	9.6	9.1	9.7	8.5	8.3	4.6	18.3
1964-65	2647,67	233,09	9.2	8.5	6.7	9.4	8.0	8.6	5.6	18.7
1965-66	2886,48	230,60	8.7	7.5	7.0	10.2	9.6	19.2	6.9	19.7

(Contd)

Table 23 (Contd)

(1)	(2)	(3)	(4)	(5)	(6)	(7)	(8)	(9)	(10)	(11)
1965-66	3143,10	—	—	—	—	—	—	—	—	27.2
1966-67	3574,28	331,44	10.5	9.0	14.5	13.3	13.5	(–)0.9	(–)2.8	33.3
1967-68	3896,86	322,88	9.3	7.7	7.0	9.2	8.1	(–)0.7	(–)1.1	34.5
1968-69	4189.97	294,59	7.8	6.3	5.0	6.0	3.8	6.4	1.9	35.3
1969-70	4497,55	305,80	7.5	5.9	3.9	7.5	5.6	7.1	3.2	33.8
1970-71	4805,87	304,26	6.9	5.1	2.9	8.8	7.4	4.6	1.8	31.5
1970-71	5099,43	—	—	—	—	—	—	4.2	—	43.0
1971-72	5483,24	376,21	7.4	5.8	3.8	6.2	7.9	5.8	0.3	42.0
1972-73	5979,32	467,74	8.5	6.4	6.6	8.2	6.2	1.6	3.1	41.7
1973-74	6524,95	525,40	8.8	6.1	7.5	8.6	11.1	2.1	1.8	41.1
1974-75	7274,79	690,94	10.7	5.9	12.6	12.1	20.2	4.4	(–)1.8[R]	38.7
1975-76	8043,72	747,23	10.4	5.6	10.1	9.5	7.3	10.0	1.0[P]	40.8

Notes: R = Revised estimates. P = Provisional. (–) = Not available. * Adjusted for revaluation. ** Organised manufacturing sector.

Sources: (a) For columns (2) to (4), (6) to (8) and (11), see the Reserve Bank of India's regular studies on the *Finances of Medium and Large Public Limited Companies*. (Data cover only those sample serieses.)

(b) For column (5), see CSO's *National Accounts Statistics: 1960-61 to 1974-75.* (Here deflator is based on gross fixed capital formation at 1960-61 and current prices and not domestic capital formation.)

(c) For columns (9) and (10), see earlier tables on Industrial Output and Employment.

period saw a shift in favour of larger inventories, even the decline in the rate of fixed assets formation was largely made good, resulting in continued high rate of gross capital formation. In any case, the gross fixed assets formation itself improved almost to its historical level–nearly 9 per cent in 1972-73 and 1973-74 and over 10 per cent in 1974-75 and 1975-76.

It is true that these rates have been based on the figures of gross fixed assets formation at current prices. When the same are reduced to 1960-61 prices as per the CSO's implicit investment deflator for gross fixed capital formation, it is found that the gross fixed assets formation of the companies sector works out to a steady annual rate of about or over 6.0 per cent since 1968-69 which compares with the average rate of a little over 8.7 per cent for the preceding seven-year period since 1960-61. The rate of assets formation in real terms during the recent period has been only slightly lower than that in the earlier period; it has certainly been far higher than the rates of employment and output growth.

During the entire decade from 1965-66 to 1975-76, industrial output in the private sector is estimated to have increased by 30 per cent[42] and industrial employment of the private sector under the head of 'manufacturing' rose only by about 7.4 per cent,[43] but gross fixed assets formation (with due adjustments for revaluation following devaluation of currency) of the medium and large public limited companies in the private sector galloped by 130 per cent in current value and by 70 per cent when the asset formation is deflated at 1960-61 prices. This brings out the enormity of economic powers acquired by the private corporate sector–about Rs 4,500 crore addition to gross fixed assets in current value in a decade–without at the same time being made to undertake the most crucial socio-economic responsibility of employment generation.

This brings us to the second issue of the sources of these funds, particularly the role played by the term-financing institutions in this respect. A preponderant part of private industrial investment in recent years has been financed by loans from public sector financial institutions. The contributions from share capital and internal savings of the companies have been meagre. The promoters' contributions to the project costs have been allowed, as a policy, to be kept at unusually low levels. Secondly, the colossal amounts of loans granted by the term-financing institutions have been palpably disproportionate to the meagre impact seen in industrial investment and output growth in real terms and particularly in employment. Thirdly, the easy availability of investible funds at relatively cheap cost, accompanied by the low personal stake of the promoters, seems to have induced higher capital intensity, siphoning off of funds and general lack of cost consciousness. Lastly, this phenomenon of capital wastage and diversion accompanied by distortions in the patterns of investment and production has been encouraged by an atmosphere of laxity in government discipline and regulations for the private sector.

This brings us to the crucial question as to whether such neck-deep involvement of the public financial institutions in the private sector projects has been desirable. The answer may differ depending on one's views about the extent to which the public sector should help in building private assets in the country. However, what is unlikely to be controversial is the nature of certain specific socio-economic benefits expected from private investment primarily based on public sector advances.

An objective reading of the situation would present the following disquieting trends. First, despite such colossal amounts of public sector lendings since the mid-sixties, there has hardly been any significant impact on industrial investment, output and employment; this is distinctly so with regard to employment growth in the private industrial sector (which includes employment even in very small factories). Curiously enough, this sluggishness in industrial investment, in output and particularly in employment, has coincided with a period when term-financing institutions and commercial banks have sunk disproportionately large amounts of scarce investible funds in private sector enterprises.

Secondly, it could be argued a priori that in fact the easy availability of funds on a massive scale has been at least partly responsible for the galloping projects costs for, otherwise, in a situation of recession and sluggish investment demand when the supplies of key investment goods have been easy, there should have been no reason for such increase in project costs. The argument that rising wage costs have been responsible for pushing up prices of investment goods can be only partly true because in every one of the basic and capital goods industries, total remuneration to employees (including non-worker employees) has been as low as 16 per cent or less.[44]

If such colossal funds disbursed to the private sector had resulted in better utilisation of capacity in the basic and capital goods sectors, there would have probably been some reduction in their production costs. Also, rise in import cost cannot be the explanation because we are considering the increase in investment cost considerably after the devaluation of the Indian rupee in 1966. We are considering particularly the period since the beginning of the seventies, when disbursements by term-financing institutions (for sectors other than the public sector) have gone up at a compound rate of 25 per cent per annum with no perceptible impact on the investment climate. It is not doubted that some of these factors including the oil price increases of 1973 and 1974 may have played a part in cost escalation, but obviously all of them put together cannot explain the absorption by the private industrial sector of such massive amounts of investible funds without making any perceptible impact on the overall investment climate generally and on the ouput of basic and capital goods industries in particular, leave alone on employment.

This situation can perhaps be explained by two plausible developments of the period, viz, the preference for higher capital intensity by project promoters and the siphoning off of funds through infalted project costs and fictitious cost overruns. There is some indirect evidence on both of these possibilities.

During the years 1970 to 1972 when there was relative stability in investment cost, capital per worker in the IDBI-assisted concerns had shown a steady increase. Interestingly, the highest increase of nearly 90 per cent in capital per worker in just two years, 1971 and 1972, took place in the traditional 'textiles (including jute)' industry. Similar increase have taken place in many other industries such as fertilisers, manufacture of machinery (both electrical and non-electrical), chemical and other chemical products, and basic metal industries. While this is a very limited piece of information on the subject with many limitations, it nevertheless provides some indication of the trend in regard to the sharp decline in employment content of medium and large-sized projects financed by the term-financing institutions.

The liberal availability of public funds at relatively cheap cost has apparently also encouraged promoters to siphon off funds, through inflation of project costs, fictitious cost overruns and such other devices. The use of these devices in turn appears to have got a fillip in the atmosphere of permissiveness in public policies concerning private investment and from the manner of disposition of the nation's investible resources, whether in the public or private sector. It is, of course, almost impossible to present any systematic data on this subject, because the siphoning off of funds is effected under technically permissible heads of expenditure and the published data would, therefore, neatly hide the fact. Nevertheless, if the use of such devices have gone on uninhibitedly on a sizeable scale for a fairly long period, as they seem to have since the mid-sixties, it would be difficult for it to get hidden entirely.

The entire situation is aptly summed up in an in-depth study of the trends in corporate finances in recent years:

Despite such large inflow of funds from external sources, which has the effect of reducing the stake of the promoters of companies, the growth of employment in organised industry in the private sector has been dismal. Data on employment in organised industry show that total employment in the private sector was 68.49 lakhs in March 1973, whereas by March 1976 this had actually declined to 68.30 lakhs. During the same period public sector employment increased by 11.2 per cent from 111.75 lakhs to 133.18 lakhs.

These data bring out the rising capital intensity of industry which has been encouraged by government policies. The most important of these policies are (i) asset-based tax incentive schemes, such as development rebate and initial depreciation allowance and (ii) liberal grants of loan capital and other investible funds by the public sector financial institutions at relatively cheap rates of interest, resulting in (a) higher capital intensity and poor employment content of investment, (b) encouragement of uneconomical use of scarce capital, (c) reduction of the stake of the promoters and consequently the absence of cost consciousness among them, (d) substantial siphoning off of funds from the public limited companies into the promoters' proprietary concerns, and (e) growing concentration of ownership of corporate enterprises.

Despite their neck-deep involvement in the financing of private sector investment, the public financial institutions have not been able to prevent even to the slightest extent the distortions in the production and investment pattern and in the employment content of investment or the monopoly and concentration of economic power. The easy availability of public funds has made leeches of the semi-feudal entrepreneurial classes in the country. Sickness in industry is attributable mainly to this phenomenon as is evident from the fact that generally those in control of sick units have become richer and richer even as their units have been brought to the verge of closure. It is widely known how most promoters of projects clandestinely recoup their contribution to the capital in the projects' construction stage itself. These and other malpractices are greatly facilitated by intercorporate investments and interlocking of directorships. The public financial institutions have not been able to insist upon some of the most obvious reforms such as banning of intercorporate investments and insisting that no person shall be director of more than one company. These measures, particularly the second one, would also encourage the induction of professional managers as directors of companies.[45]

Relaxation of Industrial Controls

The above analysis brings home a crucial point, namely, that mere pumping in of large financial resources without a sound policy direction regarding their deployment is sure to turnout to be counter-productive. This vacuum in policy has emerged precisely since the mid-sixties. Following the strains and stresses experienced by the economy due to the droughts of 1965 and 1966, a view was canvassed very successfully, that industrial controls were inhibiting production and growth and that, therefore, the controls had to be relaxed. *The Economic Survey for 1966-67* reported that after the major devaluation of the rupee 'a number of changes were made in the regulations governing the establishment and utilisation of industrial capacity. There were modifications in the industrial licensing regulations, the import control system, and controls on distribution and prices of industrial products.'[46]

But it was not realised that as mere additional funds could not achieve higher investment and growth, the relaxation of industrial controls would also fail to do the trick. It was clear to any careful observer of the economic scene that laxity in government regulation of the private sector would only further accentuate the distortions in the economy. As had been brought out by the Mahalanobis Committee, the Monopolies Enquiry Commission, R K Hazari and finally, by the Dutt Committee, if despite the existence of a fairly comprehensive system of controls during the Second and Third Plans, there had arisen certain distortions such as inappropriate production and investment patterns, pre-emption of industrial licences, public funds and other scarce real sources by the large industrial houses, and concentration of economic power mainly because the system generally favoured the large entrepreneurs, there was no reason to believe that removal and relaxation of controls would reduce the power of these entrepreneurs and eliminate the distortions. Once the process of relaxations began, the vicious circle of relaxations leading to further economic difficulties and distortions and these in turn creating pressure on the government to loosen discipline and control, has passed through many rounds during the past decade.

One of the most crucial relaxations systematically carried out since the mid-sixties relates to industrial licensing policy. This potent instrument designed to establish some priorities for private sector investment and output has been systematically blunted over the years. In May 1966, a major departure was noticed in the thinking of the government in this respect. Reflecting this thinking, a Departmental Committee of the period came up with a curious answer to the problem of alleged heavy workload imposed on the government by the licensing system: '...this [reduction of workload] could be achieved *inter alia* by relaxing controls to the maximum extent possible, retaining only those which are essential for the implementation of Plans and policies'. The Committee laid down two principles for such relaxation: (i) '....generally speaking, industries which do not involve the import of capital goods or of raw materials should be exempted from the licensing provisions'; and (ii) 'it should, by and large, be left to the economic judgment of the entrepreneur to decide whether or not he will enter in these fields and make an investment and to what extent. In these fields, the targets laid down by the Planning Commission would serve as indicative targets and as a factor to be considered by the prospective investor in his assessment of demand and other economic data.'[47] Following this new thinking, government announced in May 1966 a list of industries which were exempted from industrial licensing; this list was enlarged in July 1966 and again in November 1966 and by May 1969 as many as 41 industries had been delicensed.[48]

These considerations in effect went counter to the basic framework of regulating and channelising domestic industrial investment by the private sector on the basis of plan priorities. First, the primary purpose of control was to ensure proper allocation of scarce resources, whether domestic or foreign. The domestic availabilities of investment goods having increased sizeably during the first three plan periods and in the absence of controls on the deployment of domestic funds, the scope for misallocation of investment had enormously increased.

Secondly, it was naive to expect that investment decisions, when they are left to the economic judgment of the entrepreneur, would result in establishment of the right kind of priorities and ensure a socially desirable pattern of investment and output. This was particularly so when the personal stake of the private entrepreneurs was being reduced to insignificant proportions as a result of cheap and liberal finance provided by the public sector financial institutions.

Despite it being so obvious that the principles enunciated by the Departmental Committee were antithetical to a developmental strategy based on economic planning, the government had accepted them and followed them in its industrial licensing policies almost throughout the period since the mid-sixties. This new thinking was endorsed by the Planning Commission, whereas the Dutt Committee placed renewed emphasis on the instrument of licensing as essential for industrial planning.[49] 'The Planning Commission had suggested further extension of delicensing to cover all industries which would not require much foreign exchange either for setting up new capacity or for current production. As against this, the ILPIC had recommended a purposeful but clear-cut use of industrial licensing and had even recommended reintroduction of licensing in the delicensed industries' [Paranjape, 1976].

The final version of the Fourth Plan, which reproduced the government decision on the Dutt Committeee Report, also reiterated the above principles: (i) 'Regulation of industrial development has to be considered primarily in relation to the allocation of foreign exchange... The supply of a variety of industrial commodities has considerably eased and the need is one of stimulating demand and production. With the broader industrial base and growing availability of capital equipment and raw materials from within the country, the need to control further expansion in industries which are largely based on domestic resources has less importance'; and (ii) 'within the broad framework of control in strategic areas, there is advantage in allowing the market much fuller play'.[50] That such an approach would put at naught the whole concept of industrial planning based on national priorities and optimal use of scarce domestic resources was predicted by many, including the Lok Sabha's Estimates Committee (1972-73): 'Until March 1970, government were in the matter of industrial licensing following the policy of capacity restraints on the basis of indicative demand and production targets given in the Five-Year Plan documents. Therefore, at least in some cases, the shortages could have been due to production targets being based on a faulty assessment of the demand by the Planning Commission. To meet the situation, government have, since March 1970 given up the policy of applying rigidly capacity considerations in the issue of industrial licenses. The Committee are, however, of the view that the new policy of freeing industrial licensing from the limitations of assessed demand and indicative production targets given in the plan may be justified as a short-term measure to tide over the current shortages of goods but in the long run this policy is fraught with danger inasmuch as it would generate undue pressure on scarce resources and may well lead to excess capacity. Besides, it would set at naught the whole concept of development through planning.'[51]

Despite the position being so clear, the government went about relaxing industrial licensing regulations.[52] A lackadaisical attitude was exhibited towards working of the licensing system as a whole after 1972. It started with the most obnoxious of the recent relaxations. A scheme was introduced initially for 54 selected industries in January 1972 and subsequently extended to 11 more industries in October 1972 whereby industrial undertakings were permitted to get their licences endorsed for increased capacity in terms of relaxations for fuller utilisation of installed capacities. This meant in a good many cases outright regularisation of illegal capacities built. The Industry Ministry's Annual Report for 1972-73 reported that by December

1972 as many as 787 applications had been received under the scheme and they covered a wide range of industries like boilers and steam generating plants, prime movers, electrical equipment, textile machinery, ball and roller bearings, electronic instruments, paints and enamels, chemicals and pharmaceuticals, transport equipment including automobile components and ancillaries, etc.

A recent study by the Estimates Committee has brought to light how government has taken a very lenient view of the creation of capacity much beyond what was licensed. 'Information furnished to us by the DGTD indicating cases where the actual capacity is much beyond the licensed capacity provides further evidence of the gradual erosion of the control expected to be exercised by industrial licensing over the creation of capacity in differernt industries.'[53]

Yet another set of industries have been totally exempted from industrial licensing with some conditions. Diversification of production has been permitted in industrial machinery, machine tools, electrical equipment, steel casting and steel forgings industries though within the overall licensed capacity of a particular undertaking. Cement manufacturers have been permitted to fabricate cement machinery for their own use. Fifteen engineering industries have been allowed to expand automatically at the rate of 25 per cent in the Fifth Five-Year Plan period (5 per cent per annum) over their licensed capacity. This was in addition to the normal permissible limit of 25 per cent expansion over the licensed or registered capacity. In cases where increased output is in consequence of the replacement of old equipment, 'necessary amendment in the industrial licence will be granted liberally'. Industrial undertakings would be allowed to expand capacity based on the results obtained by their research and development efforts. In this respect, undertakings covered under MRTP Act and FERA would also be covered on merits.

In the light of all these relaxations, the question has been raised: 'What is left now of the licensing system? In the middle and small-scale sectors, there is no licensing. The monopoly and large industrial houses and foreign companies have to take out industrial licences but once they acquire a licence, they can build any capacity–to the extent of 100 per cent in excess of the formal licensed limit in the name of diversification, 25 per cent by normal expansion, another 25 per cent in five years by automatic expansion and, lastly, to virtually any extent by unauthorisedly installing capacity which will be regularised promptly by the administrative ministries. Would it not have been more straightforward to have abolished licensing altogether?'[54]

These relaxations were all in addition to the streamlined system of industrial approvals, whereby a majority of the applications for industrial licences have been cleared over the past few years, and as a result of which the number of industrial licences issued rose from 363 in 1970 to 626 in 1971, 725 in 1973-74, 1038 in 1974-75 and 1026 in 1975-76. By that time, as the Industry Ministry's *Annual Report for 1975-76* reported, against 2,500 outstanding industrial licence applications at the end of 1973 and 1,000 applications at the end of 1974, the number of such applications at the end of 1975 was only 168.[55] Hence in 1976-77, only 641 licences were issued. 'What one needs to be sceptical about, however, is the attempt to elevate the whole operation to the level of a major initiative in the field of industrial planning. This attempt is based on a number of very questionable premises: that the administrative procedures which are sought to be streamlined can exert a major influence on industrial investment, output and employment; that it is the delays in the granting of various clearances and approvals, not the actual content of these clearances and approvals, which are the bane of industrial planning in the country; and finally, that the delays themselves occur only, or mainly, because of inefficient procedures.'[56]

The damage done by these relaxations to industrial development between the mid-sixties and the mid-seventies can be summed up thus: (i) The building up of illegal capacity and its subsequent regularisation have become a regular feature of the industrial scene. (ii) The scope for diversification and expansion has created such vast possibilities for creation of additional capacities by the large and medium scale industries that the whole system of licensing has been reduced to a farce. (iii) Investment propositions are almost entirely left to be decided by private entrepreneurs without any consideration for priorities, which has ties built in different industries. (iv) Output and investment patterns have increasingly moved against consumption goods. (v) The scope for diversification and expansion as well as the tendency to build unauthorised capacities by the large and foreign firms have done incalculable harm to the investment climate, particularly because of uncertainty arising from lack of knowledge about the existing and prospective capacities in particular industries for new entrepreneurs. (v) Finally, the concentration of industrial capacity as well as that of economic power has increased sizeably.

Diversification and automatic growth in specific situations may be desirable, but indiscriminate expansion with or without licensing has created a series of problems for the metallurgical industries as well as many others. Unfortunately, even the term-financing institutions, which have provided enormous amounts of public funds, have not been able to enforce even a modicum of priorities in this respect. One of the important causes of growing 'sickness' in industries related to this indiscriminate expansion with the help of public funds and with very meagre personal stake of the promoters. All of these put together have brought industry to an impasse and generated considerable uncertainty in the investment climate.

Concurrently, there has been a gradual shift of investment in favour of commodities which have relatively low social priority. In the textile industry, it is the man-made fabrics sector that has absorbed the bulk of the investment since the mid-sixties. For instance, in the 'silk and rayon textiles' industry, net fixed assets formation ranged from 4.6 per cent to 2.2 per cent between 1962-63 to 1965-66 but since then in all the years from 1966-67 to 1974-75 it has ranged from 6.2 per cent to 16.7 per cent. The man-made fibre industry has been listed as a 'core' industry for licensing purpose. Similarly, in 'breweries and distilleries' the rate of net fixed assets formation worked out to an average of 10.8 per cent per annum for the entire period from 1966-67 to 1975-76 when the corresponding rate for the 'cotton textiles' industry averaged 5.6 per cent for the same period.[57] Because of the very broad industrial classification adopted for many of the macro-level studies, it is almost impossible to disaggregate the picture sufficiently and indicate the investment trends in regard to many other non-essential products. But the overall picture is unmistakably one of serious distortion in the production pattern during the past few years.

This had to be so because the licensing authorities have deliberately permitted it. Let us take three or four extreme examples of room air-conditioners, refrigerators, passenger cars and breweries. *The Guidelines for Industries for 1973-74* had said that the capacity for room air-conditioners as well as domestic refrigerators would be trebled by 1978-79 from 35,780 to 90,000 and from 1.85 lakhs to 4.80 lakhs.[58] On passenger cars, the *Annual Report of the Ministry of Industrial Development* put it quite explicitly: 'In the case of passenger cars, there is still a large gap between the demand and indigenous production. With a view to filling the gap, steps have been taken to create additional capacity. In pursuance of a decision announced in Parliament on 10th August, 1970, to encourage growth of indigenous talent and resources by issuing letters of intent to such of the parties in the private sector as were prepared to take up the manufacture of passenger cars based on completely indigenous design without requiring import of capital goods or allocation of foreign exchange for components or raw materials, eleven parties have been granted letters of intent for manufacture of cars.'[59]

The following two examples of (i) cosmetics and toiletry, and (ii) the beer industry, reflect the height of official connivance in the emergence of a patently distorted production and investment structure. On the import content, however small, permitted for cosmetics and toiletry industries, some data have been cited earlier. It is also officially admitted that these industries are largely dominated by foreign concerns and MRTP houses. On top of it all, these very industries have been allowed to continuously expand their output beyond their licensed capacity. According to the statistics contained in the Industry Ministry's *Annual Report for 1977-78*,[60] 'The eleven tooth paste units in the organised industry had installed capacity of 4,193 tonnes, whereas their output was 9,079 tonnes in 1977, or more than double the sanctioned capacity. The same is true of a number of other industries such as soap, talcum and face powder, tooth powder, etc, which are dominated by foreign companies and large houses. Output in these industries in 1976 and 1977 was in excess of the licensed capacity. In these circumstances, where large industrial units are allowed to expand capacity unauthorisedly and the illegally installed capacity is subsequently regularised by government, there is little hope for village and small industries.'[61]

Coming to the case of beer industry, the Industry Ministry's *Report for 1972-73* wrote thus: 'As a result of the announcement of liberalised licensing policy of 1970 a number of beer units have been licensed and registered. At present 11 breweries are in operation with a total capacity of 44,342 kilo litre per year. License/letters of intent have been granted to 9 units for a total capacity of 44,000 kilo litre per year. Besides 24 units with a total capacity of 100,500 kilo litre per year have been registered with the DGTD out of which 12 units having a capacity of 46,340 kilo litre were registered during 1972. These schemes are under implementation. The production of beer is likely to increase substantially in the coming years as new units are expected to go into production.'[62] Many more such examples could be cited of brisk investment and expansion of capacity in low priority areas with official support: luxury hotels, soft drinks, cosmetics, baby food, room airconditioners, domestic refrigerators, passenger cars and so on.

Such is the story of the distorted development of the decade since the mid-sixties with all the attendant perversities. Obviously it has done considerable damage to the developmental processes and a good part of the damage appears to be of a permanent nature because there is some degree of irreversibility about many of these distortions under the present socio-economic set up. How will the economy move from here and what is required to be done to recover the lost ground at least partially are vital questions but they are not the subject matter of this study, though our analysis suggests by implication the path policy-makers have to tread if any progress is to be achieved in regard to the objective of removal of poverty and unemployment.

NOTES

[The author expresses his gratitude to the National Institute of Bank Management for the facilities provided for undertaking this research study. The views expressed here are entirely the personal views of the author.]

1 One such important study is that of T N Srinivasan and N S S Narayana: 'Economic Performance Since the Third Plan and Its Implications for Policy', *Economic and Political Weekly,* Annual Number, February 1977, pp 225-39.

2 In this paper the author has attempted to include, to the extent data are available, the year 1976-77 also as it appropriately belongs to the period of analysis chosen in the Pai Panandiker-Varde study. Data on saving and investment ratios are from RBI, *Annual Report 1976-77*, p 3. The CSO's quick Estimates for 1976-77 have confirmed this phenomenon.

3 *Economic Survey, 1975-76*, p 6.

4 Ibid, p 6.

5 Ibid, p 224.

6 See *Economic Survey, 1976-77*, p 59.

7 'Land Reforms: Tasks Ahead', *The Economic Times,* September 11, 1975.

8 *Draft Fourth Five-Year Plan,* 1969-70 (Part II), p 43.

9 *Draft Fifth Five-Year Plan,* 1974-79, p 23.

10 C H Hanumantha Rao, *Technological Change and Distribution of Gains in Indian Agriculture,* Institute of Economic Growth and Macmillan Co of India Ltd, Delhi, 1975, pp 139-40.
Also see S L Shetty, 'Deployment of Commercial Bank and Other Institutional Credit: A Note on Strutural Changes', *Economic and Political Weekly,* May 8, 1976, p 701. Quoted in it is also C D Datey's observation: 'Even in co-operatively advanced States, co-operative credit has been flowing pronouncedly in favour of the large cultivators to the neglect of medium and small farmers.' See *Industrial Times,* June 9, 1975, p 29.

11 See the results of Geoffrey Swenson and K Subbarao quoted in M L Dantwala, 'Agricultural Policy in India since Independence', *Indian Journal of Agricultural Economics,* October-December 1976, p 40.

12 The Government of India's latest *Economic Survey* has succinctly put it: 'Till now, although there has been a great deal of concern for employment, employment generating programmes have always been conceived of as appendages rather than as an integral part of the development strategy. The emphasis has been on special programmes for generating employment.' *Economic Survey: 1976-77,* p 48. The same thought was expressed in *Economic Survey: 1975-76.* p 8.

13 'Distribution of Rural Income', *Economic and Political Weekly,* September 20, 1975, p 1493. See also *Economic Survey, 1975-76,* p 8.

14 CMIE, *Basic Statistics Relating to the Indian Economy,* Vol I: All-India (October 1976), Table 13.3.

15 'Distribution of Rural Incomes', *Economic and Political Weekly,* September 20, 1975, pp 1495.

16 This information is being collected regularly on a quarterly basis since March 1961 by the Directorate General of Employment and Training, Ministry of Labour and Employment, Government of India, through their Employment Market Information (EMI) under the provisions of the Employment Exchanges (Compulsory Notification of Vacancies) Act 1959 from all establishments in the public sector and from those private sector establishments in the non-agricultural sector employing 25 or more workers up to March 1966, or 10 or more workers thereafter. Those not covered are agriculture, self-employed household establishments, establishments in the private sector employing less than 10 workers and defence forces. For a detailed study, see S R Krishna Iyer, 'Employment Growth in the Organised Sector', *Reserve Bank of India Bulletin,* August 1970.

17 In fact, it should be lower because a part of the increase is statistical arising from the extension of the coverage also to units employing 10 to 24 workers.

18 The well-known limitations are: (i) there has occurred considerable improvement in coverage which is reflected in a steady increase in the number of Employment Exchanges covered; (ii) all the unemployed do not get themselves registered with the Exchanges; (iii) there are at times registrations by those already in some employment; (iv) some of those registered also belong to 'rural' areas; and (v) despite the Employment Exchanges (Compulsory Notification of Vacancies) Act enforced in 1959, requiring all public sector units employing 25 or more workers to notify their vacancies to the Exchanges, many employers do not do so. Nevertheless, the Employment Exchange statistics are reliable indicator in this respect particularly because by the early 1960s, a fair degree of coverage was achieved and every district in the country was having at least one Exchange. Planning Commission (Government of India), *Report of the Committee of Experts on Unemployment Estimates,* New Delhi, 1970, pp 27-28. See also 'Growth of Employment: 1950-51 to 1968-69', *Reserve Bank of India Bulletin,* December 1969.

19 See Raj Krishna, 'Rural Unemployment: A Survey of Concepts and Estimates for India' (mimeo), April 1976. Quoted in A Vaidyanathan, *Indian Economy: Performance and Prospects',* Centre for Development Studies, Trivandrum.

20 See Raj Krishna's Presidential Address at the 32nd Annual Conference of the Indian Society of Agricultural Economics on 'Unemployment in India', *Indian Journal of Agricultural Economics,* January-March 1973, footnote on page 11.

21 Amartya Sen, *Dimensions of Unemployment in India.*

22 Raj Krishna, op cit, Table II, p 7. To quote Raj Krishna: 'I would earnestly urge that the widespread impression that no meaningful figures of the

magnitude of the unemployment problem in India are available has no basis... Including the wholly unemployed and the severely underemployed available for additional work nearly 2.15 crores of our workers are unemployed–about 1.93 crores in the rural areas and 22 lakhs in the urban areas.' Ibid, p 8.

23 Ministry of Labour and Rehabilitation (Government of India): *Report of the Committee on Unemployment,* Vol I, Part A, New Delhi, May 1973, pp 155-59.

24 Amartya Sen's other estimate which he calls the 'biggest estimates' came from the production approach suggesting about 42.4 million rural unemployed in 1971. Amartya Sen, op cit.

25 Dantwala Committee itself noted that the NSS procedure 'would have a tendency to underestimate the degree of unemployment actually prevailing ...'. Op cit, p 17. See also Raj Krishna (1973), op cit, p 8.

26 For instance, the average household size increased from 3.87 in rural areas and 2.63 urban areas for the top decile to 5.88 and 6.58, respectively, for the lowest expenditure group (0-5), according to the 20th Round of the NSS (July 1965-June 1966). See NSS, *Tables with Notes on Household Consumer Expenditure, Enterprise and Demographic Particulars,* New Delhi, 1975, pp 35 and 93.

27 Though the wholesale price index has1960-61 = 100 as base, it should not make any difference as there was price stability between 1960-61 (99.8) and 1961-62 (100.0).

28 K M Tripathi and A S Bharadwaj, op cit, p 1463.

29 Size of the Fifth Plan investment as originally proposed and as revised are shown in Table below:

Table: Fifth Plan Investment as Originally Proposed and Revised

(Rs crores)

	As Proposed in the Draft Fifth Plan (at 1972-73 Prices)	As Revised in the Final Fifth Plan (at 1974-75 Prices for 1974-75 and at 1975-76 Prices for the Subsequent Four Years)	Revised Plan Investment Deflated to 1972-73 Prices
Public Sector	31400	36703	22987
Private Sector	16161	27048	16940
Total	47561	63751	39927

The CSO's investment deflator with base 1960-61=100 rose from 191.4 in 1971-72 to 281.8 in 1974-75 and to 305.6 in 1975-76. Accordingly, the real investment in the final version of the Plan gets reduced by about 16.0 per cent from the original amount; the shortfall in the Public Sector works out to 27 per cent. Secondly, even this size in the revised version was made possible because of the striking increase effected in private sector investment, which was just a formalisation of the higher savings of the households sector revealed in the meantime; it was not known as to how such savings and consequential investment would partake the form of Plan investment.

30 We are aware that this is a rough comparison as NDP is not the same thing as net disposable income of the public sector. Even so the argument is very much valid.

31 Development expenditure comprises expenditure for the functional category of 'social and economic services'.

32 This was not due to rising debt services either. In the Central budget, if there are interest payments on the expenditure side, there are also a sizable amount of interest receipts on the receipts side.

33 Unallocable tansfers are those current transfers even outside the head of 'social and economic services' (development expenditure) in the two-way Economic and Functional Classification of the Central budget. See, for example, *Economic-cum-Functional Classification of the Central Government Budget, 1977-78,* pp 18-19.

34 *Fourth Five-Year Plan 1969-74,* p 370.

35 Ibid, p 369.

36 Ibid, pp 369-70.

37 Ibid, pp 369-70.

38 *Draft Fifth Five-Year Plan: 1974-79,* p 92.

39 Government of India, *Economic Survey: 1971-72,* p 40.

40 See M V Raghavachari: 'Excess Capacity and Production Potential in Selected Industries in India', *Reserve Bank of India Bulletin,* April 1969, pp 471-92 and 'On Recent Recessionary Trends in Organised Industry', *Reserve Bank of India Bulletin,* July 1968. See also S L Shetty: 'Recent Recovery in Industrial Output', *ReserveBank of India Bulletin,* May 1969, pp 615-32.

41 While separate figures of output in the public and private sectors have not been presented in the Table, there is evidence to show that the performance of the public sector in this respect during the past decades has been relatively better than that of the private sector. See, for instance, the behaviour of GDP orginating in 'manufacturing' segments of the two sectors. CSO *National Accounts Statistics: 1960-61 to 1974-75,* pp 14-15 and 48-49.

42 Total industrial output expanded by 42 per cent during this period. Increase in private sector output has been estimated on the basis of CSO's estimates of net domestic product by industry of origin.

43 Coverage of employment data is obviously far wider; they include under 'manufacturing' all non-farm establishments employing 25 or more workers on a compulsory basis and even those employing 10 to 24 workers on a voluntary basis. According to the Annual Survey of Industries (1974-75), factory employment in private organisations, other than 'companies', accounted for one-fourth of the total private sector factory employment and this is also growing. Ibid, p 12.

44 See 'Finances of Medium and Large Public Limited Companies', *Reserve Bank of India Bulletin,* September 1977, p 551. For earlier years, see S L Shetty: 'Trends in Wages and Salaries and Profits of the Private Corporate Sector', *Economic and Political Weekly,* October 13, 1973, pp 1864-90.

45 See 'No Check on Managements', *Economic and Political Weekly*, January 7, 1978, pp 8-10.

46 Government of India, *Economic Survey, 1966-67,* p 15. 'After the devaluation of the Rupee in June 1966, certain follow-up measures have been taken which include liberalisation of imports and exemption of certain industries from the licensing provisions of the Industries (Development and Regulation) Act, 1951.' Ministry of Industrial Development, *Annual Report, 1966-67.*

47 These experts are quoted in Government of India (Ministry of Industrial Development), *Report of the Industrial Licensing Policy Enquiry Committee, Main Report* (Chairman: Subimal Dutt), July 1969, p 35.

48 Ibid, pp AL-AP. For the list, see Indian Investment Centre: *Industrial Licensing: A Guide on Procedures,* March 1968, pp 23-24.

49 'If industrial development is to take place as a part of an overall development Plan and at the same time we have to attempt to achieve the objectives enunciated in the Constitution and spelt out in the Industrial Policy Resolution of 1956, it is essential to have an instrument for industrial planning as the one forged through the Industries (Development and Regulation) Act, 1951.' The Dutt Committee Report, op cit, p 185.

50 Planning Commission (Government of India), *Fourth Five-Year Plan, 1969-74,* p 305.

51 Lok Sabha Secretariat, *Twenty-Seventh Report of the Estimates Committee* (1972-73), New Delhi, Februay 1973, p 5.

52 These facts are obtained from two main official sources, viz, (i) *Annual Report of the Union Ministry of Industrial Development*; and (ii) *Guidelines for Industries*, an annual publication introduced by the same ministry, beginning from 1973-74, the latest issue being for 1976-77.

53 *Report of the Industrial Licensing Policy Enquiry Committee, Main Report,* p 37.

54 See 'Elusive Investment and Output', *Economic and Political Weekly,* November 22, 1975, p 1785. A series of articles in this journal have presented a systematic account of the developments in this respect. See (i) 'After This Why Talk of Planning?', September 22, 1973, p 1699; (ii) 'Why Have Licensing?', November 10, 1973, p 1983; (iii) 'Industrial Development: Accent on Administrative Trivia', April 13, 1974, pp 585-87; (iv) 'Industry: End of Licensing', January 18, 1975, p 45; (v) 'Ashes of Licensing', July 17, 1976, p 1949; and 'Industry: On the Wrong Tracks', April 8, 1978, pp 601-02.

55 Ministry of Industry and Civil Supplies, Government of India, *Annual Report, 1975-76,* p vii.

56 'Why Have Licensing?', *Economic and Political Weekly,* November 10, 1973, p 1983.

57 Derived from RBI studies on company finances.

58 *Guidelines for Industries, 1973-74,* pp 162-63.

59 Ministry of Industrial Development: *Annual Report, 1972-73,* p 88-89.

60 Ministry of Industrial Development: *Annual Report; 1977-78,* p 226.

61 'Industry on the Wrong Tracks', *Economic and Political Weekly,* April 8, 1978, pp 601-02.

62 Ministry of Industrial Development: *Annual Report, 1972-73,* p 111.

REFERENCES

Dandekar, V M and Nilakantha Rath (1970): *Poverty in India,* The Ford Foundation, New Delhi, December.

Dantwala, M L (1976): 'Agricultural Policy in India since Independence', *IndianJournal of Agricultural Economics,* October-December.

Datta Roy Choudhury, Uma and Grace Majumdar (1977): 'Alternative Measures of Economic Development for Inter-State comparison: An Exploratory Study', paper submitted at the Eleventh General Conference of the Indian Association for Research in National Income and Wealth held at Shillong on October 28-31.

Dave, S A (1973): 'Measuring the Performance of Five-Year Plans', *Economic and Political Weekly,* July 28, pp 1357-59.

Divatia, V V (1976): 'Inequalities in Asset Distribution of Rural Households', *Reserve Bank Staff Occasional Papers,* June, Vol I, No 1, p 20.

Hanumantha Rao, C H (1976): 'Changes in the Structural Distribution of Land Ownership and Use (Since Independence)' (Rapporteur's Report), *Indian Journal of Agricultural Economics,* October-December, p 22.

– (1977): 'Agricultural Growth and Rural Poverty: Lessons from Past Experience', *Economic and Political Weekly,* Special Number, August, p 1369.

Laxminarayan, H and S S Tyagi (1976): 'Some Aspects of Size Distribution of Agricultural Holdings', *Economic and Political Weekly,* October 9, p 1639.

Minhas, B S (1974): *Planning and the Poor,* S Chand and Co, New Delhi.

Mukherjee, M, N Bhattacharya and G S Chatterjee (1974): 'Poverty in India: Measurement and Amelioration', *Commerce Pamphlet Series,* Bombay, January.

Mukherjee, M and G S Chatterjee (1973): 'On the Validity of NSS Estimates of Consumption Expenditure', a paper submitted at the Lucknow Conference of the Association for Research in National Income and Wealth.

Narain, Dharm (1972): 'Growth and Imbalance in Indian Agriculture', *Economic and Political Weekly,* Review of Agriculture, March, p A-3.

– (1976): *Growth of Productivity in Indian Agriculture*, Cornell University, June, p 1.

Pathak, R P, K R Ganapathy and Y U K Sarma (1977): 'Shifts in Pattern of Asset Holdings of Rural Households, 1961-62 to 1971-72', *Economic and Political Weekly,* March 19.

Pai Panandikar,V A and S A Varde (1977): 'The Indian Economy under the First Three Prime Ministers', *Prajnan,* April-June, Vol VI, No 2, pp 133-48.

Paranjape, H K (1976): *Poverty of Policy,* Somaiya Publications, p 113.

Raj, K N (1976): 'Growth and Stagnation in Industrial Development', *Economic and Political Weekly,* Annual Number, February, p 223.

Shah, C H (1976): 'Growth and Inequality in Agriculture, *Indian Journal of Agricultural Economics,* October-December.

Vaidyanathan, A (1974): 'Some Aspects of Inequalities in Living Standards in Rural India', quoted in Mukherjee *et al* (1974): op cit.

– (1977): 'Performance and Prospects of Crop Production in India', *Economic and Political Weekly,* Special Number, August, p 1355.

Annual Number February 1978

8

Industrial Development in India

Some Reflections on Growth and Stagnation

Deepak Nayyar

I

INTRODUCTION

AT first sight, the record of industrial growth in India since Independence appears impressive. In the quarter century from 1950 to 1975, industrial production more than quadrupled. What is more, this growth was accompanied by a marked diversification of the industrial structure, which is reflected in the wide range and complexity of goods now manufactured in India. However, a mere glance at the aggregate data reveals that the pace of industrial development has been somewhat uneven over time. In the period 1951-65, industrial production increased at an average rate of 7.7 per cent per annum. This rate dropped rather sharply to 3.6 per cent per annum during the decade 1965-75.

In retrospect, it is clear that the poor performance, which became discernible in the middle and late 1960s, was neither an aberration nor a temporary deviation from the trend, but the beginning of a long-term structural problem. The sluggishness of industrial growth, which has persisted for more than ten years, can no longer be attributed to short-term problems and obviously needs systematic analysis. While the problem area is vast, the object of this paper is a limited one. It seeks to analyse the factors underlying the marked deceleration in the rate of industrial growth, which transformed a scenario of rapid industrialisation into a situation of persistent quasi-stagnation.

Section II examines the trends in industrial production and establishes the fact of deceleration in growth. Section III provides a critical review of the alternative explanations for stagnation in the industrial sector. Section IV attempts to focus attention on factors which have, in a relative sense, been neglected by the literature on the subject, and explores the relationship between income distribution, the demand factor and industrial growth. Section V is directed towards developing a unified hypothesis about the sluggishness of growth in India's industrial sector since the mid-1960s.

II

TRENDS IN INDUSTRIAL PRODUCTION

It is rather difficult to outline the trends in industrialisation because there is no complete time series on the index numbers of industrial production which spans the entire period. In fact, changes in base years make inter-temporal comparisons problematic. All the same, there is overwhelming evidence in support of the proposition that the mid-sixties witnessed a dramatic decline in the rate of industrial growth: the average annual rate during the decade beginning 1965 turned out to be less than half what it was in the preceding fifteen years. However, it might be argued that starting from a small base, all growth rates appear unusually large and therefore, one might be overstating the degree of deceleration in growth. In an attempt to circumvent this legitimate problem, the present essay considers 1955 as the base year for all comparisons. While such a method might not eliminate the bias altogether, it should certainly reduce the magnitude.

Table 1 sets out the available data on the indices of production in the industrial sector. A slackening of growth is discernible from a cursory study of the table, and is confirmed by a few simple computations. During the decade 1955-65, total industrial production increased at an average annual rate of 7.8 per cent, while manufacturing output increased at 7.6 per cent. In the following decade, 1965-75, the rates dropped to 3.6 per cent and 3.1 per cent respectively. These are point to point compound growth rates. In order to take account of all the observations in the two periods, we fitted a semi-log trend to the indices for both total industrial production and manufacturing (Series B), only to find that the results were remarkably similar.

The reader would notice that the above exercise on growth rates ignores 1976, a year in which industrial production registered an unprecedented increase of 10 per cent over the preceding year. This omission is deliberate, because the revival of 1976 was more apparent than real. It was the outcome of a phenomenal bumper harvest and the unusual political circumstances of the time. The government stepped up public sector production irrespective of whether the output could be utilised, so that there was a rapid accumulation of stocks in intermediate goods such as steel and coal. A higher level of output and improved capacity utilisation followed from government policy towards its workforce, when the Emergency laws were used extensively to eliminate strikes and all other forms of industrial disputes.[1] But these policies did not transform the industrial scene in the private sector. Indeed, private corporate investment during 1976-77 was, in absolute terms, significantly lower than it had been in 1975-76.[2] Given this context, it would be reasonable to infer that the industrial performance in 1976 did not mark the beginning of the end of stagnation.[3] Nor did it mean a return to the trend rate witnessed earlier, quite simply because the factors which propped up growth in 1976 were not sustainable in the long run. As such, it is hardly surprising

Table 1: Index Numbers of Industrial Production

	Series A: 1956=100		Series B: 1960=100		Series C: 1970=100	
Year	General Index	Manufacturing	General Index	Manufacturing	General Index	Manufacturing
1955	91.9	91.6	(72.7)	(73.8)		
1956	100.0	100.0	(78.4)	(79.6)		
1957	104.2	103.3	(82.7)	(83.4)		
1958	107.7	106.2	(84.4)	(84.8)		
1959	116.8	114.9	(90.3)	(90.5)		
1960	130.2	127.9	100.0	100.0		
1961	141.0	137.9	109.2	109.2		
1962	152.9	149.2	119.8	119.6		
1963	167.3	162.9	129.7	129.1		
1964	177.8	173.6	140.8	141.2		
1965	187.7	182.3	153.8	154.0		
1966	192.6	186.0	153.2	151.7		
1967			152.6	149.6		
1968			163.0	158.7		
1969			175.3	170.6		
1970			184.3	178.9	100.0	100.0
1971			186.1	178.9	104.2	104.2
1972			199.4	191.4	110.2	110.1
1973			200.7	193.4	112.0	112.2
1974			(210.7)	(202.2)	114.3	113.0
1975			(219.9)	(207.7)	119.3	116.1
1976					131.6	127.7

Note : For Series B, the figures given in brackets are derived from Series A and C respectively. Those relating to the period 1955-59 are based on 1960 weights and have been taken from *Commerce*, Annual Number, Bombay, 1968, p 287. The figures for 1974-75, however, are unweighted and calculated simply by using the ratio of the 1970 index in Series B to that in Series C as the conversion factor.

Source: CSO, *Statistical Abstract, India*, annual issues.

that industrial output in 1977 is expected to be just about 4 per cent higher than the previous year.

From the above, it seems obvious that 1976 was an abnormal year which cannot serve as a point of reference or comparison. In the following discussion, therefore, we shall focus attention on the trends in industrial production until 1975. Our choice of terminal year is perfectly justifiable, particularly as the primary purpose of this paper is to analyse the long-term shifts in the pace of industrialisation.

In order to pinpoint changes in the rate of industrial growth, for the period 1955-1975, we fitted the equation Log Y = a + bt + ct² to the data in Table 1, Series B, where 'Y' is either the general index of industrial production (I_{ip}) or the index of manufacturing (I_m), and 't' is the time period. The following results were obtained from the exercise:

$$\text{Log } I_{ip} = -4.6440 + 0.2387t - 0.0014t^2$$
$$\qquad\qquad\qquad (0.0338) \quad (0.00026)$$
$$\bar{R}^2 = 0.99; \quad DW = 1.03$$

$$\text{Log } I_m = -4.8486 + 0.2480t - 0.0015t^2$$
$$\qquad\qquad\qquad (0.0371) \quad (0.00029)$$
$$\bar{R}^2 = 0.99; \quad DW = 0.95$$

In both cases, the estimated values of 'c' turned out to be negative, and significant at the 1 per cent level of probability, thereby providing definitive evidence of a deceleration in the rate of growth.

The picture of deceleration is substantiated further if we examine data at a disaggregated level. Table 2 outlines the trends in output starting from the two-digit level of the CSO industrial classification. While the composition of industrial production certainly changed over time, taken together, the ten manufacturing industry groups selected for the table contributed approximately 90 per cent of the total output in manufacturing, throughout the period under review.[4] A comparison of the average annual growth rates in the period 1955-65 with the corresponding ones in 1965-75 conclusively shows that the slow-down in growth occurred across the board in the industrial sector, though it might have been more pronounced in some industries than in others.

The mid-sixties were, obviously, the turning point. This is brought out even more clearly in Table 3, which is based on an alternative industrial classification but the source of primary data is the same. From the viewpoint of macro-economic analysis, a use-based classification is certainly more interesting; unfortunately, however, data in this series do not extend back beyond 1960. Nevertheless, the available statistics do highlight the dramatic deceleration in growth

Table 2: Composition and Time Profile of Industrial Growth in India

Industry Group	Weights (1960=100)	Index Numbers of Production (1960=100)			Average Growth Rate (Per Cent Per Annum)	
		1955	1965	1975	1955-65	1965-75
Food products	12.09	75.9	122.2	171.2	4.9	3.4
Beverages and tobacco	2.22	61.7	147.6	200.9	9.1	3.1
Textiles	27.06	94.1	114.8	112.0	2.0	–0.5
Chemicals and chemical products	7.26	60.1	152.6	306.9	9.8	7.2
Non-metallic mineral products	3.85	53.7	149.1	243.3	10.8	5.0
Basic metals	7.38	53.3	180.9	242.3	13.0	3.0
Metal products	2.51	54.1	205.6	310.0	14.3	4.2
Non-electrical Machinery	3.38	35.5	320.9	623.6	24.6	6.9
Electrical machinery and appliances	3.05	49.0	208.2	443.8	15.6	8.0
Transport equipment	7.77	99.2	205.3	149.4	7.6	–3.2
All Manufacturing	84.91	73.8	154.0	207.7	7.6	3.1
Mining and quarrying	9.72	74.6	131.7	189.8	5.9	3.7
Electricity	5.37	51.5	190.9	461.8	14.0	9.2
Total industrial production	100.00	72.7	153.8	219.9	7.8	3.6

Note : The figures in the last two columns of the table have been computed as point to point compound growth rates.

Sources: (a) For the 1960 weights and for 1965 index numbers, CSO, *Statistical Abstract, India, 1974*, pp 127-31. (b) For 1955 index numbers, *Commerce*, Annual Number, Bombay, 1968, pp 287-90. These figures are derived from the 1956 series using 1960 weights, and have also been compiled by the CSO; *cf: Basic Statistics Relating to the Indian Economy, 1950-51 to 1974-75,* NewDelhi, 1976, p 46. (c) The index numbers for 1975 have been calculated from the 1970 base series, as reported in the CSO *Monthly Abstract of Statistics*, July 1977, pp 27-30. To convert them to 1960 base, we have used the relevant ratio of the 1970 index in the two series, for each industry group, as the conversion factor.

Table 3: Deceleration of Growth in Industrial Sector, 1960-1975
(average annual percentage increase in production)

Industry Group	Weights (1960=100)	1960-65 (1)	1965-70 (2)	1970-75 (3)
Basic industries	25.11	10.4	6.2	5.2
Capital goods industries	11.76	19.5	−1.7	5.1
Intermediate goods industries	25.88	7.0	2.5	2.6
Consumer goods industries	37.25	5.0	3.9	1.6
(i) Durable goods	(5.68)	10.7	8.4	2.4
(ii) Non-durable goods	(31.57)	3.8	2.7	1.5
Total industrial production	100.00	9.0	3.3	3.6

Notes: (a) The figures in the table have been calculated from the index numbers of industrial production, as point to point compound growth rates. (b) Columns (1) and (2) are derived from the series on index numbers of industrial production with 1960 as base year, whereas column (3) is derived from the new series with 1970 as base year.

Source: RBI, *Report on Currency and Finance, 1974-75*, Volume II, p 26 and 1975-76, Volume II, p 28.

of the capital-goods sector. The table also shows that the fate of intermediate goods industries was roughly similar, although the drop in the growth rate was not as steep. The basic industries group (constituted by electricity, mining, fertilisers, heavy chemicals, cement and basic metals), on the other hand, fared a little better insofar as the rate of growth remained at a reasonable level even after the deceleration set in. It is worth noting that growth in the consumer goods industries was always significantly below the average for the industrial sector. In the 1960s, it was sustained at a respectable level by a rapid expansion in the output of consumer durables. However, even the modest growth disappeared in the 1970s as the pace of expansion in the durable goods industries slackened markedly.

It needs to be stressed that the evidence presented so far relates only to the organised factory sector. Given the paucity of published data, it is almost impossible to assess how the performance of the small-scale sector would influence the overall trends in industrial production. Available information suggests that small-scale industries account for roughly 15 per cent of the total value of industrial production.[5] Thus, it would seem that the statistical evidence outlined in the preceding pages is a reasonable indicator of the trends in industrial output. In any case, the performance of the small-scale sector should be reflected in the level of industrial production (originating in registered large-scale units) insofar as it provides inputs to, or purchases them from the factory sector.

As a starting point for discussion, it might be useful at this stage to recapitulate the salient features of the pattern of industrial development in India over the past three decades. In the years following Independence, infrastructural developments and import substitution in the consumer goods sector stimulated industrial production. After that phase, in the late 1950s and early 1960s, the high rate of industrial growth was sustained by investment in the capital goods sector and in basic intermediate goods industries. Starting around 1965, there was a marked deceleration in the rate of growth, which led to a near stagnation of industrial output in the early 1970s. The little growth that did take place in the period 1965-1970 was largely attributable to infrastructural basic industries and to consumer durables. However, the expansion in luxury goods industries also came to an end thereafter. The ostensible revival in 1976 was a consequence of special circumstances, and did not mean a return to the trend growth rate of earlier years.

III

ALTERNATIVE EXPLANATIONS OF DECELERATION AND STAGNATION

Several explanations have been advanced to account for the sluggishness of industrial growth since the mid-sixties. Of these, in my view at least, two sets are clearly inadequate essentially because they do not get to the core of the problem. On the other hand, there are explanations which are perfectly plausible and merit careful discussion. Before we move on to such a critical review, however, a brief sketch of the inadequate hypotheses about industrial stagnation might be worthwhile.

Soon after the slow-down in growth became discernible, the problems of the industrial sector were frequently attributed to exogenous factors or random occurrences. While this view is not widely held now, its adherents have not disappeared altogether. The emphasis has varied but, *inter alia*, short-term analysis draws attention to the following: (a) the wars of 1962, 1965 and 1971 which diverted potential public investment into unproductive uses; (b) the successive droughts of 1965-66 to 1966-67, and later 1971-72 to 1972-73, which restricted the supply of raw materials and the demand for industrial goods from the agricultural sector; (c) supply constraints which became more pronounced in the late 1960s, in the form of infrastructural bottlenecks (power and transport) or shortages of intermediate goods; and (d) the oil crisis of 1973 which led to considerable industrial dislocation and severe balance of payments difficulties.

In the early stages, it is hardly surprising that policy-makers in government and economists outside stressed the importance of these occurrences.[6] It would be naive to deny that such occurrences had a significant impact on the level of industrial production at the time. With the benefit of hindsight, however, it seems fairly obvious that the aforesaid random factors cannot account for the persistence of stagnation, simply because the economy should have returned to even keel after the event. It did not. In retrospect, it is clear that the disappearance of the short-term problems has not meant a revival of industrial growth.

There is a second, more long-term, view of industrialisation in India, which does not concern itself with the problem of deceleration in growth, but stresses the difficulties arising from the industrial policies pursued by the government. The volumes by Bhagwati and Desai (1970) and Bhagwati and Srinivasan (1975) provide an elaborate exposition of this view. It is argued that the complex bureaucratic system of licensing, restrictions and controls led not only to inefficiencies but also to a misallocation of resources. What is more, the cumulative effect of these policies became an obstacle to growth. Thus, Bhagwati and Srinivasan (1975, p 245) conclude that:

> India's foreign trade regime, in conjunction with domestic licensing policies in the industrial sector, led to economic inefficiencies and impaired her economic performance.
>
> The policy framework was detrimental, on balance, to the growth of the economy by adversely influencing export performance, by wasteful inter-industrial and inter-firm allocation of resources, by permitting and encouraging expansion of excess capacity and by blunting competition and hence the incentives for cost-consciousness and quality improvement.[7]

Such analysis, however, does not throw much light on the problem posed in this essay. One can, after all, ask: (1) Why did the industrial sector perform satisfactorily until 1965, in spite of these policies, and why did it not respond to liberalisation thereafter, or now? (2) Why did other economies, operating in a framework similar to that of India, achieve significantly higher rates of industrial growth? These questions are seldom raised, let alone answered, primarily because the authors are interested in a completely different set of issues.

Much of the literature cited above is preoccupied with an evaluation of import substitution strategies and the economic efficiency of industrialisation. It is hardly surprising, the refore, that relatively little attention is paid to the process of growth. In any case, neo-classical writing on the subject is essentially static in conception, and largely ignores inter-temporal considerations. Even the limited analysis of growth effects is often derived from static allocative efficiency criteria.[8]

Other hypotheses about the deceleration of industrial growth since the mid-sixties with a few exceptions, hinge on two basic themes: the performance of the agricultural sector and the level of investment in the economy. Detailed discussion of these contributions to the literature is a task outside the scope of this paper. For our purpose, it would be sufficient to provide a critical review of the more important contributions, with a focus on salient features, and examine the extent to which they provide satisfactory explanations.

A *Performance of Agricultural Sector*

For an economy such as India, the importance of the agricultural sector arises, in principle, from its overwhelming share in production and consumption. Quite apart from that, however, its performance has a direct impact on the pace of industrialisation, through the following mechanism. A slow increase in agricultural production would act as a brake on industrial growth if: (i) a surplus of wage goods and/or investible resources is not forthcoming; (ii) the supply of agricultural raw materials is restricted; or (iii) the demand for industrial goods is constrained. On the other hand, a rapid expansion in agricultural output would, through the same linkages, provide a sustained stimulus to growth in the industrial sector.

It is only to be expected that different authors would emphasise different factors and outline different mechanisms through which such linkages operate. Following this general line of argument, however, a number of scholars, notably Chakravarty (1974), Raj (1976) and Vaidyanathan (1977) have sought to explain the sluggish growth of industrial output, since the mid-sixties, in terms of the meagre growth in agricultural production. It is possible to argue about the numbers and debate about the trends, as indeed a few economists have,[9] but it is difficult to dispute the basis of such a fundamentalist explanation. Once the fact of deceleration in the growth of agricultural output is accepted, there remains the question of factors responsible for it, which, in turn, have been discussed at length in the literature; they range from technological factors on the one hand, to the institutional framework and property relations in agriculture on the other. It would involve too much of a digression to enter into a discussion of these issues here. For the sake of analysis, therefore, let us grant the proposition that there has been a slackening of growth in the agricultural sector and that this may have had an adverse effect on industrialisation in the recent past. Available evidence, on balance, probably lends support to such a hypothesis.

Nevertheless, it is important to pose the simple question: is this a sufficient explanation for the persistence of industrial stagnation? For if it were, a resumption of steady growth in agriculture would revive and stimulate industrial production. In my view, however, the explanation is only partial, on account of the reasons set out below. Thus, while agricultural expansion might be a necessary condition for sustained industrial growth, it is by no means a sufficient condition in the present Indian context.

Technical change, improved inputs, more resources or even successive bumper harvests would increase agricultural production. If there is a balanced growth in crop output, it would almost certainly increase the marketed surplus of raw materials and food, but these surpluses might not be available on the terms necessary to revive industrial growth. Past experience suggests that a secular movement of the inter-sectoral terms of trade in favour of the agricultural sector, operating through a squeeze on profits, might have held back industrial expansion. Chakravarty (1974) notes this point in his analysis, but ascribes the shift in relative prices to the deceleration in growth of agricultural output. However, it is likely that the landlord class, through political influence, manipulated the inter-sectoral terms of trade in its favour [Mitra, 1977], and might well do so in the future. In such circumstances, an improved performance in agriculture would not ensure industrial growth. An increase in agricultural production may not be sufficient on other counts either. While it would lead to an increase in the total income of the farm sector, there can be little doubt that the bulk of increments in income would be appropriated by those who own the means of production: landlords and rich farmers. But unless incomes accrue to the poor, the demand for industrial wage goods from the rural majority cannot revive. We shall return to this issue later in the paper.

B *Level of Investment*

During the decade 1955-65, real investment in the economy increased rapidly but the pace of expansion slackened markedly thereafter, notably in the public sector.[10] The share of gross domestic capital formation in GDP which attained a peak level of 19.7 per cent in 1966-67, declined a little in subsequent years and fluctuated around an average level of 17 per cent in the period 1967-68 to 1974-75 [Government of India, 1976, pp 30-31]. The trend was much the same for gross fixed capital formation in the public sector. Thus some economists have attempted to explain the slow-down in industrial growth in terms of the stagnation in investment. There are two, rather different, variants of this hypothesis.

Consider first, the paper by Srinivasan and Narayana (1977). They start from two sets of observations for the period since the mid-sixties: (i) a slackening of real investment, particularly in the public sector; and (ii) a deceleration in the rate of industrial growth. It is stressed that these developments constituted a marked departure from the trends established in the first three five-year plans. The authors go on to argue that the stagnation of real investment, especially public investment, is among the principal causes of sluggish industrial development, and if the economy is to surmount its present crisis there should be a vigorous expansion of public investment. Towards that end, they believe, recourse to deficit financing is perfectly possible given the enormous reserves of food and foreign exchange.

The thesis is somewhat simplistic. It does not even attempt to analyse the factors underlying the slow-down in public investment, nor does it trace the reasons why this failure of the public sector restrained industrial growth. Reading between the lines, one can discern an implicit view that large net inflows of foreign aid until 1965 sustained high levels of public investment, which, in turn, had complementarities with private investment. Problems arose once the sources of aid began to dry up, ultimately leading to stagnation.

Such analysis is open to criticism on two counts. First, it assumes that aid supports investment alone and not, even in part, consumption. As a matter of fact, substantial aid inflows in the period 1955-65 might have provided the government with a soft option, enabling it to avoid mobilising domestic resources to the extent it should have. Second, net aid inflows rose very sharply in the 1970s, from their lowest ever level of Rs 159 crore in 1972-73 to Rs 1,153 crore in 1975-76, around which level they have since remained,[11] but public investment has failed to pick up.

Patnaik and Rao (1977) put forward a much more perceptive and interesting hypothesis about industrial stagnation. They advance an explanation in terms of the circumstances leading to (i) a decrease in public investment, and (ii) a loss of stimulus for private investments; both these occurrences, it is suggested, were a natural consequence of the earlier growth process. The impressive industrial growth until

1965 followed from a rapid expansion of public investment on the one hand and public expenditure on the other. While the former ensured the supply of basic industrial inputs, the latter generated a demand for goods manufactured in the private sector. At the same time, the strategy of import substitution implemented through protection, virtually guaranteed a market for domestic producers, thereby providing a steady stimulus for private investment. This process of growth was not sustained for two reasons. In the first place, import substitution was nothing but a transient stimulus which lasted so long as the local markets remained uncaptured. Second, and possibly more important, there was a marked deceleration in the growth of public investment and expenditure. During the period 1960-61 to 1964-65, gross fixed capital formation in the public sector increased at 9.1 per cent per annum whereas total expenditure of the government increased even faster at 13.2 per cent per annum, both expressed in terms of constant prices. In the following years, 1964-65 to 1973-74, these rates dropped to 0.7 per cent and 2.0 per cent respectively [Patnaik and Rao, p 126]. As a result, basic inputs manufactured in the public sector became scarce, while the demand for several outputs manufactured in the private sector tapered off. In this manner the deceleration in investment led to a deceleration in industrial growth. The authors are careful to tie up the loose ends in the argument. They explain that the level of investment stagnated primarily because the government failed to mobilise resources for the public sector. On the other hand, the private sector, which appropriated the increments in the economic surplus and was therefore capable of investment, channelled resources into speculation, luxury goods, construction and the like.

In the framework set out above, stepping up the rate of investment in the public sector should provide an obvious solution to the problem of industrial stagnation. However, Patnaik and Rao believe that there are limits on the expansion of public investment. In the short run, given the reserves of food and foreign exchange, deficit financing might appear simple enough, but it does imply a serious threat of inflation,[12] which would restrict the room for manoeuvre. Anyway, in the long run, a sustainable increase in public investment must be backed by a mobilisation of domestic resources or, in effect, a major shift of the economic surplus from the private sector to the public sector.

The basic thrust of this hypothesis is perfectly acceptable but, as an explanation and prescription, it remains incomplete. The reasons underlying my view are as follows. First, the failure on the part of the private sector to invest its accumulating resources productively cannot be attributed to the stagnation in public investment alone. Surely, the profitability of private investment is a relevant consideration which depends, among other things, on the pattern of consumer expenditure and demand in the overwhelmingly important home market. Second, even if we assume that resources could *somehow* be mobilised to step up public investment, would it revive industrial growth on its own? Possibly not. Public investment may have made for rapid industrial growth until the mid-sixties and its decline may have been responsible for the stagnation thereafter. It does not, however, follow that public investment by itself would do the trick now, simply because the nature of the problem is different. Let me elaborate. In the early stages of industrialisation, outlets for public investment posed no problem and resources were used to develop basic industries. But, at the present juncture, the avenues for public investment in the industrial sector are not unlimited. There already exist substantial underutilised capacities in the capital goods and intermediate goods industries. More public investment along the same lines would only create further excess capacity and compound difficulties, unless there is a growth in the final goods sector which absorbs these capacities. In other words, the supply of investible resources in the hands of the government is not the only constraint on public investment. A demand for such investment is as crucial; for public investment is not something autonomous which can be stepped up irrespective of appropriate outlets, nor can it create its own demand. It is worth stressing, however, that the composition of public investment does provide the government with a policy variable insofar as it determines the extent of direct and indirect employment creation which, in turn, would determine the growth in consumer demand. Hence, the investment-mix in the public sector would matter as much as the rate of investment.

To recapitulate, it would appear that the best of the hypothesis about sluggish industrial growth, outlined so far, are partial and somewhat incomplete. If this was not the case, stagnation should have disappeared by now. After all, there have been no exogenous shocks since the oil crisis in 1973; licensing, controls and trade policies have all been liberalised; the constraints imposed by agricultural production have been significantly relaxed by a succession of good monsoons; the limit on public investment is not as rigid any more, what with the existing reserves of food and foreign exchange. Yet, there is little evidence of sustained industrial growth on the horizon. Thus it is imperative that we probe further and work towards a coherent and unified hypothesis.

IV

INCOME DISTRIBUTION AND DEMAND FACTOR

It is my contention that a satisfactory explanation of stagnation cannot afford to ignore the relationship between income distribution, the demand factor and industrial growth. So far, relatively little attention has been paid to this aspect of the problem. The only exceptions are a paper by Bagchi (1970), parts of a recent book by Mitra (1977) and, to some extent, an article by Raj (1976). In this section, therefore, I shall attempt to sketch a preliminary hypothesis which concentrates attention on consumer demand and income distribution as possible factors underlying the persistent sluggishness of growth in the industrial sector. Prima facie demand factors might appear somewhat unusual, even Keynesian, as an explanation of low levels of industrial output in an economy such as India, but they might well be very significant at the present stage of development.

Given the overwhelming importance of the agricultural sector, private consumer expenditure obviously depends, to a large extent, on farm incomes. It follows that slow growth in agriculture could restrain the demand for manufactured goods and, consequently, hold back industrial expansion. This point is stressed by Raj (1976), who notes that regions characterised by moderately high and stable rates of agricultural growth have also experienced high growth rates in industry.[13] Looking at aggregate demand, however, might be slightly misleading, and it is important to consider it in the context of income distribution. The reason is simple. In an economy where the bulk of the consumption, production and investment decisions are made through the market mechanism, it is income distribution which determines the pattern of consumer expenditure as well as demand and, hence, the composition of industrial output.

The Bagchi (1970) thesis, which derives from this basic proposition, is as follows. The unequal income distribution (that exists) is reinforced by the process of growth, for, it is the private sector which owns the means of production and, as such, appropriates the increments in income. The government is unable to exercise effective control over the allocation of resources between: (a) consumption and saving–as reflected in the failure to mobilise domestic resources for investment; and (b) 'essential' and 'non-essential' consumption–as revealed by the excessive importance of luxury goods in industrial production. Therefore, it is not possible for the government to maintain a high rate of investment irrespective of the unequal income distribution and the demand pattern generated by it. In this analysis, Bagchi considered the period 1951-68, towards the end of which the slow-down in growth was just about discernible. The primary object of his paper was to highlight the problems which arose in the execution of the Mahalanobis strategy, and to pinpoint the reasons for its failure to generate a balanced and sustained industrial growth.

Given the fact of persistent quasi-stagnation, which has been with us for a decade, we can take the argument further. Up to a point, it is possible to bring about rapid industrialisation through import replacement in the consumer goods sector and through investment in the creation of a capital- and intermediate-goods sector. Ultimately, however, the pace of industrialisation can only be sustained if there is a growth in the domestic market, because the production capacities created in the investment goods sector must be absorbed by final consumer demand. But, in a market economy where the distribution of income is unequal, the demand base might be very narrow in terms of population spread. That was and, indeed, is the case in India. For the year 1964-65, using National Sample Survey data, it has been estimated that, in the rural sector, the richest 10 per cent of the population was responsible for 32.2 per cent of the total consumption of industrial goods, whereas the poorest 50 per cent accounted for only 22 per cent of the total. Consumption inequalities were even more pronounced in the urban sector, where the top decile purchased 39.3 per cent of the industrial goods and the bottom five deciles absorbed just 19.9 per cent of the total.[14]

Clearly, a large proportion of the demand for industrial products originates from a narrow segment of the population. However, manufactured goods sold to the relatively few rich can use up only so much, and no more of the capacity in the intermediate- and capital-goods sector. Only a broad-based demand for mass-consumption goods can lead to a full utilisation of capacity (and generate sustainable increases in output), but that in turn requires incomes for the poor. Thus an unequal income distribution, operating through the demand factors, might well restrict the prospects of sustained industrial growth. As an aside, let me stress that one does not have to be an underconsumptionist to hold this view. What has just been described is not uncommon to crises in capitalist economies. From time to time, it is possible that inadequate demand might constrain growth. While higher wages for workers might improve the situation, they would lead to a squeeze on profits and investment. In other words, solving one problem exacerbates the other.

The hypothesis outlined above can only be tested through careful empirical work and further research. Of course, the assimilation of direct, quantitative evidence on the relationship between income distribution and industrial growth might turn out to be an elusive pursuit. Indeed, for this particular issue, one might have to rely on indirect evidence. But even that would require another paper: a task we shall set aside for the future. For the present, it is sufficient that the hypothesis is plausible and, given available information, cannot be rejected out of hand. The recent work of Ashok Mitra posits a mechanism through which a worsening income distribution might have retarded industrialisation in India. A statistical analysis by Ranjit Sau, though somewhat out of date, provides limited evidence in support. The persistent sluggishness of industrial growth, in a situation otherwise characterised by plenty, further points to income distribution and the demand factors as important elements in a complete explanation of stagnation.

It has been argued by Mitra (1977) that the redistribution of income attempted in the country via the manipulation of relative prices in favour of agriculture and against industry is a major factor responsible for the deceleration in industrial growth since the mid-sixties.[15] He suggests that: "the shifting terms of trade have been instrumental in eroding the level of real incomes of the majority of the population in both urban areas and the countryside". The causation is straightforward enough. An increase in foodgrain prices, which accompanied the change in inter-sectoral relative prices, squeezed the non-food expenditure of the urban as well as the rural poor, because there was no corresponding increase in their incomes and food remained a preponderant item in their budget.[16] After a time, higher prices of agricultural commodities, operating through an escalation of raw material and wage costs, led to an across-the-board increase in industrial prices, so that the demand for manufactured products was squeezed further. The end result was that the demand for mass consumer goods in the economy levelled off.

In principle, the industrial sector could have been compensated for this loss by an expansion in demand on part of the rich, who appropriated the bulk of the growth in income. But this did not happen because their avenues for further consumption were limited. For them, luxury consumer goods industries were the only outlet, apart from speculation, trade and construction. The point relates clearly to the urban industrial bourgeoisie and the large affluent farmers. In this context, however, the rich peasantry in the countryside remains a puzzle, for it is unlikely that their consumption of basic industrial goods reached saturation point so quickly.

Available evidence on inter-sectoral resource flows reveals some interesting trends in demands. On the basis of data drawn from the NSS, Sau (1974) has shown that the percentage of per capita consumer expenditure spent on industrial goods declined over the period 1952-53 to 1964-65, rather sharply in rural India but less markedly in the urban sector. More important, he found that the decline was far more pronounced in the case of the poorer sections of the population, particularly the bottom five deciles. From these findings, Sau concludes that the market for industrial consumption goods was shrinking over the years, which is, in a sense, correct. But it is worth noting that these trends did not disrupt the process of industrialisation. Indeed, this was also a period of rapid industrial growth. One can only presume that the industrial expansion occurred in spite of the constraints imposed by income distribution and consumer demand; I shall return to this issue towards the end of the essay.

From our viewpoint, it would be far more interesting to examine the changing pattern of consumer expenditure and the trends in demand during the period 1965-75. While such an exercise is not possible here, a rough calculation from the CSO's *National Accounts Statistics* does suggest that an increase in relative food prices did squeeze the demand for manufactured goods after 1965. In terms of current prices, the proportion of private final consumption expenditure in the economy devoted to cereals and cereal substitutes rose from 27.4 per cent in 1965-66 to 32.7 per cent in 1974-75, whereas the proportion spent on industrial goods fell from 23.1 per cent to 19.3 per cent.[17]

The dilemma of the Indian economy in the late 1970s, more than anything else, highlights the importance of the demand factor in industrial performance. There have been three successive bumper harvests, the stockpile of food is estimated at 18 million tons, and foreign exchange reserves stand at an unprecedented level of Rs 4,500 crore. Where does all this point to? Is the economy poised for a period of uninterrupted growth, which represents a break from industrial stagnation? Probably not. While overt healthy signs provide policy-makers with considerable room for manoeuvre and there exists a potential, industrial capitalism in India today faces problems that have become familiar in the past decade. Indeed, the nature of the crisis has not changed very much.

None of the occurrences referred to above have created incomes for the poor, either in the urban sector or in the rural sector. Thus there is no new demand for manufactured wage goods which could sustain industrial growth. Consider, for a moment, the rural poor. Successive bumper harvests might have increased incomes in the agricultural sector. But whose incomes? There can be little doubt that much of the benefit has accrued to large landowners and rich peasants; not to the rural poor. Even in the heyday of the green revolution, therefore, stagnation in the industrial sector was not transformed into growth. As for the urban poor, among whom it is possible to identify the industrial working class, the situation probably deteriorated during the Emergency regime. A stringent incomes policy coupled with the compulsory deposit scheme and the legislation on bonus payments effectively squeezed the real income of this group.

While the government has done almost nothing towards raising the incomes of the poor, a large number of recent policies have been directed towards stimulating consumption of the higher income groups and encouraging investment in the private corporate sector. The policies introduced to meet these objectives are: reduction of indirect taxes on luxury goods, a substantial cut back in income taxes payable by the rich, a delicensing of industries, and an open door policy towards multinational corporations. However, the response of the economy has been slow and investment in the industrial sector has not revived. Consequently, the government is rather puzzled by the fact that investment has failed to pick up in spite of policies designed to remove all possible constraints and to create an environment conducive to industrial growth.[18] But the static level of investment is not surprising in the context of our hypothesis. After all, an increased production of consumer goods destined for the richer sections of the population can utilise the existing production capacities only to a limited extent: it cannot bring about a sustained increase in industrial output.

The argument presented so far has one important lacuna; it also has an underconsumptionist flavour that may not appeal to some. Critics might well ask if it is possible for India to circumvent the demand problem at home and repeat the Brazilian experience of 'successful' capitalist development. Given an underutilised intermediate- and capital-goods sector, a declining rate of investment, and a luxury goods sector that has run out of steam, the Brazilian model must appear as a rather attractive option to policy-makers. Such a path of development, *inter alia*, has three essential ingredients: (a) external markets–which are necessary to get around the domestic demand bottleneck; (b) foreign capital–which provides resources as well as technology; and (c) a dominant class of industrial capitalists–in whose interest state power is exercised. Their consumption forms the basis of the home market and they also provide the savings for investment. Consider each in turn.

Export-led growth is a curiously naive prescription for the problems faced by the Indian economy, and is not a feasible proposition. The reasons underlying my view have been developed, at length, elsewhere [Nayyar, 1976]. Suffice it to say that the problem of Indian exports is a problem of production. In the ultimate analysis, exports can be increased on a sustainable basis only if there is a growth in real national income. Therefore, export performance is likely to be determined by economic growth rather than the other way round. There is also very little evidence to suggest that foreign capital would flow into India in large amounts. This is because transnational corporations are extremely cautious about their decision to relocate production where it affects global operations, as in export-oriented manufacturing. The same international firms are far less worried about choosing sites for a horizontal spread, and setting up production units in India to cater for local markets. The essential point is that the internationalisation of production is limited to a finite number of countries, of which Brazil is one, but it will be long time before it spreads to India. In the Indian context, however, the most important problem is the difficulties that will arise in the fostering of an urban industrial elite at the expense of the rest of the population. It would mean a rupture of the ruling class alliance and a dumping of the rural oligarchy somewhere along the line. Recent policies such as the subsidy on fertilisers, priority in public investment to irrigation, and high procurement prices, all point to the continued existence of the rural oligarchy as a potent force in the Indian polity.[19] Unless there is a change in the class character of the Indian state, and the government opts squarely for industrial capitalists, the Brazilian model is unlikely to materialise in the sub-continent.

The moral of the story, if one emerges, is that in an economy such as India, where the domestic market is overwhelmingly important, steady and continuous industrial growth requires a broad-based and increasing mass consumer demand. In a fundamental sense, therefore, sustained industrialisation can only be based on a growth of the internal market.

V

TOWARDS A POSSIBLE HYPOTHESIS

The preceding discussion sought to focus attention on income distribution and the demand factor simply to compensate for the relative neglect in the existing literature. The intention was not to minimise the importance of other factors. Indeed, no explanation for the uneven pace of industrial development, in the Indian context, can be logically complete without reference to both public investment and the agricultural sector. Therefore, it would be useful to recapitulate and draw together the strands of the different arguments outlined so far. Such an approach, to the extent it provides a macro-economic view of the growth process, should, hopefully, facilitate our understanding of the problem and might even suggest policy prescriptions. Towards this end, I shall attempt to formulate a unified, albeit tentative, hypothesis about the factors responsible for the transition from rapid industrial growth to the point of quasi-stagnation, and for the persistent sluggishness of growth in the industrial sector since the mid-sixties.

The impressive expansion of industrial output in the period 1950-65 can be explained as follows. Public investment, in large doses, created an infrastructure and set up intermediate goods industries, so as to ensure a supply of inputs to the private sector. In doing so, it carried out a task the domestic capitalists could not have on their own [Chattopadhyay, 1970]. At the same time, an ever-increasing level of public expenditure gave rise to a demand for outputs manufactured in the corporate sector. As an aside, it is worth noting that this *modus operandi* of fostering industrialisation was not different from the tactics of state capitalism elsewhere in the world, though it might have been at a later stage in history. But that was not all. The policies of import substitution, implemented through protection, reinforced the demand stimulus. Local capitalists were not only guaranteed existing markets but were also ensured a future insofar as the excess demand attributable to import restrictions would continue to provide markets, at least in the medium term. Given this background, the sequence of industrial development is hardly surprising. In the years following independence, infrastructural developments and import substitution in the consumer goods sector stimulated industrial production. Thereafter, the high rate of industrial growth in the late 1950s and early 1960s was sustained by investment, on the part of the government, in the capital goods sector and in basic intermediate goods industries. During this phase of rapid development, a reasonable rate of expansion in agricultural output ensured the *supply* of food–the basic wage good–and raw materials, thereby allowing industrialisation to be sustained at a moderate pace which was, against the back-drop of colonial history, unprecedented. However, it should be stressed that the growth in industrial production was more directly attributable to public investment and protection.

In retrospect, the negative impact of agricultural performance on industrial development turned out to be far more significant. Starting around the mid-sixties, growth in the agricultural sector began to slow down, for reasons that have been discussed at length in the literature. Food prices began to rise and raw materials became scarce, so that the indirect support provided by agriculture to industrialisation diminished markedly. As the inter-sectoral terms of trade shifted in favour of the agricultural sector, even the reduced support was now available to the industrial sector on less favourable terms. Difficulties were compounded by the fact that the principal sources of industrial growth in the first phase also waned in their impact. There was a dramatic deceleration in the growth of real public expenditure and investment.[20] The proximate causes of this occurrence might appear to lie in the wars which diverted investment to unproductive uses, or the successive droughts of the mid-sixties which generated unforeseen consumption needs, but, in the ultimate analysis, it was a direct consequence of the government's failure to mobilise domestic resources.

A question immediately springs to mind: is it possible that accelerated investment in the private corporate sector could have sustained growth? In the circumstances, the answer is a definite no. In the first place, the complementarities between public and private investment in India have always been rather important. Moreover, the market stimulus provided by import substitution also disappeared. It was, almost by definition, a transient stimulus which could last only so long as the existing markets were uncaptured and excess demand remained. Once these opportunities were taken up, a growth of the domestic market was essential. Even after import substitution ran out of steam, for a while, investment could be sustained by expansion in the capital goods sector and in basic industries, as indeed it was during 1960-65. But, it was not possible to continue with the creation of capacities in these sectors, for ultimately, even their existence depends upon demand in the final goods sector.

It would be perfectly legitimate to ask why industrial growth came up against the demand barrier since 1965 and not earlier for, after all, income distribution was unequal right at the start, so that the majority of the Indian population was not in the market for industrial products.[21] The answer is relatively straightforward. Irrespective of the income distribution at the time, there was an assured domestic market, the size of which was determined by the level of imports and the state of excess demand for importables. This guaranteed source of demand was exhausted once import substitution in consumer goods was virtually complete, and the capacities created in the capital goods and intermediate goods transcended the prevalent needs of the final goods sector. The demand for industrial goods generated by the elite did, to some extent, support the process of growth in the 1960s, but it was only a limited and temporary solution: limited because it could use only so much and no more of the capacity in the capital- and intermediate-goods sector; temporary because the demand for luxury goods on the part of a small fraction of the population is likely to reach saturation point. The alternative of export-led growth, we have noted earlier, is not feasible in the Indian case. Therefore, the utilisation of excess capacity and sustained industrial growth both require a demand for mass consumption goods. In this context, it is worth stressing that creating incomes for the poor is not a simple matter of redistribution through taxes and subsidies, for in a market economy such as India the distribution of incomes is closely related to, and cannot be divorced from ownership of the means of production.

The demand factor needs to be singled out not only because it has received little attention so far, but also because it does explain, in part, the present crisis in the economy and the persistent sluggishness of industrial growth. Moreover, it has obvious policy implications. Successive bumper harvests, the unprecedented stockpile of food and massive foreign exchange reserves have, at least for the time being, removed the supply constraints. Yet there is little evidence of a return to the earlier trend rate or of sustained industrial growth. Why? *Inter alia*, it is because the lack of a mass domestic demand for industrial goods has surfaced as a problem.

Given the political aspects of the situation, a radical redistribution of income might be unattainable. What about stepping up the rate of investment which is frequently thought of as a possible solution? Such a strategy is clearly difficult in the case of private investment, because investment decisions in the corporate industrial sector follow signals provided by the market mechanism; hence, they depend on the state of demand, the pattern of consumer expenditure and, ultimately, the existing income distribution. On the other hand, in terms of policy, public investment does provide some room for manoeuvre. In the long run, however, the rate of public investment itself depends on the ability of the government to mobilise domestic resources, for otherwise a serious threat of inflation remains; the reserves of food and foreign exchange do not entirely solve this problem once speculation enters the picture. What is more, even if the rate of investment in the public sector could be stepped up, it would not suffice unless adequate attention is paid to the composition of investment, so that it leads to employment creation and incomes for the poor, if not directly at least as a second-order effect.

Let me conclude. For sustained industrial growth, it is essential not only to mobilise savings of the rich for investment but also to channel increments in income to the poor which, in turn, would generate a broad-based demand for industrial goods. Unless these conditions are satisfied, stagnation will only reappear after a time. Stepping up of public investment, supported by an inflow of foreign resources, can only be a temporary and partial solution. It cannot generate a process of sustained industrialisation in India.

NOTES

[Some of the ideas developed in this essay were first outlined in a note prepared for an informal discussion group at University College, London, in January 1977, and a preliminary version of the paper was presented to a seminar on 'Industrialisation in India' at the Centre for Studies in Social Sciences, Calcutta, in December 1977. I would like to thank the participants in both places for their critical comments and searching questions, which enabled me to revise the paper for publication.]

1 Statements originating in official sources provide confirmation. For instance, the government's *Economic Survey* for 1975-76 stressed the fact that the number of man-days lost through industrial disputes fell from 6 million in July-September 1974 to 1.5 million in July-September 1975. It also emphasised the progressive decline in work time lost since July 1975 as a possible factor underlying the spurt in industrial output.

2 It has been estimated that net capital formation in the private industrial sector during 1976-77 was Rs 537 crore as compared to Rs 848 crore in 1975-76 ; see *The Economic Times*, New Delhi, January 1, 1978, p 1. These figures, it is worth noting, are in terms of current prices.

3 For a careful and convincing exposition of this view, see Patnaik and Rao (1977).

4 The share of manufacturing in total industrial production, however, declined a little over time, from 88.85 per cent in 1956 to 84.91 per cent in 1960 and 81.08 per cent in 1970.

5 The latest census of small-scale industries estimates the gross value of their output at Rs 2,603 crore in 1972 [Government of India, 1977, p 2]. Unfortunately, data for the corresponding period are not available in the case of factory sector because the usual annual survey of industries was not carried out in 1972. But we do know that in 1971-72 the gross value of output in the registered manufacturing units was Rs 14,980 crore [Government of India, 1976, p 103]. Thus, the share of the small-scale sector in the gross value of *total* industrial output works out at 14.8 per cent. While this figure might not be entirely accurate, it is a reasonable approximation.

6 See, for example, *Economic Survey, 1968-69*, Government of India, New Delhi, pp 10-11. For a critical evaluation of this view, see Bagchi (1970), pp 184-87.

7 Bhagwati and Desai (1970), p 499 are more elaborate in discussion but less definite in conclusion. Their final chapter begins as follows: "It seems to

us manifest, even though policy analysis in economic questions can rarely be as definitive as in the natural sciences, that Indian planning for industrialisation suffered from excessive attention to targets down to product level, and a wasteful physical approach to setting and implementation thereof, along with a generally inefficient framework of economic policies designed to regulate the growth of industrialisation."

8 See, for instance, Bhagwati and Srinivasan (1975), Ch 13; also p 175.

9 See Srinivasan (1977) and the subsequent interchange with Vaidyanathan (1977) in *Economic and Political Weekly.*

10 For evidence on this point, see Raj (1976) and Srinivasan and Narayana (1977).

11 Cf *Economic Survey, 1976-77,* Government of India, New Delhi, 1977, p 44.

12 According to Patnaik and Rao (1977), the danger of inflation arises once we allow for speculation. Corresponding to the 18 million tons of foodstocks and Rs 3,800 crore of foreign exchange reserves, there is an enormous amount of liquidity in the economy. In this context, deficit financing might generate inflationary expectations which, in turn, might induce people holding these liquid resources to switch from money into commodities, thereby pushing up prices.

13 Apart from the demand factor, Raj also specifies other linkages between agricultural and industrial growth. For an interesting, but different, analysis of how a shortage of agricultural wage goods would affect the demand for industrial goods, see Patnaik (1972).

14 *Cf* Sau (1974): the richest 20 per cent accounted for 48.4 per cent of the total consumption of industrial goods in rural India, and 55 per cent of the same in urban India.

15 For a detailed and succinct exposition of the argument, see Mitra (1977), Chapter 10, pp 141-69.

16 *Cf* Patnaik (1972). It is assumed, of course, that the absolute level of food consumption is maintained; in fact, it might also be cut back if the erosion of real incomes is large enough.

17 The proportion devoted to food (excluding edible oils, sugar and salt which are also manufactures) increased, at the same time, from 51.3 per cent to 55.2 per cent. These percentages have been computed from the data in Government of India (1976), pp 26-27. In our calculation, the category of industrial goods includes pan, tobacco, intoxicants, clothing, footwear, fuel, power, furniture, furnishings, household equipment and miscellaneous goods.

18 See, for example, a recent statement by H M Patel, the finance minister: "We have in fact removed all constraints on investment. We have not put any fresh hurdles to investment. If it does not pick up, the reasons are somewhat deeper to seek. I frankly confess I have not found an answer to my satisfaction", *The Times of India,* New Delhi, February 10, 1978, p 1.

19 For a lucid discussion on the political power of the rural oligarchy and its implications for economic development in India, see Mitra (1977).

20 The factors responsible for the reduction in public expenditure are discussed in Patnaik (1972).

21 Even in 1952-53, the richest 10 per cent of the population was responsible for 32.7 per cent of the total consumption of industrial goods in the rural

sector and 36.8 per cent of the total in the urban sector. The share of the poorest 50 per cent was 23.6 per cent and 19.7 per cent respectively; *Cf* Sau (1974).

REFERENCES

Bagchi, A K (1970): 'Long-Term Constraints on India's Industrial Growth, 1951-1968' in E A G Robinson and M Kidron (eds), *Economic Development in South Asia*, Macmillan, London.

Bhagwati, J and P Desai (1970): *India: Planning for Industrialisation*, Oxford University Press, London.

Bhagwati, J and T N Srinivasan (1975): *Foreign Trade Regimes and Economic Development: India,* National Bureau of Economic Research, New York.

Chakravarty, S (1974): *Reflections on the Growth Process in the Indian Economy,* Administrative Staff College of India, Hyderabad.

Chattopadhyay, P (1970): 'State Capitalism in India', *Monthly Review*, March.

Government of India (1976): *National Accounts Statistics: 1960/61-1974/75,* Central Statistical Organisation, Ministry of Planning, New Delhi.

– (1977): *Report on the Census of Small-Scale Industrial Units,* Development Commissioner, Small-Scale Industries, New Delhi.

Mitra, A (1977): *Terms of Trade and Class Relations,* Frank Cass, London.

Nayyar, D (1976): *India's Exports and Export Policies in the 1960s,* Cambridge University Press, London.

Patnaik, P (1972): 'Disproportionality Crisis and Cyclical Growth', *Economic and Political Weekly*, Annual Number, February.

Patnaik, P and S K Rao (1977): '1975-76: Beginning of the End of Stagnation?', *Social Scientist*, January-February.

Raj, K N (1976): 'Growth and Stagnation in Indian Industrial Development', *Economic and Political Weekly*, November 26.

Sau, R (1974): 'Some Aspects of Inter-Sectoral Resource Flows', *Economic and Political Weekly*, Special Number, August.

Srinivasan, T N (1977): 'Constraints on Growth and Policy Options: A Comment', *Economic and Political Weekly*, November 26.

Srinivasan, T N and N S S Narayana (1977): 'Economic Performance since the Third Plan and Its Implications for Policy', *Economic and Political Weekly*, Annual Number, February.

Vaidyanathan, A (1977): 'Constraints on Growth and Policy Options', *Economic and Political Weekly*, September 17 and December 17.

Special Number, August 1978

9

On the Question of Home Market and Prospects for Indian Growth

Sukhamoy Chakravarty

I

THE purpose of this note is to discuss whether there are reasons to believe that the problem of a 'narrowing' home market poses a serious problem so far as India's growth prospects are concerned.

At the time of formulation of the Second Five-Year Plan, such a query would have been dismissed as prima facie pointless inasmuch as there was a general consensus that developing countries were subject to the operation of Say's Law. That this was not a view exclusively held by orthodox economists is well attested by the fact that as late as 1965, M Kalecki wrote the following lines which have recently been republished: "The crucial problem facing the under-developed countries is thus to increase investment considerably, not for the sake of generating effective demand, as was the case in an under-employed developed economy, but for the sake of accelerating the expansion of productive capacity indispensable for the rapid growth of the national income".[1]

Consonant with this basic diagnosis, the principal questions were viewed as those of increasing the rate of saving as well as bringing about its conversion into an appropriate mix of capital goods which will be consistent with a process of accelerated growth. There were, of course, many and varied debates about how the increase in savings could be brought about. Whether it could be done by mobilising the so-called 'disguised unemployed' into productive work was debated in some depth as this method, under certain assumptions, could be shown to involve a relatively small marginal impact on the required savings rate. More importantly, in the Indian case, following the adaptation made by Mahalanobis of Marx's two-departmental scheme, it was argued that a higher priority should be given to the growth of investment goods industry. Briefly known as the 'heavy industry thesis' it was the subject of a very lively debate, one that has not subsided even to this date.

Different strategies were, however, proposed to overcome certain 'real', i e, non-monetary, constraints which were generally regarded as inhering in the structural features of the Indian economy. Briefly stated, these could be described as 'food' and 'foreign exchange' bottlenecks. These constraints affected the rate at which the economy's stock of productive assets could be built up, because the very process of capital formation implies the development of 'men and machines' which produce non-consumable output. Since in the Indian case, availability of men was deemed a non-problem, the question related to the method of 'feeding' them as there was a limit below which the consumption of a productively engaged person cannot fall. On a first approximation, this meant the existence of a 'food' surplus. Likewise, if a country's balance of payments situation was such that it could import the necessary 'machines' by increasing its export earnings without depressing its terms of trade excessively, in operational terms, the need for building up a 'capital goods producing sector' could be significantly obviated. At one time, it was however felt that while the 'food problem' could be taken care of through changes in agrarian relations, creation of 'infrastructure' through community development programmes and greater provision of public irrigation facilities, the problem of 'foreign exchange' was likely to remain until India could develop an adequate potential for exporting manufactured goods. To take care of the growing requirements of capital goods and heavy intermediates, it was decided to follow a two-pronged strategy which relied on building up a capital goods base at an accelerated rate while relying on an inflow of foreign aid during an intervening period.

The details of this strategy which broadly prevailed during the ten-year period spanning two five-year plans (1955-65) underwent significant changes in the course of the late sixties. However, at no time was it doubted that India's growth prospects significantly depended on the availability of food and 'foreign exchange'. It is, of course, true that there was a period of recession during the sixties which significantly affected the degree of capacity utilisation in most industries, especially capital goods producing industries, but recession was regarded as a process of adjustment consequent on severe harvest failures. Market problems, in an intrinsic sense, were not seriously raised although some vague references to 'disproportionality crisis' were heard.

The climate of discussion changed somewhat in the early seventies when some economists started to talk about the limits of an import-substituting strategy of industrialisation. The question of 'markets' was felt to be intrinsic to this discussion, as the main point at issue was whether India should not change its policy framework so as to make it more 'outward looking'. Two sets of data were generally adduced in support of this contention. One referred to the fact that the rate of growth of industrial production did not respond positively to improvements in food production which marked the years 1967-71. The second point related to India's poor performance on the 'export front' relative to the performance of several other south and east Asian economies. It was felt that given the fact that India had followed a policy of producing at home manufactured commodities which could be produced much more cheaply abroad, because of scale economies and other related advantages, the rate of growth of industrial production could not be stepped up on a sustained basis because neither the 'home market' nor the foreign market could absorb them. While the inability to push exports was considered to be closely related to the lack of competitiveness of Indian manufactured exportables, the limitations of the domestic market were supposed to reflect the unevenness in the distribution of incomes. This last point was a relatively new one in the Indian case, because up to that time while equity was considered to be a desirable objective in itself, it was generally thought to be negatively correlated with growth, a proposition which is regarded by many as the central maxim of classical theory of economic policy.

While in regard to developed countries, Keynes was thought to have shown a positive association between growth and equity, because of capital shortages the proposition was generally held to be inapplicable to India at the present stage of its growth.

While the argument for giving an outward looking orientation to our commercial policies has persisted as an important component of much subsequent thinking, events of the years 1972-74 succeeded in re-establishing the earlier argument relating to the primacy of the supply side, especially in food, fuel and necessary intermediates. However, of late, India has experienced a somewhat unprecedented set of conditions which has included piling up of a high level of foreign exchange reserves along with accumulation of large quantities of food stocks. While the growth rate over the period 1974-79 has averaged 5 per cent per annum, the composition of the growth rate suggests that easing of the so-called primary bottlenecks may not have done much to boost up investment in fixed assets, more particularly equipment. While savings have increased, investment has not increased to the same extent. More importantly, a part of the increase in investment has been due to an increase in inventories, which has taken place because of the absence of a profitable market.

Against this background, the question of markets has once again been raised. It is, however, possible that the immediate occasion for these queries, i e, the so-called 'reserves', will prove quite transitory in character, as they may have resulted largely from a combination of several accidental factors. If prices once again resume their upward course, of which there is some evidence already, these reserves can be eaten up fairly quickly, and the economy may return to its previous 'supply-constrained' state. Is it then merely of academic interest to discuss the problem of demand deficiency as a constraint on growth? There are good grounds for such scepticism.

However, there are at least three reasons why a discussion would appear to be necessary. First of all, it is useful to know why easing of supply constraints on two occasions failed to trigger off growth spurts over a longer period. After all, some successful cases of industrialisation have taken place because of windfall gains, as to a certain extent was the case of Japan in the 1890s. If it does not happen in the Indian case, it at least requires explanation. Secondly, the question of export-led growth as a strategy for India would remain a moot question, for judging which it is necessary to have a proper idea regarding the nature of the domestic 'market' problem. Finally, the question of income distribution and its relationship to growth is an issue that is likely to persist, no matter what short-term changes take place on the economic scene.[2]

II

How does one define the 'market' problem? In Marxian terms, the 'market problem' is considered to be a problem of the realisation of 'surplus value' as distinct from its 'production'. In the language introduced by Keynes, the problem is one of deficiency of 'effective demand' which generates idle capacity implying a loss of 'potential output'. Or put differently, it is the problem of insufficiency of investment in relation to the 'full-employment level' of savings. That these two approaches are closely related was shown by Kalecki, who arrived at conclusions similar to Keynes while starting from the Marxian schemes of reproduction.[3]

In Marxian terms, the argument that the 'market problem' is a relatively minor one in the developing countries rests on the implicit assumption that the production of surplus value is in some sense more basic than the problem of realisation of surplus value. In the language of Keynes, the argument rests on the greater strength of inducement to invest relative to the capacity to save.

It is necessary to judge in what sense these propositions are valid before we turn once again to the Indian situation.

In her argument regarding the logical impossibility of positive net investment within a pure capitalist environment, Rosa Luxemburg had used the Marxian expanded reproduction schemes which were left in an unfinished state at the time of Marx's death. She used these schemes to show that in the absence of a so-called 'third' market, sometimes referred to as the 'external market', growth cannot take place. If her argument were correct, then the problem of 'market' is a critical problem both for early capitalism as well as for late capitalism. There would, then, be no reason to characterise the market question as relevant only for 'mature capitalism'. In fact, several Russian economists had precisely argued along similar lines in the nineties of the last century.[4] Rosa Luxemburg's argument was more sophisticated than the relatively crude arguments used by some 'Narodnik' economists which ran more on 'under-consumptionist' lines. Nevertheless, discussion on the market problem dates back at least nearly a century, even if one ignores for the time being the Ricardo-Malthus controversy and also the contemporary contribution of Sismondi which ran on somewhat different lines.

But the moot point is whether Rosa Luxemburg was correct in drawing her conclusions from the reproduction schemes. On the basis of extensive discussions which have taken place on this question, it can be shown that in a purely formal sense, the Marxian schemes of expanded reproduction may be shown to be consistent with steady growth, accelerated growth or disproportional growth that leads to a breakdown of the process of capital accumulation. If we define accumulation to include both savings and investment, different outcomes would depend on initial conditions, and the values of crucial technological and behavioural parameters.[5] As a matter of fact, as we have noted already, the so-called priority for heavy industry can be obtained from an application of the reproduction schema, provided only additional assumptions are made.[6]

The decisive question relates to the factors governing the process of accumulation. Marx made no specific study of inducement to invest although he emphasised the critical role of endogenous technical changes. However, his position on the question of Say's law was not uniform throughout all the three volumes of *Capital.* In several places, he dismisses it as 'childish nonsense'. But there are other places where he appears to have implicitly assumed it. Rosa Luxemburg was not prepared to assume it in any form in her discussion. This is why the issue of where the demand, i e, demand for net investment, is going to come from was her most pressing question. However, it is not possible to go the whole way with her for a variety of reasons which need not detain us here. Suffice it to note here that there is nothing in the functioning of the capitalist system which requires consumption to be rigidly fixed over time. While allowing for consumption to increase over time even though in a limited and lopsided manner allows us to overcome the logical impasse, the point about the 'external' market may still remain a very crucial insight in explaining several problems pertaining to early as well as late capitalism.

However, it is quite essential to be clear about one point. Rosa Luxemburg did not use the term to mean only foreign markets in a geographical sense of the term. Using this concept, it is possible, as we shall show, to distinguish between 'early' and late capitalism in terms of the magnitude of the need for an 'external' market as well as of the type of the 'external' market that may be relevant for different phases of growth.

On the basis of this preliminary discussion, it is now possible to turn to the developing country scene to sketch out a broad scheme that can correlate the more obvious facts pertaining to the growth experience of such countries.

It is undoubtedly true that the productivity of labour in the principal wage-good producing sector, i e, food, in most developing countries is low in relation to the consumption requirement of a gainfully occupied worker. Along with the 'high dependency' ratio that is nearly universal throughout many such economies, the total quantum of real surplus, i e, surplus of wage-goods, that is available for feeding workers who may be employed in producing outputs belonging to department of industries is, therefore, limited. In this sense, therefore, a Ricardo-like situation prevails. Traditionally, it has been argued that in this situation, all that is necessary to ensure that sustained growth takes place is to increase the potential for generating surplus in agriculture. However, such a conclusion may not always be warranted. Much depends on whether there is a desire to capitalise the 'surplus' in the form of adding to directly productive investment. This, in its turn, is a function of the rate of profit in relation to the rate of interest on lending money. Furthermore, even when the rate of profit is reasonably high, long-term growth in demand will depend on the character of the innovation which creates the basis for a long-run upward push. Here we can distinguish between different situations. First, we may think of the Smithian 'vent for surplus' type of argument which operates through commercialisation of agriculture. 'Food crops' may be replaced by 'cash crops' which have a market abroad, thus triggering off an initial spurt of growth whose source in a way is external to the home economy. Realisation problem does not arise at least initially but the process may not lead to any significant capitalisation of agriculture, let alone the emergence of a domestic capital goods producing sector. Growth may, in such cases, prove quite transitory in nature. Secondly, profit opportunities may be created by the appearance of innovations which are of a predominantly labour-saving character. In this case, productivity per unit of labour increases but so does the body of dispossessed rural workers. Capitalisation of agriculture increases in this case, giving rise to the emergence of a domestic capital goods sector along with occupational differentiation of the labour force. In this case, no market problem need arise, at least initially, because of the high rate of growth of Department I along with the creation of a tertiary sector which is known to be income elastic in nature. However, the situation is likely to prove highly unstable unless the rate of reabsorption of the displaced labour force into non-agricultural occupations is high, or the consumption of the productively employed labour is allowed to rise over time.

Thirdly, innovation may be such as to lead to an increase in productivity per acre. In this case, labour displacement is not inevitable. However, if the beneficiaries of technical change are limited in number, the solution of the 'realisation' problem may take the route of inducing a changed pattern of preferences favouring the domestic production of luxury goods or of imports which directly or indirectly cater to luxury goods. The new employment effect of this pattern of growth will probably be adverse in general because the labour content of luxury goods production is generally low in present-day developing countries. Labour-content of agricultural output is also, on balance, likely to decline unless special types of non-market intervention are being envisaged, which go beyond the 'rules of the game' permitted by capitalism.

Our analysis would seem to suggest that while the ability of agriculture to generate surplus is crucial to sustain growth or to accelerate it, it is by no means a *sufficient* one in a private enterprise economy. There must exist both a mechanism as well as a motive for capitalisation of the surplus. If we assume the operation of a traditional market mechanism, then the rate of interchange of the output between agriculture and industry or 'Dept I and Dept II' must also enter our calculation. Secondly, if profit is the determining motive, then demand does enter the picture via the influence that it exercises on profitability of different types of decisions, including decisions to hoard, which affect the long-term rate of interest. Leaving out state intervention as well as exceptionally favourable situations on the 'foreign trade' side, growth is likely to be modest, especially in over-populated agricultural economies with hierarchical agricultural structures. This may be because of the operation of a 'terms of trade effect', a phenomenon much emphasised by Ricardo,[7] or because of the presence of a market problem, which enters the picture as soon as we relax the assumption that all surplus is automatically reinvested.

There may be situations, where the demand problem remains only a latent one as it is overwhelmed by a strong inducement to invest arising from opportunity to exploit an exceptionally profitable innovation. If institutional-financial arrangements of the society permit widespread diffusion of the particular innovation, and demand patterns prove sufficiently flexible, the economy may experience rapid growth for some time. The length of the period is determined by a whole host of factors, which include the relative rate of interchange between the produce of the sector experiencing innovation and the output of the rest of the economy.

There have been, historically speaking, episodes of growth when innovations have covered a wide front. In these cases, booms have lasted much longer, stretching sometimes over decades. There have been economists who have been much impressed by the presence of 'long waves' in the history of capitalist economies whereas others have remained unimpressed as to whether they constitute a separate analytical category or not.[8]

Just as we may have situations when the demand problem may remain only a latent one, we can have situations when the demand problem may turn out to be the most important one. Generally, 'mature' economies are the ones which are regarded as prone to 'demand deficiency', but even at earlier stages of development such difficulties may arise. In late capitalism, the problem of inducement to invest is negatively correlated with the existing stock of capital, which can involve a so-called 'junking effect' when additions to capital stock take place. If the market is of an oligopolistic character and there is a strong preference to maintain 'capital values', the strength of an innovation has to be correspondingly greater to overcome the inhibition to invest. In early capitalism, one may be inclined to dismiss such junking effect as prima facie unimportant and thus view the problem of demand as possessing much less importance. One can, then, argue on Ricardo that the tendency to a decline in the rate of profit depends crucially on the strength of diminishing returns to agriculture, which operates through the 'terms of trade effect'. While motive to accumulate and the rate of growth are affected adversely, there is no 'market' problem in relation to what is produced.[9]

However, in contemporary developing countries, the market problem can arise insofar as savers are not necessarily the investors. In addition, many of them possess an industrial structure which is significantly oligopolistic in character. Furthermore, even in agriculture, interference with the market mechanism may cause problems in relation to surplus absorption. Thus, technical innovation even in agriculture, especially food, which should normally expand the market may fail to be insufficiently stimulating because of various 'support operations' carried out by the political authorities in the name of maintaining adequate incentive to invest. Along with a highly skewed distribution of property in land and other capital assets, the propensity to save may increase without there being a corresponding increase in the inducement to invest. Inventory investment assumes a critical role, which is largely determined by the role of the government as a 'buyer of the last resort'. In addition, there may be a preference for acquiring functionally unproductive assets, such as 'gold' and other precious metals, or for illegal export of capital.

In situations where the inducement to invest begins to flag, the role of the 'third market' acquires critical importance. We have already pointed out the importance of support price operations, which effectively implies a third market. When producer interests even in agriculture begin to operate on an organised basis, the rules of the economic game acquire a different character. In principle, an active and energetic state can in such situations play an important role by expanding capacity in Department I industries which pay off only in the long run and undertaking redistributive measures to increase the consumption demand of the disadvantaged strata, thereby increasing the volume of offsets to saving. As a matter of fact, superficially it may look that with an increase in the potential surplus of agriculture, not merely rapid growth but even growth with equity is on the cards as the economy is likely to operate well within the 'inflation barrier'.

However, in practice, things may work out much less smoothly even in situations where the Ricardian fear may be temporarily absent. Even ignoring, for the time being, traditional doubts regarding the character of the state,[10] there are certain important considerations that must be borne in mind. First, how does the state finance its spending? There are, in principle, several possibilities. However, only such possibilities need to be included as would reduce surplus consumption of the affluent, an expression which has to be fairly broad-based in terms of coverage.

However, a system of taxation, which is based on an operational application of this idea, should only include direct taxation of the propertied classes of the society on a progressive basis as well as graduated taxes on 'luxury commodities' or commodities of superior quality. In such a system, while additional consumption of a particular segment will be restrained by extra taxes, the net effect on consumption as a whole will show an increase inasmuch as public investment is likely to generate additional wage demand. Furthermore, additional wage demand will involve greater demand for articles such as food and other mass consumer goods whereas real resources released by taxation will have a somewhat different composition. Given the non-malleability of capital equipment, at least in the short run, the problem of financing will be eased to the extent that scarce intermediate goods and foreign exchange may be used for building up productive assets. To the extent these assets lead to an increase in output of food and essentials, there can be non-inflationary growth at a rate determined jointly by the income elasticity of demand for essentials, particularly food, and the rate of growth of 'food' production per capita. The above policy package is merely a logical deduction from the maintained hypothesis that 'food' constitutes the major bottleneck.

However, there can be three major hitches in the process. First, and an obvious one, is the large-scale evasion of taxes that may take place. Secondly, property-owners may reduce their savings rather than consumption. In that case, real resources may not be effectively released. If, to counteract these influences, one maintains low rates of taxation and also gives considerable exemptions for savings, if they are not altogether left out of the tax net, both the growing wealth effect as well as the resulting volume of transfer expenditure via the increasing tax burden will have to be allowed for in case deficit in expenditure is sought to be met by extra market borrowing. Thirdly, raising resources through taxes does not automatically imply increasing public investment because the government's propensity to increase current expenditure is by no means a factor that can be ignored. In the event of government's current expenditure going up on a 'loan financed basis' the market problem may be solved in a manner of speaking but there can be worsening of unemployment in the long run, especially in situations where population is growing fast. In practice, out of different possibilities, heavy reliance is placed on indirect taxes especially on those commodities whose demand is relatively inelastic and on different forms of borrowing, particularly on borrowing from the central bank. The effect is inevitably mixed since to the extent that prices rise, real incomes of fixed income recipients, including those of the salariat, fall which leads to a decline in consumption demand while incomes of owners of property increase which leads to increase in their consumption. But in compositional terms, consumption declines are not matched by consumption increases and hence disproportionalities appear, even if there is no overall decline in demand. There is, in general, an overspill into the market for foreign exchange. Certain productive assets may get created by the government, depending on the nature of its expenditure pattern, but their utilisation cannot be assured because there is usually an element of instability associated with public expenditure financed by such methods. Because as soon as inflation begins to be anticipated, state invervention degenerates into 'stagflation' because there is usually an attempt to mollify the most aggressive claimants to the national cake. Thus, while state intervention may serve in logic a crucial role in steering clear between the pulls of 'inflationary' and 'deflationary' tendencies the extent of controllability of the economy may be much too small for it to succeed in most developing countries.

At this stage, it is necessary for us to look into the question of 'foreign trade', even though briefly. It may look on the face of it quite plausible that 'exports' can play a strategic role in the whole process. On the one hand, it can provide a market for sectors where output has increased and, at the same time, it can provide the capacity to import additional capital goods. Thus, both the demand problem and the capacity problem can be taken care of through the mechanism of international trade.

The possibility of an 'export-led' growth has, therefore, attracted a great deal of attention in the literature. It is also one of the standard policy prescriptions doled out to developing countries by multinational aid-giving agencies. That there is something plausible about this argument has been shown by the growth experience of certain developing countries.

Since most of these arguments are well known, it is not necessary for us to repeat them here. It is only necessary to mention that both the ability to expand exports as well as to secure favourable terms of trade have usually depended on rather exceptional circumstances. These include the phase of the economic cycle through which developed countries are passing, the nature of the product demand and the course of technological change. Arthur Lewis has argued that the terms of trade have fallen for the tropical producers because their productivity in food growing has remained constant relatively to 'commercial crops'. In addition, one can refer to the competition from the synthetic products which have profoundly affected prospects of developing country exports of primary products. As regards manufacturing exports, the degree of protection engaged in by developed country producers has figured very prominently in most recent discussions. Finally, the growth of multinational corporations has affected the very nature and volume of trade understood as 'arm's length' transactions.

Our analysis of the 'market problem' has indicated that while it cannot be ignored as soon as we distinguish between decisions to save and decisions to invest, and that the classical assumption that all savings are automatically invested, leading to expansion of productive assets, is too much of a simplification, which can sometimes grossly distort our perspectives, the market question is not usually an independent problem to be tackled by methods which operate only on the demand side. The 'market problem' is best viewed as part of a more general conditioning framework which encompasses questions relating to the nature and the type of the accumulation process that prevails in a particular developing country.

III

Our general discussion of the 'market problem' permits us to make here some observations in relation to India. Our discussion relates largely to domestic demand, because we shall leave out the question of export growth except for some brief observations. Let us first make an attempt to state the problem in concrete terms.

Given the fact that the Indian economy is still largely dependent on agriculture in terms of the percentage of labour force that is gainfully occupied and also the fact that final consumption expenditure is largely devoted to agricultural and agro-based products, the market problem in the Indian context could possibly be stated as follows. Assume that we have information which enables us to estimate probable increases in acreage, cropping pattern and yield rates, based on the past trend. The increase amounts to a rate of growth of agricultural production which is fairly close to the rate at which population has been growing. Let us now consider a situation when for technological reasons, it becomes possible for us to step up the rate of growth significantly over the past trend. More concretely, let us take the case of 'food'. Assume that food production has been growing at about 2.5 per cent per annum. Let the hypothetical growth rate be 4 per cent per annum, a possibility which is technologically on the cards. Can this increase be sustained by demand over a sufficiently long period of time, say, at least a decade?

The variables that would have been considered relevant in this context would include the rate of growth of population, the rate of growth of consumption, and the elasticity of food demand with respect to per capita consumption. If the savings-income ratio is assumed to be constant, then the rate of growth of income equals the rate of growth of consumption. In that case, it can be shown that with the usual estimates of Engel elasticity for food, a rate of growth of income between 5 and 5.5 per cent per annum will ensure that no 'demand problem' arises. The main problem is then one of ensuring how best this increase can be brought about.

However, this procedure is subject to very many limitations, most of which are well understood. But despite these, it is frequently used as a check as it fits in with our general preconceptions about the operative role of a 'food bottleneck' in the case of an over-populated agrarian economy.

As we have noted, there are, however, reasons to believe that the above calculation may go wrong outside a planned economy for reasons that have something to do with demand. In the Indian case, the growth of population which is supposed to lead automatically to an increase in demand is not a correct assumption since paupers cannot consume in a market economy unless special transfers are made. It is well known that, outside the family, there are no such mechanisms in operation, not even Poor Laws. Secondly, the distribution of incomes can be adversely affected by the process of growth, which can have further reflex action on the economy. There are several mechanisms at work here which require to be explicitly stated. One refers to changes in the share of marketed surplus. This share may go up if the bigger farmers are the ones who have largely benefited from the yield-raising innovations, which is the case in India. The share may remain constant or fall if the poorer farmers are the ones who have benefited, an alternative implied in certain policy pronouncements of the government. In the first and realistic case, capacity to save in real terms will have gone up. Whether there will be sufficient offsets to savings will determine whether the production level will be maintained at increasingly higher levels, barring of course an increase in unproductive expenditure which is no answer outside a short-term context. In the second case, food demand is less of a problem. There may be problems regarding meeting demand for industrial products which may be required on the margin in raising food production. The second case is likely to lead to a situation of disproportionality rather than to one of overall demand deficiency. However, disproportional growth processes develop a tendency towards 'crisis', which means at least a temporary disruption of the growth process.

Apart from the share of marketed surplus changing as a result of the nature of the growth process there is also the related question of the terms of trade which we have also noted in our general discussion.[11]

On this question four factors may be regarded as particularly important, technology, relative factor endowment, market form and ownership pattern of land. To the extent that product markets are considered to be perfect and a perfectly competitive lease market for land services is being postulated, we have the Ricardian situation where the ultimate rate of growth is zero even though its approach can be postponed for a long time to come by means of a sequence of land-saving innovations. The medium-term growth rate depends on the strength of historical diminishing returns on the one hand and propensities to save of the rent owners and profit receivers, on the other side.

However, the problem of demand deficiency is assumed away in traditional treatments rather than demonstrated because of the reliance on the assumption that savers are necessarily the same as investors or, alternatively, by evoking the presumed equilibrating role of the interest rate.

In the Indian context, neither of these assumptions listed above to validate Say's law holds. Furthermore, there are important departures from the assumption of perfect competition in the product markets, including even agriculture, after price support operations were accepted as a part of the rules of the game since the late sixties. Finally, one cannot assume that the Indian land market bears any similarity to Ricardian assumptions, as Richard Jones pointed out even in the 1830s.[12]

All these imply that the terms of trade between industry and agriculture cannot be any longer regarded as corresponding to the ratios of marginal costs of production. Rather they should be regarded at least in part as political parameters.[13]

This implies that we can have a general deterioration in the distribution of incomes, arising partly from a differential distribution of output gains intra-sectorally and partly from differential incidence of price changes inter-sectorally. These considerations suggest that the 'demand' problem may arise inasmuch as the force of overall inducement to invest may not be matched by the capacity to save. This can, of course, go either way in principle.

In the Indian context, however, inducement to invest on the part of private investors is significantly affected by the behaviour of public investment. The critical role of the state as an investor and the dual role of state investment in sustaining demand as well as creating capacity is not envisaged in the simple Ricardian model nor in the Marxian schemes of expanded reproduction. The requirements of agricultural growth in the Ricardian schemes could be largely defined in terms of the amount of 'corn' that was directly or indirectly needed for producing a unit of 'corn'. This was because the role of fixed capital in agriculture was relatively a minor one, at least conceptually. 'Capital' largely meant advances to 'labour' along with the 'seed corn' that was planted.

Mark, of course, fully allowed for the role of 'fixed capital' in the form of instruments to assist labour. But he was dealing with a situation where the pressure of ruthless competition was supposed to lead to a situation of growing capital intensification in agriculture with a predominantly labour saving bias. Growth of agricultural output took place through mechanisation which was also correlated with a growth in the size of farms.

In the Indian case, facts of demography and compulsions of an agro-climatic character require different types of investment in agriculture, which include prominently items such as irrigation, fertilisers, better seeds, pesticides, etc. Some of these capital inputs such as irrigation works often require to be organised on a very large scale which makes state intervention essential. Along with these yield-increasing investments, there is the need for investment in infra-structure such as transport and electricity which enlarge the market and provide a suitable energy base for sustained growth.

Transforming agriculture, therefore, means growing public investment involving a suitable mix of directly productive capital and social overhead facilities. While, in principle, this form of investment planning can do the job so far as raising agricultural growth is concerned, the question of how the public investment is to be financed becomes a crucial factor specific to India. Among the necessary conditions, one must have a mechanism for channelisation of a part of the growing agricultural surplus into state hands. Herein lies a possibility of a major hitch between the increased capacity to save of the farmers who have benefited, a relatively small group, and the capacity to invest on the part of the state. The problem, of course, gets more complicated if the capacity to save on the part of those who have benefited from public investment can be maintained only on the basis of an 'administered price system' which diverts investment away from directly productive channels into investment in holding stocks. Furthermore, an extra amount has to be deducted from the potential savings of the public sector in the form of subsidies for political reasons; urban consumers have to be provided with foodgrains at relatively stable prices even when the food has to be procured at rising prices.

It may, however, be argued that growing agricultural production makes its contribution to the exchequer indirectly by increasing income and hence capacity to pay taxes through its backward and forward linkages. However, this does not very much change the overall dimensions of the problem or its nature.

The accompanying table demonstrates the extent of the gap between 'capital formation' and 'saving' on a net basis which had to be bridged by resort to draft on private savings, foreign assistance and 'deficit financing'. The figures in the table pertain to the years from 1960-61 to 1971-72. The table reveals the situation as it existed up to 1971-72. However, there is no reason to doubt that the same trend persists in the late 1970s.[14]

For our purpose, it is sufficient to note that in future, if the growth momentum acquired in the economy towards the end of the 1970s has to be sustained, the problem of financial intermediation is going to be more acute because the disproportionate relationship between

Table

(Rs crore, current prices)

Year	Capital Formation	Saving	Deficit
1960-61	1021	309	–712
1961-62	1038	363	–675
1962-63	1306	408	–898
1963-64	1501	539	–962
1964-65	1714	611	–1103
1965-66	1967	592	–1375
1966-67	1853	407	–1446
1967-68	1999	355	–1644
1968-69	1810	522	–1288
1969-70	1846	645	–1201
1970-71	2346	822	–1514
1971-72	2759	804	–1955

Source: Uma Datta Roychoudhury and Pratap Narain, 'Current National Income Statistics: What They Tell', *Economic and Political Weekly*, September 27, 1975.

costs and prices is nowhere more serious today than in public enterprises almost across-the-board. On the other hand, the share of subsidies in the expenditure of public sector has gone up from 5.9 per cent in 1970-71 to 9.6 per cent in 1976-77, whereas the combined share of interest on public debt, subsidies and current transfers has gone up from 20.8 per cent in 1970-71 to 26.8 per cent in 1976-77. During this period, it is of interest to note that taxes as a percentage of total net product have also gone up significantly.

Thus, we can say that one of the basic problems in maintaining demand as well as creating capacity to take care of the requirements of growth is to work out a framework of monetary and fiscal policy that restrains growth of consumption expenditure in upper income brackets, diverts a part of their savings to the state and allows for growth of consumption in lower deciles.

It is, however, important to note that insofar as realised savings in the private sector depend on the extent of public expenditure managed through deficit financing and indirect taxation which leads to an upward bias in prices, the distribution of incomes is worsened, which tends to do the opposite, i e, reduce consumption demand where it should not and promote it where it has little leverage in terms of demand for staples.

It is only to the extent that public investment expenditure becomes more labour-intensive that, via an employment effect, one can expect to partially offset the disequalising process. We know, however, that of late government investment has taken partly the form of building up inventory of finished products, especially food. This has, however, had the effect of accentuating the inequality between surplus farmers and those who are net purchasers of food in rural areas. To keep up effective demand for food in such a situation would, then, require at the least a public works programme. The latter has to be so designed as to meet both requirements of demand as well as of additional capacity creation. That there are obvious limits in this direction is shown by the fact that during a period when food surpluses piled up significantly, the outlay on irrigation was increased proportionately to a much lesser extent.

While the pattern of public investment can play an important role in Indian agriculture, on the demand side far more significant effects can be obtained in a long-run sense by changes in agrarian relations. In Japan during the fifties, it is generally agreed that among the significant factors promoting demand was a reduction in landowner's rent consequent on implementation of land reform laws. In India, so far as public pronouncements go, changes in the distribution of incomes in the countryside requiring reforms of various sorts, starting from tenancy regulation and greater unionisation of rural labour to more ambitious programmes of land reform, have often been mentioned. However, it is not clear that much has been achieved on the field. It is symptomatic of the situation that while the net availability of cereals per capita per day has gone up from 403.1 gms in 1970 to 427.8 gms in 1978, procurement has gone up from 6.71 million tonnes in 1970 to 11 million tonnes in 1978. In 1976 the corresponding figures were 406.6 gms and 12.85 million tonnes, respectively. During the entire period 1970-78, the amount released through the public distribution system has not exceeded 11.74 million tonnes. An average for the period as a whole will be slightly below 10 million tonnes annually.

These figures are broadly indicative of the fact that while bad years cause great strains on the public distribution system necessitating large-scale imports of grain, good years do not lead to any expansion. This is partly as it should be because for the affluent in a good year it makes little difference whether he buys from a fair price shop or from the open market when prices are more or less the same; but it is equally clear that this function, howsoever important it may be, has little to do with widening the market. Investment in procurement operations, then, reduces to a form of investment against downward change in grain prices so far as the producer is concerned. While one need not minimise the importance of this investment from the social point of view, one has to recognise it for what it is and not expect the mechanism to serve as a solution of the farm surplus absorption problem by providing the needy with the required amount of grains.

It may be argued that increases in agricultural output, even when they are confined to relatively bigger producers, have many advantages through the linkage effect on the economy. This is partly true inasmuch as increases in output can allow for import substitution in grains, generate demand for locally produced industrial products and provide the basis for savings, and therefore contribute to the growth process. But the crucial question is the cost at which these gains are being achieved. If public investment that is needed for this purpose is being financed through deficit spending and to a larger extent by taxation of necessities, which reduce the real wage rate through induced increases in prices, then a part of the gains of growth is being offset by a deteriorating distribution of income. In other words, increase in savings which matches the extra investment is going to be in part inflation-induced, which can lead to additional distortions in the productive structure.

We have no precise information on the distribution of incomes which can be utilised to throw light on the question of how the increase in the rate of domestic savings has been brought about in recent years.

We know from the data published by the CSO that the implicit price index of net domestic product has risen from 100 in 1970-71 to 165 in 1976-77. This information, along with such other information that we have about the decline in the share of labour income in the value added of the organised sector from 71.2 to 66.4 over the same period whereas for the unorganised sector the distribution of factor incomes has remained almost unchanged, is consistent with the inference that at least a part of the increase in the savings rate has been brought about through reduction in the consumption levels of the poorer sections of our society which consist of agricultural labourers, small farmers, urban unorganised labour, etc. However, alternative explanations are also conceivable although they do not look as probable.

In this context, it is also worthwhile to refer to the very extensive literature on rural poverty. We have the recent results of Ahluwalia which show that even in the case of Punjab and Haryana, the percentage of people living below the 'poverty line' has not declined even though agricultural net value added per person has gone up very sharply over the period 1960-61 to 1973-74.[15] At the all-India level, too, there has been no significant decline in the proportion over the years, which implies an increase in absolute numbers over all these years. While there are many who would go beyond Ahluwalia in suggesting growing immiserisation, his data also do not suggest that a mere increase in net output of agricultural sector per capita leads to an automatic improvement in the standard of living of the poorest segment of rural population.

Can we infer from the above pieces of information that the home market problem is quite a serious one for India? Not necessarily, unless we have looked into the factors governing investment demand. Here we note that both public and private investment have been increasing. Although when one takes into account the fact that the implicit price deflator for gross fixed capital formation has increased more sharply than the overall net domestic product deflator, part of the recorded increases may be optical in character.

What then are the prospects for sustained growth? Here we should note the fact that the government is finding it necessary to resort to an increasing extent to borrowings. The data given in the *Economic Survey* bear out this trend and there is no evidence that this process is going to reverse soon. Furthermore, the private corporate sector is also finding it necessary to borrow increasingly from the household sector. Reduction of corporate sector's capacity to finance its investment from its internal saving is a fact which can be explained through a combination of factors in which government's inability to raise public investment sufficiently plays an important role along with the changes in the pattern of financing capital expenditure decision. Thus we get back to the question as to how long this pattern of development can continue. It is not impossible that government's ability to tap household savings will decline sharply if inflationary expectations become prominent. In that context, while public savings will diminish further due to upward escalation in wages and salaries and a larger subsidy burden, the net accretion of deposits will slacken implying a change in the preference pattern of asset receivers. Hence, the process of financial intermediation, even with its in-built bias, will cease to be effective in a situation of expected inflation.

With weather cycles playing their usual role and instability in the international economic environment, the cushion currently available like food and foreign exchange may not stay too long, necessitating cut-backs in investment. Such an outcome is rendered all the more likely because of the large increase in liquidity which has taken place from government's own budgetary operations over the last several years.

Multiplier effect of reduction in public investment will lead to emergence of further idle capacity in capital goods sector and push down the gross profit margin because of the possible increase in overhead charges and the prices of raw materials. There can be possibly some increase in demand for industrial products needed for residential construction which can lead to capacity bottlenecks in certain sectors such as cement, special types of steel, etc. In addition, there can be some increase in demand for consumer durables, a possibility which has been noted by many.

We have neglected in this discussion the question of export growth. This is because a reasonably complete analysis will have to take into account recent developments in the international economy which we cannot discuss within the compass of the present note. Secondly, while the share of exports in current prices has gone up in recent years, this has been due to a conjuncture of several accidental factors. Unless something of the nature of a big structural break is postulated, for which there is as yet no evidence, it is quite unlikely that exports can play a dimensionally critical role given the nature of the country's resource endowment and size. Finally, if the government's commitments to village and cottage industries along with its declared objective of meeting the requirements of low end poverty are to be implemented, export strategy will require suitable alteration whose outlines are not yet available.

IV

Is there any specific sense in which we can then say that we have a market problem today which suggests a qualitatively different situation from what prevailed in the fifties and mid-sixties? Arguments based on 'absolute immiserisation' are often invoked to support the position that we are faced with a new situation. This may well have been true in certain parts of the country but the data would not support a simple immiserisation thesis on the scale of the country as a whole although it would be granted that the total number of 'absolutely' poor people has been going up over the years. But considering the deterioration in the employment situation over the economy as a whole which is often commented upon, it could be argued that 'effectual demand' for labour is not increasing or is increasing slowly even when and where output, especially agricultural output, has increased at significant rates. This would suggest that 'labour absorption' is taking place in agriculture at a very slow rate which is creating along with a natural growth of rural population a larger reserve army of labour. This implies two possibilities. A growing proliferation of footloose labour as has been happening in the eastern region which, through migration, can keep down wages even in prosperous rural areas, thereby preventing any significant change in the distribution of factor incomes. Secondly, it could mean a compensating increase in the size of Department I where labour displaced from agriculture can find productive employment. If, food surpluses are emerging and men are 'in surplus', we could have in principle witnessed much larger growth rates of investment, thus helping to project a rising level of domestic demand. Unfortunately, in the initial period of new agricultural strategy dating from the late sixties, public investment was kept as a whole on a low key while government entered the area of price support operations. Thus the state had to assume a new and important role in the realisation of surplus produced per man as distinguished from its earlier role of setting up industries in key sectors for raising the productivity per worker.

In the initial absence of effective financial intermediation that was necessary for mobilising rural savings in productive investment, capacity to invest by public agencies had declined along with the capacity to save induced by an adverse movement in the terms of trade against the non-agricultural sector. In the seventies up to 1973-74, the economy experienced a series of shocks such as war, drought, a sharp deterioration in external terms of trade, resulting in a price inflation which redirected incomes away especially from unorganised industrial workers, small farmers who were net purchasers of food, agricultural labourers, etc. Household savings, especially financial savings in the form of net accretion of deposits, however, began to display a buoyancy which they have continued to maintain, supported meanwhile significantly by remittances from abroad. In the meantime, however, the government's newly acquired role in solving the realisation problem has also increased. It has been instrumental in preventing a fall in prices in the economy in years of plenty. This is shown by the fact that the implicit deflator for final consumption expenditure has been going up, which is probably a more accurate measure of the cost of living. Meanwhile, of course, the economy has acquired certain assets such as food stocks and foreign exchange reserves.

The culmination of this process has been reached in the late 1970s when investment has fallen short of savings, suggesting an apparent inability to absorb higher levels of investment. While this phase can be called a 'demand constrained' one in a fairly straightforward sense, there is little reason to believe that such a conjuncture will last much longer.

Should a couple of harvests prove inadequate and oil prices increase further, there can be a very big change in the economic scenario which will almost certainly compel reduction in the rate of growth of public investment for a fresh stretch of time. This will imply a slowing down in the overall rate of growth of fixed capital formation and consequent reduction in the rate of employment creation and slowing down of the growth of demand for major industrial products with the possible exception of certain consumer durables.

In a long-term sense, the demand problem is thus much better viewed as an important tendency that has got built into the system rather than as a projection of the experience since the mid-1960s. Structurally speaking, the factors that tend to produce 'demand deficiency' in relative terms have a lot to do with a growing rigidity in the structure of prices throughout the economy, both agricultural and industrial, with an upward trend imparted through a highly permissive monetary policy, insufficient generation of employment opportunities, absence of bargaining power on the part of rural poor, and the myopic character of private investment. On the other hand, through its commanding position in the process of financial intermediation, the state has acquired an ability to invest significantly in excess of its savings. This, along with an increasing inflow of foreign aid, can keep the rate of investment at a higher level than would have been possible otherwise. However, as we have seen, there is an inherent element of instability about such a process of growth, which can be easily aggravated by exogenous factors. Besides, viewed in the long-run sense, such a system cannot possess the kind of dynamism that marks processes of capital accumulation which are based on rapid absorption of labour into relatively more productive work and/or permit real wages to increase in terms of those goods whose costs decline as a result of capital accumulation.

In the absence of these trends, the process of growth is not only likely to be inequitable but also a slow one as well. It is in the combination of these two features that the main departures from the 'classical model' lie, and the source of the market problem has to be located.

NOTES

1 See M Kalecki, *Essays on Developing Economies,* The Harvester Press, Sussex, England, 1976, p 23.

2 In the Indian context, there are several economists who have highlighted the distributional problem in the context of growth. We can mention, in particular, A K Bagchi, L Lefeber, K N Raj and Deepak Nayyar. See A K Bagchi, 'Long-Term Constraints on India's Industrial Growth' in E A G Robinson and M Kidron (eds), *Economic Development in South Asia*, Macmillan, London, 1970; L Lefeber, 'Income Distribution and Agricultural Development' in J Bhagwati and R S Eckaus (eds), *Development and Change*, Allen and Unwin, 1972; K N Raj, 'Growth and Stagnation in Indian Industrial Development', *Economic and Political Weekly*, Annual Number, February 1976; D Nayyar, 'Industrial Development in India: Some Reflections on Growth and Stagnation', *Economic and Political Weekly*, Special Number, August 1978.

3 See M Kalecki, *Essays in the Theory of Economic Fluctuations*, Allen and Unwin, 1939. Kalecki reverted to the theme on many occasions in his later writings.

4 There is an extensive literature on this subject. Rosa Luxemburg presents a critical assessment in her *The Accumulation of Capital*, English translation, 1951 with an introduction by J V Robinson. Lenin's most penetrating discussion is possibly his essays on the market question (1893) which were lost for a while and then subsequently included in his *Collected Works*, Vol I, Moscow.

5 For a recent restatement, see D J Harris, 'On Marx's Scheme of Reproduction and Accumulation', *Journal of Political Economy*, 1972, pp 505-22; also reprinted in *The Economics of Marx*, edited by Howard and King, Penguin Books, 1976.

6 The usual derivation suffers from dimensional confusions as well as from failure to distinguish between 'value accounting' and 'price accounting'. In addition, we should distinguish between applications in the context of planning and applications aimed at deducing the 'laws of motion' of a capitalist economy.

7 See particularly Ricardo's 'Essay on Profits' and 'Essay on Protection' for policy-oriented discussions.

8 See Schumpeter's *Business Cycles,* Vol I, and also recent discussion on Kondratieff waves by contemporary authors such as Mandel. See also the highly critical review that Kuznets had written of Schumpeter's business cycles volumes, *American Economic Review*, 1940.

9 This comes out clearly in the correspondence between Ricardo and Malthus: see volume IX of Ricardo's *Work and Correspondence* edited by P Sraffa.

10 Kalecki brought a new perspective to the discussion by introducing the concept of an 'intermediate regime'. It is however not clear that the concept provides an adequate conceptualisation of the issues at stake.

11 See S Chakravarty, 'Reflections on the Growth Process in the Indian Economy', Foundation Day Lecture, Administrative Staff College of India, Hyderabad, 1974; also reprinted in C D Wadhwa (ed), *Some Problems of Economic Policy*, Tata-McGraw Hill, 1977.

12 See R Jones, 'An Essay on the Distribution of Wealth', available also as a Kelley reprint.

13 Interactions between the political and economic factors in fixing 'support prices' and their relevance for determining the 'terms of trade' between industry and agriculture have been argued at length by Ashok Mitra in his recent monograph *Terms of Trade and Class Relations*, Frank Cass, 1977.

14 The figures for recent years have been given in CSO's 1979 publication.

(Rs crore, current prices)

	Net Domestic Capital Formation (1)	Saving (2)
1971-72	3166	762
1972-73	3611	740
1973-74	4815	1082
1974-75	5978	2442
1975-76	7754	2829
1976-77	8127	3196

15 See M S Ahluwalia, 'Rural Poverty and Agricultural Performance in India', *Journal of Development Studies*, 1978, pp 298-323 and other references cited therein.

10

Factors Underlying the Slow Growth of Indian Industry

Ashok V Desai

NOT all the economists who have contributed to the debate on industrial growth and stagnation in India put forward their arguments with equal clarity, subtlety, or rashness. But readers would, it is hoped, recognise the following sequence to be a logical description of events as seen by a set, authors with a particular perspective. The more cautious among these authors would couch the argument in dynamic terms, substituting rates of change for the absolute magnitudes of output.

(1) Rich farmers earn a large proportion of their income from sale of their agricultural surplus. They have considerable influence on the government. Under their influence, the government raised agricultural prices by means of support operations and by stockpiling.

(2) This rise was reflected in the prices of wage goods and industrial raw materials. It reduced the real incomes of consumers of food, especially the rural and the urban poor on the one hand, and it squeezed profit margins in agriculture-dependent industries.

(3) Real wages being already, near the minimum subsistence level, could not be greatly reduced. Hence the rise in the prices of wage goods was reflected in money wages; it thereby reduced the real income of the government and profits of industry.

(4) The fall in the government's real income reduced its savings and its investment, while the fall in rural and urban real wages reduced the demand for industrial mass consumer goods.

(5) The shift in income distribution, from the poor to the rich, raised the demand for luxury consumer goods, whose output increased. But investment in luxury industries rose even faster; as a result, there was underutilisation of capacity and a fall in the rates of profit.

(6) The net effect of (5) and (6) was to reduce the demand for industrial goods. Hence industrial prices could not be raised as much as agricultural prices, and terms of trade turned against industry.

This argument is wrong in its two essential premises–viz, that terms of trade have moved in favour of agriculture and against industry, and that income distribution has worsened. I shall demonstrate this by using the statistics and the sources used by the proponents of the argument themselves.

I

TERMS OF TRADE

Ashok Mitra (1977) has written the most cogent exposition of the view that rich farmers use the (central) government to raise agricultural prices. To counter the view that supply and demand influence agricultural prices, he argues that the government buys and sells at the 'margin' where small transactions have a large effect on the price, and that its declarations of procurement and support prices influence expectations and thereby bring forth speculative sales and purchases which swamp the influence of harvests and of consumption [Mitra, 1977: p 112]. However, this market sensitivity evidently does not extend across crops. For, if it did, a rise in wheat procurement prices would have pushed up rice prices and left Mitra (1977: pp 125-28) with no grounds, for suspicion that rice growers were discriminated against. He must, therefore, believe that the effects of government operations are crop-specific.

To begin with, it should be stressed that there has been no continuous improvement of the terms of trade of agriculture against industry. As the series in Table 1 shows, agricultural terms of trade worsened in the early fifties, improved in the sixties, worsened again in the early seventies, and were about the same at the beginning and the end of the 30-year period. Thus, anyone who believes that the farmers' lobby raised agricultural prices and improved their terms of trade must also believe that the influence of the lobby declined or that powerful countervailing factors emerged in the 1970s. This apart, agriculture is too large a sector for its product prices to rise without generating general inflation, the final effects of which on relative prices are not easily predicted.

Next, take Ashok Mitra's (1977: 131) assertion that wheat prices rose more than rice prices because the marketed surplus of wheat is produced on larger holdings and their producers have greater political influence. Actually, the ratio of wheat prices to rice prices fell in the fifties, rose in the sixties, and fell again in the seventies; over the three decades it recorded a net decline (Table 1). Thus all the political influence of the big wheat farmers of Punjab did not serve wheat better than the political impotence of the small rice growers.

A comparison of the course of cotton and jute prices is rendered difficult by the fact that jute is subject to short and violent price fluctuations. But here, again, the behaviour of prices has been different from Ashok Mitra's (1977: pp 130-31) reading. Relatively to the index of agricultural prices, the cotton price index fell sharply between the mid-fifties and mid-sixties, rose equally sharply in the late sixties and fluctuated without a trend in the seventies. The course of cotton prices is parallel to that of a number of dry crops, whose output rose more rapidly in the early years of area expansion than in the post-1965

Table 1: Some Price Index Ratios, 1951-1979

Year	Agr/Mfg	Rice/Wheat	Cotton/Agr	Jute/Agr
1951	94.6	94.7	109.3	151.4
1952	87.7	94.0	109.0	108.5
1953	87.6	99.0	104.2	86.3
1954	82.1	98.1	117.3	99.2
1955	80.0	97.8	117.1	131.9
1956	82.9	97.1	117.7	116.0
1957	84.8	103.2	109.4	120.7
1958	86.0	100.4	98.4	104.0
1959	86.6	89.4	96.6	97.2
1960	83.4	107.5	101.6	141.4
1961	73.2	105.1	107.7	181.3
1962	82.8	111.2	96.1	94.4
1963	80.3	119.9	99.6	97.0
1964	89.1	101.3	89.8	95.0
1965	94.9	89.2	82.2	116.2
1966	97.0	102.8	75.6	139.4
1967	84.6	95.2	84.7	108.9
1968	97.1	101.3	81.5	107.5
1969	102.4	96.1	84.0	118.3
1970	101.9	97.3	91.8	99.9
1971	92.7	105.6	111.4	94.4
1972	89.2	106.5	84.5	99.1
1973	97.9	121.9	83.8	80.8
1974	101.2	106.6	98.5	59.8
1975	94.4	111.1	84.4	67.9
1976	88.9	102.9	117.9	81.5
1977	96.9	104.9	115.5	83.5
1978	96.9	102.7	100.4	86.8
1979	89.7	110.4	89.9	96.1

Sources: Calculated from Chandhok, H L (1978); Ministry of Industry (1980).

period, when output increases have been concentrated in wet and irrigated crops. The jute price index, on the other hand, was steady till the mid-sixties and then declined till the mid-seventies. Thus Mitra's conclusion that cotton prices rose more than jute prices depends closely on his choice of years.

II

INCOME DISTRIBUTION

A variety of evidence has been adduced to show that the real income of the poor has declined or that income distribution has worsened. The most commonly used statistics are from the National Sample Survey.

The large number of studies of rural distribution of consumption has been surveyed by Ahluwalia (1978). He fitted trend equations to two indexes of poverty for the country as well as for the states from 1956-57 to 1973-74: the proportion of people with a real consumption level below Rs 15 per head at 1960-61 prices, and the Sen index of relative inequality. He found no trend in either index for India as a whole. The trends were insignificant in all states except four–in Andhra Pradesh and Tamil Nadu where one or both indexes showed a decline in poverty, and in West Bengal and Assam where one or both showed an increase. As he points out, a number of authors obtained contrary results–showing both increases and decreases–by choosing different benchmark years; but, once all observations for the 18 years are given equal weightage, there is no reason to believe that poverty has increased or consumption distribution has worsened.[1]

Another result established by Ahluwalia is that growth of agricultural productivity is clearly associated with a reduction in the proportion of the poor as well as in relative inequality. This conclusion goes against the Lewis model which would lead us to expect that a rise in productivity in a labour-surplus economy would accrue to profits.[2] This result, so contrary to received wisdom, entails that the ratio of wages to agricultural output should rise as productivity increases in the short run. It implies that the supply of labour to agriculture is inelastic enough to drive up the product wage when a large crop has to be harvested; further, it indicates that neither the propensity of rich farmers and speculators to hoard nor the storage capacity of the government is sufficient to prevent a fall in local prices and a rise in real wages in good years.

A second piece of statistical evidence cited is in respect of agricultural real wage rates. The most comprehensive statistics, compiled by

Jose (1974), refer to wage rates of male agricultural workers at the peak of agricultural season, deflated by statewise consumer price indexes for agricultural labourers. He found that, between 1956-57 and 1971-72, real wage rates rose substantially in six states, changed little in five, and fell significantly in one. On the basis of alternative unpublished estimates made by Ashok Mitra [1977: p 124], he claims that real wage rates declined nearly everywhere in India. According to our own reading of Jose's figures, the year-to-year fluctuations are so great that any claim of a long-run rise or decline is unwarranted. Apart from this, *daily wage rates* at the peak of the season can hardly give any indication of the *annual earnings* of agricultural workers or their household income, and to treat such wage rates as an indicator of standards of living is erroneous.

In industry, we have earnings of workers earning less than Rs 200, which were used by the National Commission on Labour (1969) to demonstrate that real industrial earnings had been more or less constant between 1951 and 1964. From 1962 onwards, the Bureau of Labour Statistics started another series of earnings of workers earning less than Rs 400, which could be used to show that their real earnings rose little between 1962 and 1970. Madan (1977) argued that both these series had a downward bias, and constructed a series of real earnings of workers covered by the Census of Manufacturing Industries and the Annual Survey of Industries, which showed a rise of 35 per cent between 1951 and 1970. Ranjit Sau (1977), in his review of Madan's book, argued that Madan went too far in rejecting the BLS series, which also contained 'useful information'. To illustrate what information it contained, Sau concluded from a comparison of the BLS and the CMI-ASI series that the earnings of lower-paid workers rose less rapidly: 'The dice is loaded against the poor, as it were.'

This conclusion shows that Sau has in fact been misled by precisely the bias that Madan has pointed out. An unbiased idea of the course of earnings can best be obtained by taking the average of earnings of an unchanging group of workers in various periods. Such an average is never available; what we get, instead, is the average earnings of workers classified by industry or occupation or place. The movement of this average between two periods is influenced by three factors: (a) the rise of earnings of workers included in both periods, (b) the earnings of workers who left the group between the two periods, and (c) the earnings of new entrants. If the average earnings of leavers exceed those of new entrants an index of earnings for the entire group will understate the rise in the earnings of an unchanging group of workers, and vice versa.[3] Ordinarily, a group of workers will be large enough for the annual movements into and out of it to be relatively small. But, if a maximum wage is used as an upper cut-off point to define a group of workers, the earnings of leavers will be invariably above average, and the bias will be downward; and if the proportion of leavers is substantial, so will be the bias.

So it is. For, the proportion of employees earning less than Rs 200 a month was 64.5 per cent in 1949 [Madan, 1977: p 25]. If the wage distribution had remained unchanged, the number of these lower-paid workers would have risen to 3 million by 1964 instead of 2.5 million; if we chose to believe that the distribution must have worsened, the rise would have been even greater. Thus the unchanged upper limit did lead to the exclusion of a substantial proportion of workers and hence, probably, to a significant bias. Thus the BLS series do not give information, but misinformation.

Finally, a variety of evidence has been presented to show that income distribution must have worsened because the consumption of luxury goods rose faster than that of necessities, and the inference drawn that income distribution must have worsened. To begin with, this inference is itself based on the fallacy of the unchanging basket: it assumes that people will continue to buy goods in the same proportions whatever happens to their income or to prices.[4] If per capita income increases, the purchases of luxuries will rise faster than the consumption of necessities even if income distribution remains unchanged, because all income groups spend their incremental income on less 'necessary' goods than those on which they spend their income. Further, it is necessary to look more closely at the consumption of necessities and luxuries.

On the production of foodgrains there has been a controversy between Vaidyanathan (1977a; 1977b; 1977c) and Srinivasan (1977; 1978; 1979). The welter of trend equations fitted by the two is fit to make one's head reel, but the conclusion of the debate is that the growth rate of foodgrain production rose between 1949-50 to 1964-65 and 1965-66 to 1977-78, and fell between the first period and 1967-68 to 1977-78 (that is, excluding the drought years 1965-66 and 1966-67), but that the difference in either case was statistically insignificant [Srinivasan, 1979: p 1284]. However, the question before us is whether per capita output and consumption rose, to which Table 2 gives a simple answer. Per capita foodgrain output was 5 per cent higher in 1965-66 to 1977-78 and 9 per cent higher in 1967-68 to 1977-78 than it was in 1950-51 to 1964-65; but the year-to-year fluctuations were such that the increase was not statistically significant. Per capita apparent consumption showed an insignificant rise. The rise in output was not reflected in consumption because per capita imports fell.

Two comments on these figures are called for. First, output figures are reduced by 12.5 per cent when calculating apparent consumption. By this convention, therefore, more than a ton of domestic production is required to replace a ton of imports. Second, the population estimates used to calculate per capita figures are interpolated from census figures up to 1971, but are projections thereafter. Hence post-1971 per capita figures will not be known with any degree of accuracy till after 1981.

Subject to these qualifications, one can say that whilst per capita foodgrain consumption has 'stagnated', this is not because per capita output has not risen, but because there has been import substitution. Output has risen rapidly enough not only to replace imports but also to occasion a shift in terms of trade against agriculture in the 1970s. In the circumstances, the constancy of per capita foodgrain consumption is perfectly consistent with a slow growth of per capita income, and does not in itself support any supposition of worsened income distribution.

Next, consider the argument that a fall in the per capita consumption of mass consumer goods must imply a worsening of distribution. This argument can apply only to textiles, for no other mass consumer goods shows such a fall: there it is based on a logical fallacy. The quantity of cloth purchased per household rises with income in both urban and rural areas [Textiles Committee, 1979: pp 29-30]; so must per capita consumption since household size varies inversely with income, as repeatedly confirmed by National Sample Survey. Hence a fall in per capita cloth consumption would signify an *improvement* in income distribution rather than a worsening–if distribution were the only variable. Actually, it was not. The fall in per capita consumption coincided with the rise in relative cloth prices in the late sixties, which

Table 2: Changes in Per Capita Foodgrain Output and Consumption

	Production		Consumption	
	Mean	sd	Mean	sd
1950-51 - 1964-65	465.3	40.0	439.5	27.6
1965-66 - 1977-78	486.7	44.4	441.8	23.8
1967-68 - 1977-78	502.0	28.4	448.5	19.3

Sources: Calculated from Ministry of Agriculture (1979); Ministry of Finance (1970; 1980); World Bank (1978).

in turn would be traced to the rise in cotton prices discussed in Section I above.

Lest an impression of a fall in the consumption of mass consumer goods may be gathered from Sau's figures (1974) purporting to show that "the base of the market for industrial consumer goods is narrowing...", it should be made clear that they show no such thing. The proportion of consumer expenditure devoted to 'industrial goods' shows no pronounced trend for any fractile group in rural or urban India, if we look at all the figures in Sau's Tables 1 and 2; the impression of a fall is created only by low figures for 1964-65, Sau's terminal year. So if relative prices had not changed, real purchases of industrial goods would have risen more or less at the same rate as per capita real incomes. But, in fact, prices of agricultural goods rose relatively to those of industrial goods in that period [Thamarajakshi, 1969: p A-98]. Thus the presumption is that the market for industrial consumer goods expanded, if it changed at all. Further, Sau's (1974: p 1284) figures of urban consumption of agricultural consumer goods are only about half of Thamarajakshi's (1969: p A-94) figures of non-agricultural consumption of agricultural consumer goods. Whilst it is impossible to decide which of them is right, we can fairly say that until concepts are clarified and calculations repeated, judgment on Sau's proposition is best suspended.[5]

Finally, let us come to luxury consumption. Shetty cites large increases in the output of certain luxury goods between 1975 and 1976 [Shetty, 1978: p 198]. However, it is hardly appropriate to read long-term trends into two consecutive years' figures.[6] According to figures computed by Mitra (1977: p 164) from Reserve Bank statistics, the weight of consumer durables in the index of industrial production rose from 2.21 per cent in 1956 to 5.68 per cent in 1960, 7.84 per cent in 1970, and 8.09 per cent in 1972. According to Reserve Bank of India (1977a: p 212), however, their weight was only 2.92 per cent in 1970! Actually, neither Mitra's nor RBI figures permit a fair comparison. Industrial output statistics are organised by establishment and squeezed into a classification based on industries, which the RBI then regroups into a user classification. Naturally there are a number of industries which fall into more than one group and which the RBI puts arbitrarily into one group or another according to current whim. Thus we have among luxuries (*pace* Mitra as well as RBI) electric bulbs, professional scientific instruments, spectacles, 'metals', and products of industries not elsewhere classified.[7] Besides, the change of index weights tells us nothing about trends over time, for it is affected by changes in prices as well as quantities.

Even were we to look at quantities only, official statistics are by now a misleading indicator of output. For the combination of differential excise duties and labour laws has given such an edge to unregistered industry that the output of registered firms is a diminishing proportion of total output in some industries. By and large, the less 'luxurious' the consumer durables, the greater the underrecording. For instance, there is little unregistered production of motor cars or air-conditioners, but substantial output of bicycles, sewing machines, and radios; the output of coolers and furniture is not recorded at all. Output statistics of many of the 'luxuries' of the poor are not even collected; for instance, plastic footwear, aluminium utensils, or unpressured kerosene stoves, whose sales have increased manifold in recent years.

No one has put forward evidence to show that capacity utilisation in luxury industries has been lower than in others. But here too it is necessary to warn excavators before they get caved-in. In the sixties, when many materials were allocated on the basis of capacity, there was an incentive to overstate capacity. From the late sixties onwards, there were curbs on the expansion of big business groups and foreign firms which led them to understate actual capacity. In the seventies, as shortages emerged from time to time, these firms were allowed to expand capacity *ad hoc*; then declared capacity figures were often raised abruptly without fresh investment. Public enterprises plagued by criticism in parliament of their low capacity utilisation, have a standing incentive to understate capacity.

III

CAPITAL-OUTPUT RATIOS

I have presented evidence to show that the thesis under review is wrong in its two fundamental premises—viz, that terms of trade have moved in favour of agriculture, and that income distribution has worsened. It may be argued, however, that a cyclical mechanism in which agriculture acts as a constraint would nevertheless be applicable to Indian industrial growth. Such a cycle was the basis of Patnaik's (1972) model, and was proposed by me in Desai (1966).

The explanation must depend on what is to be explained. Industrial growth till the mid-sixties was subject to severe supply constraints, and it was natural to think then in terms of supply-constrained models. The three constraints that were most popular were savings, foreign exchange, and agricultural output. The theoretical predilections of their protagonists have continued to guide their thinking on more recent events. Undersavers have become underconsumptionists, trade-backers have continued to be liberals, and ruralists have turned into structuralists.

It is quite all right for old habits of thought to die hard. But to my mind, the problem has changed. What is to be explained is not cyclical fluctuations in industrial growth, but a persistently low rate of industrial growth since the mid-sixties.[8] The rate fell from 9 per cent in 1960-65 to 3.7 per cent in 1965-70 and in 1970-75, and in 1975-79 it was slightly higher at 5.7 per cent (Table 3).[9] An explanation of this long-term slowing down must be looked for in more permanent factors, and

Table 3: Sectoral Growth Rates of Industrial Output

(Per cent per year)

	1951-55	1955-60	1960-65	1965-70	1970-75	1975-79
General index	5.7	7.2	9.0	3.7	3.7	5.7
Use-based classification						
Basic goods*	3.8	12.0	10.5	6.3	5.2	6.6
Capital goods	15.1	13.7	19.7	–1.7	5.1	5.9
Intermediate goods	6.4	6.2	7.0	2.5	2.6	5.3
Non-durable consumer goods	3.7	3.8	3.8	2.6	1.5	5.4
Durable consumer goods	12.3	25.5	10.8	8.5	2.4	8.5
Input-based classification						
Agriculture-based	3.6	3.6	3.8	1.6	1.1	3.5
Metal-based	10.9	14.0	18.3	0.5	4.2	6.4
Chemical-based	8.1	9.7	9.0	9.7	5.2	9.2
Transport equipment	11.1	10.5	14.2	–2.6	3.0	3.7
Electricity and allied	8.5	16.0	14.7	11.8	5.6	10.0

Note: * Includes minerals, cement, heavy chemicals, metals and electricity.
Sources: Central Statistical Organisation (1965: pp 153-58); Reserve Bank of India (1970: pp 992-95; 1977: pp 32-33; 1980: pp 5266-67).

not in cyclical ones. Kulak power, favoured by structuralists, would be an excellent horse to back–if only it would get up and run.

The fall in the growth rate was particularly severe in the case of capital goods whose absolute output fell between 1965 and 1970. Contrary to Deepak Nayyar's (1978: p 1271) impression, this fall had little to do with the end of import substitution, which continued till the end of the sixties as Table 4 shows; it was due to the fact that real investment in machinery, which rose at 11 per cent a year in 1960-61 to 1965-66, itself fell in the next five years. The fall was greater in public investment. This persuaded Srinivasan and Narayana (1977) to the view that a fall in public investment was the root cause, and to advocate an increase in it. Srinivasan (1977) has little regard for those who want revolution or nothing, but if the view we shall put forward is correct, greater public investment will inevitably bring revolution or nothing—or both.

However, we now have more recent statistics, which prove the hiatus in machinery purchases to have been short-lived (Table 5).[10] In the late sixties, the share of investment in machinery in GNP was slightly lower than in the early sixties; in the seventies it rose to ever-higher levels, until it reached 10.3 per cent in 1978-79 when industrial value added was 22 per cent of GNP.[11] A persistently high rate of industrial investment, combined with a low rate of industrial growth, must indicate high capital-output ratios.

Just how high they were is shown by Table 6.[12] Capital-output ratios in India have generally been high by international standards. The ICOR in registered industry at constant 1970-71 prices was 7.5 in the second plan period and 5.6 in the third. In the following 10 years, however, it jumped up to about 12. In mining the ICOR rose from 4.9 in the Third Plan period to over 13 in the subsequent years. In public utilities—power and railways—it was never below 15; after mid-sixties it hovered around 20.

Table 4: Gross Investment in Machinery and Its Import Intensity, 1960-61 to 1977-78

Year	Gross Investment in Machinery (Rs bn)		Machinery Imports (Rs bn)	Share of Imports in Investment (Per Cent)
	At 1970-71 Prices	At Current Prices		
1960-61	15.1	8.2	3.3	40.7
1961-62	16.7	9.5	3.7	38.6
1962-63	19.3	11.2	3.9	34.7
1963-64	21.4	13.8	4.4	31.7
1964-65	24.6	16.2	4.8	29.4
1965-66	25.5	17.7	4.9	27.8
1966-67	21.8	18.5	5.4	29.0
1967-68	21.5	20.5	5.0	24.6
1968-69	22.3	21.5	5.1	23.9
1969-70	23.7	22.9	4.0	17.3
1970-71	23.5	23.5	4.0	16.8
1975-76	34.0	60.3	8.8	14.6
1977-78	41.4	74.2	11.2	15.1

Sources: Central Statistical Organisation (1975: p 23; 1980a: pp 32, 148); Reserve Bank of India (1969: pp 5132-33; 1971: pp 5144; 1977b: p 144).

The implications of such high capital-output ratios are unmistakable. If the life of equipment is 25 years, an investment with a capital-output ratio of 12 would give a 4 per cent return net of depreciation *even if it required no paid workers to operate it*. With a capital-output ratio of 20, it would give 1 per cent on the same assumption. If employees take two-thirds of value added, to take a typical proportion, no investment with a capital-output ratio of over 8.33 would give a positive net return.

A positive *nominal* return could be earned on them if the product wage was depressible–that is, if product prices could be raised relatively to wages. This would require an acquiescent and weakly organised labour force, and an absence of more efficient competitors. Competitors can be eliminated by means of import and industrial licensing, and used to subsidise inefficient enterprises by means of state-imposed differential prices, but employers in India's major industries can hardly wish away organised labour. Further, raising industrial prices is feasible only as long as such industries are an

Table 5: Share of Investment and Its Components in GNP, 1960-61 to 1978-79

(Per cent)

Year	Machinery		Construction		Inventories		Total Gross Investment		
	Public	Private	Public	Private	Public	Private	Public	Private	Total
1960-61	2.7	3.1	4.8	4.7	0.6	2.4	8.1	10.2	18.3
1961-62	2.4	4.0	5.1	4.8	0.3	1.6	7.8	10.4	18.1
1962-63	2.5	4.6	5.8	4.0	0.9	1.6	9.2	10.2	19.4
1963-64	2.3	5.3	6.4	3.5	0.7	1.5	9.4	10.3	19.6
1964-65	2.7	4.9	5.9	3.7	0.6	1.4	9.2	10.0	19.2
1965-66	3.1	5.0	6.3	4.5	0.8	0.6	10.2	10.1	20.3
1966-67	2.9	4.4	5.2	5.8	0.3	2.7	8.4	12.9	21.3
1967-68	2.6	4.3	4.2	6.5	1.1	0.1	7.9	10.9	18.8
1968-69	2.7	4.4	4.2	6.9	0.2	0.8	7.1	12.1	19.2
1969-70	2.0	4.7	4.4	6.8	0.2	1.1	6.6	12.6	19.2
1970-71	1.8	4.7	3.2	7.6	1.0	1.7	6.0	14.0	20.0
1971-72	2.0	5.5	3.8	7.1	0.9	2.5	6.7	15.1	21.8
1972-73	2.5	5.4	4.3	6.7	–	1.1	6.8	13.2	20.0
1973-74	2.1	5.6	3.9	5.3	1.5	2.8	7.5	13.7	21.2
1974-75	2.5	5.8	3.1	6.3	2.8	3.5	8.4	15.6	24.0
1975-76	3.6	5.6	3.3	8.3	3.5	1.5	10.4	15.4	25.8
1976-77	3.9	5.6	4.0	8.6	2.0	1.5	9.9	15.7	25.6
1977-78	3.6	5.7	4.0	8.4	–	2.6	7.6	16.7	24.3
1978-79	3.8	6.5	4.8	8.2	0.5	2.1	9.1	16.8	25.9

Source: Central Statistical Organisation (1975: p 23; 1980a: p 30; 1980b: pp 138-39).

insignificant part of the economy. If the rise in industrial prices becomes sufficiently general, it must lead to general inflation, and raise both wages and capital goods prices. At that point, even positive nominal rates of return would vanish.

IV
AN EXPLANATION

Why were the capital-output ratios high? In Vaidyanathan's (1977b, p 1647) view, inadequate investment resources were spread too thinly, gestation lags were increased, and the backlog of unfinished projects raised the capital-output ratios. He may be right, but capital-output ratios have been high in investments that went into production.

Table 6: Sectoral Incremental Capital-Output Ratios at Constant Prices: Five-Year Periods, 1950-1978[*]

(Rs million at 1970-71 prices)

	1950-51/ 1955-56	1955-56/ 1960-61	1960-61/ 1965-66	1965-66/ 1970-71	1970-71/ 1975-76	1975-76/ 1977-78
Primary	2.1	2.1	**	1.5	4.0	5.0
Agriculture	2.0	2.1	**	1.3	3.9	4.3
Forestry and logging	3.5	1.0	0.8	3.3	1.1	1.2
Fishing	4.1	5.7	6.6	6.0	3.3	**
Mining and quarrying	3.9	2.1	4.9	13.0	8.9	40.9
Secondary	4.4	5.3	5.1	9.4	12.3	4.7
Manufacturing	4.0	5.8	4.9	11.5	12.2	4.7
(1) Registered	6.1	7.5	5.6	12.9	17.8	4.6
(2) Unregistered	1.1	1.9	2.7	8.3	6.6	5.1
Construction	3.0	1.7	2.0	1.9	4.4	0.78
Electricity and gas and water supply	17.2	15.2	18.4	16.6	20.9	23.4
Transport, storage and communication	8.4	9.8	10.4	9.3	8.2	9.1
Railways	19.6	16.0	18.4	22.4	11.6	5.0
Transport by other means and storage	4.7	6.3	7.6	7.1	7.6	16.3
Communication	4.2	4.1	3.9	6.1	6.3	5.9

Notes: * Gross capital formation cumulated over five years, divided by the rise in value added in those five years. For instance, the first column represents capital formation in 1951-52 to 1955-56 divided by the difference in value added between 1950-51 and 1955-56.

** Value added declined.

Sources: Central Statistical Organisation (1979: pp 140-43; 1980a: pp 150-53).

The view is common among the authors reviewed here [for instance, Patnaik, 1972: pp 335-36; Bagchi, 1977: p 233; Mitra, 1977: p 163; Nayyar, 1978, pp 1273-75; Shetty, 1978, p 218] that excessive private investment in luxury consumer goods has led to excess capacity and high capital-intensity. They too may be right; we should not get too discouraged by the quality of their evidence scrutinised in this paper. But it is also true that high capital-intensity is characteristic of public sector investment in basic industries. In Table 7, value added is estimated at current prices and gross fixed assets at historical prices. Hence it will show lower capital-output ratios than Table 6 as long as prices are rising. But it is clear that capital-output ratios are higher in the public than in the private sector in the same industries, and that despite inflation some of the public sector ratios are comparable to those in Table 6.

So the question narrows itself down to: Why are capital-output ratios in public sector industry high? Here, a number of alternative, though by no means mutually exclusive, answers are available.

There are those who believe that the root cause is corruption among politicians and bureaucrats, which takes the form of taking a cut on capital equipment and construction as well as of siphoning off of profits through distribution of permits. I would not argue against this view. My impression is that capital costs of public sector fertiliser, aluminium, and steel plants were generally higher than those of private sector plants built around the same time, though not enormously so.

The public authorities' explanation of higher capital costs is the 'social responsibilities' borne by public sector plants–which means workers' and officers' housing for which below-commercial rents are charged, subsidised schools for their children, subsidised canteens, etc. Whatever view one might take about the social desirability of these investments, they are indisputably consumer goods and services supplied by public enterprises to their employees at a subsidised price; to this extent they should reduce the supply price of labour to the enterprises. And, in fact, the general impression is that public sector wages and salaries are lower than those in the private sector. If the enterprises nevertheless are not profitable, it is because their capacity utilisation is low; and in steel, fertilisers, cement, aluminium or power, where there are chronic shortages or continuing imports, it is no use arguing that underutilisation of capacity is due to a 'realisation problem'.

Having run through all the explanations, it is only fair that I should offer one of my own, however speculative and heretical it may sound. It is that the reason for high capital-output ratios in the public sector

Table 7: Average Capital Output Ratios in Government and in Public Limited Companies, 1960-61 to 1975-76

	Government				Public Limited			
	1960-61	1965-66	1970-71	1975-76	1960-61	1965-66	1970-71	1975-76
Agriculture and allied activities	—	—	—	—	2.70	2.91	2.22	1.67
Mining and quarrying	—	3.01	7.42	3.40	1.94	1.80	1.74	1.26
Processing and manufactured: food-stuffs, textiles, tobacco, leather, etc	—	—	—	—	2.65	2.84	2.73	2.31
Processing and manufactured: engineering metals, chemicals, etc	—	5.91	7.77	7.72	3.98	3.68	3.84	3.31
Engineering	3.55	3.29	5.64	3.22	2.71	2.73	2.95	2.60
Transport equipment					3.04	3.35	3.65	3.46
Electrical machinery					2.35	2.43	2.37	2.11
Non-electrical machinery					2.46	2.88	2.42	2.12
Foundries and engineering workshops					2.07	2.26	4.70	4.67
Ferrous/non-ferrous metal products					3.30	2.98	2.94	2.72
Chemicals	7.66	3.00	12.25	14.18	4.02	4.23	4.44	3.95
Processing and manufacturing not elsewhere specified					5.52	5.15	4.66	3.59
Cement					6.16	5.84	10.48	4.91
Other industries	—	12.92	8.32	9.02	5.16	4.85	4.77	5.58
Construction					1.54	1.53	1.88	1.77
Electricity generation and supply					16.19	14.95	13.39	12.89
Miscellaneous	—	1.72	6.34	6.71	—	—	—	—

Sources: Reserve Bank of India (1963: pp 1267-76; 1967: pp 1563-1607; 1968: pp 1141-58; 1973: pp 2040-77; 1975: pp 771-818; 1979: pp 481-516; 1980: pp 356-94).

is the same as that for low productivity: Where labour is underutilised, so will concomitant capital.

In my view, the strongest political force in this country, even more powerful than the kulak, the bourgeois and the capitalist combined, is the petty-bourgeois haute-proletarian with a little education and less property. It was this class that inherited power from the British. It promptly set about multiplying by setting itself up schools and colleges. The capital-intensity of education was low; the gestation lags were short, and its output was limited only by the ample fertility of the petty-prole, to use a convenient abbreviation. Within 20 years, a vast army of aspirant petty-proles was created, all clamouring for jobs. The preference for jobs was not confined to petty-proles. I do not believe that there is much unemployment in the country: I have earlier cited Ahluwalia's results to suggest that there is a shortage of agricultural labour in the peak season. But all who are not rich enough to do what they like–or what keeps them rich–have a perfectly rational preference for a job, for getting regular pay in return for regular work, or idleness, as the case may be.

This pressure for jobs had a strong effect on politicians, most of whom were petty-proles themselves. Those who were in power would press industrialists to absorb their friends and relatives, but this channel proved inadequate. Finally, they turned to two institutional means–small enterprises and public enterprises. Small enterprises are another, equally scandalous story. Here we shall stick to public enterprises.

The same forces that led to the proliferation of public enterprises also led to their overmanning, which became irremediable because, once appointed, no employee of a public enterprise could be dismissed. Overmanning had two effects. First, since no one wanted to be found overtly doing nothing, a work ethic grew up among employees, by which everyone worked less than he could. Second, any voluntary sharing out of work would leave some with more work than others. This led to mutual jealousies which were a strong force to keep down the average work-load. And when workers were working with machines, their underemployment also entailed the underemployment of the machines.

Overmanning increased the managerial work-load. Getting work from workers, whose interests and ideology were oriented towards idleness, was a laborious and troublesome task, which was shared unequally among managerial staff. Line supervisors bore the brunt, while accounts and sales staff not only escaped the burden, but also often had lucrative opportunities of corruption. This led to the growth of the same minimum-work ethic among white-collar as among blue-collar workers.

Not only did overmanning lead to below-capacity operation, it also made improvement of technology more difficult. It is well known that much technological improvement in industrial countries arises in small changes in operating plants. This is virtually absent in Indian public enterprises; the steel plants, for instance, were found to have fallen technologically behind similar plants built in their home countries by the foreign collaborators. The reason is that the technologists in steel plants were too busy just keeping them running to think of improvements, and too scared to take the risk of trying out variations.

Thus the high capital-output ratios are one of the consequences of the attempt of the petty-proles to squeeze in ever growing numbers into an industrial base that is not growing fast enough, and the high ratios in turn led to grossly inadequate rates of return and ploughback. The low returns entail that the bulk of public industrial investment must be financed from general revenue, as it has been and continues to be. And in enterprises, whose surplus does not cover replacement cost

Table 8: Share of Investment in Machinery in GNP at Constant 1970-71 Prices: 1961-62 to 1977-78

	Debtors (1970-71 = 100)		Share of Machinery Investment in GDP	
	GDP	Investment in Plant	Current Prices	1970-71
1961-62	56.3	56.9	6.4	6.3
1962-63	58.6	57.7	7.1	7.1
1963-64	63.7	64.4	7.6	7.5
1964-65	69.4	66.1	7.6	8.0
1965-66	75.9	69.4	8.1	8.9
1966-67	86.8	84.6	7.3	7.5
1967-68	94.1	95.0	6.9	6.8
1968-69	94.2	96.3	7.1	6.9
1969-70	98.1	96.6	6.7	6.8
1970-71	100.0	100.0	6.5	6.5
1971-72	105.2	103.7	7.5	7.6
1972-73	117.2	112.2	7.9	8.3
1973-74	139.1	122.1	7.7	8.8
1974-75	161.8	157.7	8.3	8.5
1975-76	154.8	177.6	9.2	8.0
1976-77	165.6	177.4	9.5	8.7
1977-78	171.2	179.1	9.3	8.9

Sources: Central Statistical Organisation (1975: pp 15, 25; 1979: p 142; 1980a: p 150).

depreciation, investment even to maintain capacity would eventually have to come out of general revenue. When government revenue turns inadequate, funds must be, and are, obtained at near-zero real rate of return from the credit system, which the government has monopolised. Hence a situation may eventually be reached when government investment is just sufficient to maintain a vast and inefficient industrial base and no expansion of industrial employment is possible. That is when the petty-prole class will rise in revolt and destroy the system that employs them, but fails to exploit them.[13]

Lest this sounds too apocalyptic, I would point out that 'students', an omnibus category whose only common feature is that they are all aspiring to enter the petty-prole class, have been the most potent disruptive force in the recent history of this country. They were the backbone of the Samyukta Maharashtra agitation.[14] They were the core of the Naxalites, and the storm-troopers of Youth Congress (I). They were JP's right hand in the pre-Emergency agitation. They have kept the central government at bay in Assam for a whole year. The greatest strike of the post-Independence period was organised in 1975 by petty-proles par excellence, the railwaymen. Smaller petty-prole strikes, pen-down strikes, and work-to-rule agitations, are too numerous to count. The revolution I predict is in daily rehearsal. A visitor to India may well say, 'I have seen tomorrow, and it is unworkable.'

NOTES

1 However, it is not disputed that the *absolute* number of people with real consumption below the threshold has risen, any more than that the total population has increased. Nor is it claimed that the income distribution is good, or was, or will be: simply that it has not worsened.

2 Another implication of the Lewis model, that the overall savings ratio should increase, has been borne out in the seventies. This does not establish its validity, but Sukhamoy Chakravarty's (1974) explanation of its failure is both unnecessary and rests on the fiction of terms of trade turning in favour of agriculture. Similarly, Amiya Bagchi's (1970) explanation of a constant savings ratio in terms of "some kind of permanent income hypothesis... combined with the operation of national and international demonstration effects" no longer has any facts to explain. This is not, however, to deny international intellectual demonstration effects, so righteously excoriated by Raj (1976: p 231), with which the literature surveyed here is replete.

3 An (unconstrained) index of average earnings will be biased downwards in the case of workers whose earnings tend to go up with age. In the case of workers whose earnings decline with age, as may happen in unskilled occupations requiring physical strength, the index will have an upward bias.

4 Thus, Shetty (1978: p 202) takes the decline in the share of coarse grains in foodgrain output, as well as in the share of coarse cloth in mill output (which,

incidentally, leaves out of account handlooms' and powerlooms' output of coarse cloth) as an indication of a decline in the standard of living of the poor.

5 Amiya Bagchi's (1977: p 221) flamboyant hypothesis of 'last-resource subsistence farming and increasing pauperisation', insofar as it rests on Sau's (1974) evidence, may be stronger than weak-minded empiricists can stomach.

6 Even Amiya Bagchi (1975: p 159) indulges in comparisons between convenient points in support of this view.

7 Whilst the pioneering quality of his work must be appreciated, Bharat Hazari's (1967) classification of imports into necessities and luxuries also has an arbitrary element. Besides, the import-intensity of the consumption of no class is immutable, as assumed by Amiya Bagchi (1977: 220); it depends on the extent of excess demand for various goods and on how far the government allows it to be met out of imports. In the years when India was heavily import-dependent for foodgrains, the marginal import intensity of the consumption of the poor must have been far higher than that of the rich. Finally, Hazari himself did not show that luxuries are more import-intensive than necessities; nor has anyone else to our knowledge.

8 And not 'structural retrogression' [Shetty, 1978], which has been disproved by Rao (1979), nor deceleration in agricultural growth, which has been refuted by Srinivasan (1979).

9 Some may argue that the rise in the growth rate in the last four years shows that it is a cyclical phenomenon and no permanent depression of the growth rate, and may point out that constant-price ICORs in industry fell to pre-1965 levels in 1975-76 to 1977-78. They may be eventually proved right, but the figures for the last two years are too unstable and tentative to infer a reversal of the trend. Further, they are not so low to suggest that the surplus capacity built up in 1965-66 to 1975-76 was being utilised. See also footnote 12.

10 Whilst the share of machinery in gross investment, which was about 40 per cent in the early sixties, then fell and did not regain that level till the late seventies, the corresponding rise was not all in inventories as supposed by Shetty (1978: p 216) and Chakravarty (1979b: p 1241). Inventory investments were high in the inflationary period of early seventies, but construction also increased its share. In any case, investment in food stocks was high only in a single year, 1975-76 [Ministry of Finance, 1980]. It was clearly due to an abrupt rise in output, and is no indication of chronic excess supply of foodgrains.

11 The estimates in Table 5 are at current prices. Estimates of the share of machinery investment in GNP at 1970-71 prices, shown in Table 8, show a considerably slower rate of increase, but nevertheless show a rising trend since the late sixties.

12 The neglect of lags introduces a certain degree of approximation in this table. But an underestimation of ICOR in one period will be associated with an overestimation in an adjacent period; over five-year periods such biases should largely cancel out. It should be stressed, however, that the terminal years of the periods of high and low capital-output ratios indicated by this table are approximate.

13 This argument should not be interpreted to mean advocacy of private investment. If an interpretation must be imposed, what is advocated is the

destruction of the petty-prole class, whose membership includes every author cited in this paper, including myself.

14 I can testify to this at first hand, having once been playfully beaten up by the police who quite reasonably assumed that a student in a wrong place must be an enemy of order. Sharad Joshi of the onions fame, also a fellow-Sydenhamite at that time, received his political training in the same agitation.

REFERENCES

Ahluwalia, Montek S (1978): 'Rural Poverty and Agricultural Performance in India, *Journal of Development Studies,* 14(3).

Bagchi, Amiya Kumar (1970): 'Long-Term Constraints on India's Industrial Growth, 1951-1968' in E A G Robinson and Michael Kidron (ed), *Economic Development in South Asia,* Macmillan, London.

–(975): 'Some Characteristics of Industrial Growth in India', *EPW,* X (6-7).

–(1977): 'Export-Led Growth and Import-Substituting Industrialisation', *EPW,* XII (6-8).

Central Statistical Organisation (1965): *Statistical Abstract of the Indian Union.* 1963 and 1964, New Delhi.

–(1975): *National Accounts Statistics,* 1960-61/1972-73, New Delhi.

–(1979): *National Accounts Statistics,* 1970-71/1976-77, New Delhi.

–(1980a): *National Accounts Statistics,* 1970-71/1977-78, New Delhi.

–(1980b): *Monthly Abstract of Statistics,* 33(5), New Delhi, May.

Chakravarty, S (1974): 'Reflections on the Growth Process in the Indian Economy' in C D Wadhwa (ed) (1977): *Some Problems of Indian Economic Policy* 2nd edition, Tata McGraw-Hill, New Delhi.

(1979a): 'Keynes, 'Classics', and the Developing Economies' in C H H Rao and P C Joshi (eds), *Reflections on Economic Development and Social Change: Essays in Honour of Professor V K R V Rao,* Allied Publishers, Bombay.

–(1979b): 'On the Question of the Home Market and Prospects for Indian Growth', *EPW,* XIV (30-32).

Chandhok, H L (1978): *Wholesale Price Statistics India 1947-1978,* Volume 1, Economic and Scientific Research Foundation, New Delhi.

Desai, A V (1966): 'Growth and Fluctuations in the Indian Economy 1951-1964', *EPW,* I(14).

Hazari, B R (1967): 'Import Intensity of Consumption in India', *Indian Economic Review,* NS, 2(3).

Jose, A V (1974): 'Trends in Real Wage Rates of Agricultural Labourers', *EPW,* IX(13).

Madan, B K (1977): *The Real Wages of Industrial Labour in India,* Management Development Institute, New Delhi.

Ministry of Agriculture and Irrigation (1980): *Bulletin of Food Statistics 1979,* New Delhi.

Ministry of Finance (1970): *Economic Survey 1969-70,* New Delhi.

–(1980): *Economic Survey 1979-80,* New Delhi.

Ministry of Industry (1980): *Revised Index Numbers of Wholesale Prices in India,* New Delhi.

Mitra, Ashok (1977): *Terms of Trade and Class Relations,* Frank Cass, London.

National Commission on Labour (1969): Report, New Delhi.

Nayyar, Deepak (1978): 'Industrial Development in India: Some Reflections on Growth and Stagnation', *EPW,* XII (31-33).

Patnaik, Prabhat (1972): 'Disproportionality Crisis and Cyclical Growth', *EPW,* VII(5-7).

Rao, V K R V (1979): 'Changing Structure of the Indian Economy: As Seen through National Accounts Data', *EPW,* XIV (5).

Raj, K N (1976): 'Growth and Stagnation in Indian Industrial Development', *EPW,* XI (5-7).

Reserve Bank of India (1963): *RBI Bulletin,* Bombay, October.

—(1967): *RBI Bulletin,* Bombay, December.

—(1968): *RBI Bulletin,* Bombay, September.

—(1969): *Report on Currency and Finance, 1968-69,* Bombay.

—(1970): *RBI Bulletin,* Bombay, June.

—(1971): *Report on Currency and Finance, 1970-71*, Bombay.

—(1973): *RBI Bulletin,* December, Bombay.

—(1975): *RBI Bulletin,* Bombay, September.

—(1977a): 'Index Number of Industrial Production Revised Series' *RBI Bulletin,* Bombay, February.

—(1977b): *Report on Currency and Finance, 1976-77,* Vol II, Bombay.

—(1979): *RBI Bulletin,* Bombay, August.

—(1980): *RBI Bulletin,* Bombay, May.

Sau, R (1974): 'Some Aspects of Intersectoral Resource Flows', *EPW,* VI(31-33).

—(1977): 'Share of Wages', *EPW,* XII (26).

Shetty, S L (1978): 'Structural Retrogression in the Indian Economy since the Mid-Sixties', *EPW,* XII (6-7).

Srinivasan, T N (1977): 'Constraints on Growth and Resource Options: A Comment', *EPW,* XII (48).

—(1978): 'Constraints on Growth and Resource Options: Further Comment', *EPW,* XII (1).

—(1979): 'Trends in Agriculture in India 1949-50 to 1977-78', *EPW,* XIV (30-32).

Srinivasan, T N and Narayana N S S (1977): 'Economic Performance since the Third Plan and Its Implications for Policy', *EPW,* XII (6-8).

Textiles Committee (1979): *Consumer Purchases of Textiles 1978,* Bombay.

Thamarajakshi, R (1969): 'Intersectoral Terms of Trade and the Marketed Surplus of Agricultural Produce, 1951-52 to 1965-66', *EPW,* IV (26).

Vaidyanathan, A (1977a): 'Performance and Prospects of Crop Production in India', *EPW,* XII (31-33).

—(1977b): 'Constraints on Growth and Policy Options', *EPW,* XII (38).

—(1977c): 'Constraints on Growth and Policy Options: Reply', *EPW,* XII (51).

World Bank (1978): 'India: Occasional Papers', *World Bank Staff Working Paper,* No 279, Washington.

Annual Number 1981

11

Industrial Growth: Another Look

C Rangarajan

AN aspect of the Indian economy that has been a cause for concern is the deceleration in the rate of growth of industrial production since the mid-1960s. It is to this question that this paper is addressed. In many ways, India's industrial performance since independence has been impressive. Notwithstanding the difficulties faced in the measurement of industrial output over a long span of time–an issue to which we shall come later–there is enough evidence to indicate that aggregate industrial output has increased five-fold over a 30-year period, giving a compound rate of growth of 6 per cent per annum.

The performance looks even more impressive if it is judged by the criterion of the range and sophistication of the output manufactured. The output of capital goods industries, which consists primarily of machinery, had a weight of less than 5 per cent in the index of industrial production in 1956; its weight has increased to almost 16 per cent in 1970. The output of basic and capital goods industries, taken together, accounted for 50 per cent of the total value added in industrial production in 1980. This striking change in the composition of industrial output is also reflected in India's exports. Engineering goods had a negligible share in India's total exports in 1950. In 1980, they have a share of almost 11 per cent.

While India's performance in the industrial sector is certainly impressive since independence compared to the rate of growth of 2 per cent per annum experienced by the country in the previous 50 years, there are some disturbing trends in the rate of growth of industrial production which call for serious attention. A feature of industrial performance which has been the subject of many writings and discussions has been the fact that, while industrial production increased at an average rate of 7.8 per cent in the decade following 1955, the rate of growth fell to 3.7 per cent in the next decade 1965-75. Even if we include the second half of the 1970s, when performance has been slightly better, the rate of growth comes to only

4.3 per cent. The data on industrial production, available for 15 years since 1965, indicate that of the 15 years, there are two years in which the growth rate was negative and four years in which the annual rate of growth was less than 2 per cent.

Violent fluctuations in agricultural output are understandable in a country which is highly dependent on the bounties or otherwise of nature. But sharp fluctuations in industrial output have raised the question whether there is something endemic in the economic system which has been responsible for this or whether it is simply a coincidence of circumstances.

Before taking up the various hypotheses that have been offered to explain the phenomenon of deceleration, let us briefly highlight some of the features of industrial performance that deserve attention in this context. As mentioned earlier, there are difficulties in computing any index over a long time-span. The weights keep changing, and that makes comparison between one time period and another very difficult. We can construct an index based on common, unchanging, weights but that does not present a true picture of the situation. Also, the index of industrial production underestimates the level of output because the index is based largely on the data derived from the registered manufacturing organisations. The output in the unregistered sector in manufacturing does not get fully reflected in the index. We, therefore, constructed a different series taking the data on value added in manufacturing both in the registered and unregistered sectors, and compared it with the index of manufacturing which is a sub-set of the index of industrial production. Over a 15-year period, it is found that the annual rates of growth according to the two series are in agreement in most years (Table 1). There are, however, some exceptions–such as 1966–when the data on value added in manufacturing shows a positive growth rate whereas the index of manufacturing shows a decline in growth rate.

When one looks at the index of industrial production, it is seen that the best period was between 1961 and 1965. In this period the annual average rate of growth was nearly 9 per cent (Table 2). There was not even a single year in this period when the growth rate was less than 8 per cent. The sharpest increase was in the capital goods industries, where the average annual rate of growth was nearly 20 per cent. The basic goods industries rose by 10.5 per cent during this period and the output of consumer goods industries rose by 5 per cent. The sharp downturn occurred between 1966 and 1970, when the average growth rate fell to 3.7 per cent. And the most noticeable decline was in the capital goods industries where, over the five-year period, the average rate of growth turned out to be negative. The rate of growth of consumer goods industries, at 4 per cent per annum, was only a small decline from the previous period. During 1971-75, the growth rate of industrial production was 3.6 per cent per annum—which was no different from the growth rate achieved in the previous five-year period. During this period, while the basic goods industries and capital goods industries maintained a rate of growth of 5 per cent, the rate of growth in consumer goods industries fell to 1.6 per cent per annum. Thus while the period 1966-70 was marked by a sharp decline in capital goods industries, the subsequent five-year period was marked by a steep fall in the output of consumer goods industries. During 1976-80, the average rate of growth rose to 4.8 per cent. This was more or less the rate of growth experienced by all segments of industries. Thus, while undoubtedly the rate of growth of industrial production since 1966 has been much lower than what

Table 1: Rates of Growth in Manufacturing

Year	Index of Value Added in Manufacturing[1]	Index of Manufacturing in Industrial Production[2]
	1960 = 100	1960 = 100
1961-62	9.5	8.4
1962-63	6.1	9.1
1963-64	7.8	9.4
1964-65	7.9	8.9
1965-66	1.3	2.6
1966-67	1.9	1.2
1967-68	3.1	–0.1
	1970=100	1970=100
1971-72	2.7	6.2
1972-73	4.2	3.9
1973-74	4.8	2.1
1974-75	2.4	1.2
1975-76	2.4	3.8
1976-77	9.5	10.9

Notes: 1 Data on value added from manufacturing, in registered and unregistered sectors, in rupees at constant prices, are available (see *National Accounts Statistics,* October 1975 and February 1980). These have been added to obtain value added for the entire manufacturing sector.

2 Data on industrial production available on the monthly basis have been used to construct the index for fiscal years.

The growth rates for 1968-69, 1969-70, and 1970-71, have not been calculated since monthwise data on industrial production are not readily available.

Table 2: Year to Year Rates of Growth in Industrial Production

Year	All Industries	Basic Goods Industries	Capital Goods Industries	Consumer Goods Industries
1961	9.2	12.7	18.0	6.6
1962	9.7	13.3	29.6	1.3
1963	8.3	14.2	11.1	2.2
1964	8.6	3.8	17.7	7.4
1965	9.2	8.6	22.0	7.5
Average	9.0	10.5	19.7	5.0
1966	-0.4	5.2	-13.9	2.9
1967	-0.4	2.1	-2.3	-4.3
1968	6.8	10.2	3.4	4.9
1969	7.6	8.9	1.7	10.2
1970	5.1	4.6	4.9	6.4
Average	3.7	6.2	-1.4	4.0
1971	4.2	4.6	5.5	3.2
1972	5.7	8.0	0.9	4.7
1973	1.6	-3.1	15.8	-0.5
1974	2.0	3.9	4.3	2.2
1975	4.7	13.3	0.5	-1.5
Average	3.6	5.3	5.4	1.6
1976	9.9	14.3	10.5	10.2
1977	5.2	5.1	5.5	6.4
1978	6.9	4.8	2.7	10.0
1979	1.3	2.3	2.7	-2.2
1980	0.8	-1.0	4.6	0.4
Average	4.8	5.1	5.2	4.9

was experienced in the previous period, in trying to provide an explanation for this, it is important to note that the impact on different segments has been different in the different time periods.

The explanations that have been offered cover a wide spectrum. At one end, there are those who locate the cause for deceleration in the periodic shocks that the economy had received in the form of war in 1965 and 1971, the oil crisis in 1973, and the droughts in 1965 and 1966. According to them, it is these shocks which prevented the economy from gaining momentum and achieving a higher rate of industrial growth.

But at the other end, there is the explanation offered by economists influenced largely by the Marxian analysis. These assert that the crisis in industrial growth is rooted in the path of development that India has adopted and that there is no way out unless the fundamental property relations and structure of income distribution are altered. It may be convenient to deal with the various hypotheses and explanations suggested, by grouping them into two broad categories, viz, those that stress the supply constraints on growth and those that stress the demand constraints. We shall therefore proceed first to state the various hypotheses, test them with the help of empirical data available, and finally formulate our own position on the issue.

The explanation emphasising supply constraints basically argues that the growth rate of industrial production has been hampered primarily by the non-availability of critical inputs such as power, imported raw materials, and agricultural raw materials. The agro-based industries had a weight of approximately 60 per cent in the total industrial production in 1950. It has declined sharply over the years, but its weight, circa 1980, is still 33 per cent. It is therefore not improbable that fluctuations in agricultural output, insofar as they affected the supply of raw materials required by the agro-based industries, might have had an impact on industrial production. Needless to say, availability of power is another critical factor. Disturbed industrial relations can also be regarded as a constraint operating on the supply side. Those who think that the supply constraint has been the most important impediment—this includes, in the main, economists who speak for the government—do not necessarily argue that the same bottleneck has been faced from year to year.[1] The constraints that operate on the supply side might change from year to year. Their main contention is that, but for these constraints some of which are man-made and some acts of God, the growth rate would have been higher.

In the early phase of the development of the country, the question of demand constraint was never raised. However, in recent years, fears have been expressed that the real constraint on industrial growth in India may be operating from the demand side. If this is so, it has serious consequences for the future growth of industrial production. The concept of demand constraint, however, does not lead to a single explanation. The factors leading to demand restriction are seen to be different for basic and capital goods industries and for consumer goods industries.

In relation to capital goods industries, it has been argued that, by 1965, the possibilities of import substitution had been exhausted, and that further growth in the output of capital goods industries could therefore come only from an increase in demand which perhaps was not forthcoming. Import substitution, in the early phase, implies only the substitution of the foreign source of supply by domestic source of supply. Consequently, while the growth of capital goods industries up to 1965 had been helped by a strategy of import substitution which did not require a fresh increase in demand, in the subsequent period, growth of these industries has been hampered by the lack of generation of additional demand.[2]

Another stream of thought, bearing on the demand constraint in relation to capital goods industries, is that a high level of demand for these industries can be maintained only if investment is growing at a reasonably high rate. It is pointed out, therefore, that the sharp decline in public investment, noticed after 1966, was mainly responsible for the decline in the growth of capital goods industries.[3] Another strand of thinking intertwined with this is that private investment in India moves more or less in unison with public investment and that public investment stimulates private investment. Thus this theory postulates a complementary relationship between the two sectors rather than the usual approach which says that public investment 'crowds out' private investment. If this proposition is true, a decline in public investment will result in a decline in private investment as well, and the two together have a serious impact on the output of capital goods industries.

Turning to the demand constraint operating on the output of consumer goods, a major link is sought to be established between the demand for consumption goods and the performance of the agricultural sector. This hypothesis centres on the nature of the interrelationship between industry and agriculture.[4] As mentioned previously, agriculture influences industry on the supply side, through the availability of raw materials needed for industries. But another important influence is via the demand route. If, under the category of industrial consumption goods, we include such output as clothing, footwear, sugar and edible oils, then rural consumption of these commodities is nearly two and a half times that of urban consumption. It should not be surprising, then, if fluctuations in agricultural output have had a considerable impact, may be with some lag, on the demand for industrial consumption goods. If agricultural output increases and agricultural income grows as a result, the demand for these goods rises. On the other hand, poor agricultural performance will affect adversely the demand for industrial consumption goods.

These effects are plain enough to see, but there is another route through which demand can be influenced–and that is through the terms of trade between agriculture and industry. By terms of trade, we mean the ratio of agricultural price to the price of manufactured goods. One will have to trace the impact of a change in terms of trade on three different classes of people—the urban group, the rural poor, and the rural upper class. A rise in food price in relation to manufactures affects adversely the demand for non-food items in urban areas. The cross-elasticity of demand is negative, and this is all the more so in lower income groups in urban areas where food consumption is a sizeable part of the budget. In the case of the lower income groups in rural areas, the impact is likely to be the same as that in urban areas, since this segment of rural population also buys food. In the case of upper income groups in rural areas which have a marketable surplus, the negative effect on demand resulting from the rise in terms of trade in favour of agriculture can be offset by the increase in income arising from the improvement in agricultural prices. Thus the overall effect on the demand for industrial consumption goods because of the rise in terms of trade will depend upon the combined effect on all three groups we mentioned.

Agricultural performance can also affect the demand for capital goods by affecting the level of savings and investment of the household, government, and corporate sectors. Savings and investment of rural households may be helped by a rise in the terms of trade in favour of agriculture. On the other hand, a rise in agricultural prices relative to manufactures may have a negative influence on the corporate sector. First, a relative increase in non-food prices, by increasing the cost of production, may affect adversely the profitability of agro-based industries. Second, a relative increase in foodgrains prices may push up the wage cost and also thereby reduce the profitability. The savings of the government sector will be influenced both by agricultural output and the terms of trade. The rise and fall in agricultural output has an impact on government revenue and expenditures. A severe decline in agricultural output may force the government to undertake several relief measures, thereby forcing it to increase expenditures. A rise in foodgrains price will affect government expenditure through the impact it has on the compensation payable to the government employees. Thus there are several channels through which the impact of agricultural performance will be felt on industry. The argument of some has been that there has been a fall in the rate of growth in agricultural output since 1966 and that it is this which has been responsible for the slow-down in the rate of growth of industrial production.

Let us conclude the list of hypotheses by including one more which traces the demand constraint on industrial consumption goods to the unequal income distribution[5] and reaches the conclusion that the base of the market for industrial consumer goods in India is not only narrow but is shrinking. The argument quite simply is that the market for industrial consumption goods is concentrated in the top 10 per cent of the population, and that as this income group gets saturated with consumption there will be no further expansion in demand. Once the demand for consumption goods begins to fall, in the subsequent stages the demand for machinery and capital goods will also fall. And a crisis will then automatically develop. A continued growth in the demand for industrial consumption goods is possible only if the market widens. This can be accomplished, according to this hypothesis only by a drastic redistribution of income. This group of analysts sees in the improvement in the terms of trade in favour of agriculture the rising power of kulaks and the pauperisation of the urban proletariat and the rural poor.

We have just outlined the basic premises of the various hypotheses suggested and we shall now try to show how far these various theories stand the test of empirical verification. It must be noted that, not all these theories are mutually exclusive. Nevertheless, each of the hypotheses certainly seems to say that the factor emphasised by it is the key factor responsible for the deceleration in industrial growth.

Taking the supply constraint hypothesis first: It is easy to identify several years following 1966 when output was held back because of the non-availability of critical inputs. It is worth noting in this context that electricity generation, which had maintained an average annual rate of growth of 14 per cent during 1960-65, declined to an average 6.3 per cent in 1970-75 (Table 3). In fact, looking at the performance of industry in the current year and the two previous years, it is quite obvious that what has helped industrial production achieve a rate of growth of 10 per cent in the current year has been the removal of infrastructure constraints. Thus a year-by-year analysis of the factors inhibiting growth clearly indicates that, since 1966, one can easily identify six or seven years where the cause of deceleration can be traced to supply bottlenecks. These bottlenecks have arisen, in most years, not so much from inadequate investment as from an inefficient use of existing investment. Nevertheless, it must be noted that supply availability is only a necessary but not a sufficient condition for industrial growth.

Talking of demand constraint on the output of capital goods, the import substitution hypothesis does sound plausible as an explanation of the earlier growth and the later deceleration. But it really overstates the case. With the virtual ban on certain kinds of output, there is no

Table 3: Year to Year Rates of Growth in Select Variables

(In percentage)

Year	All Crops	Foodgrains	Non-Foodgrains	Electricity Generated
1961-62	0.0	0.8	–0.2	18.3
1962-63	–0.2	–3.1	1.8	14.0
1963-64	2.4	0.6	2.6	17.4
1964-65	10.6	10.8	11.7	10.1
1965-66	–16.7	–19.0	–11.4	11.6
1966-67	0.0	2.6	–3.2	10.3
1967-68	21.5	28.0	11.5	13.2
1968-69	–1.5	–1.0	–2.1	15.1
1969-70	6.7	6.7	6.4	9.6
1970-71	7.2	8.9	5.1	7.4
1971-72	0.0	–1.0	2.0	9.1
1972-73	–8.0	–8.2	–7.8	5.9
1973-74	9.9	7.8	14.4	3.3
1974-75	–3.2	–5.4	1.1	5.2
1975-76	15.2	22.0	2.5	13.0
1976-77	–7.0	–9.0	–2.6	11.5
1977-78	14.4	15.5	12.6	3.4
1978-79	3.5	4.3	1.4	12.2
1979-80	15.5	–18.2	–9.4	2.1

doubt that some of the industries must have been helped a great deal by such a policy. But there is no evidence to indicate that the policy came to so sudden an end in 1965-66 as to cause a sharp fall in the production capital goods. The index of machinery imports, with the base 1960-61 = 100, rose from 103 in 1961-62 to 143 in 1965-66; between 1966-67 and 1970-71, it declined from 101 to 74 (Table 4). Thus, in the latter period, imports declined at a sharp rate, whereas in the former period, machinery imports actually increased. The share of imported machinery to investment in machinery declined from 38.6 per cent in 1961-62 to 27.8 per cent in 1965-66. But it continued to fall during the next five years–from 29 per cent to 16.8 per cent. Thus it is difficult to sustain the proposition that it is the exhaustion of the possibilities of import substitution that brought about the collapse in the growth of capital goods industries between 1966 and 1970. A commodity-wise analysis does not show any negative correlation between the rate of growth in imports and the rate of growth in production. Thus this hypothesis has a very limited role in explaining the behaviour of even one segment of industrial production, viz, the output of capital goods industries.

The link between industrial performance and agricultural growth is crucial in an economy such as ours, where income originating in agriculture still contributes 45 per cent of the national income and where agriculture is still subject to severe exogenous shocks from time to time. Many studies in the past have shown that the link between agriculture and industry, based on the input and output relationship, has not been strong in India. This is the conclusion that the Second Asian Agricultural Survey also reached. For example, in 1968-69, the total value of the output of agriculture and allied activities was Rs 1,972 crore. The total value of inputs used by them was Rs 4,840 crore. However, of this, Rs 3,571 crore was the value of inputs coming from agriculture and allied activities themselves. Thus inputs worth Rs 1,269 crore alone came from industry and services sectors. This constituted no more than 6.4 per cent of the value of total agricultural output. Again, the flow of agriculture and allied activities to other sectors constituted only a small proportion of the total value of their output. Only output worth Rs 2,489 crore went to non-agricultural sectors as inputs. This is approximately 13 per cent of the total output of agriculture and allied activities. Dividing the economy into three sectors–agriculture, manufacturing and services and by taking into account the direct and indirect requirements, it is found that a rupee increase in the final demand of agriculture results in an increase in

Table 4: Index of Imports

(1960-61=100)

Year	Machinery
1961-62	103
1962-63	114
1963-64	125
1964-65	132
1965-66	143
1966-67	101
1967-68	95
1968-69	88
1969-70	73
1970-71	74
1971-72	96
1972-73	140
1973-74	87
1974-75	76

Source: Vidya Pitre, 'A Study of Trends in India's Imports, 1960-61 to 1974-75', *Economic and Political Weekly*, May 9, 1981.

the output of manufacture by rupee 0.09 and of services by rupee 0.02, whereas a one rupee increase in the final demand of manufacture results in an increase in the output of agriculture by rupee 0.26. These data indicate that the dependence of industry on agriculture is greater than that of agriculture on industry. Dependence of agriculture on industry for inputs varies with the level of technology used in agriculture. Similarly, the dependence of industry on agriculture for inputs varies with the growth of various processing industries. At the present moment, the link through the input-output relation does not appear to be very strong. This, however, is only a partial picture. Even a cursory glance of the data relating to rates of growth in industry and agriculture will show the kind of impact agriculture has had on industry. During 1961-65, agricultural output fell in 1961 and 1962, and the output of consumer goods industry fell in the following years 1962 and 1963. Moreover, the sharp decline in agricultural output in 1965-66 and 1966-67 is reflected in the slower growth rate in consumer

Table 5: Imports of Machinery and Fixed Capital Formation

(Rs crore in current prices)

Year (1)	Gross Domestic Fixed Capital Formation in Machinery and Equipment (2)	Imports of Machinery and Transport Equipment (3)	(3) as Percentage of (2) (4)
1961-62	952	368	38.6
1962-63	1116	387	34.7
1963-64	1378	437	31.7
1964-65	1623	478	29.5
1965-66	1772	492	27.8
1966-67	1887	536	28.4
1967-68	1976	503	25.4
1968-69	2040	516	25.3
1969-70	2221	395	17.8
1970-71	2346	328	14.0
1971-72	2810	376	13.4
1972-73	3352	432	12.9
1973-74	4099	557	13.6
1974-75	5171	696	13.5
1975-76	6031	935	15.5
1976-77	6810	1048	15.4
1977-78	7419	1110	14.9

Sources: Column 2, CSO, *National Accounts Statistics*.
Column 3, RBI, *Report on Currency and Finance*.

goods industries in 1966 and 1967. Even in the more recent period, the decline in agricultural output in 1972-73 and 1974-75 is reflected in the fall in the output of consumer goods industries in 1973 and 1975. Thus, with a lag of one year, agriculture seems to affect directly the output of consumer goods industry with some exceptions (see Tables 2 and 3). The fall in agricultural output in 1969 did not result in a decline in the output of consumer goods industries in 1969. However, to isolate the various types of influences, there is need to construct a broader framework of analysis.

We had mentioned, earlier, the various channels of influence having a bearing on the demand for industrial produciton. Both agricultural output and terms of trade influence the demand for industrial consumption goods–the former positively, and the latter negatively on some groups and positively on others. Both these again influence savings and investment of the household, government, and corporate sectors–and thereby influence the demand for the output of basic and capital goods industries. In order to understand the total effect, a macro model was constructed where all these relationships were explicitly postulated and estimated.[6] In the model, agricultural output was treated as exogenous, since the purpose was to study the impact of agriculture. The terms of trade were determined within the system and so, too, the output of the different segments of industrial production. Data tend to confirm the a priori hypotheses stated earlier. Agricultural output has a positive impact on the demand for industrial consumption goods. On the other hand, the total effect of foodgrains' terms of trade, after taking into account both the rural and urban impact, is found to be negative. But the elasticity is negligible. Agricultural output and terms of trade have a positive impact on household savings and investment. This means that a rise in agricultural prices in relation to manufactures prices promotes rural savings. This should not come as a surprise, because a survey conducted by the National Council of Applied Economic Research in 1967-68 showed that rural household savings were 1.83 times urban savings.[7] The terms of trade elasticity with respect to household investment was 1.5. A rise in agricultural prices in relation to manufactures prices, operating through cost and profitability, has an adverse effect on corporate investment. And the elasticity works out to –1.5. The rise in the foodgrains' terms of trade has a significantly negative impact on government savings. A rise in agricultural output has a positive influence both on government savings and corporate investment.

The negative impact of a rise in the foodgrains' terms of trade on urban non-food expenditures is also evident from an analysis of the

National Sample Survey data. A disaggregated analysis in relation to cloth consumption also brings out this fact. But in relation to both expenditures, the rural response is positive to changes in terms of trade. Taking the model as a whole, it is seen that the positive and negative effects of a rise in terms of trade tend to cancel out. What then is the total effect of agricultural performance on industrial growth? We simulated the model to find out what the rate of industrial production would have been, had the agricultural growth rate been one per cent higher than what was historically experienced. The conclusion that emerges is that an increase in the agricultural growth rate by one per cent will have an effect of slightly less than one per cent on national income. This implies that a one per cent rate of growth in agriculture results in the industrial output rising by close to one per cent. This must be deemed to be a sizeable impact, even though magnitude might be less than what some agricultural fundamentalists may believe it to be. A one-shot increase or decrease in agriculture has its reverberations on the economy for the next three to four years.

There is considerable difference of opinion among agricultural economists as to whether there has been any decline in the trend rate of growth in agricultural production. Various kinds of trend equations have been estimated in support of either position. Without entering into this argument, our study shows that fluctuations in agricultural output can have a significant impact on industrial performance. However, it would be wrong to conclude that the behaviour of industrial production since 1966 can be explained purely in terms of agricultural performance. The dynamics of industrial growth is more complex. But it is apparent that, unless agriculture grows at a steady and reasonable rate, industrial growth will itself run into problems.

Those who argue that income distribution is the root cause of deceleration argue that the demand base for industrial goods is very narrow in terms of population coverage. For example, in 1964-65, using National Sample Survey data, it has been estimated that in the rural sector the richest 10 per cent of the population was responsible for 32.2 per cent of the total consumption of industrial goods, whereas the poorest 50 per cent accounted for only 22 per cent of the total. The consumption inequalities were even more pronounced in the urban sector where the top 10 per cent purchased 39.3 per cent of the industrial goods and the bottom five deciles absorbed just 20 per cent of the total. While these data show that the market for industrial consumption goods is concentrated in the upper income segments of the population, it still does not prove that the market is narrowing or shrinking.

To support the hypothesis of a shrinking market, two sets of data are provided. The National Sample Survey provides data on different types of consumption expenditure for different expenditure classes. Using these data, the percentage of per capita consumption expenditure spent on industrial consumption goods is computed for different deciles of population in the rural and urban areas. Such a computation, according to one estimate, shows that while the lowest six deciles spent around two-fifths of their consumption expenditures on industrial goods in 1952-53, 12 years later the ratio was around three-tenths.[8] A similar trend is noted for urban India. Second, once again using the NSS data, the share of each decile in the total market of industrial goods is computed and such an analysis shows that, in the aggregate consumption of industrial goods in rural areas, the lower six deciles were consuming proportionately less of the total consumption in 1964-65 than in 1952-53. Thus the conclusions drawn are: (i) the ratio of expenditure on industrial consumption goods to total expenditure of consumption goods is falling, and (ii) the lower deciles of population are slowly withdrawing from the market for industrial goods. The two, together, portend a dangerous trend for industrial growth.

Even though there is some evidence to show that there has been a decline in the percentage of consumer expenditure spent on industrial consumption goods, the trend does not appear to be strong, especially if we extend the data beyond 1964-65. We replicated the study by extending the analysis up to 1973-74. i e, the 28th round of NSS.[9] The analysis shows a small decline in the percentage of expenditure on industrial consumption goods. But, strangely enough, this decline occurs not only in the lower deciles of the population but also in the top decile of the population. The basic reason adduced for the decline in the percentage of per capita expenditure on industrial goods is that, as food prices rise, they pre-empt the income in favour of food, leaving less available for other expenditures. One would have expected that the expenditure on consumption goods by the upper deciles would have increased since the rise in the terms of trade in favour of agriculture ought to have benefited at least the upper income group. In fact, even the per capita rural expenditure on industrial consumption goods shows a decline for the upper income groups as well. It is well known that NSS data for the top income groups is quite suspect. Moreover, our analysis of the percentage of the total market in each fractile class shows that, as far as the urban areas are concerned, the share of middle deciles has clearly gone up. However, in the rural areas, no distinct trend was noticeable.

Table 6: Growth of Production and Imports in Some Select Industry Groups

	Production			Imports			Production			Imports		
	1961	1965	Average Annual Growth Rate	1961	1965	Average Annual Growth Rate	1966	1970	Average Annual Growth Rate	1966	1970	Average Annual Growth Rate
Non-electrical machinery	121.1	238.8	19.1	121.0	157.0	9.6	295.5	369.5	9.4	120.4	71.0	–14.28
Electrical machinery	110.0	204.4	15.4	108.0	184.0	13.2	225.1	362.7	12.2	131.0	162.0	14.40
Transport equipment	116.7	204.3	15.7	81.0	96.0	2.72	156.0	132.0	–7.9	42.0	31.0	–13.90
Manufacture of metals	112.4	205.6	16.2	79.0	71.0	1.6	208.4	219.0	6.3	48.0	24.0	–11.70

The decline in the percentage of per capita consumption expenditure on industrial consumption goods does not lead to the conclusion that the market in any absolute sense is narrowing. Even if the percentage were decreasing, the total market can expand so long as this decline is offset by a rising population. In absolute amount, even for the bottom deciles there is no decline in the consumption of industrial goods. The poorest decile of population in the rural areas consumed in 1960-61 Rs 77.7 crore of industrial goods. The same section consumed Rs 98.1 crore in 1973-74. (Tables 7A and 7B). In fact, the crisis in the system can develop only if a stage is reached where the withdrawal of the lower deciles of the population is not compensated by the increase in the upper decile. This can happen only if the top 10 per cent of the population reaches a saturation point with respect to consumption of industrial goods. It is hard to accept this argument, since the per capita consumption expenditure of the top 5 per cent of the rural population in 1973-74 was still less than Rs 75 per month at 1964-65 prices. Undoubtedly, a different distribution of income would have resulted in a demand package which is different from the current package of industrial consumption goods. However, at the present level of per capita income of the top decile, it is difficult to sustain the proposition that the distribution of income, as such has set a limit on industrial growth.

It is also worth noting, in this context, that one of the basic premises of this approach–viz, that terms of trade had improved in terms of agriculture continually–is also not confirmed by the data. The behaviour of terms of trade has not always been in one direction in this period. Agricultural terms of trade worsened in the early 1950s, improved till early 1970s, and perhaps has declined thereafter. However, this excursion into the data of NSS does indicate one thing: and that is, that organised industry at the present moment is catering to only a very limited segment of the population. This is partly reflected in the higher rate of growth of durable consumption goods. The creation of a mass market will imply that organised industry will have to produce products that can go to satisfy at least the middle deciles of the population.

The hypothesis that decline in public investment is the cause of the deceleration of economic growth found much acceptance in the early 1970s. The gross fixed capital formation in the public sector reached a peak in 1965-66, and thereafter it started to decline in real terms till 1972-73. Thus, between 1950-51 and 1965-66, public fixed capital formation grew at 12.2 per cent and private fixed capital formation at 4.2 per cent per annum (Table 8). The overall compound

Table 7A: Market Size for Industrial Consumption Goods (Rural)

(In millions at 1964-65 prices)

Fractile Class	Rounds									
(Percentage)	16	17	18	19	20	21	22	23	24	25	28
0-5	325.16	366.99	390.37	368.39	388.85	336.07	336.07	323.67	333.14	356.20	424.28
5-10	452.68	522.43	483.97	447.67	455.65	421.32	395.81	423.06	458.07	460.21	557.39
10-20	1131.70	1157.77	1164.27	1113.93	1097.38	1032.61	1005.72	1075.49	1150.38	1164.82	1369.90
20-30	1460.53	1472.34	1483.87	1463.49	1446.04	1178.73	1249.68	1284.47	1369.00	1398.82	1674.94
30-40	1750.93	1821.86	1835.43	1822.37	1722.84	1432.01	1503.60	1508.75	1639.60	1742.02	1841.32
40-50	1990.08	2105.84	2063.72	2227.86	2009.18	1782.71	1847.13	1840.06	1983.24	2147.63	2456.95
50-60	2630.66	2481.57	2401.59	2507.51	2371.88	2099.31	1986.54	2288.61	2316.38	2563.64	2606.68
60-70	3096.16	3045.16	2972.31	3057.48	2915.94	2352.60	2648.72	2747.35	3164.86	3177.25	3538.45
70-80	4150.98	4342.75	3702.83	3793.89	3545.89	3268.31	3116.73	3287.64	3732.64	3770.06	4114.16
80-90	6012.95	5915.57	4967.55	4996.38	4576.73	4047.63	4361.43	4470.17	4997.14	4986.88	6322.62
90-95	4516.12	4198.57	3362.68	3688.59	3502.06	3165.24	2959.90	3631.70	3789.50	3598.45	4506.25
95-100	9916.24	9830.16	10049.24	8657.23	8652.67	6651.87	5451.78	9264.01	8953.22	8343.53	10082.22

Note : The term 'Industrial Consumption Goods' is taken to include the following categories of the NSS data: (1) clothing, (2) footwear, (3) fuel and light, (4) durables, (5) miscellaneous goods and services.

Source: Siddharth Roy, 'Demand for Industrial Consumer Goods in India: A Study of Linkages' (a thesis submitted to Indian Institute of Management, Ahmedabad under the Fellow Programme).

Table 7B: Market Size for Industrial Consumption Goods (Urban)

(In millions at 1964-65 prices)

Fractile Class (Percentage)	Rounds 16	17	18	19	20	21	22	23	24	25	28
0-5	98.43	105.49	100.22	186.48	101.62	81.26	90.17	97.90	111.38	110.40	147.43
5-10	148.62	136.66	145.82	141.80	135.66	105.85	128.42	138.74	158.22	156.23	188.07
10-20	364.66	388.41	381.85	339.91	321.61	257.68	323.52	336.78	407.84	391.23	473.98
20-30	496.84	484.31	468.05	436.15	409.61	295.10	409.86	436.36	506.08	520.35	555.27
30-40	588.71	626.25	595.33	531.37	468.28	345.35	474.34	523.63	606.61	626.23	684.79
40-50	691.83	756.68	759.70	665.49	566.75	451.20	560.69	640.00	822.23	755.35	799.15
50-60	854.00	909.17	939.10	828.28	652.65	539.95	707.14	763.08	928.77	1047.16	1000.37
60-70	1059.31	1183.45	1111.48	1013.60	819.20	622.27	921.36	968.95	1198.38	1236.97	1092.62
70-80	1440.84	1496.10	1409.15	1356.59	1073.79	835.04	1178.21	1280.00	1659.91	1679.85	1532.16
80-90	2114.86	2091.67	2272.08	1970.89	1588.16	1124.80	1779.34	2244.47	3312.47	3596.00	2135.65
90-95	2313.13	1557.96	1698.80	1839.84	1459.83	825.42	1367.29	1633.56	2004.91	1845.77	1500.47
95-100	2382.97	3610.31	3413.13	2916.41	2088.91	1408.67	2325.27	2303.77	3036.50	2798.03	2872.42

Note : The term 'Industrial Consumption Goods' is taken to include the following categories of the NSS data: (1) clothing, (2) footwear, (3) fuel and light, (4) durables, (5) miscellaneous goods and services.

Source: Siddharth Roy, 'Demand for Industrial Consumer Goods in India: A Study of Linkages' (a thesis submitted to Indian Institute of Management, Ahmedabad under the Fellow Programme).

Table 8: Rates of Growth in Gross Fixed Investment

	1950-51 (at 60-61 Prices)	1965-66 (at 60-61 Prices)	Compound Rate of Growth (Per Cent)	1965-66 (at 60-61 Prices)	1971-72 (at 60-61 Prices)	Compound Rate of Growth (Per Cent)	1970-71 (at 70-71 Prices)	1977-78 (at 70-71 Prices)	Compound Rate of Growth (Per Cent)
Gross fixed investment									
Total	1140	3333	7.4	3333	4059	3.3	6305	9412	5.9
Public	293	1649	12.2	1649	1603	–0.47	2394	4078	8.0
Private	847	1684	4.7	1684	2456	6.5	3911	5311	4.5
Corporate	97	324	8.4	324	459	5.97	545	7811	5.3

rate of growth for fixed capital formation was 7.4 per cent. This rate fell to 3.3 per cent during the six years following 1965-66. Public investment started declining in absolute amount, and reached again the level achieved in 1965-66 only in 1972-73. The gross fixed capital formation by the public sector stood at Rs 293 crore in 1950-51, and the private sector investment in that year was nearly three times at Rs 847 crore (Table 9A). Because of the more rapid growth in investment in public sector, by 1964-65 public investment was approximately equal to private investment.

Then began the sharp decline in public investment. The increase in public investment prior to 1965-66 was made possible both by a rise in public savings and by a substantial inflow of real resources from abroad (Table 10). The decline in public investment was triggered by the severe droughts of 1965 and 1966, and was further compounded by the fall in capital inflows from abroad. As mentioned previously, some people postulate a complementary relationship between public investment and private investment. Public investment affects private investment in two ways. Both of them in the current period compete for the savings that are available; and so, the more one has, the less will be available to the other. On the other hand, public investment of the previous periods can stimulate private investment in the current period, because of the growth in the demand generated by public sector investment and expenditure. To the extent that public sector investment is in infrastructure facilities, it can also lead to a lowering of the cost of producing private sector output. Thus, in trying to understand the relationship between the two sectors, one has to take into account both the 'crowding out' effect and the 'stimulation effect' and find out which, in the long run, will be more dominant. It may be noted that, during 1966-72, when public investment was declining, private investment surged forward. In 1972-73, once again, private sector investment was higher than public investment. However, when one compares private corporate investment with public sector investment one sees a much closer positive relationship between the two (Table 9A and Chart).

There are a number of ways of testing the relationship between public investment and private investment.[10] One simple way of trying to understand the relationship is to regress the private sector investment or corporate investment on public sector investment of the previous period and on savings less public investment of the current period. Estimated equations in this respect show that, in the case of private investment, the positive and negative effects almost cancel out each other; whereas in the case of private corporate investment the

Chart

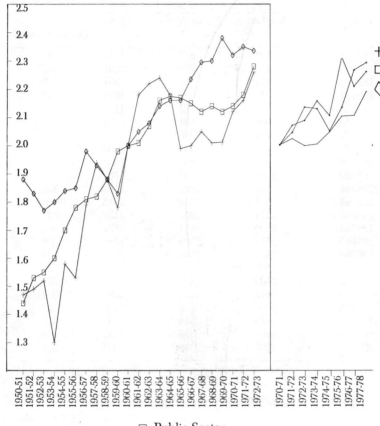

□ Public Sector

◊ Private Sector + Private Corporate Sector

positive effect seems to dominate the negative.[11] The investment stagnation hypothesis, which may seem to provide an explanation of the phenomenon that occurred between 1966 and 1972, fails to carry conviction when we go beyond that period. In fact, public investment started moving up from 1971-72, and during the next six-year period public investment grew at 8 per cent per annum and private investment continued to grow at the trend rate of growth of 4.5 per cent per annum (Table 9B). The crucial question that arises, then, is why has industrial production not picked up even after a growth rate of 6 per cent per annum is maintained in gross fixed capital formation.

Table 9A: Gross Fixed Capital Formation

(Rs crore at 1960-61 prices)

Year	Public Sector	Private Sector	Total	Private Corporate Sector
1950-51	293	847	1140	97
1951-52	356	741	1097	103
1952-53	374	617	991	112
1953-54	421	695	1040	65
1954-55	504	779	1185	129
1955-56	668	804	1472	115
1956-57	714	1058	1772	196
1957-58	716	968	1684	291
1958-59	810	827	1637	217
1959-60	1018	749	1767	192
1960-61	1055	1101	2156	326
1961-62	1061	1254	2315	492
1962-63	1214	1265	2479	376
1963-64	1390	1411	2801	565
1964-65	1570	1586	3156	509
1965-66	1649	1684	3333	324
1966-67	1492	1854	3346	329
1967-68	1400	2136	3536	373
1968-69	1417	2174	3591	353
1969-70	1400	2638	3758	347
1970-71	1448	2316	3764	415
1971-72	1603	2456	4059	459
1972-73	1987	2346	4333	561

Source: See R N Lal, *Capital Formation and Its Financing in India*, pp 107 and 116.

Table 9B: Gross Fixed Capital Formation

(Rs crore at 1970-71 prices)

Year	Public Sector	Private Sector	Total	Private Corporate Sector
1970-71	2394	3911	6305	545
1971-72	2648	4038	6686	634
1972-73	3166	3893	7059	655
1973-74	3134	3926	7060	758
1974-75	2678	4245	6923	671
1975-76	3161	4571	7732	1093
1976-77	3927	4842	8759	745
1977-78	4078	5334	9412	781

Note: 1980. Figures in current prices for all the series have been deflated by a common index.

Source: CSO, *National Accounts Statistics*, February,

Whatever the factors that might have operated in the past in holding down the industrial growth rate, the critical question to ask now is why has not the industrial growth rate picked up even after a substantial rise in investment?

Before we attempt to answer this question let us summarise where we stand in relation to the past. The problem with many of the explanations offered is that the proponents of each theory tend to believe that there is just one explanation that will account for the entire sequence of events that happened over the 30-year period. While it is important to isolate the critical from the accidental, it is also not wise to search for a single explanation. The period 1960-65 was marked by a high growth rate in industrial production because public investment was rising at a very sharp rate, aided partly by the sizeable inflow of real resources from abroad. The demand constraint in relation to capital goods industries was not operating at least in part because of the policy of import substitution. Although agricultural production was not behaving well during this period, foodgrains prices still ruled low because of the import of concessional foodgrains. The output of consumer goods industries, except in two years, maintained a fairly high rate of growth. The decline in industrial growth during 1966-70 could be traced mainly to the droughts of 1966 and 1967, and the subsequent inability to raise public investment. The period 1971-75, when public investment once again picked up, the basic and capital goods industries showed a moderate rise. But the consumer goods industries suffered severely as the general price level rose to unbelievably new heights. The period 1976-80 was marked by a moderate rise in industrial production, and more or less all segments of industrial production maintained the same rate of growth. However, this period on the whole was plagued by various kinds of infrastructural constraints, which prevented it from achieving the full benefits of the investment increase.

In the early years of plan formulation in this country, the biggest constraint in the way of economic growth was seen to be in the low savings ratio which was considered inevitable in the low income countries. Over the years, through a variety of techniques and efforts, the country has been able to raise the savings and investment ratio. Gross capital formation, as a percentage of gross domestic product at current market prices, rose from 10 per cent in 1950-51 to 21.8 per cent in 1979-80. The savings rate achieved by India is comparable to the rate achieved in middle income and even some high income industrialised countries. The investment stagnation hypothesis does not seem right, when one looks at the investment-income ratio. In spite of the substantial jump in the investment-income ratio, gross fixed capital formation has been growing only at 5.9 per cent in recent years as compared with 7.9 per cent in the period 1950-51 to 1965-66. Since income growth rate is lower, total investment is not rising at a faster rate as compared with the previous period, in spite of stepping up the ratio of investment to income.

In fact, what lies at the root of all this is the rising incremental capital-output ratio. The rise in incremental capital-output ratio has nullified the output increase that could otherwise have come from the increase in the share of investment to income. The capital-output ratios actually experienced in the economy had turned out to be much higher than those anticipated in the plan documents. The calculation of the capital-output ratio is beset with many statistical problems. A comparison over time raises more issues. Changing relative prices can affect the ratio. One can also get different results depending on

Table 10: Capital Inflows and Public Savings

(Rs crore at 1970-71 prices)

Year	Gross Fixed Capital Formation in Public Sector	Net Capital Inflows	Public Savings (Gross)
1952	374	–40.2	171.4
1953	421	–15.9	155.2
1954	504	28.4	186.3
1955	668	63.7	210.7
1956	714	416.6	268.1
1957	716	526.8	271.7
1958	810	400.0	242.8
1959	1018	241.6	199.8
1960	1055	481.0	425.0
1961	1061	332.4	389.2
1962	1214	412.2	530.2
1963	1390	392.7	632.9
1964	1570	515.1	701.0
1965	1649	482.7	652.0
1966	1492	663.7	480.4
1967	1400	571.3	455.0
1968	1417	276.9	571.0
1969	1400	152.9	655.0
1970	1448	233.2	742.0
1971	1603	272.7	718.0
1972	1982	157.8	705.0

Note: Data in current prices have been deflated by CSO's investment deflator.
Source: Current prices data: R N Lal, op cit, pp 107 and 207.

whether the ratio measured is one of net investment to increase in the net domestic product or gross investment to increase in gross domestic product. The latter will always give a higher ratio. According to the Sixth Plan document, the incremental gross capital-output ratio has risen from 3.2 in the First Plan to 5.7 in the Fourth Plan. Leaving aside other factors, such as changing lag pattern and weather-induced fluctuations in output, changes in the aggregate incremental capital-output ratios over time are influenced by two factors: One, change in the incremental capital-output ratio of the different sectors, and two, change in the output mix. The rise in incremental capital-output ratio due to change in the output mix can be policy-induced, as happened between the First and the Second Plans. The sectoral capital-output ratios presented in the Sixth Plan document are again revealing (Table 11). In almost every sector, even the planned ICOR is very high. In sectors such as electricity and transport and communication, the ratios are as high as 34.3 and 11.1, respectively. If past experience is any guide, the 'realised incremental capital-output ratios may turn out to be larger than those implied in the Plan. We have shown in Table 12 the actual ICOR for the various sectors using the data for the period 1970-71 to 1977-78.

The rise in incremental capital-output ratio calls for a systematic analysis of the factors that have contributed to this rise. We have witnessed, the co-existence of non-availability of power and underutilisation of capacity in the power sector. While it is always possible for underutilisation to occur because of the absence of complementary investment, a significant degree of underutilisation of capacity essentially shows an inefficient use of the available capital. It can very well be argued that an improvement in capacity utilisation can only lead to a one-shot increase in output. That is true. But if the additional investment that is being added every year is more effectively utilised than is being done now, it should be possible to extract a higher growth rate from the economy. International comparisons of ICORs have problems.

It is nevertheless true that India has one of the highest incremental capital-output ratios among the developing economies. The ICOR for rapidly developing economies such as Korea is as low as 2.0. In fact, the mean for 22 industrialised countries was 4.9. The Indian ratio is close to this figure. It should also be noted that industrially advanced countries are content to grow at 2 to 3 per cent which is not the case for a country such as ours. Two things are required. First, there should be an attempt to bring down the sectoral ICORs. In this respect, greater attention needs to be paid to the efficient utilisation of capital.

Second, investment choices should also be governed by the level of ICOR. Some serious thinking is called for whether investment in some of the projects, such as petrochemical complexes or even steel plants, at certain locations are justified. The composition of investment from this angle needs a closer look. Industrial growth in future is not going to be free from the problems that may arise from fluctuations in

Table 11: Sectoral Incremental Capital Output Ratios in Sixth Plan

(Rs crore at 1979-80 prices)

	Investment (at Market Prices)	Incremental GDP (at Factor Cost)	ICOR
Agriculture	33468	7049 (25.2)	4.74
Mining and manufacturing	52090	7540 (26.9)	6.91
Construction	1760	1389 (4.9)	1.26
Electricity and Gas	23554	686 (2.5)	34.33
Transport, communications storage and trade*	26255	6733 (24.0)	3.90
Other sectors	21583	4602 (16.4)	4.69
Total	158710	27999 (100.0)	5.67
Total at market price		37994	4.20

Notes: Figures in brackets refer to percentage to total.
Since sectoral domestic product at market price is not available, investment at market prices has been divided by gross domestic product at factor cost. This will overstate the ICOR. In the next table also, the same procedure has been adopted.
* For Transport and communication alone the ICOR is 11.10.

Table 12: Sectoral Incremental Capital Output Ratios during 1970-71 to 1977-78

(Rs crore at 1960-61 prices)

	Investment (at Market Prices)	Incremental GDP (at Factor Cost)	ICOR
Agriculture	11414	2913	3.92
Mining and manufacturing	18009	2078	8.67
Construction	1070	594	1.80
Electricity, gas and water supply	5307	244	21.75
Transport and communication	11854	2167	5.47
Other sectors	13545	2018	6.71
Total	61199	10014	6.11

Source: CSO, *National Accounts Statistics*, February 1980.

agricultural output or rising terms of trade in favour of agriculture or from infrastructure bottlenecks now and then. But, having learnt to raise our investment rate to a level comparable to that in any industrialised country, we ought to turn our attention more closely to improving the productivity of capital and thereby decreasing the capital-output ratio.

The possibility of stepping up the investment rate much beyond 25 per cent must be ruled out. With the savings and investment rate stabilising at that level, higher growth rate can occur only if we learn to lower the incremental capital-output ratio. The changes in the output mix need not run into the ideological conflicts which were witnessed at the time of the Second Five-Year Plan.

The question is not whether more capital goods or more consumer goods should be produced. The question really is, which commodity can be produced at a lower capital-output ratio. Increased investment in electricity which has a high incremental capital-output ratio does not necessarily mean that the overall ratio should increase. If, for example, lack of power has been responsible for underutilisation of capacity elsewhere, the increased output flowing from electricity should generate increased output in the other sectors and to that extent the aggregate ICOR will be lowered. In planning for investment, we should really move towards a system of what can be described as 'sequential strategic sector planning'—a system of planning in which the planners identify the constraining sectors in the economy and invest more in them so that the constraints are relaxed and output growth is activated. However, the point to be made at this juncture is that, unless we are able to identify outputs and sectors in which it is possible to lower the incremental capital-output ratio, we will continue to creep along a 5 to 6 per cent growth rate even in industry.

This paper has not touched upon an issue that has been put forward vehemently by the industrialists in recent months. Many of them see in the regulatory measures the stumbling block to faster industrial growth. Also, they find the present taxation policy not providing the corporate sector with adequate funds for growth. Corporate sector investment constitutes only 10 per cent of the total investment. Nevertheless, its importance and role cannot be underestimated. In a planned economy controls cannot be dispensed with. It should be possible, however, to work out a compromise between the compulsions of social purpose and the incentives needed for private action. Much of the controversy in this regard is centred around the allocation of total savings between the corporate and the public sector.

Given the need to lower the incremental capital-output ratio, it is necessary to understand which sector is more productive for what output. While the allocation among sectors is important, the focus of this paper is on some of the fundamental factors bearing on industrial growth, such as inter-sectoral linkages, income distribution, and efficient utilisation of capital. The economy no longer operates under a low savings constraint. The constraints of yester-years have disappeared but in the place have come newer challenges.

An 8 to 10 per cent growth rate in industrial production is absolutely essential if the economy is to achieve an overall growth rate of 5 per cent. And this will come only if we can extract more out of the capital that we have so far invested and the capital that we will continue to invest. Therein lies the key to future industrial growth and this is the lesson that recent industrial experience teaches us.

NOTES

[This is a slightly modified version of the Reserve Bank of India Endowment Lecture delivered at the Indian Institute of Management, Ahmedabad, on December 1, 1981. The author is thankful to Veena Padia for her help in collecting and analysing the data.]

1 See for example, the reasons given for the decline in the industrial production in 1979-80 and the subsequent rise in the next two years in the *Economic Survey* of these years.

2 Among other things, this point is stressed by D Nayyar (1978), p 1227. For a refutation of this hypothesis, see A V Desai (1981), p 387.

3 T N Srinivasan, and N S S Narayana (1977).

4 The various links between agriculture and industry have been spelt out in A Vaidyanathan (1977), p 1644. Also see K N Raj (1976), pp 228-31.

5 D Nayyar (1978) and R Sau (1974).

6 C Rangarajan (1980).

7 I Z Bhatty and M T R Sarma (1977), p 283.

8 R Sau (1974), p 1281.

9 S Roy (1981).

10 For a full-fledged model, see V Soundararajan, and S Thakur (1980).

11 In order to find out the relationship between the private investment and public investment, we estimated the following equations using the data for the period 1952-53 to 1972-73:

Private Corporate Investment

$$= 206.350 + \underset{(2.70)}{0.227}\ PUI_{It-1} - \underset{(0.665)}{2.586}\ TT_{t-1} + \underset{(0.337)}{0.233}\ (S\text{–}PUI)_t + \underset{(1.26)}{0.313}\ \Delta Y_{NAt}$$

$$\bar{R}^2 = 0.671$$

Private Investment

$$-1182.66 + \underset{(3.07)}{0.432}\ PUI_{t-1} + \underset{(2.07)}{13.488}\ TT_{t-1} + \underset{(4.32)}{0.499}\ (S\text{–}PUI)_t + \underset{(0.14)}{0.341}\ \Delta Y_{NAt}$$

$$\bar{R}^2 = 0.953$$

Where PUI = Public Investment in real terms.
TT = Terms of trade between agriculture manufactures.
S = Savings in real terms, come in real terms.
Y_{NA} = Non Agricultural Income in real terms.
t–values are given in brackets.

REFERENCES

Bhatty, I Z and M T R Sarma, (1977): 'Saving Behaviour in India and Implications for Policy' in C D Wadhva, (ed), *Some Problems of India's Economic Policy,* second edition, pp 276-89.

Desai, A V (1981): 'Factors Underlying the Slow Growth of Indian Industry', *Economic and Political Weekly,* Vol XVI, Nos 10-12.

Nayyar, D (1978): 'Industrial Development in India: Some Reflections on Growth and Stagnation', *Economic and Political Weekly,* Vol XII, Nos 31-33.

Raj, K N (1976): 'Growth and Stagnation in Indian Industrial Development', *Economic and Political Weekly,* Vol XI, Nos 5-7.

Rangarajan, C (1980): 'Agricultural Growth and Industrial Performance in India–A Study of Interdependence' (mimeo).

Roy, S (1981): 'Demand for Industrial Consumer Goods in India: A Study of Linkages' (A thesis done under the guidance of the author and submitted to Indian Institute of Management, Ahmedabad under the Fellow Programme).

Sau, R (1974): 'Some Aspects of Intersectoral Resource Flows', *Economic and Political Weekly,* Vol VIII, Nos 31-33.

Srinivasan, T N and N S S Narayana, (1977): 'Economic Performance since the Third Plan and Its Implications for Policy', *Economic and Political Weekly,* Vol XII, Nos 6-8.

Soundararajan, V and S Thakur, (1980): 'Public Investment, Crowding Out and Growth: A Dynamic Model Applied to India and Korea', *IMF Staff Papers,* Volume 27(4).

Vaidyanathan, A (1977): 'Constraints on Growth and Policy Options', *Economic and Political Weekly,* Vol XII, No 38.

12

Aspects of Growth and Structural Change in Indian Industry

C P Chandrasekhar

THE indifferent performance of the agrarian sector during the 1980s notwithstanding, government spokespersons and some economists espouse the view that India is poised for an economic 'take-off', with industry serving as the engine for a new era of growth. Optimism of this kind is not without basis, since official statistics appear to suggest that, after long years of deceleration, the industrial sector is registering rates of growth comparable to the creditable performance during the first decade and a half of planned economic development.

The evidence, however, is equivocal. In fact, till recently, the official Index of Industrial Production (Base 1970-71=100) indicated that the deceleration in industrial growth that began in the mid-1960s was still with us. That index seemed to suggest that the creditable 7.2 per cent rate of growth per annum recorded between 1951 and 1965 came to an end with the successive droughts of the mid-1960s, after which the economy entered a phase of secular stagnation. Between 1966 and 1975, the rate of growth of the index registered a decline to 4.0 per cent. And though the period since then has seen a recovery with the figure touching 4.8 per cent, the glorious Mahalanobis years were not to be equalled. In fact, if we exclude mining and quarrying and electricity from the index, and look at the figures for manufacturing, the decline in growth has been steeper, falling from 7.1 per cent during 1951-65 to 3.7 per cent during 1966-75 and 3.8 per cent during 1976-85 (Table 1). As has been noted elsewhere, this persistence of the deceleration rendered the first 15 years of post-independence development an exceptional interlude in an otherwise long history of stagnation. Over the quarter century ending 1975-76, the net output of large industry increased by around 280 per cent, which was equal to the magnitude of increase between 1920-21 and 1945-46 [N Chandra, 1982].

However, starting from the fact that two different sources of information on industrial production–the index of industrial production with 1970-71 as base and the more reliable value added figures from the *Annual Survey of Industries*–pointed to rather different trends, the government revised the index to accommodate, ostensibly, for changes in industrial structure that have occurred in recent years.[1] The government's contention has essentially been that the earlier index of industrial production, which operated with 1970-71 as its base year, failed to take into consideration many of the critical structural changes which have occurred in recent years. Prime among these are, first, the rapid growth of industries like chemicals, petrochemicals, garments, gem-cutting and electronics; and second, the supposed major advance made by the small-scale sector in terms of its share in industrial production. While the old index ostensibly did not capture these trends, it gave undue weightage to 'sunset' industries like mill-produced textiles. Adjusting for these developments based on 1980 value added shares, according to official statements, provides a rather different picture of industrial growth. The Index of Industrial Production (Base 1980-81=100) shows up a growth rate of 7 per cent per year for the six years ending 1985-86, compared to the much lower rates of growth suggested by the earlier indices (Table 2).

Table 1: Rate of Growth of the Index of Industrial Production

Period	Industry	Manufacturing	Mining and Quarrying	Electricity
1951-65	7.2	7.1	5.9	13.6
1966-75	4.0	3.7	3.2	9.0
1976-86	4.9	4.2	7.3	7.2

Note: Growth rates (r) in Tables 1, 2, 3 and 4 have been obtained by fitting an equation of the form $\text{Log } Y = \text{Log } A + \beta t$, where $\beta = \text{Log } (1 + r)$.

Source: Computed from figures obtained from Government of India, Ministry of Finance, *Economic Survey*, various issues.

Table 2: Trends in Industrial Production

(Base 1980-81 = 100)

Item	1981-82	1982-83	1983-84	1984-85	1985-86
Mining and Quarrying	117.7	132.3	147.8	160.8	167.5
Manufacturing	107.9	109.4	115.6	124.8	136.9
Electricity	110.2	116.5	125.4	140.4	152.4
General index	109.3	112.8	120.4	130.7	142.1

Source: Publications quoted in footnote 1 and Government of India, Ministry of Finance, *Economic Survey*, 1987-88, New Delhi, 1988.

It needs to be mentioned here that a mere change in weights attached to items included in the old index would not have resulted in any significant change in the rate of growth. What is crucial is not the change in the share in total value added of a given item as a result of a change in base year, but a change in value added per unit of output of the item concerned.[2] The change in the weighting diagram for the index with 1980-81 as base involved the inclusion of 96 new items, while 95 others were dropped, which must have resulted in an increase in the value added per unit of physical output of the more dynamic sectors. Further, as far as the small-scale sector is concerned, the report of the working group set up to revise the index itself admits that the revised series would mainly reflect the growth of medium and large sectors of industry, 'as sufficient coverage for the small-scale sector could not be achieved'. The only area where coverage of the small-scale sector has been substantially increased is the weaving industry (incorporating the rapidly growing powerlooms) whose weight in the total has been raised from 0.009 to 0.042. Thus, the

Table 3: Rate of Growth of Value Added in the Registered Manufacturing Sector
(By Industry)

Industry Group	1951-52 to 1974-75	1951-52 to 1964-65	1964-65 to 1974-75
Food	4.33	5.41	3.26
Beverages and tobacco	5.50	7.64	–0.58
Textiles	1.87	2.72	1.94
Wood and wood products, furniture and fixtures	8.48	14.39	–2.56
Paper and paper products, printing and allied industries	7.14	8.57	4.93
Leather and leather products except footwear	–0.23	5.92	–10.19
Rubber, petroleum and coal products	10.62	14.40	6.04
Chemical and chemical products	9.2	9.88	8.10
Non-metallic mineral products except petroleum	8.05	10.87	4.99
Basic metal industries	8.99	12.16	3.97
Metal products except machinery and transport equipment	5.51	10.12	1.71
Machinery except electrical machinery	16.51	23.24	4.43
Electrical machinery, apparatus and appliances	14.80	17.41	10.71
Transport equipment	4.87	11.94	–4.47
Miscellaneous manufactures	10.83	12.10	4.05
Net manufactures value added	6.21	7.88	3.60

Source: Computed from figures available in Government of India, Central Statistical Organisation, *National Accounts Statistics*, various issues.

strength of the new index has to rest on the claim that it is relatively more representative of trends in the industrial sector than the earlier index. But, there is no a priori reason to accept that contention, and the higher growth rate that the new index throws up could be because of arbitrary changes in the items covered leading to increases in value added per unit of physical output in the more rapidly growing sectors.

Not surprisingly, there are considerable differences on the extent to which the earlier index underestimated the pace of growth. However, there appears to be some consensus that there has been a modest recovery in industrial growth in recent years, which the index with base 1970 did not capture, since evidence from the Annual Survey of Industries (as adjusted in the *National Accounts Statistics* of the CSO) for the registered manufacturing sector does show up such an increase (Tables 3 and 4). The rate of growth of net manufacturing

Table 4: Rate of Growth of Value Added in Manufacturing at 1970-71 Prices: 1975-85

Industry Group	Registered	Regd and Unregd
Food products	5.22	3.51
Beverages, tobacco and tobacco products	2.90	2.43
Textiles	2.95	5.97
(a) Cotton textiles	1.14	
(b) Wool, silk and synthetic fibres	8.25	
(c) Jute, hemp and mesta	2.36	
(d) Textile products	6.49	
Wood and wood products, furniture and fixtures	0.11	–4.09
Paper and paper products, printing and allied industries	1.33	3.67
Leather and leather and fur products	5.75	1.62
Rubber, plastic, petroleum and coal products	6.44	3.86
Chemical and chemical products	6.53	5.91
Non-metallic mineral products	6.24	3.57
Basic metal and alloy industries	3.48	5.48
Metal products except machinery and transport equipment	2.86	3.01
Machinery, machine tools and parts except electrical machinery	5.71	6.73
Electrical machinery, apparatus and appliances	9.28	7.05
Transport equipment and parts	8.69	2.96
Miscellaneous manufactures	9.41	–0.18
Net manufactures value added	5.18	4.59

Source: Computed from figures available in Government of India, Central Statistical Organisation, *National Accounts Statistics*, various issues.

value added in the registered manufacturing sector, which fell from 7.88 per cent per annum over the period 1951-52 to 64-65 to 3.6 per cent over 1964-65 to 74-75, rose to 5.18 per cent over the period 1974-75 to 1984-85. This does constitute a significant recovery, though the most recent trend rate is still well short of the expansion seen in the first decade and a half after the launch of planned development. However, there does not appear to be much ground for the belief that the recovery is to a large extent influenced by the growth of small-scale production, since the rate of growth of NAS figures on value added in the registered and unregistered sectors taken together is even less than that in the registered manufacturing sector alone. This holds true in all industries except for cotton textiles, which in any case was the only section of small-scale production adequately covered in the new index.

To understand what the factors underlying the recovery were, we need to turn our attention to the developments in the industrial sector over the four decades since independence. The Indian economy at independence was characterised by features typical of a backward ex-colonial country. It was predominantly agrarian, with mining, manufacturing and small enterprises contributing around 17 per cent of national income and less than 10 per cent of employment.[3] Within this relatively small contribution of the industrial sector, that of the organised factory sector stood at less than 40 per cent and that too from units which by contemporary standards were extremely small. Above all, going by weights accorded in the index of industrial production, nearly two-thirds of organised sector production consisted of traditional activities like textiles, food processing and processing of agricultural and mineral raw materials, while commodities like capital goods and intermediates had still to be procured from the international market. Not surprisingly, manufactured goods accounted for a large proportion of India's imports, and these imports met 50-100 per cent of the domestic demand for many manufactures. In terms of product groups, roughly 55 per cent of the total supply of capital goods and 27 per cent of industrial raw materials in 1950-51 were imported [Ahmed, 1968: p 355].

OBJECTIVES OF POLICY

The principal aim of state policy was thus defined by the circumstances: viz, a rapid acceleration of industrial growth, with the aim of breaking the barriers to increases in productivity characteristic of predominantly agrarian economies. In the policy perspective of the time, four initiatives were considered crucial to realise this objective. First, a widening and intensification of protection offered to manufacturing, through an across-the-board increase in tariffs and the institution of quantitative restrictions on imports. Second, a massive step up in public investment, which would not only close such infrastructural gaps as could hamper industrial development, but also result, directly through purchases of commodities and indirectly through the creation of additional incomes, in a rapid growth of the protected home market. In fact, even leading industrialists like the Tatas, Birlas, and Purushotamdas Thakurdas, who framed what has been termed the 'Bombay Plan' for post-independence development, stressed the need for a major role for the state in industrialisation. Third, a sharp increase in the rate of savings, which would be accompanied by measures that would channelise these funds to the state sector (taxation) as well as through the mediation of the state (financial institutions) to the private sector. And finally, the introduction of a wide range of controls on capacity creation, production and prices, which would ensure that these funds would be utilised in accordance with the investment-mix specified by the strategy of industrialisation adopted by the government.

Thus, the framework under which post-independence industrialisation occurred has been described as follows: 'in a regime with heavy all round protection and import control the government was to spearhead investment in crucial high-risk sectors (involving lumpy investments and long gestation lags), while making finance available to the private sector to take advantage of opportunities opened up as a consequence of its own investment and its protectionist policy' [Prabhat Patnaik, 1979]. This permitted a considerable degree of dissociation of industrial growth from the expansion of mass-markets, particularly in the rural sector.

As we saw earlier, this strategy produced an unprecedented spurt in industrialisation during the 1950s and early 1960s, with import substitution providing a major part of the stimulus for growth. According to Jaleel Ahmed, import substitution accounted for 23 per cent of the total output growth of all industries over the entire period 1950-51 to 1965-66 [Ahmed, 1968]. A detailed study by Bhagwati and Desai found that over the period 1951-63, while three of four indicators showed that import substitution was negative for 'all industries', they were positive for some sub-sectors, with the degree of import substitution being the highest in the investment goods sector. In fact till 1957, the extent of import substitution was the highest in the consumer goods sector, followed by the intermediate and investment goods sector in that order. But with the launch of the Second Plan, matters changed completely. Over 1957-63, import substitution in the consumer goods industries was the lowest followed by the intermediate and investment groups. This difference was largely due to the emphasis laid on the heavy industrial sector in the Second Plan [Bhagwati and Desai, 1970].

There were two problems that a state-engineered expansion of industry of this kind generated. Firstly, it resulted in a high degree of disproportionality between industrial and agricultural growth. Secondly, though it did result in a substantial degree of substitution of imports at the final goods stage, it set off demands for imports of capital and intermediate goods that touched India's scarce foreign exchange reserves.[4]

The extent of the dissociation between industry and agriculture comes through if we look at relative movements in industrial and agricultural output. While the rate of growth of the latter stood at just around 3.34 per cent over the first decade and a half of planned development, the former registered a rate exceeding 7 per cent overall, and nearly 10 per cent over some sub-periods. In a predominantly agrarian economy, agricultural stagnation cannot but act as a drag on industrial growth. To start with, by serving as the source of livelihood for nearly two-thirds of India's working population, agriculture does constitute a major source of demand for the products of industry. Secondly, most of India's traditional industries like cotton and jute textiles, sugar, vegetable oils and tobacco, are essentially agro-based, rendering their output directly dependent on agricultural performance and the consequent availability of agricultural inputs. Finally, agriculture remains the dominant supplier of what constitutes the 'wage basket' in a poor country like India. Indifferent agricultural performance can therefore constrain the pace of industrialisation both directly and by setting off an inflationary spiral that could squeeze profit margins as well as force the government to opt for deflationary policies aimed at holding the price line. While all these factors rendered the slow pace of agricultural growth a drag on the expansion of industry,[5] the last of them provided the basis for a cyclical process in which 'stop-go' policies with regard to public investment provided the mechanism for periods of boom and recession.[6]

If these factors did not constrain the expansion of industry over the 1950-65 period, it was partly because of the nature of industrialisation engineered by public investment (which was heavily biased in favour of non-agro-based industry), and partly because of the large imports of food under PL-480 that helped augment supplies and hold the price level.[7] Food aid rose from Rs 5.1 crore during 1951-52 to 1955-56 to Rs 544.8 crore during 1956-57 to 1960-61 and Rs 853.2 crore during 1961-62 to 1965-66. Although the figure for 1966-67 to 1969-70 is placed at Rs 861.6 crore, actual imports were much lower than in the previous quinquennium, as after the Indo-Pak war of 1965 the bulk of food aid had to be paid for in hard currency which, given the 1966 devaluation, exaggerated the rupee value of imports.[8] Averaging 5-8 per cent of availability, these imports did result in subdued price trends in the agricultural sector, which shifted the terms of trade against it and in favour of industry [Tyagi, 1987]. This provided the basis for non-inflationary growth of industry led by large-scale public investment. Over the period 1950-51 to 1964-65, while real investment in the private sector grew at a compound rate of just 3.9 per cent per annum, that in the public sector grew at a remarkable 13 per cent per annum (Table 5).

The other effect of state-engineered industrialisation, namely, the growing reliance on imports, was also visible in this phase, leading to a worsening of India's balance of payments position. There is now adequate evidence that high levels of protection and the Mahalanobis strategy notwithstanding, India's dependence on imports of basic and intermediate stage goods increased substantially over the Second Plan period. Two factors contributed to this trend. First, the fact that responding to market signals the private sector was increasingly resorting to the production of import intensive consumption goods consumed by the more well endowed sections of the population. It has been estimated that the direct and indirect foreign exchange cost of non-essential consumption amounted to Rs 200 crore or nearly 25 per cent of export earnings in 1964-65 [Raj, 1967]. And second, the government not only did not discourage this trend, but starting with the 1957 foreign exchange crisis, provided licences for capacity creation in this sector so long as entrepreneurs could find a foreign partner who would finance the foreign exchange component of the investment involved.

Thus by the time the drought years of the mid-1960s severely constrained India's manoeuvrability, a difficult balance of payments situation and rising agricultural prices were presaging an end to the years of high industrial growth. It was precisely at this point that the now well-documented reverse tilt in the terms of trade between agriculture and industry occurred, which led up to the period when the deceleration of industry inevitably began.

STRUCTURAL CHANGE

Underlying these overall trends in industrial growth were certain structural features which were crucial from the point of view of influencing the pattern of industrialisation over the first decade and a half. It hardly bears reiterating that, even by independence, Indian industry was characterised by a high degree of concentration. Besides

Table 5: Gross Domestic Capital Formation at 1970-71 Prices

Year	Total	Public	Private
1950-51	2379	530	1849
1951-52	2804	614	2190
1952-53	1838	506	1332
1953-54	2127	588	1539
1954-55	2363	868	1495
1955-56	3323	996	2327
1956-57	4271	1239	3032
1957-58	4088	1464	2624
1958-59	3382	1395	1987
1959-60	3741	1498	2243
1960-61	4523	1826	2697
1961-62	4140	1797	2343
1962-63	4808	2181	2627
1963-64	5080	2421	2659
1964-65	5581	2665	2916
1965-66	6170	2846	3324
1966-67	6675	2574	4101
1967-68	6139	2635	3504
1968-69	5758	2397	3361
1969-70	6677	2373	4304
1970-71	7177	2773	4404
1971-72	7556	2957	4599
1972-73	7130	3135	3995
1973-74	9097	3738	5359
1974-75	8244	3517	4727
1975-76	8463	4433	4030
1976-77	9316	4920	4396
1977-78	10207	4184	6023
1978-79	12304	5012	7292
1979-80	11024	5309	5715
1980-81	12227	5576	6651
1981-82	12468	6124	6344
1982-83	12652	6238	6414
1983-84	13132	6139	6993
1984-85	13846	6842	7004
Growth Rates			
1950/51-64/65	7.0	13.1	3.9
1964/65-74/75	4.0	3.2	4.7
1974/75-83/84	5.3	5.8	5.0

Source: Government of India, Central Statistical Organisation, *National Accounts Statistics*, various issues.

focusing on this concentration, the work of R K Hazari and its elaboration by Aurobindo Ghose, provided a number of valuable insights that can be usefully referred to.[9] The most significant of these was the identification of the 'business group' as the representative unit of Indian capital. The group in this view consisted of a large number of legally independent companies operating in a number of related and, more significantly, unrelated areas, controlled by a single, central decision-making authority and thereby functioning as a co-ordinated organisation. This meant that besides a high degree of product concentration, monopoly in India consisted of the predominance of a few representative units of capital in most areas of industry.

Even as far back as 1964, the Monopolies Inquiry Commission had reported that of a total of 1,298 products studied by it, 87.7 per cent were in the hands of oligopolists, with 437 being produced by only one firm each and 229 by two firms each.[10] In fact, excepting for food products, cotton textiles and jute textiles, almost the whole of Indian industry was characterised by monopoly, duopoly and oligopoly. But that was not all. Given the extremely diversified and technologically integrated structure of the business group, a few houses tended to monopolise most areas through firms under their control. According to Hazari, in 1958, out of 22 rudimentary categories of actual business, the Tatas as a group were present in 21, the Birlas in 25, Bangurs in 19, Thapars in 15, JK in 18, Shriram in 7, and so on. As a result he found that in most industries, the same set of business groups appeared to predominate, though each time with a different pattern of market shares.[11]

Given their wide interests and their financial strength, past performance and ability to bear the costs of obtaining information, the large business houses have always had an edge over other entrepreneurs in a system where capacity is licensed with the aim of achieving plan targets. Not surprisingly, therefore, periodic enquiries have shown that the government's stated objectives notwithstanding, these business houses have been able to corner a disproportionate share of licences issued by the government in all areas of industrial activity.[12]

But cornering these licences did not necessarily lead to the creation of capacity. Rather, the business houses have always followed a two-fold strategy. In the more dynamic areas where profit margins are high, the business houses have adopted an *offensive* strategy of obtaining licences, establishing capacity and bidding for a dominant share in the area concerned. But in areas where demand is slowly growing or profits lower either because of slack market conditions or price controls, they have pre-empted capacity by obtaining licences, preventing entry by others, but not translating their own licences into installed capacity. This *defensive* strategy permits retaining earlier bases of monopoly power without actually investing in productive capacity or helps ensure a foothold in an area which can be exploited any time in the future when market conditions turn more buoyant.

This pre-emptive behaviour of the business group had a number of implications. To start with, it implied that government efforts at diverting investment in certain directions and not others, in keeping with the priorities defined in its plans, through the use of the licensing mechanism, were never realised.[13] Independent of the licences issued, investments made and capacities installed tended to correspond to market signals. With the highly skewed distribution of income in the country providing a lucrative market for manufactured luxury consumer goods including consumer durables, private investment flowed in those directions. On the other hand, sunset industries like coarse textiles, which in the context of trends in income and its distribution were facing a slowly growing market, became the source of surplus for investments in other dynamic areas, but were themselves deprived of much needed investments for modernisation.

The immediate impact of this situation was that productive capacity fell short of targets and even actual demand in many cases. In response to this the government not only resorted to stricter scrutiny of application, but also to the practice of 'over-licensing' based on an assessment of the share of approved applications that have 'pre-emption' as their motive. But given the rather wide range of firms through which the business group could apply for licences in any one area, this only led to a spiral where the share of pre-emptive applications and the extent of over-licensing increases over time. This whole process defeated the purpose for which licensing was adopted, resulting in an implicit breakdown of the licensing system.

The impact of this investment behaviour of the business group was also visible in the case of price control. Being in a position to pre-empt capacity as well as having the option of 'investing in a rather wide range of areas, the response of the business group to price control has been that of choking of production in the areas concerned. Since price control inevitably means lower profits than could be earned in the manufacture of uncontrolled luxury consumer goods and their intermediates, the business group has most often left units in areas like textile, sugar, cement and paper 'dormant', while diverting surpluses to more lucrative avenues. This did not imply that the group did not obtain licences for manufacture in these areas–rather they pre-empted them to an extent where, even with over-licensing, there were persistent shortages of controlled items. The consequent growth of a black market was then used as the instrument of manoeuvre to get the government to go back on controls, either partially or fully. A typical instance of this tendency is the cement industry where, prior to partial decontrol, inadequate capacities and shortages were a major problem. And even though the government was repeatedly issuing licences, which were promptly being accepted by the leading business groups in and outside the cement industry, there was no effort to implement these licences till control was relaxed. The immediate response to this relaxation was the implementation of accumulated licences resulting in a transition of the industry from a situation of shortage to one of glut in the matter of a few years.

Thus government intervention notwithstanding, the growth of the large industrial sector not only corresponded to effective demands on the market, but more specifically to those areas which assured some 'target' rate of return. However, even in these areas, given the rapidly diversifying demand for manufactures in the upper income groups and the fact that the business group had access to a wide range of them, there was a tendency to spread the utilisation of the investible resources of the group across a number of areas. At any debt-equity level, this tendency to spread risks resulted in a specific investment level, which pre-determined the scales of production. Even though in most cases these scales were uneconomic, utilising the protection offered by the government, business houses chose to establish capacity, resulting in the highly uneconomic units operating in a number of areas like synthetics, plastic intermediates and automobiles.[14] This only aggravated the tendency towards uneconomic scales resulting from the practice of dividing licences for targeted capacities among a number of applicants with the aim of curbing monopoly in an already concentrated industry.

But that is not all. The tendency of the business group to leave certain areas of industry dormant so long as it did not offer some target rate of return, left open a number of niches for the small-scale sector even in areas where it had no technological or market-size advantage. Not surprisingly, there are areas of industry where small-scale production has tended to proliferate, even though that may not be the most efficient or cost effective way of producing the commodity concerned.

This experience no doubt has some significant implications for the political economy of industrialisation. It suggests that, while the state, independent of the interests it represents, has a substantial degree of autonomy *vis-a-vis* the private corporate sector, its ability to ensure investment of a kind that goes beyond short-run profit maximisation is limited by the strength of the corporate sector itself. In alternative situations like that of South Korea for example, the relative weakness of private industry has helped the state mould the quantum, direction and nature of industrial investment, while providing substantial concessions to the private sector. In the Indian case, however, while concessions are not negligible, efforts at influencing investment behaviour have in most cases been unsuccessful. In understanding this difference it may be useful to recall that while most of South Korea's industrial leaders were post-war creations, well before independence in 1947, leading Indian industrialists had sat together and formulated a plan of action for the post-independence state. It is this factor that ensured that the relatively high growth of the Mahalanobis years notwithstanding, not only did the actual pattern of production in industry not correspond with the planned,[15] but also large chunks of industry tended to be characterised by backward technologies and inappropriate scales. These were the features that were to come into focus when the high growth of the earlier years were to give way to a decelerating trend.

THE PUBLIC SECTOR

The behaviour of the private corporate sector and the consequent developments with regard to the commodity composition of industrial output also crystallised the role to be played by the public sector. Though the industrial policy resolutions and statements with regard to the 'commanding heights' role of the public sector suggested that it was to play a leading role in industrial development, in practice it merely adjusted to an inevitable residual role in an industrialisation process where market signals and private decision-making determined the direction of growth. Even if investments in the public sector were tailored to the requirements of the Mahalanobis model, so long as the private sector could not be either guided or coerced into meeting the requirements set for it, such investments would either remain unutilised or its fruits diverted to areas which were 'non-priority' in the perspective of the time. In which case, its role would be that of providing certain crucial infrastructural inputs which otherwise would have either constrained the pace of industrialisation or had to be imported, since the private sector would have been unwilling to invest, given its investment behaviour, in areas which involved lumpy investments, long gestation lags and low returns.

The government's own realisation of the supportive role to be played by the public sector was reflected in the Third Plan which stated that such investment was required since 'a number of basic industries which require large investments and extensive collaboration with foreign firms or governments and which could be undertaken only on the assurance of future prospects, with no immediate gain in sight, would not normally be started if reliance was to be placed entirely on private enterprise'.[16] The state therefore chose to play a dominant role in the infrastructural sector, owning in time more than 60 per cent of all productive capital, 8 of the top 10 units, and employing two-thirds of the workers in the organised sector [Bhardhan, 1984].

The objectives underlying the creation of a public sector influenced its character. At the end of financial year 1966, which could be seen as the end of the first phase of public investment-led growth, steel (40.62 per cent), engineering (20.29), chemicals (9.11), petroleum (12.22), mining and minerals (7.49) and aviation and shipping (4.97) accounted for more than 90 per cent of the cumulated investment in public sector projects.[17] This composition of public sector output endowed the former with a high capital-output ratio. In addition, this output was till recently sold at prices that indicated the government's concern for offering infrastructural inputs at relatively low prices to the private sector. Not surprisingly, while the public sector's share in total physical assets increased quite sharply over the years, its share in production increased from around 2.5 per cent in 1950-51 to only around 26 per cent by 1965-66. One concomitant of this tendency was an extremely low margin over costs, which could easily turn to a loss either if costs rose due to overmanning or inefficiency, or administered prices were not increased fast enough to accommodate changes in the costs of inputs.

Besides carrying the burden associated with serving as the supplier of infrastructural inputs, the supportive role of the state is seen in its attitude *vis-a-vis* the investments of financial institutions. By virtue of holding through the financial institutions more than 25 per cent of the paid-up capital of private joint-stock companies, the state was in a position to wield considerable influence over the private sector. But unlike the case in South Korea for example, the control over financial resources has never been utilised to influence investment decisions in the private corporate sector. In fact, the financial institutions have accepted the yardstick of a short-run profit maximiser in a protected market to assess the viability of individual projects, contributing to the perpetuation of tendencies of the kind noted above.

INDUSTRIAL GROWTH

Earlier analyses have suggested that two factors have been responsible for bringing the high growth of the first decade-and-a-half after independence to an unacceptable low. To start with, the stimulus arising from protection had exhausted itself. This was not surprising, since import substitution results in a once-for-all increase in indigenous output. Once domestic markets have been captured by indigenous producers from foreign ones, any further growth depends on the growth of the market as a whole.

The element of exhaustion of import substitution possibilities come through from the available evidence on import-availability ratios.[18] By 1965-66 the share of imports in domestic availability exceeded 20 per cent in only 4 out of 20 industrial groups: petroleum products, basic metals, non-electrical machinery and electrical machinery. A large part of this significant but residual reliance on imports may be explained by the fact that import substitution occurs most often only at the final stages of production, while dependence on imports for certain initial, second and subsequent stage goods, where the size of the domestic market may completely rule out indigenous production, continues. That is, the possibility of substituting imports that were meeting existing domestic demand were extremely limited.

TRENDS IN PUBLIC INVESTMENT

Thus if the rapid pace of expansion of industry had to be sustained, public investment had to grow at an even faster rate than before, to balance for the exhaustion of the transient stimulus that import substitution provided. In practice capital formation in the public sector, which registered a rapid rate of increase till the mid-1960s, decelerated sharply subsequently and grew at a compound rate of just 3.2 per cent per annum in the period till the late-1970s (Table 5).

Given the role that public investment had played in an India-type mixed economy, the impact of the deceleration of such investment was two-fold: first, it resulted in a slower growth of the home market and therefore a slower growth in the demand for products of the private sector; second, it resulted in a slow-down in capacity creation in certain crucial sectors like power, transport and irrigation. The slowdown in investment in irrigation obviously limited the pace of growth of production in general and foodgrains production in particular. And the cut back in investment in infrastructural areas resulted in infrastructural bottlenecks whenever the economy, after a good harvest, found itself on an upswing. The inflationary potential that these two sets of bottlenecks built into the economy meant that any boom was soon accompanied by an inflationary spiral that cut it short by forcing a reduction in public investment and expenditure aimed at holding the price level.

Short-run cycles are thus understandable. But why was public investment restricted over the decade and a half that followed the recession of the mid-1960s? The answer essentially lies in: (a) the introduction of procurement at cost plus prices as part of the new agricultural policy, which set a high rising 'remunerative' floor to open market prices that set themselves on an upward trend [Patnaik and Rao, 1977]; and (b) the fact that, by that time, a whole complex of price and budgetary policies had limited surpluses earned by the public sector, reduced revenues from taxation and increased current expenditures through transfer payments of one kind or another to different sections of the population. While the latter ensured a squeeze on the resources available with the exchequer, forcing the government to rely on inflationary means of financing for stepping up plan outlays, the former set ceilings on the pace of growth of public outlays in order to moderate inflationary pressures. One way in which this problem could have been circumvented was to resort to large imports of essentials aimed at holding the price level. However, this precisely was the time when worsening relations with the US led to a tapering off of PL 480 aid, while the difficult balance of payments situation foreclosed the option of using India's own foreign exchange reserves for the purpose.

The role of declining public investment in explaining the deceleration in industrial growth is corroborated by trends in the composition of industrial output as well. In the 1950s and the early 1960s industrial growth occurred across-the-board. While consumer goods as a whole grew at a pace slower than the basic, capital and intermediate goods sectors, consumer durables, sustained by upper income group demand, registered extremely high rates of growth, going up to nearly 11 per cent per annum during the period 1960-65. However, after the mid-1960s, though the consumer goods sector as a whole did record a slight deceleration, consumer durables continued to grow at a creditable 6.2 per cent per annum, which was much higher than the rate of growth of the capital and intermediate goods sectors (Table 6). That is, in the period after the mid-1960s industrial growth has come to depend on the expansion of the middle and upper income markets for consumer durables, rather than on public investment which at least till the mid-1970s had lost its role as the locomotive of industry. It naturally follows that even to the extent that the public sector spewed out infrastructural goods like steel, chemicals and power, they did not go to sustain the growth of a basic goods sector for which they were created, but rather served the needs of those industries which, with effective demands on the market, were identified as the forerunners of growth.

This shift in the commodity composition of industrial output has perpetuated industry's relative degree of independence *vis-a-vis* the pace of agricultural growth.[19] The kind of consumer demand that has to serve as the engine of growth consisted not of 'agro-based' products, in the sense that they are dependent on agriculture for their inputs, but items that are 'chemical-based' such as synthetic textiles, plastic goods and pharmaceuticals, or 'metal-based' such as motor cycles and cars, electrical appliances, radios and television sets. The rate of growth of agriculture need not constrain the rate of growth of the output of these products, provided the demand for them is rising

Table 6: Annual Compound Growth Rates in the Index of Industrial Production

Industry Group	1951-55	1955-60	1960-65	1965-76
Basic goods	4.7	12.1	10.4	6.5
Capital goods	9.8	13.1	19.6	2.6
Intermediate goods	7.8	6.3	6.9	3.0
Consumer goods	4.8	4.4	4.9	3.4
Consumer durables	–	–	11.0	6.2
Non-durables	–	–	–	2.8
General index	5.7	7.2	9.0	4.1

Source: S L Shetty, 'Structural Retrogression in the Indian Economy since the Mid-Sixties', *Economic and Political Weekly*, Annual Number, February 1978, Table 1, p 186.

Table 7: India's International Commercial Borrowing

(Million US Dollars)

End of	External Bank Claims	Non-Bank Trade Related Claims	Total	Increase (1985-86 and 1986-87)
June 87	8330	1829	10159	1630
June 86	6747	1782	8529	2151
June 85	4800	1578	6378	–

Source: Organisation for Economic Co-operation and Development and Bank of International Settlements, *Statistics on External Indebtedness: Bank and Trade-Related Non-Bank External Claims on Individual Borrowing Countries and Territories,* Paris and Basle, Issues dated January 1987 and 1988.

rapidly enough and the necessary intermediate goods (chemicals, metals, etc) are available in adequate quantity.

However, the growth of demand for luxury consumer goods and consumer durables in particular was inadequate to offset the slower growth in demand for industrial products as a whole as a result of the deceleration in public investment. In the net, we saw the decline in rates of growth noted earlier. Thus, by the mid-1970s, it appeared that the industrial sector had run up against a demand constraint that could not be met unless there was a rapid expansion in exports or a breakthrough in the agricultural sector that raised incomes to levels that could set off an industrial boom.

THE 1980S RECOVERY

However, there have been signs of a reversal in recent years. As mentioned earlier, there has been a recovery in the rate of growth of industry during the late-1970s and early 1980s, with the evidence pointing to a possible shift away from the period of slow growth. Clearly, a step up in agricultural growth does not underlie this recovery. Ignoring the unusual years of the mid-1960s, the rate of growth of the index of agricultural production, which stood at 3.34 per cent during the first 15 years of planned development, declined to relatively lower levels of 2.44 and 2.94 per cent respectively during the periods 1970-71 to 1977-78 and 1977-78 to 1985-86. The corresponding figures for foodgrain production were 3.17, 2.37 and 2.94 per cent per annum respectively.[20] That is, the recovery over the last decade points to a return to the period of dissociation between industrial and agricultural growth–a phenomenon that was most visible during and after the drought year 1987-88.

Thus, if past experience is any guide the stimulus to industrial growth must have come from elsewhere. Capital formation in the public sector does not appear an adequate explanatory variable either. In fact, during the 'industrial recovery' since the mid-1970s, capital formation in the public sector in real terms has grown only at 5.8 per cent per annum, as compared with the 13 per cent recorded in the first decade and a half of planned development. However, this is not true of public outlays as a whole. The non-development outlay in the budgets of the centre, states and union territories, grew at a compound rate of 16.6 per cent per annum in current prices over this period. In terms of shares in GDP non-plan revenue expenditures had grown from about 8 per cent of GDP in the first half of the 1970s to nearly 11 per cent in 1979-80 and a whopping 14.01 per cent in 1987-88.[21]

Needless to say, this must have played a major role in setting off the recovery of the 1980s. Interestingly, much of the increase in public expenditure has been concentrated on public administration and defence–a fact which has influenced movements in the sectoral shares in national income as well. If we take the years 1970-71 to 1984-85, while the contribution of the primary sector (consisting mainly of agriculture and allied activities) to GDP at constant prices grew at 2.26 per cent per annum and that of the secondary sector (dominated by manufacturing) by 3.92 per cent, the contribution of the tertiary sector (consisting mainly of services) grew by a remarkable 5.82 per cent. That is, the recovery of the 1980s was not the result of an acceleration in the principal commodity producing sectors, but of a faster growth of the service sector. And within the latter, a significant share of the acceleration is explained by the growth of non-productive government expenditure on public administration and defence, whose contribution to GDP grew at a compound rate of 8.97 per cent during the period 1970-71 to 1985-86.[22]

Interestingly, this sharp increase in public expenditure has not resulted as much in an increase in employment as in real incomes in the organised sector. Organised sector employment which grew rapidly (5.08 per cent per annum) in the early 1960s, has since risen at a much slower rate of around 2.25 per cent. However, per worker income in the organised sector has registered impressive increases. Public sector workers more than doubled their real income between 1960-61 and 1984-85, while the real incomes of the private organised sector rose by 60 per cent over this period [Sen, 1988; Mitra, 1988]. This increase in incomes in the middle and lower-middle income groups would have spilled over into enhanced demand for manufactured consumer goods, including consumer durables, resulting in the diffusion of such consumption to lower ranges of income. That is, unlike in the early years of planning when the diversion of public revenues to investment purposes resulted in direct demand for plant and equipment, the new phase of public expenditure-led growth sustains essentially consumption demand for manufactures.

This provides a fillip to precisely those changes in the commodity composition of industrial output of the type noticed since the mid-1960s, which however occurred despite the government's then-proclaimed intention of curbing such growth. Now unlike earlier, food products, synthetic textiles, leather and fur products, electronics, modern telecommunications, chemicals and automobiles, constitute the 'leading sectors' both in terms of growth and in the perception of the government as well (see Table 6). But the latter's role in stimulating them till recently was only indirect—that of providing jobs and incomes to a burgeoning middle class by creating a sprawling administrative empire. The difference between the most recent phase of such growth and what occurred earlier is that its mediation through the state permits a degree of percolation down to slightly lower income levels of the demand for commodities which were earlier consumed only in the highest income segments of the population.

THE CONSTRAINTS

A boom of the 1980s kind can run into an upper bound for two reasons. Firstly, the likelihood of its sustaining itself depends on the ability of the state to maintain rising levels of public expenditure and investment without setting off an inflation. And second, since most manufactured luxuries are known to be import intensive in character either because they are based on collaborations that provide access to international brand names or because they use intermediates and components that are not produced locally (examples, television sets, fuel efficient automobiles and personal computers), the government would have to provide for an adequate volume of foreign exchange outgo to sustain the boom.

It needs to be said here that though the growth scenario has changed considerably in recent years, with a revival in growth rates, the problem of inadequate resources with the state still remains. The essential features of the financial crisis facing the government have been defined rather clearly in the Long Term Fiscal Policy (LTFP) statement of the government released in 1986. While the current revenues of the government (tax and non-tax) had stagnated at around 10.5 per cent of GDP since the mid-1970s, non-plan revenue expenditures had grown from about 8 per cent of GDP in the first half of the 1970s to nearly 11 per cent in 1984-85.[23] This rapid growth of non-developmental expenditure has essentially been due to a few items under the head of current expenditures. To be more specific, in recent years, nearly 70 per cent of non-plan expenditures have been on four items: defence, interest payments, subsidies on food and fertilisers. Thus there are essentially two options before the government when seeking to come to terms with the resource crunch. That of raising revenues through higher rates of taxation and measures (like the taxation of agricultural incomes) that widen the tax net; and that of reducing the outlays on those items of non-developmental expenditure that are eating into its limited resources. However, higher tax rates obviously are not a thrust area within the philosophy of the new fiscal regime instituted in the 1980s, under which the government has advanced the process of providing fiscal concessions in the form of reduced direct and indirect tax rates in order to expand markets and provide incentives to the corporate sector to exploit these new markets. This leaves only the option of raising revenues through raising public sector prices and thereby increasing public sector surpluses—an option that the LTFP, not surprisingly, stressed.

As for the possibility of reducing non-developmental expenditure, with defence outlays being determined by a set of perceptions that are not easily altered and interest payments being the price of past profligacy, the only decision left with the government is that of reducing subsidies of various kinds. Thus the LTFP made clear that, within its perspective of growth there was only one set of hard decisions available to wriggle out of the resource squeeze: that which emphasised a double-edged policy of cutting subsidies and raising administered prices, even though it would be received adversely at the popular level.

Irrespective of how, or why, the government did not implement these 'hard' decisions, the resource crunch remains a major constraint on development. But the 1980s have seen a rather simple solution to the problem—that of raising public expenditure by resorting to large doses of deficit financing and large-scale borrowing from the market. Deficit financing rose from Rs 1,417 crore in 1983-84 to Rs 3,748 crore in 1984-85, Rs 4,490 crore in 1985-86 and a whopping Rs 8,265 crore in 1986-87. This sharp increase occurred precisely at a time when the government's reliance on market borrowings was registering a phenomenal increase. Gross market borrowing which stood at less than Rs 100 crore during the 1960s, touched Rs 2,296 crore by 1979-80, rose to Rs 2,949 crore in 1980-81, Rs 4,584 crore in 1984-85, Rs 5,543 crore during 1985-86 and an estimated Rs 6,350 crore during 1986- 87.[24]

THE SQUEEZE ON AGRICULTURE

What is surprising is that the overhang of liquidity created by this runaway increase in deficit spending did not provide a spur to inflation, even though the pace of agricultural growth was by no means remarkable. Rather, throughout this period foodgrains prices remained depressed, shifting the terms of trade once again against agriculture and in favour of industry.[25] The main explanatory factor is no doubt the comfortable levels of foodstocks with the government over much of this period. The stocks themselves, however, were not due to any major breakthrough in agriculture. After the bumper crop of 1983-84, which took foodgrains production to 152.37 million tonnes, the monsoon has remained indifferent culminating in the drought of 1987-88, and output has never regained that level. Yet foodstocks with the government touched record levels and even till mid-1987 were well above the 20 million tonne mark. Part of the reason is no doubt the large-scale imports of foodgrains during the early 1980s aimed at holding the price level. While the increase in the level of foodstocks between January 1, 1982 and January 1, 1986 works out to 12.7 million tonnes, the net imports of foodgrains during this period amounted to 7.7 million tonnes. However, even granting the role played by these stocks in enhancing availability, we find that the problem of explaining the situation of glut still remains.[26] As has been noted by many studies the per capita availability of foodgrains in the country has in fact stagnated since the mid-1960s. Thus, increase in foodgrains output and large-scale imports have not been adequate to raise availability in physical terms above the per capita consumption levels of the 1950s. The explanation for the surplus and therefore for the relatively depressed level of food prices must lie in the realm of inadequate 'effective demand', backed by adequate purchasing power. And any such explanation must turn to the extremely uneven distribution of agricultural growth since the mid-1960s that has left deficit regions in rural India with inadequate incomes to absorb the surpluses generated in the more successful states [Utsa Patnaik, 1988; Prabhat Patnaik, 1988]. The squeeze on agriculture which was a direct fall-out of the strategy of agriculture pursued has helped sustain public expenditure at levels adequate to fuel the moderate recovery of the 1970s and 1980s.

What is crucial is that in a macro-economic sense, during the two periods of relatively high industrial growth, though public investment and expenditure have provided the proximate causes for such growth, the burden of financing the process of growth has fallen on the agricultural sector which has been the loser in a process of inflationary financing of industrial growth. That is, the shift in the terms of trade between agriculture and industry in favour of the former, which formed the basis for explanations of the deceleration of industrial growth in the decade after the mid-1960s, was just a brief interlude in a longer term process of growth where agriculture bore the burden of financing industrial development.

THE EXTERNAL CONSTRAINT

While the domestic constraint on deficit financed industrial growth has been met in the manner discussed above, the external one, influenced by the import intensiveness of consumer durables, has been sought to be overcome by financing a burgeoning trade deficit with borrowing from abroad. In fact, a part of the balance of payments problem, both prior to the mid-1960s and during the 1980s, was a fall-out of the policy of 'pump-priming' industry without setting off an inflationary spiral. For, a trade deficit *ceteris paribus* is anti-inflationary. However, the problem assumed alarming proportions with the introduction of changes in import policy that watered down quantitative restrictions and reduced tariffs, with the aim of providing domestic producers access to cheaper capital equipment and intermediates, as well as pressurising indigenous suppliers to reduce costs and improve quality.

The massive saving in India's oil import bill notwithstanding, India has in recent years seen a worsening in her balance of payments situation. The trade deficit that rose to an alarming Rs 8,700 crore in 1985-86 (79.2 per cent of export earnings), as compared with Rs 5,200 crore in 1984-85 (44.3 per cent of export earnings), declined to just Rs 7,512 crore in 1986-87 (60.8 per cent of export earnings). A significant part of the explanation for the persistence of a large trade deficit is no doubt the resort to imports as part of the strategy of trade liberalisation aimed at sustaining the new manufactured consumer goods boom. Not surprisingly, the liberalisation measures, whether in the form of removal of restrictions on imports or in the form of reduced tariffs, have applied essentially to components, intermediates and capital goods, rather than the final product. That is, import liberalisation has helped lubricate the consumer boom, though at the expense of the balance of payments. As a result, the last few years have seen a major entry by India into the market for international commercial bank credit. According to the Bank of International Settlements, Basle, between June 1985 and June 1987, India tapped international markets to the tune of \$3.8 billion—a sum that is large by any standard, but particularly relative to India's borrowing experience in the past.

NEW INDUSTRIAL POLICY

The process of lubricating the 'recovery' over the last decade has not just consisted of a relatively freer access to imports but the adoption of a package of policies that would provide greater flexibility to the private sector. These measures, which in the debate on policy within the country have been captured by omnibus terms like the 'new economic policy' and liberalisation, have essentially three elements to them. First, a set of measures that enlarges the economic space open to the private sector and increases its flexibility relative to the government.

While this dilution of government intervention was occurring partly as a result of the resource crisis spoken of above, the process was considerably accelerated by deliberate efforts at dismantling controls over prices, production, capacity creation and foreign collaboration and by opening up areas previously reserved for the private sector. Second, certain direct and indirect tax concessions (as in the case of synthetics, automobiles and electronics) that are expected to stimulate consumer demand as well as raise the profitability of private production, with the aim of raising investment and growth in the private sector. And finally, the withdrawal of controls on the closure of firms, so that the process of restructuring industry is not hindered by the inability of private capital to abandon outdated plants and obsolete technologies.

A number of measures adding to a package of this kind have been implemented. In March 1985, the government announced the delicensing of 25 broad categories of industries, and a few more (including 82 bulk drugs) have been added since. Delicensing in these areas was subject to the restrictions that the applicant did not fall within the purview of the MRTP Act or the Foreign Exchange Regulation Act (FERA). However, the definition of an MRTP company was changed to cover only those units that had assets of Rs 100 crore and above as compared with the Rs 20 crore that prevailed till then. In addition, in May 1985 the government exempted MRTP companies in 27 industries from sections 21 and 33 of the act, thereby permitting them to directly seek a licence under the IDRA, without obtaining any special clearance from the department of company affairs. And in December 1985, delicensing was extended to 22 of these 27 industries, provided that the units were located in an area declared backward by the central government. All these measures no doubt considerably narrowed the range of licensing.

These measures were accompanied by another set of changes under which the government has: (i) accorded the facility of 'broadbanding' to a large number of industry groups, starting with 29, which allows units to diversify into the production of similar products without obtaining new licences (e g, all synthetic fibres); (ii) announced a modified capacity re-endorsement scheme that permits units that had achieved 80 per cent capacity utilisation during any one of the five years preceding March 31, 1985, to re-endorse their licences raising capacity by one-third of the highest production achieved during these years; (iii) permitted units to apply and obtain without difficulty licences for expanding capacity to pre-specified economic scales of production; (iv) announced a simplified procedure for cases where modernisation/replacement or renovation results in an increase in capacity by up to 49 per cent of that originally licensed; (v) expanded (to 30 industry groups) the list of 'Appendix-I' industries, where MRTP and FERA companies are permitted to set up capacities; and (vi) liberalised the conditions permitting FERA and MRTP companies to establish non-Appendix I industries in backward areas.

Other measures have carried this process forward. To start with, in the case of non-MRTP, non-FERA companies, the number of industries for which entry requires compulsory licensing has been reduced from 56 to 26. Secondly, the lower bound for investments that need to be licensed even in regulated industries has been increased from Rs 5 crore to Rs 15 crore in non-backward areas and Rs 50 crore in backward areas. Finally, companies deemed to be 'dominant' undertakings have been freed from the industrial licensing policy restrictions applicable under the MRTP Act. This has in a sense reduced by 69, the total of around 1,730 corporate entities that fall under the purview of the MRTP Act.

All these measures help the strategy of consumer-goods led industrial growth in a number of ways. First, they substantially enhance the extent to which and the pace at which all sections of industry including the large business groups can diversify their activity and grow. Secondly, for firms already established in any particular segment of industry, it provides the option of reordering their product-mix in keeping with the new demands that the market is setting, without having to go through a complex licensing procedure. And finally, to the extent that the new growth process provides opportunities for growth of the large-scale sector in areas previously reserved for the small-scale sector, it seeks to leave those options open for the former through the process of dereservation.

While this liberalisation does help in doing away with archaic control systems in areas where they are now proving a fetter, it in itself does not constitute a stimulus for growth. While liberalisation can help lubricate a boom of a certain kind, it cannot offer the stimulus for that boom. That requires the persistence of the process of expansion of manufactured consumption goods demand through the increase of incomes in the relevant range and the percolation of such demand to even lower income groups of the population. Given the fact that the state has already over-extended itself this is difficult to ensure.

It is in this context that the interest in consumer credit on the part of a banking system flush with funds has to be viewed. The private sector is demanding the extension of such credit on the grounds that it can help stave off a recession. But even if such a process of stimulating demand is attempted, it would involve large-scale borrowing in international markets to cover the foreign exchange component of an import intensive path of industrialisation. Postponing one problem—that of sustaining deficit financed growth of the kind spoken of above (partly at the expense of the balance of payments)—only brings to the fore the other constraint that has always operated on Indian industrialisation—that of the balance of payments. And so long as Indian industry remains caught between the wedge of these two interlinked constraints, a partial recovery of the late 1970s, early 1980s kind does not offer ground for the optimism, in some circles, noted at the beginning of this paper.

NOTES

[This is a revised version of a paper presented at a seminar on 'Four Decades of Economic Development', organised by the *Social Scientist.* Comments by Deepak Nayyar and Prabhat Patnaik on earlier drafts of the paper are gratefully acknowledged.]

1 Government of India, *Report of the Working Group on the Revision of the Index of Industrial Production,* mimeo; and Government of India, Press Information Bureau, *Revised Index of Industrial Production with 1980-81 as Base Year*, Press Note Number. T-11014/1/86-ISD (IIP) dated February 20, 1987.

2 See in this connection T N Srinivasan and A Vaidyanathan, 'A Note on the Index of Industrial Production' in C R Rao (ed), *Data Base of Indian Economy: Review and Appraisal*, Vol I, Statistical Publishing Society, Calcutta and The Indian Econometric Society, Hyderabad, July 1972, pp 69-83.

3 Figures are from Reserve Bank of India, *Report on Currency and Finance*, Bombay, 1956, p 127; and J Krishnamurthy, 'Secular Changes in Occupational Structure', *Indian Economic and Social History Review*, New Delhi, June 1965.

4 See in this connection, V V Desai, 'Pursuit of Industrial Self-Sufficiency: A Critique of the First Three Plans, *Economic and Political Weekly*, May 1, 1971; and Nirmal Chandra, 'Western Imperialism and India Today', *Economic and Political Weekly*, Annual Number, February 1973.

5 This has been analysed by a number of scholars. See, for example, Sukhamoy Chakravarty, *Some Reflections on the Growth Process in the Indian Economy*, Administrative Staff College of India, Hyderabad, 1974; Ashok Mitra, *Terms of Trade and Class Relations*, Frank Cass, London, 1977; K N Raj, 'Growth and Stagnation in Indian Industrial Development', *Economic and Political Weekly*, Annual Number, 1976; and A Vaidyanathan, 'Constraints on Growth and Policy Options', *Economic and Political Weekly*, September 17, 1977.

6 See in this connection, Prabhat Patnaik, 'Disproportionality Crisis and Cyclical Growth', *Economic and Political Weekly*, Annual Number, 1972; and A K Bagchi, 'Long Term Constraints to India's Industrial Growth,

1951-68' in E A G Robinson and M Kidron (eds), *Economic Development of South Asia*, Macmillan, London, 1970.

7 This is not to neglect the role that import substitution of capital intensive consumption goods for the upper income groups played in sustaining the growth of an industry that was relatively independent of agriculture and the impact that the subsequent exhaustion of these possibilities could have had on the rate of growth. Deepak Nayyar, 'Industrial Development in India: Some Reflections on Growth and Stagnation', *Economic and Political Weekly*, Special Number, February 1978, pp 1265-78.

8 Pramit Chaudhuri, *The Indian Economy: Poverty and Development*, Vikas Publishing House, New Delhi, 1978, pp 96-102. For an assessment of the impact that increased supplies through food aid would have had on prices; see also K N Raj, 'Price Behaviour in India, 1949-66: An Explanatory Hypothesis', *Indian Economic Review*, 1966.

9 The reference here is to R K Hazari, *The Structure of the Private Corporate Sector: A Study of Concentration, Ownership and Control*, Asia Publishing House, Bombay, 1966; A Ghose, 'Monopoly in Indian Industry: An Approach', *Economic and Political Weekly*, June 8, 1974; and A Ghose, 'Investment Behaviour of Monopoly Houses', *Economic and Political Weekly*, October 26, November 2, and November 9, 1974.

10 Government of India, *Monopolies Enquiry Commission Report*, Vols I and II, Delhi, 1965.

11 Hazari, op cit.

12 See for example, Government of India, *Industrial Licensing Policy Inquiry Committee Report* (Dutt Committee), Delhi, 1969; and Government of India, Planning Commission, *Industrial Planning and Licensing Policy*, Final Report, Delhi, 1967.

13 Aurobindo Ghose and Arvind Vyas, 'Industrial Structure and Industrial Policy' in Kerala State Planning Board, *Alternative Policies to the Fourth Five-Year Plan*, Trivandrum, 1969, pp 227-44; Amiya Bagchi, 'Long Term Constraints ...', op cit; and S L Shetty, 'Structural Retrogression in the Indian Economy since the Mid-Sixties', *Economic and Political Weekly*, Annual Number, February 1978, pp 185-244.

14 See in this connection, C P Chandrasekhar, 'Investment Behaviour, Economies of Scale and Efficiency under an Import-Substituting Regime', *Economic and Political Weekly*, Annual Number, May 1987.

15 For evidence in this regard refer, Aurobindo Ghose and Arvind Vyas, op cit.

16 Government of India, Planning Commission, *Third Five-Year Plan*, New Delhi, 1961.

17 Pramit Chaudhuri, op cit.

18 The evidence is provided in I J Ahluwalia, *Industrial Growth in India: Stagnation since the Mid-Sixties*, Oxford University Press, New Delhi, 1985.

19 The shift does not show through in the relative weight of the durable consumer goods sector in the use-based indices of production with 1960 and 1970 as base because of the inclusion under the consumer durables in the 1960 classification of items that did not properly belong there. Amiya Bagchi, *Public Intervention and Industrial Restructuring in China, India and Republic of Korea*, ILO-ARTEP, New Delhi, March 1987, p 124.

20 Figures computed from data obtained from Government of India, Ministry of Finance, *Economic Survey*, various issues.

21 Figures from *Economic Survey*, various issues; and Government of India, Ministry of Finance, *First Report of the Ninth Finance Commission (For 1989-90)*, New Delhi, July 1988.

22 Figures calculated from, Government of India, Central Statistical Organisation, *National Accounts Statistics*, various issues.

23 Government of India, Ministry of Finance, *Long Term Fiscal Policy*, New Delhi, 1986.

24 Figures obtained from Government of India, Ministry of Finance, *Economic Survey*, various issues; Reserve Bank of India, *Report on Currency and Finance*, Bombay, various issues; and *Budget Papers* for different years.

25 For figures on the terms of trade refer D S Tyagi, 'Domestic Terms of Trade and Their Effect on Supply and Demand for the Agricultural Sector', *Economic and Political Weekly*, Review of Agriculture, March 28, 1987. See also Jayati Ghosh, 'Intersectoral Terms of Trade, Agricultural Growth and the Pattern of Demand', *Social Scientist,* 179, New Delhi, April 1988, pp 9-27.

26 Figures from Ministry of Finance, *Economic Survey*, various issues.

REFERENCES

Ahmed, J (1968): 'Import Substitution and Structural Change in Indian Manufacturing Industry; 1950-66', *Journal of Development Studies*, Frank Cass, London, Vol 4, No 3.

Bardhan, Pranab (1984): *The Political Economy of Development in India*, Oxford University Press, Delhi.

Bhagwati, J and P Desai (1970): *India: Planning for Industrialisation*, Oxford University Press, New Delhi.

Chandra, Nirmal (1982): 'Long-Term Stagnation in the Indian Economy', *Economic and Political Weekly*, Annual Number, April.

Mitra, Ashok (1988): 'Disproportionality and the Service Sector', *Social Scientist* 179, April, pp 3-8.

Patnaik, Prabhat (1979): 'Industrial Development in India', *Social Scientist* 83, June.

–(1988): 'A Perspective on the Recent Phase of India's Economic Development', *Social Scientist* 177, February.

Patnaik, Prabhat and S K Rao (1977): 'Towards an Explanation of a Crisis in a Mixed Underdeveloped Economy', *Economic and Political Weekly*, Annual Number, February.

Patnaik, Utsa (1988): 'Some Aspects of Development' *Social Scientist* 177, February.

Raj, K N (1967): *India, Pakistan and China: Economic Growth and Outlook*, Lal Bahadur Shastri Memorial Lecture, 1966, Allied Publishers, Bombay.

Sen, Abhijit (1988): 'A Note on Employment and Living Standards in the Unorganised Sector', *Social Scientist* 177, February, pp 50-59.

Tyagi, D S (1987): 'Domestic Terms of Trade and Their Effect on Supply and Demand of Agricultural Sector', *Economic and Political Weekly*, March 28.

Index